RABIN AND ISRAEL'S NATIONAL SECURITY

RABIN AND ISRAEL'S NATIONAL SECURITY

EFRAIM INBAR

THE WOODROW WILSON CENTER PRESS
WASHINGTON, D.C.

THE JOHNS HOPKINS UNIVERSITY PRESS
BALTIMORE AND LONDON

EDITORIAL OFFICES

The Woodrow Wilson Center Press
One Woodrow Wilson Plaza
1300 Pennsylvania Avenue, N.W.
Washington, D.C. 20004-3027
Telephone 202-691-4010
wwics.si.edu

ORDER FROM

The Johns Hopkins University Press
P.O. Box 50370
Baltimore, Maryland 21211
Telephone 1-800-537-5487
www.press.jhu.edu

2 4 6 8 9 7 5 3 1

Library of Congress Cataloging-in-Publication Data

Inbar, Efraim, 1947–
    Rabin and Israel's national security / Efraim Inbar.
        p.   cm.
    Includes bibliographical references (p.   ) and index.
    ISBN 0-8018-6217-5 (cloth : alk. paper)
    1. Rabin, Yitzhak, 1922–1995.   2. National security—Israel.
3. Israel—Military policy.   4. Israel—Defenses.   5. Arab-Israeli
conflict.   I. Title.
DS126.6.R32I63   1999
956.9405'092—dc21

                                                                          99-22113
                                                                          CIP

ABOUT THE CENTER

The Center is the living memorial of the United States of America to the nation's twenty-eighth president, Woodrow Wilson. Congress established the Woodrow Wilson Center in 1968 as an international institute for advanced study, "symbolizing and strengthening the fruitful relationship between the world of learning and the world of public affairs." The Center opened in 1970 under its own board of trustees.

In all its activities the Woodrow Wilson Center is a nonprofit, nonpartisan organization, supported financially by annual appropriations from the Congress, and by the contributions of foundations, corporations, and individuals. Conclusions or opinions expressed in Center publications and programs are those of the authors and speakers and do not necessarily reflect the views of the Center staff, fellows, trustees, advisory groups, or any individuals or organizations that provide financial support to the Center.

To Rivkale

CONTENTS

PREFACE   XI

ACKNOWLEDGMENTS   XIII

INTRODUCTION   1

CHAPTER 1
THE APPROACH TO INTERNATIONAL POLITICS AND THE
    ARAB-ISRAELI CONFLICT   7

CHAPTER 2
THE AMERICAN ORIENTATION IN ISRAEL'S
    FOREIGN POLICY   34

CHAPTER 3
BUILDING A CONVENTIONAL MILITARY FORCE   58

CHAPTER 4
THE USE OF MILITARY FORCE   84

CHAPTER 5
WEAPONS OF MASS DESTRUCTION   114

CHAPTER 6
RABIN OF THE 1990s: THE CHANGING STRATEGIC
    ASSESSMENT   133

CONCLUSION   167

APPENDIX A

AFTER THE GULF WAR: ISRAELI DEFENSE AND ITS
SECURITY POLICY (ADDRESS BY YITZHAK RABIN AT
THE BEGIN-SADAT CENTER FOR STRATEGIC STUDIES,
BAR-ILAN UNIVERSITY, 10 JUNE 1991)   172

APPENDIX B

POLICY STATEMENT BY PRIME MINISTER YITZHAK RABIN
TO THE KNESSET, 3 OCTOBER 1994   179

NOTES   191

BIBLIOGRAPHY   247

INDEX   267

PREFACE

I wrote this volume with mixed emotions, for in many ways it closes a personal and academic circle. In June 1967 I was a young soldier savoring the great victory; the enthusiasm and admiration that I, like many of my contemporaries, felt for my commander-in-chief could be summed up in the popular song "Nasser Is Waiting for Rabin." My admiration gradually transformed into a more adult and sober appreciation of the man—his analytical qualities, his weaknesses, and his middle-of-the-road political views. This led, inter alia, to my first serious academic endeavor: a Ph.D. dissertation at the University of Chicago (completed in 1981 under the guidance of the late Albert Wohlstetter), which focused on the national security policies of Yitzhak Rabin's first government (1974–77).

During the research for my dissertation, Rabin was in the political wilderness—an opposition backbencher—and I was fortunate enough to meet him and investigate his views at length. He has been an object of my professional attention ever since, as part of my study of various aspects of Israel's national security predicament. Rabin was a very reserved person, but through my research I felt that I acquired a certain familiarity with the man, his views, and the nuances of his complex personality. My hero of the Six-Day War turned into an object of serious academic research. Many years after the 1967 war, which precipitated many of Israel's contemporary security dilemmas, Rabin was murdered by a right-wing fanatic. Bewildered at the tragedy and not fully clear about its meaning for my society, I was left, as were many others, to wonder what had happened to the sense of elation and unity of 1967. Rabin's sad removal from the political stage also ended my familiarity with one of Israel's foremost leaders.

The deep personal loss felt by my countrymen, and so acutely by myself, led me to pay tribute to Rabin in the best way academicians know—writing about him. With Rabin (a veteran of the War of Independence) gone, a change of guard has taken place in Israel's leadership. The current leaders of the two largest parties, Likud and Labor, belong to a new generation. Furthermore, the structural changes in Israeli electoral law (allowing for direct election of the prime minister), which Rabin supported wholeheartedly (it is far from clear that the changes are for the better), have heralded an age of new politics. Since the 1967 war, within the span of thirty years, Israel underwent many societal and political changes; it also improved relations with most of the Arab neighbors who were once intent on destroying it. With Yitzhak Rabin gone, an epoch has ended for Israel, as well as for my research agenda.

ACKNOWLEDGMENTS

I owe much gratitude to numerous people for enabling me to complete this book. The many interviewees showed much patience, even when the questions touched on sensitive issues. I thank Stuart A. Cohen, Yehezkel Dror, and Avi Kober for reading all the chapters and for making innumerable excellent remarks and suggestions. Yehudit Auerbach, Barry Rubin, and Shmuel Sandler made valuable comments on parts of the manuscript. Shmuel Gordon clarified some military details. The Begin-Sadat (BESA) Center for Strategic Studies at Bar-Ilan University has been a fertile intellectual home and of great logistical help. Hava Koen, Avi Rembaum, and Alona Rozenman proved once again to be a hard-working and helpful team. Ruth Shashoua and Elisheva Brown were intelligent and indefatigable research assistants. Lyle Goldstein polished parts of the manuscript and made important comments. I also benefited enormously from Haim Wazman's editorial skills. The research for this book was supported by the Schnitzer Foundation for Research on the Israeli Economy and Society and the Ihel Foundation at Bar-Ilan University. I also thank the Israel Defense Force (IDF) Spokesman Office for allowing me access to the IDF Archives and the Library of the National Security College. Finally, the Woodrow Wilson International Center for Scholars provided, during the summer of 1996, an extremely hospitable physical and intellectual environment for beginning to write on this subject. There I also received valuable research help from Nadia Jaser. Most important, the Wilson Center encouraged me to expand my research into a book. This is the product of that encouragement.

As a humble academician, I owe the reader a caveat. It is probably too early to write the definitive work on Yitzhak Rabin. One reason is the lack of access to primary, still classified materials. Because of Rabin's tragic end, the present tendency in interviews and in other sources is to emphasize favorable explanations and views, which may have some distorting effects. Some of the accounts, particularly those on sensitive security matters, are provisional until archives and other materials become available. Nevertheless, a contemporary account still attuned to the political-military context in which Rabin operated will be vital for balancing the image that will emerge from reading documents years after they were recorded.

INTRODUCTION

Prime Minister Yitzhak Rabin was shot to death in Tel Aviv on 4 November 1995 as he left a mass rally supporting his peace policies. Sixty heads of state attended his funeral, among them U.S. President Bill Clinton, British Prime Minister John Major, French President Jacques Chirac, and German Chancellor Helmut Kohl. No less striking was the attendance of representatives of seven Arab countries—Egypt, Jordan, Mauritania, Morocco, Oman, Qatar, and Tunisia. That so many high-ranking statesmen honored Rabin's memory with their presence was a tribute to the prime minister and his recent policies, but sadly, it took the tragedy of Rabin's assassination to demonstrate Israel's enhanced international status in the mid-1990s.

For more than forty years Rabin played a critical role in the shaping of Israeli national security policy and military doctrine. Born in 1922, he began his career in 1940 as a soldier in the Palmach, the elite underground unit of the Yeshuv (the Jewish community in Palestine); in the 1948 War of Independence, Rabin first commanded the Palmach Harel Brigade, which fought to clear the way to Jerusalem and within the city, and later served as deputy to his mentor, Yigal Allon, at southern front headquarters. Like many of his colleagues, Rabin had received little formal military training, but over time he developed into an influential officer in the Israel Defense Force (IDF).

Rabin reached the apex of the military hierarchy when he was appointed chief of staff in 1964, and in that capacity he led the Israeli army to its 1967 triumph. This was a personal victory for him as well, for in 1948 he had been unable to keep Jerusalem united under Israeli rule. Now he became, in his own mind and in the minds of Israelis, "the liberator of Jerusalem." As chief of staff (January 1964–December 1967), as ambassador to the United States (February 1968–March 1973), as defense minister in several governments (September 1984–March 1990, July 1992–November 1995), and twice as prime minister (June 1974–June 1977, July 1992–November 1995), he was among Israel's primary decision-makers on defense issues, foreign affairs, and the Arab-Israeli conflict, and he dominated Israeli thinking on national security affairs after the 1973 Yom Kippur War. Indeed, he was the only man to serve as chief of staff, defense minister, and prime minister. Rabin, who in the 1980s came as close to being a centrist as seems possible in the Israeli political system, gradually became Israel's most popular politician. His public standing finally persuaded the Labor Party to put him at its helm, a move that led in 1992 to the only decisive Labor electoral victory in the past two decades. His views commanded the respect of Israelis of all political colors, as well as many leaders abroad. Indeed, he was perceived to be the ultimate Israeli: a tough soldier who yearned for peace.

The decision-making pattern in Israel, particularly in national security affairs, amplified Rabin's influence because of his presence in the small, sometimes informal forums that weighed the main options and reached the critical decisions. Israeli decision-making in defense matters has always been extremely centralized and has remained the coveted privilege of the very few.[1] The political constellation of the mid-1960s propelled Rabin, then chief of staff, to become the senior and most trusted national security adviser to the new prime minister, Levi Eshkol (in 1965). While serving as ambassador in Washington, D.C., Rabin continued to exert influence; both Eshkol and his successor, Golda Meir (1969–74), sought Rabin's advice. His direct link to the prime minister, as well as his unpolished assertiveness, generated a long feud with Abba Eban, at that time foreign minister.

The shock of the 1973 military failure, which discredited Israel's leadership, ushered in a new generation of leaders. The Labor Party apparatus, looking for a candidate untainted by the blunder of the 1973 October War, catapulted Rabin to the position of premier in 1974. In April 1974 he won (by a small margin) the contest within the Labor Party against Shimon Peres—a rivalry that became central to Labor politics for the next two decades. This personal dispute was one of the reasons for Labor's inability to win elections in the 1980s. Actually, neither of the two large parties, Likud and Labor, won a clear victory in the 1984 and 1988 national elections, a situation that led to the national unity governments (1984–90) in which Rabin served as defense minister. This was the political post he felt most comfortable in, as he surrounded himself with army officers and dealt with security affairs, paying only minimal attention to his party and to domestic politics.[2] This was the period when he acquired a public reputation as an undisputed expert in national security affairs and as a respected political leader.[3] Although he had been a respected voice on these issues earlier, the deaths of Moshe Dayan and Allon left him as the major authority on national security.

The apex of his influence on Israeli national security policy came when he served as defense minister. Like other ministers in the Israeli cabinet, the defense minister has almost exclusive authority within his ministry; only in exceptional circumstances do others, such as the prime minister or senior cabinet members, have access to the defense decision-making process. When, in 1992, Labor finally won a national election, this time under Rabin's leadership, he kept the defense minister position for himself.

Rabin's views had a strong impact on Israeli policies in the past, and they are likely to remain influential well into the future. His thinking has heavily permeated the political sphere. Furthermore, Rabin was personally responsible for the promotion of many senior IDF officers who have themselves become important politicians.[4] Many of them were deeply influenced by Rabin, whose authority on defense matters was hardly ever challenged. For example, the present Likud defense minister, Maj. Gen. (Res.) Yitzhak Mordechai, an influential politician, displays a picture of Rabin in his office rather than photographs of venerated Likud personalities. Similarly, Labor's current leader, the former chief of staff Ehud Barak, considers Rabin to have been his mentor and portrays himself as continuing in Rabin's course, blending a strong defense policy with political pragmatism. Indeed, Rabin's views had an impact on Israel's entire strategic culture: he was "Mr. Security" for much or most of the defense establishment and the public at large.[5]

This book is not a political biography, and the political fortunes of Rabin are not its focus. As a matter of fact, Rabin's career as an Israeli politician was not particularly impressive. During his first tenure as prime minister, Rabin failed to exploit his initial popularity to establish himself as a national and political leader. He also failed to build a solid base of power within his own Labor Party. Inexperienced at the Israeli political game, he made many mistakes that cost him political capital in the party and among the electorate. His government was further weakened by several financial scandals, as well as his habit of expressing himself tactlessly and even rudely in public. He later admitted that he had not been, during his first tenure as prime minister, experienced enough to handle domestic challenges. The fall of Rabin's government led to early elections and to the political upheaval of the Likud victory in June 1977.[6] During the electoral campaign, he even relinquished the post of premier and the leadership position of his party because he and his wife, Leah, were involved in a violation of foreign currency regulations.[7]

In his second term, many failings from his first tenure reappeared. After the 1992 electoral victory, Rabin failed to establish a broad-based government that included parties to the right of Labor. This ran counter to Labor's tradition of playing a centrist role in government coalitions and in Israeli politics. By deviating from this political dictum and gravitating toward the left, he missed a historic opportunity to restore Labor's pivotal position in Israeli politics.[8] His dependence on support from the left increased until, at the time of his death, he headed a minority government that depended on the support of communist and nationalist Arab Knesset members outside the coalition—something he had refused to contemplate earlier. During the last two years of his government, Rabin adopted policies on the peace process that had been advocated by Peres and the dovish wing in his party.[9] These policies were encountering growing domestic political resistance. The September 1993 Oslo Agreement, to be credited primarily to Peres, and particularly its sequel of September 1995 (Oslo II) elicited much criticism. Government policies could have been better marketed domestically, and a wiser, more tolerant attitude to opposition groups could have done much to reduce antagonism. Nonetheless, Rabin's political stature was so great that much of the public accepted some of Rabin's altered positions and Israel's concessions to the Palestinians in the peace process.

Rabin was not a polished politician. He lacked good speaking and public relations skills and an eye for what was politically feasible domestically.[10] Certain aspects of Rabin's personality were the opposite of those needed by a charismatic leader who can sway the masses. Having neither the desire nor the ability to develop close ties with new acquaintances (particularly if they lacked a military background), Rabin was shy, even introverted, and never felt comfortable with crowds.[11] He was most at ease at work, where there was a clear hierarchy and where his dealings with others were for the purpose of accomplishing his goals. Amorphous social situations were much more difficult for him.[12] Rabin had little patience for interparty political negotiations and never paid much attention to what was happening in his own party. Generally, the rate of support for Rabin in the

Labor Party was lower than among the Israeli public at large. He was extremely suspicious of new people he met and of those working for him, and he tended to be short-tempered. Rabin was known to be hesitant and very cautious, quite different from the bold and even reckless stereotype of the Israeli officer.

Nevertheless, Rabin's gruff style won him many supporters, and his frank, rough, and occasionally insensitive language appealed to the Israeli psyche, which values candor and bluntness. His great attraction to Israelis across the political spectrum lay precisely in their perception that he was not a typical Israeli politician. His candidness antagonized some, however, who felt he was not attuned to the concerns of those Israelis who disagreed with him. Many of the interviewees for this book, including some of his longtime friends, described him as rough and unusually stubborn.

Yet whatever their feelings about Rabin, they could not ignore him. His logical and systematic treatment of all major issues, coupled with his ability to master an immense amount of detail, powerfully and effectively impressed both supporters and opponents. Even though the latter sometimes scorned him for his keen ability to analyze only the past, they could not deny his intelligence and personal integrity. His tremendous dedication to the job, his patriotism, and his sense of mission were unquestionable.

Many prominent Israeli leaders have been prolific writers—David Ben-Gurion, Moshe Dayan, Yigal Allon, and Shimon Peres. Rabin, however, did not leave behind a written strategic legacy. He did not have such an intellectual drive. He was, however, often interviewed in the military press and the general press. His speeches were occasionally published in *Maarachot* (the IDF professional journal),[13] in Labor Party organs, and in newspapers, and in 1979 he published an autobiography.[14] After his death a collection of his "peace" speeches was published to secure his place as a "peacemaker" in Israel's historiography,[15] though his main concern over the years was in fact Israel's national security. Peace was a corollary of security in Rabin's view—an important national goal but not a core value. His priorities were ordered around his defense concerns; "maximum security constitutes the true peace," he declared.[16] Nevertheless, he was always cognizant that (as he often reminded senior army officers) security is only the means, critical as it may be, for realizing other, more important values inherent in the slogan "the return to Zion."[17] Security was needed to secure the building of a Jewish state in the midst of much surrounding hostility.

No systematic study of Rabin's strategic thinking and his policies is currently available. The purpose of this work is to fill this lacuna. It is an attempt to present and analyze Yitzhak Rabin's strategic legacy by looking at his record of thought and action on key strategic issues. The first chapter analyzes his approach to international relations and his outlook on the Arab-Israeli conflict over the years. The second chapter reviews Rabin's preference for an American orientation in Israel's foreign policy and his treatment of U.S.-Israeli relations when he was in office. Chapter 3 assesses his contribution, during his army career and afterward as prime minister and defense minister, to forging the IDF into a mighty military machine. Chapter 4 analyzes Rabin's Clausewitzian approach to the use of force and his preference for measured military force commensurate with political goals. The fifth chapter focuses on Rabin's views on Israeli nuclear strategy and his responses to the introduction of long-range missiles and weapons of mass destruction into the Middle East. Chapter 6 concentrates on Rabin's evaluation of the strategic equation in the 1990s and identifies changes that occurred in Rabin's attitudes and positions concerning the Arab-Israeli conflict. The conclusion evaluates Rabin's contribution to Israel's national security. It also assesses his personal transition from warrior to peacemaker and offers a few thoughts on how he should be remembered. Since Rabin played key roles in Israel's defense establishment at important junctions in its history, this analysis is also a prism for acquiring a better understanding of the national security challenges that Israel has faced and of its responses over four decades.

CHAPTER ONE

THE APPROACH TO INTERNATIONAL POLITICS AND THE ARAB-ISRAELI CONFLICT

From the outset, Israeli policy-makers have been keenly aware of the pervasive threat to the integrity of national borders in the international system and have assumed that over the long run, no state can ever be certain of its security. Israel's foreign policy elite has always perceived the anarchical nature of international politics. It has been pessimistic about the behavior of states and organizations in the Middle East and skeptical about attempts to introduce rules of international behavior similar to those governing the domestic arena. Most Israeli leaders have realized that in the real world, threats to national security are omnipresent and that all states attempt to widen their margins of security, even at the expense of their neighbors. This approach was primarily the result of experience accumulated in the Arab-Israeli conflict rather than the outcome of an abstract and/or systematic study of world politics.[1] Thus, within the Israeli political elite, political realism became the dominant conceptual framework for understanding regional and international politics.[2]

THE ATTITUDINAL PRISM

Yitzhak Rabin's sober realism in his approach to international politics was not exceptional in the Israeli context. Born in Jerusalem in 1922, Rabin grew up in the Jewish community in Palestine, a society that daily experienced the hostility of its Arab environment. He later recalled that at a very young age (preschool), it was "naturally clear" to him that there were Jews and Arabs. "And with all our desire to live peacefully, we were always provoked, and sometimes even hit, by Arab boys."[3] As a high school student he first learned to use a gun and participated in the effort to defend his school, Kadouri, from the attacks of neighboring Arab villagers. After he finished his high school studies, his sense of duty and patriotism compelled him to give up a scholarship to study engineering in the United States and to stay home to cultivate the Land of Israel and to defend, by arms, the Zionist enterprise.[4] At the end of 1940 he enlisted in the Palmach. Thus, like many other Israelis of his generation, Rabin learned that national security was the key to his country's future, and this perspective was reinforced by his long military career. This was Rabin's prism through which he viewed world politics and the Arab-Israeli conflict.

Jewishness has also been an important element in the attitudinal prism of many Israeli leaders,[5] including Rabin. He was not versed in Jewish orthodox tradition and lacked the capacity to link easily with fellow Jews. Nevertheless, his personal identity was very Jewish.[6] He grew up in an ardent Zionist family and took great pride in the Jewish revival in its ancient homeland after two thousand years of exile.

The Jewish historic experience of this century and of previous epochs amplified Israel's sense of insecurity and reinforced the realpolitik tendency. Similarly, it made isolation an easily "evoked set" of individual and collective memories.[7] The biblical prophet Balaam's declaration that Israel "is a people that shall dwell alone, and shall not be reckoned among the nations" (Numbers 23:9) is well rooted in the political culture of contemporary Israel. The news about the fate of the Jews in Europe at the end of World War II strengthened Rabin's assessment that the Jews would be left on their own after the war, despite the fact that the Jewish community in Palestine had mobilized to serve the British war effort: "We will fight over our destiny in the Land of Israel and only our independent force will be available."[8] Rabin, chief of staff during the 1967 Six-Day War, experienced the feeling of isolation as he faced an Arab attempt to destroy the Jewish state. Several years later, recollecting the developments leading to the 1967 war, he said: "In fact we had no one to rely on, but ourselves . . . we were on our own, and we alone were responsible for our fate."[9]

In 1974 Rabin, by then prime minister, again acutely sensed Israel's isolation: "We should have no illusions and we should know that we are quite isolated in the world. Out of the 137 member states of the UN [United Nations], less than ten support us. Israel shall dwell alone and only our military might guarantees our existence."[10] In Rabin's final analysis, Israel could not rely on the gentile world but only on its own military power. Because of this experience of solitude in the world arena, Rabin felt an obligation to help the Kurdish minority in its national struggle within Iraq. On 9 March 1975, when Rabin explained to his government that as result of the Iran-Iraq agreement, Israel had to end this assistance to the Kurds, he pointed out that the cooperation had lasted twelve years not only because Israel was interested in weakening Iraq but also because "we are Jewish."[11]

Rabin's Jewish outlook was most evident in his reaction to the November 1975 UN resolution equating Zionism (the Jewish national revival movement) with racism: "The whole world is against us—when was this not so?"[12] Another example occurred when Rabin rejected the international criticism of his order to use clubs against Palestinians in dispersing violent demonstrations during the early stages of the Intifada. In February 1988 he said: "In general, beating a Jew is unimportant in the eyes of the world. But when a Jew beats somebody, then it is news."[13] Like David Ben-Gurion, Rabin developed a deeply rooted, suspicious attitude toward the outside world, an attitude accentuated by his Jewish prism.

Raison d'État was obviously paramount in Rabin's considerations. Yet he was not oblivious to the destiny of Jews outside the Jewish state. He admitted that his time in Washington and his meetings with American Jewry during that period had strengthened his link to the Jews living in the Diaspora.[14] In 1976, Rabin explained that one reason Israel should preserve good relations with the United States was the role played by America in facilitating access to Jewish communities in countries with no diplomatic relations with Israel.[15] Prime Minister Yitzhak Shamir was pleasantly surprised that Rabin's approach to the Soviet Union in the 1980s had a Jewish aspect. Rabin valued the emigration of Jews to Israel and seemed to be genuinely moved by meeting Jewish activists in Moscow.[16]

THE INTERNATIONAL ARENA

Rabin's military background and Jewish prism combined to make him see the world and the Arab-Israeli conflict through realpolitik lenses. Like Kenneth Waltz, the best-known spokesman of neorealism, Rabin assumed that states operate in a "self-help" system. He attributed no value whatsoever to international guarantees, which in his opinion were totally unreliable.[17]

In 1965, Rabin deduced from the Indo-Pakistani war that where there is hatred and enmity there is potential for war and that rational thinking does not always prevail. "This war clearly demonstrated that they [the protagonists] could rely only on their own power . . . political arrangements were irrelevant; and the result of the military campaign was determined purely by the bilateral balance of power."[18] Military force most often proved to be the final arbiter in international relations.

Rabin learned similar lessons from the setbacks experienced by the Christians in the civil war in Lebanon; these tragedies elicited no reaction from the UN and the states of the world. Rabin observed in 1975: "The future and security of over a million Christians is at stake in Lebanon, and the Christian world is silent. We have not heard even one Christian leader say something about what is expected in Lebanon."[19] It was clear to Rabin that the future of the Christians in Lebanon depended first and foremost on their ability to muster enough force to fight their enemies. Rabin's personal experiences in the Arab-Israeli conflict and his long military career conditioned him to see the use of force (analyzed in greater detail in chapter 4) as a vital dimension of the international game.

Rabin maintained that the motivating force in international politics was national interest. For example, the alliance between Muammar Qaddafi of Libya and the Kremlin was based on mutual interests rather than ideology. In his opinion, the Soviet Union cynically disregarded any ideological considerations in attempting to consolidate its influence in the world.[20] Such behavior also prevailed in the West. For example, Rabin observed that the French indiscriminately sold weapons of any quality to everybody because doing so served their interest of maintaining an arms industry.[21] In 1986, Rabin lamented the lack of international cooperation against terrorism. Though such international behavior would be laudable, Rabin said that the world was not yet ripe for it. He noted that even the United States had failed to secure the help of its NATO allies in the struggle against terrorism because these allies were unwilling to sacrifice their narrow economic and short-term political interests.[22]

Rabin's perceptions of the international arena coincided with a realpolitik outlook: states pursue their national interests ruthlessly, using force when necessary. Moreover, in such a violent world, states cannot always rely on others to come to their rescue and must develop capabilities to survive on their own. Rabin's formulations were in accordance with the classic balance-of-power prism. For many years such views formed the fundamental tenets of Israel's "activist" school in defense and foreign policy matters, a school of thought generally associated with Ben-Gurion's outlook and policies.[23] Nevertheless, in the 1960s and the 1970s, Rabin was often regarded as leaning toward policies somewhat left of center. Yet Rabin's emphasis on power politics was, from the mid-1970s, increasingly subject to criticism from the Israeli left and gradually even from the growing dovish wing in his own Labor Party. As the Israeli political spectrum shifted as a whole to the left, Rabin, who was consistent in his views, came to be perceived as more hawkish in the Israeli political context.[24]

A corollary of Rabin's realpolitik outlook on international relations was his view of secrecy as vital for successful results in international negotiations. This was also the result of his own closed personality and cautiousness in sharing information with others. In 1974, Rabin regarded face-to-face secret negotiations between Egypt and Israel as the best way to reach an Arab-Israeli agreement.[25] Twenty years later Rabin still maintained, "I think that in the international reality of today, secret personal contacts are a precondition for agreements."[26] In his opinion, the November 1977 journey to Jerusalem by Egyptian President Anwar Sadat could not have happened without the preceding secret meeting between Moshe Dayan and Hassan Touhami in Morocco. Similarly, he believed that early media reports about the Oslo discussions, which eventually led to the Israeli-PLO agreements, could easily have put an end to this process. According to Rabin, leaks to the Israeli press were counterproductive and caused Israel to lose credibility in its contacts with neighbors.[27]

Rabin's approach to the international system naturally mirrored most closely the situation in the perennially unstable Middle East. This instability had its roots in the political and social features of Arab societies. In 1975, he stated his belief that for at least the next twenty-five years the Middle East would remain unstable.[28] Furthermore, he noted: "The analysis of the facts proves that essentially what has assured Israel's existence, and will continue to do so, in the face of the hatred around it and the will to destroy it, is primarily Israel's comprehensive power, with military might as the decisive element."[29]

Rabin was famous for his thorough and comprehensive analyses of the Israeli strategic situation. In his briefings, he was always sensitive to the international power balance. He understood very well that the developments in the Arab-Israeli conflict could not be analyzed in isolation from the larger international picture and that events in the Middle East are linked to trends in world politics. He realized that Israel would be affected by global and regional circumstances. Generally, he had a good feel for the nature of Mideastern power politics.

For example, Rabin often expressed concern about the fact that Arab military capabilities were continually enhanced by the Soviet Union. According to Rabin, the June 1967 war was partly the result of a Soviet attempt to exploit regional tensions to further its own superpower interests: "Due to international developments, the Soviet Union tried, for her own reasons, to transform the Middle East into a hot arena in her global struggle."[30] Furthermore, the Soviet Union was instrumental in the rehabilitation of the Egyptian army and Egypt's regional status following the 1967 war.[31] Rabin was extremely apprehensive about the Soviets acquiring military bases in Egypt, which would enhance the Soviet naval and air reach.[32] The 1971 Egyptian-Soviet Treaty of Friendship and Cooperation was an additional source of concern and required Israel to increase the scope of its demands from the United States.[33] The ousting of the Soviet military advisers in August 1972 was met with relief by Rabin, who believed that the military option of Egypt was thus eliminated—an evaluation proved incorrect by the 1973 war.[34] In his opinion, the Soviet Union, after 1973, continued to encourage the radical forces in the Arab-Israeli arena, such as Syria and Libya, and interfered with attempts to reduce tensions in the region.[35]

Rabin's fears about Soviet involvement in the Arab-Israeli conflict grew over the years. This led him to insist in 1975 that U.S. Secretary of State Henry Kissinger include an American pledge "to deter a world power" (a veiled reference to Moscow) in a memorandum of understanding (MOU) that was part of the U.S. quid pro quo for the Israeli withdrawal from the Sinai in the framework of the Sinai 2 Agreement between Egypt and Israel. In 1981, Rabin still feared direct Soviet military involvement in Arab-Israeli wars and even envisioned, under certain geopolitical circumstances, a possible Soviet landing on the shores of Israel.[36]

As discussed at great length in the next chapter, Rabin regarded the United States as a crucial factor in the Israeli strategic equation. For many years, Rabin believed that Israeli relations with Washington were of paramount importance for the mere existence of Israel and for its dialogue with regional protagonists. The tension between the desire to maintain Israel's freedom of action and the efforts to guarantee American support accompanied Rabin's thinking and deeds for most of his adult life.

THE NATURE OF THE ARAB-ISRAELI CONFLICT

On the nature of the Arab-Israeli conflict, Rabin accepted the Zionist doctrine, formulated primarily by Ben-Gurion.[37] The conflict was considered to be an existential one, since the goal of the Arab enemies was to annihilate the Jewish state. This acute Israeli threat perception stemmed from the common belief that the Arabs' goal was the destruction of Israel as a political entity—what was termed "politicide."[38] Such a far-reaching objective was not common in international relations following World War II.[39]

In his first interview as chief of staff in January 1965, Rabin emphasized that Gamal Abdel Nasser and Egypt wanted to destroy Israel and that, unfortunately, the world was not taking Nasser's words seriously.[40] Rabin's opinion reflected mainstream thinking within Israel at that time. The "ingrained and very real hatred" toward Israel was, according to Rabin, widespread among the Arab states and represented one of the few themes that could foster Arab unity. Moreover, the Arab countries were making concrete efforts to increase their military power. According to Rabin, "The goal of the Arab weapons procurement program is clear—the destruction of Israel."[41]

In the case of Egypt, national interest reinforced this hatred, which had cultural and religious roots. In 1964, Rabin related Egypt's hostility toward Israel to the essentials of the geopolitical situation: Nasser sought to unite the Arab world, mostly east of Egypt, under his leadership, but Israel was a territorial wedge between Egypt and the Arab countries in the Fertile Crescent.[42] Thus, Israel's territorial location, which blocked the expansion of Egyptian influence eastward, created discord between the two countries.

Clearly, Rabin was realistic enough to realize that hatred was not the only motivating force in shaping the policies of the Arab states. He understood that a further precondition for war was the conclusion among the Arabs that their national interests could be pursued effectively through the use of force. Rabin recognized the paramount importance of national interests in the Arab states' behavior. Only in a situation in which there was "an active and real interest . . . to achieve an advantage: political, geographical, economic, or social," would hatred become activated and lead to a full-scale military confrontation, he believed.[43] Furthermore, Rabin understood that Arab behavior took into consideration regional and international developments. He often pointed out that Nasser believed that a crushing military defeat of Israel was predicated on building a strong military to win a large-scale war, on creating Arab unity, and on fostering Israel's international

isolation and that only after these conditions were met would the destruction of Israel become possible. This evaluation was proven correct by the
1956–67 period of quiet along Israel's border with Egypt.[44]

Nevertheless, Rabin noted that in the absence of a military option to destroy Israel, the Arab neighbors had limited objectives in their struggle
against Israel. "The main goal is to obstruct our attempts for progress, and
to prevent the continuation of our development and growth in this country."[45] He had in mind the Arab League resolutions and the Syrian attempts to divert the waters of the Jordan River in the mid-1960s. He regarded low-intensity military action against Israel on the part of Syria
(before 1967) as aimed at provoking Israel into an escalation, which would
in turn force Egypt to take a stand. Indeed, Rabin regarded the possibility
of hostilities between Israel and its neighbors as very real, despite periods
of quiet along the borders.

As chief of staff, Rabin described Israel's strategic situation since its birth
as "a dormant war," waking up every few years and turning into an active
war.[46] The armistice agreements signed with the Arab countries could easily be violated. The term "dormant war" also indicated that there was no
clear boundary between peace and war and that the use of force, such as in
retaliation raids, represented part of an ongoing "dialogue" with Israel's
neighbors.[47] The coinage became part of Israeli strategic parlance. Even
after the victory of 1967, Rabin did not preclude the possibility of another
war: "Unfortunately, I cannot say with any certainty that this war was the
last war or military round."[48]

Taking into consideration the profound Arab hostility toward the Jewish state, the option to end the conflict was not thought to be in Israeli
hands. The precondition for transforming the conflict into neighborly relations had to be Arab acquiescence to Israel's existence. Such a change
might, however, take generations. According to Rabin, Israel had always
been a status quo power, not pursuing any territorial aggrandizement.[49]
He meant that Israel was satisfied first with its 1967 borders and later with
the post-1967 territorial situation. He believed that in the last stages of the
War of Independence, Israel was already strong enough militarily to expand territorially but attempted to reach peace in stages by agreeing to negotiate first armistice agreements with its Arab neighboring states, despite
the fact that important parts of the homeland, Jerusalem in particular,
were in Arab hands.[50]

While envisioning an existential Arab threat for many years, Rabin did
not rule out change. He participated, as a lieutenant colonel, in the Rhodos

talks, which led to the armistice agreements with the Egyptians in 1949 and so ended the War of Independence. His impression was that the Egyptian officers could envision peace between the two countries but that since they were intent on achieving additional military goals and still entertained the hope of eliminating the Jewish state, it would take many more years before the Egyptian elite would accept a rapprochement with Israel.[51]

In 1964, Rabin stated in an interview that he did not believe that Arab hostility was a permanent given: "Hostility is not an eternal factor. Even today when the situation looks hopeless, we have to remember that nations hostile to each other for tens of years, found avenues to each other's heart, when the political circumstances changed."[52] It is remarkable that Rabin, known for his pessimistic nature, did entertain this hope, rooted in his analysis of international conflict, that peaceful relations with Israel's Arab neighbors constituted a real future possibility. This ambivalence—a tremendous suspicion of Arab hostile motives coupled with an advocacy for patience in the hope that the Arabs would eventually change their attitude toward Israel—was characteristic of Rabin until the very end.

Actually, on a number of occasions Rabin speculated about the regional conditions that could bring about peace between Israel and its neighbors. He was convinced that peace could be achieved only from a position of strength: "Our future power will determine the chances for peace in our region. Weakness is not a recipe for negotiations. If our neighbors come to realize that Israel is not weak, they will eventually see the rationale for mutual compromises, reconciliation and peace."[53] More specifically, Rabin viewed military superiority as a necessary, though not sufficient, condition for ending the conflict. In 1991 he still held that Israel had no chance to reach a negotiated settlement with its neighbors except from a position of strength: "No Arab ruler seriously will consider the peace process as long as he still can toy with the idea of achieving more by way of violence."[54] Knowing the importance of military force in the international politics of the Middle East, he regarded military strength as instrumental in propelling a resolution from the battlefield to the negotiating table—under conditions favorable to Israel.[55]

Another example of Rabin's belief that only Arab weakness would lead to the acceptance of Israel in the region occurred in 1987. The Iraqis had initiated contacts to bring about a meeting between Defense Minister Rabin and Saddam Hussein (the meeting never materialized). Iraq saw Israel as a useful diplomatic instrument for improving relations with the United States at a time when the Iranian army was still deep in Iraqi territory. Commenting on these events, Rabin noted: "The period was at the end of the Iran-Iraq war. Iraq was emerging from the war injured. My assumption was that it was possible to reach peace [with Baghdad] only if a situation were to arise in which there would be an interest on the other side due to weakness. . . . I assumed Saddam was weak, and that there was a chance for a change."[56] At that time there were some, particularly among the more dovish elements within the Israeli political leadership, who believed that Hussein, who had already mended his relations with Egypt, could be brought into the peace process.

In addition to the state of the military balance, the time vector played an important role in Rabin's thinking about the Arab-Israeli conflict. "Playing for time" was a central component of Israel's political strategy in its relations with the Arab world. In the footsteps of former leaders, such as Ben-Gurion and Yigal Allon, Rabin believed that Israel could wear the Arabs down over time and that, eventually, the Arabs would reconcile themselves to the existence of the state of Israel. Commenting on the extended period of the Palestinian uprising, the Intifada, he stressed: "In every protracted conflict there is a component of 'who gets exhausted first.' I believe that we will not be the first to give way."[57] It was only in his second term as prime minister that Rabin revised this evaluation of Israeli society as he came to believe that growing Israeli weariness from the protracted conflict was having a negative effect on Israel's bargaining position. (This changing evaluation is discussed in much greater detail in the final chapter of this book.) Furthermore, time was considered to be an important element in testing Arab commitments to moderation toward Israel.

In 1971, when there were diplomatic attempts to reach an understanding between Egypt and Israel on the basis of UN Security Council Resolution 242, Rabin believed that even a diplomatic breakthrough would not bring about a peace such as that between Belgium and France. A peace agreement between the parties could serve only as a framework to promote a lengthy process that could lead to "true peace."[58] When the Arab states moderated their positions against Israel and a peace process did evolve beginning in the mid-1970s, Rabin was again doubtful about the possibility of a direct transition from war to peace. Rabin was even skeptical about a radical change in Egypt's posture toward Israel after 1977. In his typically frank manner, Rabin expressed his opinion that the peace treaty, though important, represented essentially just another interim agreement, rather than an end to the conflict.[59] Furthermore, Rabin wrote in 1979, immediately after the signing of the peace treaty with Egypt: "The process of transition from war to peace will be extremely lengthy. Along with the promising chances will be serious risks. Appropriate Israeli military might is not only necessary for securing the existence of the state of Israel, but also for making sure that the peace process will not fail."[60] At that time, he regarded the peace treaty with Egypt as an important, though not necessarily permanent, element of Israel's national security.

His audiences were often reminded that Israel is located in the Middle East, where peace treaties are by and large a temporary phenomenon. A favorite example of his for this particular point was the 1975 Iran-Iraq agreement, which "ended" the border disputes between these two countries. Rabin liked to emphasize that the two Moslem countries had never even taken the extreme step of denying each other's existence. Yet, only five years later, when Saddam Hussein concluded that the fall of the Shah, coupled with the deterioration in the operational capabilities of the Iranian army in the aftermath of the Islamic revolution, had changed the military balance between the two countries, he did not hesitate to disregard the recent treaty and to unleash his invasion.[61] Thus, for Rabin, military power was a necessary condition to guarantee the preservation of treaties with Israel's neighbors in a turbulent Middle East.

Rabin rejected the "Peace Now" slogan voiced by Israel's far left, as well as the messianic impatience of Gush Emunim on the extreme right. He suggested adopting a long historic perspective on the return of the Jews to the Land of Israel[62] and insisted that a slow and gradual process was necessary to achieve peaceful relations in the region.[63] He continually appealed for patience: "Any attempt . . . to solve the problem by a single act will lead nowhere."[64] In 1989, Rabin warned Israelis against losing their patience and steadfastness in the face of prolonged threats and falling "into the trap of believing in miraculous shortcuts."[65]

Always suspicious of comprehensive plans to solve the Arab-Israeli conflict, Rabin preferred the Kissingerian step-by-step diplomatic approach. This was one of the reasons for his cool reception of the U.S. advocacy, during the administration of President Jimmy Carter, of the comprehensive approach to the Arab-Israeli conflict, as delineated in the "Brookings Plan."[66] Rabin, who was skeptical about the possibility of a quick transition to peaceful Arab-Israeli relations, saw no reason why Israel should not prolong the political process of tension reduction in the region so long as there was a chance to get a better deal. Rabin argued that Israel must have patience until a solution it regarded as desirable was accepted by its neighbors. When confronted in 1988 with the argument that his prescription for a settlement on the eastern border, a territorial compromise along the lines of the Allon Plan,[67] was a "nonstarter" in Arab quarters, Rabin answered, "Then we will wait until they will accept it."[68]

Nevertheless, Rabin gradually came to the conclusion that Israel could no longer be passive in waiting for the Arabs to change their attitudes toward Israel. The peace treaty with Egypt, which indicated a certain ripeness in the Arab world to accept Israel as a fait accompli, led him to believe that greater Israeli activism was warranted in the pursuit of peace. Whereas once the post-1967 war remark of Dayan about "waiting for a telephone call" from the Arab leaders was appropriate, Rabin stressed in the mid-1980s: "We should no longer wait for a telephone call from the Arabs. . . . We should pick up the telephone and dial in order to reach peace negotiations."[69] In 1987, speaking to his colleagues in the Labor Party's bureau (lishka), Rabin said that despite the fact that Israel lived under the shadow of war, it was the duty of Israel "to display openness and initiative to foster political processes which could bring about a dialogue [with the Arabs] and eventually peace."[70] With signs of change within the Arab world, the time had come for Israel to play a positive role in enticing the Arab states to reach agreements with their neighbor.

THE EVOLUTION OF THE ARAB-ISRAELI CONFLICT

Rabin read the history of the Arab-Israeli conflict through power-politics glasses. For him, the conflict was a power struggle punctuated by acts of violence, whose subtext was a dormant war. Nevertheless, Rabin realized that the conflict was gradually inching toward the greater acceptance of Israel by its Arab neighbors. Yet even in the last years of his life, when Rabin perceived peace to be within reach, he remained skeptical about its duration and quality. As he followed Shimon Peres into the Oslo discussions with the Palestinians, he continued to signal great ambivalence about the peace process, as is shown in the last chapter of this book.

The War of Independence created, in Rabin's view, the most important political fact: the establishment of the state of Israel. Yet the war did not end with any political agreements with Arab neighbors—only with armistice agreements. As a formative strategic experience, it reinforced Rabin's predisposition to see military force as the most important factor in Arab-Israeli relations. This was an important reason for his choosing, at the end of the War of Independence, to stay in the army and dedicate himself to a military career. This career pattern was similar to that of other sons of the founding Zionist elite.[71]

Rabin's perspective had not changed very much when he analyzed the 1956 Sinai Campaign. This war brought a decade of quiet along Israel's southern border and opened the Tiran Straits for Israeli shipping.[72] Its greatest achievement was, according to Rabin, the enhancement of Israeli deterrence. As elaborated in chapter 4, deterrence formed, in Rabin's eyes, a main pillar of Israeli security. By studying the statements of Arab leaders, Rabin reached the conclusion that the Sinai Campaign strengthened Arab awareness that a war against Israel was an extremely complicated enterprise, one demanding extraordinary means and efforts. Furthermore, such a war could be extremely costly.[73] The Sinai Campaign also placed Israel "strongly on the Middle East map, as a country that must be taken into consideration, and [established] that it is worthwhile to have relations with her."[74] The emphasis on deterrence and the conclusion that the military prestige endowed by the brilliant military victory was translated into political achievements were characteristic of Rabin's realpolitik approach to international relations. He noted, however, that Israel could not capitalize on its victory to make any changes in its borders with Egypt due to international pressure for full withdrawal; likewise, Israel's victory failed to bring about a change in Egypt's radical goals versus Israel.[75] Indeed, one of Rabin's conclusions was that there were limits on what Israel could achieve through the use of force.

The June 1967 war was of paramount military, national, and political importance, according to Rabin.[76] Rabin had no doubt that the Israeli military initiative in 1967 represented a response to an existential threat of the largest magnitude.[77] It also constituted the most impressive Arab military debacle. Furthermore, in the absence of peace, it enabled Israel "to hold the best defensive lines that can be drawn on the Middle East map, without having to withstand—for the time being—pressure from friends to withdraw."[78] In contrast to the postwar situation of 1956, after the 1967 war Israel retained the territories conquered, as bargaining cards to be bartered away only in exchange for political agreements with its neighbors. This favorable political situation was primarily the result of the three-week waiting period before the 1967 Six-Day War, a delay that proved to Israelis and friends abroad that Israel had exhausted all diplomatic means before resorting to force.[79]

Israel's next significant trial by fire was, of course, the 1973 Yom Kippur War. For Rabin, this war was a watershed in the Arab-Israeli conflict. In

1980 he emphasized that the post-1973 period had been characterized by Israel's inability to sustain by itself the economic effort needed to counterbalance qualitative and quantitative improvements in Arab military forces.[80] Therefore, Israeli dependence on the United States grew considerably. Following the 1973 war, Prime Minister Rabin believed Israel was facing one of the most dangerous periods in its history because of the unprecedented international isolation of the Jewish state. Only the United States remained a friend willing to render crucial assistance. Yet in the immediate period after 1973, Rabin saw the United States as a great power in retreat. The perception of enhanced Arab international leverage during the energy crisis, the increase in resources available for a military buildup as a result of the rise in oil prices, and the more tenuous Israeli-U.S. relations led the Israeli leadership to believe that war might be imminent. Rabin repeatedly expressed his apprehensions of an impending war during the 1974–76 period.[81]

The turning point in the Arab-Israeli conflict was the visit of President Sadat to Jerusalem on 19 November 1977. For Rabin, and for many others in the Jewish state, this event opened a new and unprecedented chapter in Arab-Israeli relations. The visit was an important psychological breakthrough, announcing to Israelis and the Arab world alike that Egypt was coming to terms with reality. Egypt, the visit proclaimed, would no longer regard Israel as an artificial entity but would instead recognize the existence of the Jewish state.

In 1978, Rabin articulated the implications of the Sadat initiative: (1) for the first time, an Arab leader declared that Israel was an established political fact, one that Arabs should recognize and with which Arabs should coexist peacefully; (2) the Israeli interpretation of the nature of peace (diplomatic relations and open borders) was accepted; and (3) an Arab state implemented the long-held Israeli principle of direct negotiations, rather than using intermediaries.[82] Rabin was particularly enthusiastic about this development because he, like most other Israeli leaders, realized the centrality of Egypt in the Arab world: "Egypt has always led the Arab world in any substantial move, whether toward war or in another direction. It was Egypt who was the first to wage war against us in the War of Independence, and it was the first to negotiate an armistice agreement with Israel at Rhodes in 1949. After 25 years, where no formal agreement was signed between an Arab country and Israel, it was Egypt first that put its signature on an Arab-Israeli agreement in 1973."[83]

The historic visit also vindicated Rabin's own approach during the 1974–77 period—an approach that he believed was shared by previous governments—in attempting to satisfy, as much as possible, Egyptian interests. The September 1975 Sinai 2 Agreement was the example frequently used by Rabin to demonstrate this point.[84] Then, Rabin led the moderate forces within the Israeli government to agree to territorial concessions in the western part of the Sinai, including the oil fields in Abu Rudeis and the western parts of the strategic Mitla and Gidi Passes, in order to consolidate the new pro-U.S. orientation of the Egyptian foreign policy. Furthermore, the Sinai II Agreement served, in Rabin's opinion, as a wedge between Egypt and Syria, minimizing the likelihood of coordination between the two Arab countries in launching, yet again, a two-front attack against Israel.[85] Yet in contrast to others, Rabin did not see the 1975 Sinai II Agreement between Israel and Egypt as a necessary step to the Egypt-Israel peace treaty. Rabin was, then, motivated primarily by the desire to maintain a friendship with the United States rather than to shape the conditions of the region.

Rabin recognized the significant strategic fact that Egypt, in the immediate and midrange post–peace treaty period, was unlikely to reopen hostilities with Israel. The changes in relations with Egypt obviously contributed to lowering his level of threat perception, as they did also for other Israelis. Later on, in 1986, he still placed a high value on the new relationship with Egypt. At that time, he maintained that the preservation of this peaceful relationship should constitute the highest priority for Israel's foreign policy.[86] In his capacity as defense minister of the national unity government, he emphasized that only because of this peace treaty had a huge $600 million cut in the defense budget been possible, allowing the rehabilitation of Israel's deteriorating economy.[87]

In contrast to the 1970s, Rabin regarded the 1980s as a decade in which Israel reached a comfortable strategic position. Despite an erosion in the Israeli margins of security, precipitated by cuts in the defense budget since 1985 and by Arab weapons-procurement plans, the generally unfavorable military balance between the Israel Defense Force (IDF) and the Arab armies was mitigated by favorable regional political trends.[88] In March 1990, at a memorial to Yigal Allon, Rabin explained this change to be the result of three factors: the peace treaty with Egypt, which had fragmented Arab unity against Israel; the long Iran-Iraq War (1980–88), which had diverted attention from the Arab-Israeli conflict; and the decrease in Soviet support to Syria, a country that was gradually becoming the largest threat to Israel. He concluded that toward the end of the 1980s, Israel's main Arab rivals were in no position to challenge the country militarily.[89] As a result of regional developments, the Arab states were in disarray. In his opinion, the danger of the Khomeini revolution and the spread of Islamic fundamentalism were of greater concern in the Arab world than the Arab-Israeli conflict.[90] In July 1985, he pointed out that Israelis had by and large failed to recognize that wars intended to destroy Israel were no longer on the Arab political agenda, though he did not exclude large-scale Arab military initiatives for limited political gains.[91]

Rabin did identify one negative trend in the 1980s: the "Palestinization of the Arab-Israeli conflict," meaning that there was to some extent a transition from an interstate conflict to an Israeli-Palestinian dispute.[92] Benefiting from hindsight, Rabin saw this process beginning in the 1982 Lebanon War, in which the destruction of the Palestine Liberation Organization (PLO) was one of Israel's main goals. Toward the end of the decade, Israel became preoccupied again with Palestinian terrorism from the Lebanese border, but beginning in December 1987, attention focused primarily on the violence generated by Palestinian civilians in the Israeli-ruled territories—the Intifada. He expressed the hope that this development would not divert Israeli energies from the search for solutions to the Arab-Israeli conflict to a concentration on the Palestinian problem.[93]

A serious national security problem, to which Rabin started paying attention in the mid-1980s, was Israeli vulnerability to surface-to-surface missiles and weapons of mass destruction, chemical weapons in particular (this issue is discussed in detail in chapter 5). This apprehension was a corollary of the Iran-Iraq War, in which both sides used hundreds of long-range missiles against civilian population centers. Furthermore, Iraq used chemical weapons and was subjected to only minimal international criticism.[94]

The missile threat amplified existential threats. In August 1989, Rabin regarded the 1948 War of Independence over Israel's existence as still in progress. "It smoldered for more than 41 years, and can be termed a *war of generations*."[95] He continued to demand from Israeli society sustained endurance to face the prolonged threat.[96] Nevertheless, as far as Rabin was concerned, the decade of the 1980s was, in strategic terms, a good era for Israel.

As analyzed in greater detail in the final chapter of this book, the 1990s were, in Rabin's view, strategically even better for Israel. The disintegration of the Soviet Union, the 1991 Gulf War, and the evolving peace process beginning with the November 1991 Madrid Conference significantly ameliorated the international circumstances in which Israel operated. Rabin definitely became more optimistic in the 1990s than he had ever been before, though he maintained a vigilant eye on persistent dangers to national security, dangers that continued to threaten Israel's very existence. Islamic radicalism, impressive conventional military capabilities in the Middle East, and nuclearization, in particular, occupied his thoughts.

THE PALESTINIAN DIMENSION OF THE CONFLICT

For many years Rabin dismissed the Palestinian question as a nonissue.[97] Rabin, like many others in the Israeli political elite, regarded the Arab-Israeli conflict primarily in interstate terms and did not accord great significance to the Palestinian issue.[98] The Arab states constituted the existential threat, and they were the address for making war and negotiating peace. Rabin was power-oriented and accordingly did not give much strategic weight to the Palestinians, who lacked military strength and engaged primarily in terrorist attacks against Israeli targets. Recognizing terror as the weapon of the weak, Rabin viewed Palestinian violence as an irksome problem that could not be solved by military means and, therefore, required patience and enduring determination on Israel's part. Strategically, the Palestinians were viewed by Rabin for many years as more of a nuisance than a rival deserving much serious attention.

At the end of 1965, Rabin identified a new wave of Palestinian nationalism as a fourth development worth paying attention to in Arab-Israeli relations (the others were Egypt's decline, the severity of threatening statements against Israel, and the massive weapons-procurement plans of several Arab countries). It is noteworthy that Rabin, unlike others in Israel, was ascribing to the Palestinians a national identity as early as the 1960s. Then, Rabin regarded the establishment of the PLO in 1964 as its expression, but the PLO represented, in Rabin's eyes, basically a political tool of the Arab countries against Israel, even though it constituted "a greater danger to Jordan."[99] In 1965, Rabin concluded that the PLO was unable to muster enough power to become a factor that could change the regional power balance.[100] He did not ignore, however, the few incursions into Israel by the PLO's armed organ, Fatah, and added cautiously, "It is not large and maybe it is not a very serious organization, but its harassment function could become severe in the future."[101]

In this 1965 interview, we can detect the substance of Rabin's approach to the Palestinian issue. Rabin recognized early the corporate identity of the Palestinians and never indulged in denying their existence as a separate group with political aspirations, as did some within the Israeli political elite. At the same time, he correctly perceived the weaknesses of the Palestinian national movement: its position as a pawn in inter-Arab politics; its threat to the Hashemite regime in Jordan; and its limited military potential versus the strength of Israel.

For many years, Rabin regarded the Palestinian problem as a by-product of the Arab unwillingness to accept Israel. In his January 1976 address to the U.S. Congress, Prime Minister Rabin noted that it was not Israel that had prevented the establishment of a Palestinian state after the 1947 UN General Assembly partition resolution; it was the Arab countries that had refrained from establishing a Palestinian state in the West Bank and Gaza, which were under the rule of Jordan and Egypt respectively for nineteen years (1949–67).[102] Then, Rabin referred to the "so-called PLO" as an organization set up by the Arab states with the goal of destroying Israel. He added: "Those who believe that the Palestinian issue is the obstacle to peace are mistaken. We will have to settle this problem as part of the permanent peace settlement, but those that claim that it is the key to peace, the formula for peace, the means to achieve peace . . . are simply misreading reality."[103] This statist emphasis reflected the prevalent view at that time toward the Palestinian issue in Israel.

According to Rabin, only in the aftermath of a change in the Arab states' positions toward Israel would there be a possibility of solving the Palestinian issue. The Arab states and the Palestinian leadership were blamed for Palestinian misfortunes. Despite Rabin's assertion that "we have to offer a reasonable solution to the Palestinian problem," he declared emphatically in 1983: "The Palestinian problem is not the heart of the Arab-Israeli conflict."[104] In 1988, following the outbreak of the Palestinian uprising, which attracted much attention to the Israeli-Palestinian dispute, he wrote an article in the Labor Party organ deploring "the transfer of the locus of the confrontation between ourselves and the Arabs, from the Arab states to the Palestinians."[105] In this article, Rabin pointed out the dangerous implication of such a change in perception. "Diverting the focus of a solution . . . to the Israeli-Palestinian level would be a serious mistake for it would mean Israel's facing the PLO."[106] He was afraid that bilateral Israeli-Palestinian negotiations would further elevate the status of the PLO as the representative of the Palestinians.

According to the state-centric view of the Arab-Israeli conflict and the associated reluctance to deal with the PLO, Rabin envisioned a solution to the Palestinian issue "in the political and geographical framework of a peace treaty with Jordan."[107] Despite the ascendance of the PLO as an international actor in the 1970s, Rabin resisted decoupling the Palestinian issue from Jordan because this would, in his view, inevitably bring about the establishment of a "third" state between Jordan and Israel, a very dangerous development.[108] In 1978, Rabin claimed that the permanent settlement had to produce a Jordanian-Palestinian state, wherein Palestinian nationalist aspirations could be expressed.[109]

This was typical of the Laborites' preference, which adhered to the notion of a territorial compromise with Jordan.[110] After the 1967 war, which resulted in Jordan's loss of the West Bank, Labor-led Israel demonstrated an interest in negotiating with Jordan's King Hussein for the return of some of the territories captured in that war. The one very brief attempt to deal directly with the Arab inhabitants of the territories conquered in June 1967, immediately after the war, contemplated the establishment of a Palestinian entity. Rabin, as chief of staff, expressed support for this unsuccessful Israeli initiative,[111] and after that failure he, like others, adopted a "Jordanian orientation." This meant that Israel was willing to cede most of the West Bank, particularly the areas heavily populated by Arabs, to Jordan, in accordance with the Allon Plan (discussed below).

The Jordanian option also meant that Israel preferred to see the Palestinians represented by Jordan rather than by the PLO. The rulers of Jordan, the Hashemites, had always displayed a greater readiness to enter into a dialogue with the Zionists than had those Arabs residing west of the Jordan River. Despite the fact that Jordan was formally committed to the anti-Israel consensus among Arab states, a complex relationship characterized by both conflict and cooperation had developed between the neighboring states.[112] Jordan was also a known political entity, and King Hussein seemed to be a more promising observer or guarantor of an agreed-upon modus vivendi than was Yasir Arafat, the PLO leader. Hussein's pro-Western orientation was also seen as preferable to the pro-Soviet orientation of the PLO.

Realizing that Jordan might have difficulties accepting the Allon Plan, Rabin was not averse to the idea of an interim agreement, under which Jordan and Israel would share responsibility for ruling over the West Bank and the Gaza Strip.[113] Another interim alternative that Rabin's government considered positively in 1974 was the Jericho Plan. The idea was to hand over to King Hussein the town of Jericho in the West Bank (this town was not part of the areas to be annexed under the Allon Plan).[114] Though the details of the Jericho plan were not made public, Rabin spoke, in an interview with the U.S. television company NBC, of his willingness to give up parts of the West Bank for an Israeli-Jordanian nonbelligerency agreement (less than a peace treaty).[115] In 1976, Rabin was ready to negotiate with West Bank Palestinians as members of a Jordanian delegation at the Geneva Conference.[116]

Rabin's Jordanian orientation was strengthened by his deep abhorrence of the PLO. He repeatedly used the expression "the so-called PLO," denying the organization its claim that it was a genuine liberation movement.[117] To Rabin, it was inherently a terrorist organization.[118] The PLO was perceived by Rabin, and by most other Israelis, as ideologically and unequivocally committed to the destruction of the state of Israel. The destruction of Israel was not only a long-range aspiration but also the PLO's operative political goal. Rabin said: "We know what its objective is. It is written in the Palestinian National Covenant, which is the PLO's constitution."[119] Rabin, like other Israelis, took the covenant, along with its many articles calling for the destruction of the Jewish state, very seriously. Therefore, the prevalent view was that the PLO was totally committed to unrealistic goals and was in addition extremely uncompromising. This left no possibility of its reaching an accommodation with the Jewish state. Rabin also denied the possibility of change within the PLO, because any PLO acceptance of Israel would undermine its whole raison d'etre.[120] His rejection of the PLO was coupled with a personal enmity for Arafat. In his first reference to Arafat in his *Memoirs,* Rabin called the PLO leader "a man to be mentioned often with disgust."[121]

Therefore, Rabin, like many others in the Israeli political elite, was adamantly opposed to any negotiations with the PLO. The success of the PLO in acquiring an observer status at the UN in 1974 was particularly disturbing to Rabin. In reaction to PLO diplomatic successes in the international community, Rabin succeeded, in September 1975, in extracting from the United States a commitment not to recognize the PLO and not to negotiate with it (unless it renounced terror and accepted UN Security Council Resolution 242) and secured a veto on inviting parties to a renewal of the Geneva Conference in order to exclude the PLO from such a gathering.

The pragmatic Rabin was not averse, however, to testing, as early as 1976 during his first tenure as prime minister, the PLO's willingness to moderate its positions. His intermediary was his friend and member of his General Staff in 1967, Maj. Gen. (Res.) Mati Peled.[122] Peled, who became very dovish in his political views and held talks with PLO representatives, persuaded Rabin to laud publicly an Arafat statement criticizing airplane hijackings and also to release jailed Palestinian terrorists if the PLO would show moderation at the UN General Assembly. As Rabin expected, the PLO did not deliver on its part of the proposed deal. In 1985, serving as defense minister, Rabin again approved approaching the PLO. Shlomo Gazit, ex–intelligence chief, was allowed to meet PLO representatives to test the seriousness of the PLO interlocutors and to gauge the amount of progress possible in negotiations with this organization. The dialogue petered out by the end of 1986 after three meetings.[123]

Prime Minister Menachem Begin's 1977 plan granting "home rule" (later dubbed "autonomy") to the Palestinians without linking them to Jordan, a plan that became an international binding document in the 1978 Camp David Accords, was not welcomed by Rabin. In January 1978 he criticized such a political arrangement as unsatisfactory in terms of the national Palestinian aspirations, which Rabin still preferred to channel into a Jordanian-Palestinian state. Furthermore, the autonomy proposal was "planting the seeds for a 'Palestinian entity' that will evolve into a Palestinian state (separate from Jordan), whose main goal will be the destruction of Israel."[124] Rabin advocated abandoning the autonomy plan and replacing it with a five-year interim arrangement of Israeli-Jordanian rule with a Palestinian administration, to be accompanied by a declaration of readiness to withdraw from parts of the West Bank.[125] He believed that such a plan could bring the Jordanians into the peace process, as well as reduce objections in the Arab world to Egypt's peace initiative.

Yet Rabin gradually realized that a "pure" Jordanian option was becoming less and less feasible and that the addition of a Palestinian element had become necessary. After the 1974 Arab summit in Rabat, where the PLO was recognized as the sole representative of the Palestinians, it was even more difficult for Jordan to play this role. Through the 1978 Camp David Accords, in which the Palestinians of Judea, Samaria, and Gaza were given a say in the implementation of the autonomy plan, their semi-independent participation in negotiations over the future of those areas was incorporated into an internationally binding document. At the end of 1980, in a party forum discussing the platform for the coming 1981 elections, Rabin had reconciled himself to a Palestinian role in a Jordanian context: "The key is partly in the hands of the leadership of the territories, maybe more than Hussein's. Therefore, I name my proposal Jordanian-Palestinian."[126] The practical question was who would be the Palestinian interlocutor to be part of a Jordanian delegation. Rabin, as defense minister after 1984, met regularly with numerous local leaders in the West Bank and Gaza, though he refrained from dealing with Palestinians clearly identified as PLO supporters and even criticized his colleague Peres for doing so.[127] These encounters came within the context of the Israeli policy of maintaining an ongoing dialogue with the local leadership in the territories and also pursuing the effort to find acceptable Palestinians who would be willing to be part of a Jordanian-Palestinian negotiating team.

In the latter part of the 1980s, Rabin believed that a moderate Palestinian leadership, with no PLO links, could emerge in the territories. The example he gave in April 1987 was Rashad A-Shawa of Gaza.[128] Ironically, he was even more optimistic after the outbreak of the Intifada in December 1987. In January 1988, appearing on television, Rabin told the nation: "The unique feature of what is happening here is that, for the first time, it is the residents of the territories who are leading the Palestinian struggle."[129] Rabin was impressed by the Palestinians' new emerging leadership and accepted the Labor Party doves' proposal for holding general elections in the administered territories. He hoped the elections would yield Palestinian representatives who were not subservient to the PLO but were willing to be part of a Jordanian-Palestinian delegation and negotiate with Israel. Indeed, before the 1988 elections, Rabin agreed to change his party platform, approving of negotiations with an independent Palestinian delegation for interim agreement. Rabin was successful in persuading Prime Minister Shamir to incorporate the election idea into the national unity government peace initiative of May 1989 to provide for a Palestinian interlocutor for the negotiations over a five-year interim agreement.[130] Yet even after King Hussein formally disengaged himself from the West Bank in July 1988, Rabin continued to envision Jordan as the principal partner in a permanent agreement because the two countries shared a common border and both were faced with a Palestinian problem.[131]

Rabin differentiated between the PLO and the Palestinians living under Israel's rule. The latter wanted "to go on living in peace regardless of their political views," according to Rabin.[132] Rabin, particularly in his role as defense minister, felt responsible for the well-being of the Palestinians under Israeli military rule. In 1985 he maintained, "We should offer those who want to make peace with us the opportunity to prosper and to develop."[133] Rabin believed that the amelioration of economic hardships of the Palestinians in the Israeli-ruled territories was an Israeli duty and could have positive political consequences, at least in the interim period until a comprehensive political solution could be found.

Opposition to the PLO was also related to the content of the group's demands. PLO insistence on Palestinian statehood and on the "right of return" of the Palestinian Diaspora was extremely threatening. The establishment of a "third state" (a euphemism used by Israelis in referring to a Palestinian state) between Israel and Jordan was seen by many in the Israeli political elite, including Rabin, as strategic folly. Such a state, Rabin believed, would be very dangerous.[134]

Rabin adhered to the Labor Party platform that specified that an independent Palestinian state would become "a focus of hostility and the inflammation of passions." Rabin used harsh terms to describe this possibility, asserting in 1988 that such a state would form "a cancer in the heart of the Middle East."[135] On a later occasion, he referred to this possibility as "a time bomb."[136] Even after he reached an agreement with the PLO in September 1993, Rabin continued to express his opposition to the establishment of such a state, though he realized that the creation of the Palestinian Authority carried the potential danger of developing into a Palestinian state.[137]

Rabin's rejection of the PLO was also motivated by the PLO's insistence that Jerusalem be the capital of the Palestinian state. After 1967, Rabin never contemplated any other arrangement but an undivided city under Israeli sovereignty. On this issue Rabin, like most other Jews, was unashamedly sentimental. The generations-long yearning for the Western Wall was central to his Jewish identity. Moreover, Jerusalem had played an important role in his life. In 1948, he had commanded the Palmach Harel Brigade that fought to open a corridor to and within the city of Jerusalem. In 1967, the IDF under his command had liberated the occupied parts of Jerusalem. For him, the days of June 1967 closed a personal cycle and constituted historic justice.[138]

THE TERRITORIAL DIMENSION

Rabin ascribed great importance to Israel's future borders. In accordance with his approach to the time factor in the Arab-Israeli conflict, Rabin insisted on negotiating patiently for peace agreements that would include defensible borders.[139] From his realpolitik perspective, peace agreements were not enough; Israel had to maintain a strong IDF and defensible borders, which would endow Israel with good defense lines and also strategic depth. The security arrangements and the topographical features of the new frontiers were no less important than open borders and diplomatic relations.

Although Rabin always displayed a readiness to part with some of the territories that Israel had conquered in 1967, his criterion for retaining land was strategic. He never accepted the dovish argument that in the age of missiles, territory had become unimportant. During his first tenure as prime minister (1974–77), his government implemented a cautious settlement policy along the lines of the Allon Plan.[140] As prime minister, he resisted, not always successfully, efforts by some of his colleagues to expand this area further.[141] At the time, his positions were to the left of those of Peres.

His conviction that certain territories were of cardinal importance to Israel's national security explains why he was not enthusiastic about the September 1978 Camp David Accords, which were in fact an abandonment of the principle of defensible borders. Israel agreed at that time to return to the international border with Egypt without any revisions. Early in 1978, when Israel was negotiating a peace treaty with Egypt, Rabin had advocated border changes. He wanted to annex limited territory adjacent to the old international border in two areas: in the Rafah salient, to block the two invasion routes into Palestine; and west of Eilat, Israel's port on the Red Sea, to improve the defense of this city. A second priority was an Israeli military presence in Sharm al-Sheikh; at the tip of the Sinai Peninsula, this city was needed to keep the Tiran Straits open for ships going to and from Eilat. Rabin was willing to consider an exchange of territory to make it easier for the Egyptians to accept the border changes.[142] Nevertheless, he cast his vote in the Knesset in favor of the Camp David Accords because of the great importance he attached to developing relations with Egypt.

On the eastern front, Rabin favored the plan put forward immediately after the 1967 war by his former commander in the Palmach, Allon. This preference was similar to that of other middle-of-the-road Laborites.[143] The Allon Plan envisioned the annexation of strategically important areas sparsely populated by Arabs. Rabin, like others, was sensitive to the need to preserve a Jewish majority in Israel by not annexing areas densely populated by Arabs—this was referred to in Israeli political parlance as the "demographic problem." Strategically desirable areas included the Jordan rift valley, areas around Jerusalem, the Yatir region (south of Hebron), and also territory needed to broaden the narrow center of the country.

In 1983, Rabin specified in public the magnitude of the proposed annexation: "About a third, more or less, of the territory of the West Bank and the Gaza Strip must be included in the context of peace, under Israeli sovereignty."[144] Rabin was not oblivious to the Arabs living in the territories intended for annexation, and he envisioned in 1988 an enlarged Israel "with an additional half million [Arabs] over and above the 700,000 [Arabs living in Israel at that time]."[145] He was willing to offer them a choice of becoming Israeli citizens or of remaining Jordanian.[146] Despite Rabin's reluctance to annex areas populated by many Arabs, he nevertheless insisted on holding on to the territories enumerated above.

Rabin differentiated between settlements beyond the Green Line (the 1967 border), which had a security value, and political settlements whose only function was to establish political facts on the ground.[147] According to Rabin, the security settlements were located along the confrontation lines (the Lebanese border, on the Golan Heights, along the Jordan River, and in the Arava) and had a defensive role in blocking routes of invasion into Israel. "We will defend Tel Aviv and Jerusalem from the security border along the Jordan River, tens of kilometers from home and not from places five minutes from Kfar Saba."[148] The settlements "five minutes from Kfar Saba" were located in Samaria and were considered to have only political, rather than security, value. Rabin had no qualms about actually dubbing the "political" settlements as a "security burden," since they required IDF protection.

Concerning the Golan Heights, Rabin was willing to make some unspecified territorial concessions. In January 1976, Prime Minister Rabin, bowing to American pressure, agreed to consider some territorial adjustments on the Golan in exchange for a nonbelligerency agreement with Syria. Rabin referred to these concessions as "a painful solution," meaning that the "dismantling of a settlement or two would not be an obstacle."[149] On May 19, 1976, he told his cabinet that he was considering a territorial compromise on the Golan, since Israel did not have to stick to the line along which the IDF was currently deployed.[150] Yet he was generally known for his opposition to substantial border changes, and only after 1993 was he to become more generous in territorial terms, as discussed in the last chapter of this book.

CONCLUSION

Throughout his military and political career, Rabin displayed a realpolitik outlook on international relations, emphasizing the pursuit of national interests and a reliance on military power. For most of his life, he believed

ALLON PLAN

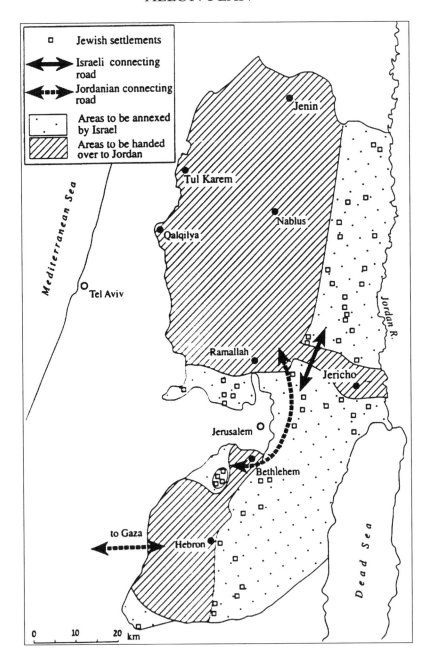

that Israel faced serious existential threats emanating from its Arab environment and that these threats had to be met primarily with military might. His naturally suspicious inclinations and his Jewish prism reinforced this conservative perspective on international affairs. Nevertheless, he could envision, even in the throes of conflict, a move toward more peaceful relations with Israel's Arab neighbors, albeit a very gradual move, which had to be predicated on unchallengeable Israeli military superiority in the region. He perceived such a historic process becoming a reality. Because of his state-centric view of the Arab-Israeli conflict and the late development of the Palestinian national movement, he only gradually learned to accept the Palestinians as a separate partner for negotiations. The PLO was not considered to be a suitable interlocutor until 1993. Rabin always favored a territorial compromise on all fronts, but he insisted on defensible borders. Toward the end of his political career and his life, in the 1990s, he changed his evaluation of the strategic environment and adopted more dovish positions on the issues of the Arab-Israeli agenda. These changes will be discussed in detail in the final chapter of this book.

CHAPTER TWO

THE AMERICAN ORIENTATION IN ISRAEL'S FOREIGN POLICY

Israel has always aspired to self-reliance in defense. Traditionally, Israeli leaders have placed little faith in the good intentions of the international community. Nevertheless, Israel has also sought to bolster its defense through an alliance with a strong world power because of sharp asymmetries between Israel and Arab states in military manpower and resources.[1]

After experimenting with a nonaligned foreign policy during the years immediately after independence, Israel began to search for an extraregional ally.[2] Israel tried to persuade the United States to lift the arms embargo it had imposed in 1948 and to increase its commitment to Israel's security.[3] Prime Minister David Ben-Gurion and his successor, Levi Eshkol, as well as Minister of Foreign Affairs Golda Meir, made continuous efforts to improve relations with the United States, despite an American policy of keeping Israel at an arm's length. The Israeli leaders' failure on this front, together with France's willingness to sell Israel advanced weapons, led in the mid-1950s to a French orientation in Israeli foreign policy.[4] Despite the 1956 Suez Campaign, which demonstrated the inefficacy of the European powers, the French orientation continued into the mid-1960s because the United States maintained its pre-1956 policies toward Israel. Abba Eban, Israel's ambassador to the United States (1950–59), aptly described the mood in the Israeli foreign policy community after the Suez Campaign: "Israeli policy makers were harshly reminded that no country except the United States could help us redress the adverse balance arising from the geopolitical predominance of the Arabs and their alliance with Soviet power."[5] Nevertheless, Israeli policymakers disagreed over the nature of the overtures to be made to the United States and the responses to American initiatives.

Yitzhak Rabin was known for his strong American orientation, and he played an important role in the gradual shift toward the United States. He worked toward good relations with Washington in all the positions he held from the time he joined Israel's political elite. After the October 1973 war, which underscored Israel's dependence on the United States, Israeli strategists' dream of self-reliance evaporated. One of the long-term implications was that the informal alliance with the United States acquired an even greater importance than before. Rabin was one of the most sensible voices in articulating the paramount need to preserve good relations between Jerusalem and Washington. Though preferring self-reliance in the use of military force, Rabin believed that Israel's freedom of action could be guaranteed only if an American understanding of Israeli positions was secured.

THE EARLY AMERICAN PREFERENCE

Rabin had, by the early 1960s, realized that Israel's military and diplomatic links with Europe were fraying and that the United States was a preferable ally.[6] On this matter he clashed with Shimon Peres, the architect of Israel's entente with France.[7] As a senior officer in the Israel Defense Force (IDF), Rabin met often with his counterparts in the French army, and he was intimately acquainted with the highest military echelons there. Yet he admitted in his memoirs: "With all fondness, friendship, sympathy, there was something in the French that eroded my confidence in them. It is probably then that my American orientation developed."[8] The French cultural ambience never appealed to the provincial Rabin.[9]

More important in Rabin's opinion, after the 1956 Suez fiasco the Europeans were of insignificant geopolitical weight, particularly in the Middle East. The field belonged to the superpowers, and only the United States counted for Israel in the strategic game. Furthermore, while he understood the importance of national interests and strategic factors, Rabin became convinced that the Americans were less cynical than the Europeans in their external relations and that moral considerations did play a role in the formulation of U.S. foreign policy.[10] A more principled foreign policy suited

Israel because the many Arab countries had much to offer American economic and strategic interests.

In concrete terms, Rabin was one of the driving forces behind the Ben-Gurion and the Eshkol governments' efforts to tap the American arms arsenal. Rabin criticized the inertia of the French-Israeli relationship, which delayed the crystallization of the politico-security awareness of the huge potential benefits that could accrue from developing closer ties with the United States. He credited Premier and Defense Minister Eshkol with overcoming this inertia and reorienting Israel's foreign policy.[11] In his memoirs, Rabin wrote: "Levi Eshkol's most historic decision was to intensify our campaign to break into the American arms market. Even if that had been his only accomplishment during his premiership (which it certainly was not), it would have sufficed to secure his fame in the chronicles of modern Israel."[12] Eshkol's foreign minister, Meir, also favored closer ties with the United States. Yet Rabin, who had been appointed by Eshkol, was Eshkol's closest national security adviser. As relations between Eshkol and Ben-Gurion (who had resigned in 1963) and Ben-Gurion's followers in the defense establishment became more tense, Rabin's influence grew.[13] His clout was greatest when Eshkol also held the defense portfolio—until just before the June 1967 war. (Then Moshe Dayan became defense minister, a post that he had to relinquish after the 1973 war, when Rabin became prime minister.)

During the late 1950s and the 1960s, Rabin preferred to diversify the sources of weapons procurement in order not to depend on the French. Furthermore, he did not consider the capabilities of the French government and military industries to be adequate, both in quantity and in quality, to counter the massive Soviet transfer of arms to the Arab countries. In addition, France was not offering satisfactory financial and credit terms.[14] In 1960, Deputy Chief of Staff Rabin supported the effort to purchase from the United States early-warning radar stations and Hawk surface-to-air missiles (SAMs), considered the best SAM system in the world.[15] He wanted primarily to solidify the break in the American weapons embargo, although he believed the SAMs could have some deterrence value against the possibility of an Arab air strike.[16] It seemed easier to overcome U.S. resistance to selling arms directly to Israel if the arms were "defensive" weapon systems, such as radar stations and SAMs. Soon thereafter, the administration of President John F. Kennedy proved to be more responsive to Israeli security needs than were previous administrations.[17]

In November 1963 Rabin, still deputy chief of staff, visited the United States and conducted a three-day strategic dialogue with American officials. This was the second such high-level military exchange of evaluations and presentation of Israel's security needs.[18] Later, in 1964, he proposed purchasing U.S.-made Skyhawk warplanes to enhance Israel's airpower,[19] and in 1966 Rabin put the Phantom F-4 combat aircraft on Israel's shopping list. He was extremely pleased with the 1965 decision by the administration of President Lyndon B. Johnson to sell "offensive" weapons also, on condition that the United States not be the only weapons supplier to Israel. Indeed, when in 1965 the Americans offered Skyhawks (less advanced than the Phantom) to Israel in return for an Israeli acquiescence to their supplying Jordan with modern tanks (with an understanding that the tanks would not be deployed in the West Bank), Rabin, as chief of staff, advised Premier Eshkol to accept the deal, despite the opposition of Deputy Minister of Defense Peres.[20] In 1966, Israel also placed an order for 250 American M-48 tanks. At the apex of his military career, Rabin became identified with the position that Israel must make every effort to establish good relations with the Americans.

MEETING AMERICA AS AMBASSADOR

A reflection of the weight that Rabin ascribed to the American factor in Israel's national strategy was his request, on his retirement from military service in 1968, to be nominated ambassador to the United States. It was unusual for a high-ranking Israeli officer to pursue a second career as a diplomat, and Rabin had to lobby hard for the Israeli ambassadorship to Washington. His object was to continue to serve his country, but on the diplomatic battleground.[21] He had little respect for diplomats and believed he could do better. Specifically, he wanted to make sure that the politicians and diplomats would not squander the military achievements of the 1967 war.[22]

Rabin's American-oriented strategic outlook was reinforced by his Americophile disposition. He had learned from his father, who spent several years in the United States, to admire that country,[23] and he had always wanted to spend an extended period there. Despite his critical attitude toward some aspects of American society, Rabin liked the United States very much and immensely enjoyed his five-year sojourn in Washington, D.C.[24] The hero of 1967 was well received in the United States. Like many other Israelis later, Rabin developed during his years as ambassador a keen interest in American affairs and a genuine feeling of closeness to the country.

Moreover, once in Washington, he learned to appreciate the U.S. political system. Later, he even sought to import some of its features into Israeli politics. (He was a staunch supporter of the direct election of the prime minister in Israel.)

Rabin had very clear plans for his task in Washington. In a memorandum he prepared for the Foreign Ministry shortly before leaving for the United States, he outlined his views on what he believed should be Israel's main goals in Washington.[25] The most important part of his mission was to make sure that the Americans would supply arms to upgrade the Israeli air force and other weapon systems to counterbalance the flow of Soviet arms to Arab countries following the 1967 war. He also believed that Israel should try to get U.S. financial assistance. In the political realm, Rabin advocated coordinating with the United States on any eventual peace negotiations and continuously taking into account American interests in devising and implementing Israeli policies. These priorities continued to define his approach to U.S.-Israeli relations in the years that followed.

In Washington, Rabin was introduced to the Nixon-Kissinger outlook on international affairs, which reinforced his own realpolitik tendencies. He had first met Henry Kissinger in 1964 when the latter was a professor at Harvard and was invited to lecture at Israel's National Security College.[26] They met again four years later, during Rabin's preparations for his move to Washington, and Rabin immensely enjoyed the opportunity to spend several hours listening to Kissinger's analysis of the world strategic situation.[27] He found a common language with Kissinger, and their business relationship developed into a true friendship.[28] Rabin also regarded the statesman as a good friend of Israel, despite Kissinger's pressuring of Israel before the conclusion of the Sinai II Agreement. In Rabin's opinion, Kissinger made "a first class contribution to Israel's security."[29]

Rabin also had a great appreciation for President Richard Nixon. Nixon's strategic preference for negotiating with the Soviets from a position of strength mirrored Rabin's views on the Arab-Israeli conflict. Rabin also appreciated the fact that Nixon saw Israel as a useful ally against Soviet expansionism.[30] He believed that Nixon was a staunch friend of Israel and even went so far as to state, in June 1972, his preference for Nixon in the presidential race—making a diplomatic faux pas. Replying to a question during an interview with Israeli radio, Rabin had said: "While we appreciate support in the form of words we are getting from one camp, we must prefer support in the form of deeds we are getting from the other camp."[31] The interview made news, and the *Washington Post* even responded with an editorial entitled "Israel's Undiplomatic Diplomat."[32] Rabin saw the Democratic presidential candidate, George McGovern, as the kind of liberal he had learned to dislike, one wanting to cut the U.S. defense budget and limit U.S. commitments around the world. Indeed, in early 1972, Rabin recommended to the Foreign Ministry in Jerusalem that it play down McGovern's stopover in Israel on the way back from a visit to the Far East. Rabin also privately lobbied among the predominantly pro-Democratic American Jewish community for President Nixon.[33] Years later Rabin continued to pay homage to Nixon, whom he visited on many occasions when he was in the United States. In 1984 he admitted to having a soft spot for Nixon, who was in his opinion a president unsurpassed in friendship to Israel.[34]

A top priority for Israel's relations with the United States immediately after the 1967 war was to secure the delivery of the fifty Phantom F-4 warplanes that had been on the Israeli shopping list. After the war, French President Charles De Gaulle imposed on Israel an arms embargo that included the much-needed and already mostly paid-for Mirage-5 warplanes. Israel could not find alternative suppliers for fighters at a time when the Soviet Union was rearming Egypt and Syria with the latest weapons, and by mid-1968, Egypt had almost reached its prewar combat-aircraft strength.[35] This Arab military strength and increasing Soviet presence were of extreme concern to the Israeli defense establishment. Dayan, the defense minister, called for a meeting at the end of May 1968 to discuss relations with the Americans; Rabin, the newly appointed ambassador, participated.[36]

Dayan and Rabin realized that the growing Soviet presence in the Middle East, partly facilitated by the Arab-Israeli rivalry, was creating concern in the United States about the potential for superpower clashes in the region. These apprehensions were generating pressures from Washington to end the Middle East conflict in ways that were not conducive to Israeli interests. Rabin reported that he hoped to counter such trends in the American capital by attempting to convince the Americans that a strong Israel would make U.S. military involvement unnecessary in case of an Israeli confrontation with the Soviet Union or a Soviet client. Dayan agreed that an Israel armed with Phantoms could deter even direct Soviet military involvement. Rabin outlined the embassy's efforts—with the White House, with Congress, and with the Jewish community—to speed the decision to supply the Phantoms. He also suggested closer cooperation in the intelligence area to acquaint the Americans with Israeli evaluations of the Soviet military presence, the developing Arab arsenal, and Israeli procurement plans.[37]

In October 1968, shortly before the presidential elections, President Johnson finally announced the U.S. government's decision to allow Israel to purchase the Phantoms (the first batch arrived the following summer). This decision also buttressed the Arab perception of the strong American commitment to Israel's security. During the 1968–69 period, the United States became Israel's main weapons supplier, something previous U.S. administrations had refused to contemplate. For Rabin, this was a great achievement.[38] The struggle to get additional Phantoms, as well as other types of military equipment, continued until the Nixon administration gradually adopted, starting at the end of the 1960s, a Middle East policy closer to Israeli preferences. The long-range agreements on delivery of weapons, agreed to by Nixon at the end of 1971, minimized tensions between the two countries.[39]

As ambassador, Rabin looked for ways to keep Israel in America's good graces and to minimize matters in dispute. For example, he lobbied Israeli leaders to adopt a tougher military reaction in the 1969–70 War of Attrition because he believed that this would help establish a better relationship with the Nixon administration, which by this time regarded Egypt, under Gamal Abdel Nasser, as a Soviet client. Rabin bombarded Jerusalem with cables urging escalation against Egypt.[40] In Rabin's opinion, the United States wanted the Nasser regime destabilized, and this was in the Israeli interest as well. Moreover, even if escalation led the Soviets to increase their involvement in Egypt in order to curb Israeli actions, this would have the beneficial effect of compelling Washington to extend further aid to Israel. His views carried great weight with Prime Minister Meir and with many others in her government because Rabin was considered to be a reliable analyst of the prevailing U.S. mood; he was also accepted as a security affairs expert, able to weigh diplomatic and security considerations.[41]

Rabin's position during the War of Attrition and his analysis of U.S. policy were criticized by many at home, particularly by Foreign Minister Eban, who disputed Rabin's evaluation of the U.S. political climate. Dayan also was reluctant to follow Rabin's advice because he feared greater Soviet involvement in the defense of the Nasser regime. But Rabin's perceptions of American preferences proved to be correct.[42] He believed that Israeli action would weaken the position of those in the U.S. administration, particularly in the State Department, who favored a Mideast solution inimical to Israeli interests.[43] Furthermore, Rabin believed that the image of a strong Israel, ready to use force in pursuing its national interests, was conducive to the quest for acquiring more weapons from the Nixon administration, which encouraged allies to withstand security challenges on their own.

Similarly, Rabin regarded Israeli readiness, at America's request, to take military action to assist Jordan in repelling the September 1970 Syrian invasion as having a far-reaching impact on U.S.-Israeli relations. "Israel's willingness to cooperate closely with the United States in protecting American interests in the region altered her image in the eyes of many officials in Washington. We were considered a partner—not equal to the United States, but nevertheless a valuable ally in a vital region during times of crisis."[44] According to Rabin, Israel later reaped benefits in terms of access to weapons and economic assistance. It is noteworthy that during the crisis, Rabin was far from being trigger-happy. He first attempted to extract various U.S. commitments, primarily a defense commitment against Soviet aggression, before recommending to Meir (then on a visit to the United States) that she accept the American request for Israeli military measures.

In his attempts to further Israeli interests, Rabin made a conscious effort to capitalize on American sources of support for Israel: the domestic political leverage of American Jewry, Americans' changing evaluation of the strategic benefits of having a strong Israel, and the widespread sympathy for Israel within the American public at large. During Rabin's tenure as ambassador to Washington in 1968–73, Israel began to profit from this pool of potential Jewish influence on U.S. policy, and the ambassador himself tried to exercise leverage within the structure of the American political system.[45]

Rabin was careful not to antagonize U.S. policy-makers. For example, he consistently mellowed the language of the embassy's bulletins (the "pink sheets" were distributed to a large mailing list) when they described American positions that Israel opposed and wanted to modify.[46] In early 1969, when Israel deliberated about the appropriate response to the U.S.-Soviet negotiations over devising guidelines to implement United Nations (UN) Resolution 242 and to the attempt to expand the negotiating forum to include the "Big Four" (adding Great Britain and France), Rabin favored a low-profile approach that minimized confrontation with the United States, in the hopes that the United States would finally begin the delivery of the Phantom F-4 combat jets. The supply of certain weapons remained, in his opinion, more important than the superpower talks.[47] Though Prime Minister Meir preferred a confrontational posture, she finally accepted Rabin's position. Another instance of Rabin's caution in dealing with the Americans, as well as an example of his clout in Jerusalem, occurred in July 1970 when he refused to deliver, to President Nixon, Meir's note rejecting the Rogers Initiative to end the War of Attrition on terms unfavorable to Israel. Rabin had learned from Kissinger to avoid head-on confrontations with the president; he directed Israel's objections to U.S. foreign policy toward lower levels within the administration, leaving the president room to maneuver and reach a compromise. Eventually, he succeeded in persuading Meir to accept the American initiative.[48]

Ambassador Rabin was also extremely successful in convincing the U.S. administration that lending financial support to Israel was in the U.S. national interest.[49] In fiscal years 1968, 1969, and 1970, the United States awarded Israel economic and military aid (almost all as loans) worth $191.4 million, $287.6 million, and $159.3 million respectively. A quantum leap in the scope of this aid took place in 1971, 1972, and 1973: U.S. aid amounted to $1,285.7 million, $838.3 million, and $818.9 million respectively.[50] Rabin's job was facilitated by changing American perceptions of Israel. Following the 1967 war, U.S. officials started seeing Israel as an effective ally against Soviet expansionism, particularly in the wake of the 1970 Jordan crisis. Furthermore, Rabin was instrumental in trying to move the U.S. Middle East policy away from the attempt to promote a comprehensive settlement to the Arab-Israeli conflict (via the Rogers Plan of December 1969, which did not take into consideration Israel's desire for secure borders and full sovereignty over Jerusalem) and toward a more modest endeavor—a partial agreement between Egypt and Israel.[51] Kissinger's ascendance in formulating the U.S. Middle East policy was, of course, the primary factor in this shift.

Rabin's unsurpassed access to policy-makers and his effectiveness in Washington were well-known. His role demonstrates that a foreign ambassador in Washington can influence the formulation of American policy.[52] *Newsweek,* at the end of 1972, named Rabin and Soviet Ambassador Anatoly Dobrinin as the two most effective envoys in Washington—a clear testimony to Rabin's success.[53] He ended his tenure as ambassador in March 1973.

CLINGING TO THE UNITED STATES

Washington acquired an even greater strategic importance for Israel after the October 1973 war, when the energy crisis enhanced Arab political power in the international arena and contributed to Israel's diplomatic isolation.[54] Rabin, Israel's prime minister during that period (1974–77), said: "I do not remember a period when we were witnesses in such a dramatic way to the collapse of Israel's foreign relations. . . . We had only one friend in the world and that was the United States."[55] Europe was energy-dependent and could neither compensate Israel, from a military point of view, for withdrawal from territory nor support Israel in the event of Arab treaty violations. Relations with Europe, Prime Minister Rabin felt, ought to be limited to economic and cultural affairs. In an interview with the German magazine *Der Spiegel*, Rabin rejected any European role in the Arab-Israeli arena and said in his curt fashion: "The less the Europeans meddle with the Middle East the better the chances are for peace."[56] Israel's European diplomacy was at that time directed primarily at neutralizing the damaging effect of European positions on the Arab-Israeli conflict. Whatever initiatives Israel introduced in Europe then were subordinate to its American orientation. Rabin accepted Kissinger's argument that Israel should be active on the European scene primarily to prevent the United States from becoming isolated in its support for Israel.[57]

At the time, Rabin reacted with pessimism to the American retreat from Indochina, its desertion of the Kurds in 1975, and its lack of support for the Christians in the Lebanese civil war. He questioned the future of the United States as a global power. Furthermore, Rabin feared that Israel might become an additional "sacrifice" of a declining West.[58] Nevertheless, he did not see any alternative to the United States in Israel's quest for diplomatic and material support. Furthermore, only the United States was considered capable of offering significant inducements to the parties involved in negotiating agreements in the Arab-Israeli arena and of compensating them for the risks taken. Basically, this evaluation was undisputed in the Israeli political elite.

Rabin bluntly stated in 1976, "Israel's very existence will be in jeopardy in case of total desertion by the United States."[59] He outlined five areas in which U.S. support was needed: (1) weapons; (2) financial support; (3) deterrence of the Soviet Union; (4) prevention of the misuse of the UN; and (5) help in maintaining contact with Jews in countries with no official Israeli presence.[60] The conclusion was loud and clear: Israel must act to guarantee America's friendship.

Post-1973, international circumstances and serious differences of opinion with the United States regarding Israel's borders and the Palestinian question made for a difficult period in U.S.-Israeli relations. Under these circumstances, Prime Minister Rabin emphasized that Israel had to nourish its relations with the United States carefully. He also sought to take advantage of the peculiarities of the U.S. political system—in particular the partial paralysis of U.S. foreign policy during election years. Israel was less likely to be pressured by an administration seeking to be reelected and courting the Jewish vote. At the end of 1974, he said: "We have to get through one year in our relationship with the United States by walking on tiptoes. If we get through 1975 successfully and reach 1976, we will gain not one year but two."[61] As noted in the first chapter, Rabin was not averse to "playing for time" and waiting for better international circumstances in the Arab-Israeli dispute.

Rabin strongly believed that U.S. support of Israel was closely related to the American conviction that Israel was sincere in searching for peace and was negotiating in good faith.[62] But he remained particularly concerned about the availability of arms. Recognizing the difficulties in purchasing weapons from the United States, Rabin commented: "The struggle to get weapons is continuous, but the United States will aid us, if it finds Israel displaying a willingness for peace."[63] This linkage dictated constant sensitivity to American perceptions and interests in the Middle East.

Yet this linkage also allowed for Israeli leverage in extracting support from the United States. For example, the 1975 memorandum of understanding (MOU) that was an integral part of the Sinai II Agreement (brokered by Kissinger) included an American promise to veto any change in UN Security Council Resolutions 242 and 338; it stated a U.S. commitment not to change policy toward the Palestine Liberation Organization (PLO); it allowed for an Israeli veto on reconvening the Geneva Conference; and it stipulated that the next Egyptian-Israeli agreement would be concerned with a full-scale peace treaty. It also promised a supply of oil, should oil be unavailable to Israel on the world market.[64] These understandings served as an example of what Rabin termed a "strategic coordination" between the two countries. The 1975 accord institutionalized the high-level American military and economic assistance that continues to this very day. The financial worth of the aid to Israel, this time mostly in grants rather than loans, for the years 1976, 1977, and 1978 was $3,476.3 million, $2,583.4 million, and $2,476.5 million respectively.[65]

Notwithstanding these achievements, Rabin did not excel at bargaining. Kissinger succeeded in persuading Rabin's team to disclose to him, early in the negotiations, the Israeli fallback position on the line of withdrawal in Sinai. Eventually, Rabin's government agreed to vacate the strategic Mitla and Gidi Passes—a territorial concession beyond the fallback position.[66]

Moreover, Rabin preferred not to submit any concrete demands on weapon systems during his negotiations with Kissinger because he was afraid that such a presentation implied acceptance of American suggestions. This pattern continued even though Kissinger, on the few occasions when Israel raised specific demands, evaded any commitment by saying that he had to check with the Pentagon on whether they could be met. As result, the discussions concentrated on Israeli concessions rather than the American quid pro quo.[67] Indeed, the MOU mentioned explicitly only the U.S. agreement to supply F-16 warplanes (which were already promised in 1974), whereas other Israeli military demands were to be considered through a "joint study of high technology and sophisticated items . . . with the view of giving a positive response."[68] Rabin did not want to emphasize the linkage between American aid and political issues (Israel had always claimed that aid should be considered according to Israel's needs only) because this connection had been used against Israel. The dilemma limited Rabin's bargaining position.

To a great extent, Rabin subordinated his policy on the Arab-Israeli conflict in the mid-1970s to the state of American-Israeli relations. There was a convergence between the need to prevent any deterioration in ties with the United States and the need to reduce the risks of another war with the Arabs, and this prompted Rabin's willingness to make territorial concessions. The Egyptian-Israeli Sinai II Agreement of September 1975, which required an Israeli withdrawal from the Mitla and Gidi Passes and also from the oil fields in the Sinai, was regarded by Rabin primarily as a measure meant to please the Americans. He signed Sinai II not to promote an act of Egyptian-Israeli reconciliation but to strengthen the U.S.-Israeli bond, to buttress Egypt's new pro-American orientation, and to introduce a wedge into the Egyptian-Syrian wartime coalition.[69]

Rabin viewed the achievement of peace between Israel and its Arab neighbors as a lengthy historic process that would take decades. He believed that continuous American friendship and support were needed to foster this process. Only a diplomatically and militarily strong Israel could bring the Arabs to terms, and the United States was crucial for projecting such an image. Even after Egyptian President Anwar Sadat's historic visit to Jerusalem and the Camp David accords, Rabin felt that the differences of opinion between the Arabs and the Israelis were unbridgeable and that continuing tensions with the United States were unavoidable because there was little American support for the border changes that Israel considered essential. Therefore, Israel had no choice but to play for time. "There is no way of finding the middle ground, even with the best intentions in the world. Our most sensible policy is to stall."[70] In 1979, Rabin viewed the peace treaty with Egypt as just another interim agreement, useful primarily for maintaining good relations with the United States. Moreover, he criticized the "low price" that Prime Minister Menachem Begin's government extracted from Washington for the Israeli withdrawal from the entire Sinai Peninsula.[71] Indeed, the American quid pro quo in 1979 was not significantly greater than the compensation that Rabin had extracted from Washington in September 1975. Then, the United States had committed itself to high levels of economic aid, the provision of sophisticated weaponry, and also limitations on American freedom of action in negotiating a resolution to the Arab-Israeli dispute.

Rabin's overwhelming emphasis on good relations with the United States extended to the symbolic level. Toward the end of 1975, he insisted on delaying his planned trip to the United States until January 1976 in order to become the first foreign dignitary to pay an official visit in the U.S. bicentennial year. Rabin wanted to underscore the cultural commonalities between the two countries—one of the pillars of their special relationship—with a symbolic "first visit" by a small democratic ally during the bicentennial celebrations.[72] In his public remarks, on his arrival in Washington and during other occasions on this trip, he emphasized that he was the first head of government to visit the United States in the bicentennial year and that this was Israel's celebration too, given the similarities between the two countries.[73]

THE BURGEONING AMERICAN-ISRAELI STRATEGIC RELATIONSHIP

The United States remained centrally important to Rabin when he returned to serve in the Israeli cabinet for six years as defense minister in Israel's national unity governments (1984–90). By then, his assessment was that only an expansion of American influence in the Middle East could contribute to a détente in Arab-Israeli relations. Only a pro-American Egypt had been able, he noted, to make peace with Israel.[74] In the political constellation of the unity government, Rabin constituted the linchpin holding the Likud-Labor government together, and due to his political stature, he enjoyed almost full autonomy in managing relations with the American defense establishment. Furthermore, Prime Minister Yitzhak

Shamir had great confidence in Rabin's judgment and agreed with his emphasis on good relations with the United States.[75]

By 1984, Israel enjoyed a burgeoning strategic partnership with the United States, nurtured by the Likud-led governments and aided by the Reagan administration's bipolar prism on international affairs.[76] In expression of the informal alliance, the two countries established (in November 1983) a Joint Political and Military Group (JPMG) as a mechanism for exchanging evaluations and for discussing matters of mutual concern.

Rabin capitalized on this framework to improve further the strategic cooperation between the two countries. Agreements were reached on military medical cooperation, the U.S. leasing of Israeli-made Kfir aircraft, joint military exercises, and the prepositioning of American military equipment in Israel. The U.S. Sixth Fleet increased the frequency and the length of its visits to the port of Haifa. In May 1986 Rabin eagerly agreed that Israel should join the American Strategic Defense Initiative (SDI), when President Ronald Reagan was looking for overseas partners to endow this program with greater legitimacy at home. Rabin was interested in showing loyalty to Washington and in acquiring access to American technology in an area of increasing importance to Israeli national security—antimissile defense. Israel was among the first foreign countries (together with Great Britain and West Germany) to respond positively to the SDI ("Star Wars").[77] American officials noted with satisfaction that in Israel there was no discernible debate over the SDI, as there was in the rest of the world, including the United States.[78] According to SDI Director Lt. Gen. James Abrahamson, Israel had by 1988 become the largest foreign participant in the SDI. Out of the total of $9 billion spent on the initiative, $165 million has been spent in Israel, mostly as part of the Arrow antitactical ballistic missile (ATBM) program, in which the United States and Israel split costs, 80 to 20 percent.[79]

Rabin's and Shamir's political clout invariably overcame any opposition from the Israeli cabinet or the military to this drive to extend strategic cooperation with the Americans. Some ministers questioned the need for close coordination, fearing the political implications of Israel being too closely identified with the United States or the possibility that the Americans would learn too much about the Israeli defense establishment.[80]

In 1987, Israel succeeded in expanding the political and legal framework for the American-Israeli strategic cooperation by formally becoming, through an act of Congress, a "Major Non-NATO Ally."[81] This led to a new MOU, signed by Israeli Defense Minister Rabin and U.S. Defense Secretary Frank Carlucci in late 1987, which eased cooperation in defense research and development and also facilitated Israeli exports of military goods to the United States. The United States has gradually become the largest market for the export of sophisticated Israeli defense items, including remotely piloted vehicles (RPVs) and Popeye standoff air-to-surface missiles. With increasing frequency, Israeli weapon producers teamed up with American defense firms to compete for U.S. defense contracts and in other arms markets. The United States also extended much financial help to Israel for the development of the Lavi aircraft and the Arrow ATBM.

In April 1988, U.S.-Israeli defense ties were given a further boost by a memorandum of agreement between the two countries. In September 1989 two additional agreements were signed: the United States allowed the use of its prepositioned equipment in Israel in times of emergency; and the United States agreed to lend Israel additional military equipment in emergency circumstances. Just as significant was the decision to announce publicly some facets of the strategic cooperation. Rabin revealed at this time that by 1989 the United States and Israel had conducted some twenty-seven joint military exercises and that Israel was interested in increasing and broadening such activities.[82] Rabin attributed great value to such maneuvers: "There is no doubt that the United States leads in all aspects of military endeavors in the Western world. Any type of cooperation that brings the IDF into contact with U.S. armed forces in the region—including training, exercises or exchanges of opinion—is helpful. It helps the IDF to better understand modern methods, equipment, and technological development."[83] He noted that the relationship was of mutual benefit: "The United States learns a lot from Israel, in terms of combat experience with the use of American and Israeli weapon systems, and studying the success of this hardware in battle against Soviet equipment."[84]

Indeed, during the latter part of the 1980s, strategic cooperation expanded considerably. Strategic interests were of course paramount in this development, but Rabin's presence at the Israeli Ministry of Defense eased the cooperation, particularly at a time when the American foreign policy establishment was not pleased with some aspects of the Shamir-led government. American policy-makers, such as Secretaries of State George Schultz and James Baker, had high regard for Rabin's moderation and political judgment.[85]

Yet this period was marred by several incidents that could have negatively affected bilateral relations. In November 1985, a U.S. Navy employee, Jonathan Pollard, was arrested in Washington for spying for Israel.

Rabin, as well as Prime Minister Peres and Foreign Minister Shamir, made a serious effort to convince the United States that Pollard was part of an unauthorized, rogue spy operation unknown to almost all of the political leadership and the intelligence community. Peres, Rabin, and Shamir successfully suppressed any notion that they knew of Pollard in advance or that they had given approval to his operation. Yet for Rabin, this incident was a "disaster" that called for a severe reprimand of Israel's intelligence agencies.[86] When Col. Aviem Sella, who had been implicated in the Pollard affair, was promoted to command the country's second-largest airbase (Tel Nof) in February 1987, the United States decided in protest to boycott this military installation. Rabin eventually bowed to American pressure, and Sella was forced to leave the IDF. Rabin's position on this matter was criticized by many Israelis as being oversensitive to the Americans.[87]

The U.S. "Irangate" affair, which revealed the unauthorized transfer of weapons to Iran and the use of the money received to fund Contra activities in Nicaragua, not only beleaguered the Reagan administration but also had an Israeli angle. In 1987 Rabin defended Israel's attempt to find an opening to Iran. As far as he was concerned, the 1985 shipments to Iran of antitank weapons and Hawk missiles drawn from Israel's arsenal and authorized by the American government were motivated by a desire to open channels of communication to the Islamic regime, to prevent the Iraqis from gaining the upper hand in the Iran-Iraq War, and also to help the United States free hostages held in Lebanon by Iran-backed groups.[88] Rabin denied that Israel shipped any arms directly to the Contras in Nicaragua.

Regarding the future of the Israeli-made Lavi jet-fighters, Rabin behaved in such a way as to minimize tensions with the United States. As American reservations to the continued development of the Lavi aircraft became more evident, he favored termination of the program.[89] His unwillingness to confront the United States on this issue, coupled with his skepticism concerning the Israeli military industries and his basic preference for American weapons (discussed in the next chapter), eventually compelled Rabin to join the struggle in the Israeli cabinet to scrap the controversial project. His weight as defense minister was crucial for gaining the necessary votes in the government to end the Lavi project in August 1987.

The desire to demonstrate Israeli friendship to the Americans also led in 1987 to Israel's acquiescence in hosting an installation of the Voice of America (VOA) broadcasting service in the Negev, where the VOA was supposed to target communist countries. (Pro-Western Arab countries refused to accommodate the American request to have it in their territory.)

Rabin was one of the strongest supporters of what was not an easy decision for the Israeli government.[90]

Rabin played no role during the 1991 Gulf War, since he was an opposition MK. However, he did support Shamir's decision to coordinate Israel's policy with the United States and to refrain from military action. (His position is analyzed in greater detail in chapter 5.) And he did have to cope with the aftermath of the Gulf War when he became premier and defense minister again in 1992.

At that time the American link continued to be cardinal for Rabin. By then the United States had become the only superpower, and its political clout in the Middle East was unsurpassed. Rabin continued to encourage American involvement in the peace process and made sure that the progress made was closely coordinated with the U.S. administration under President Bill Clinton. All photo opportunities at the peace celebrations were geared for American audiences and included a high-level U.S. presence. Rabin continued to object to a significant European political role in designing the new Mideastern architecture. Blasting at the European response to the crisis in Yugoslavia, he said: "The Europeans are volunteering to participate in peace processes all over the world, and when there is trouble at their doorstep, where are they? Where is the European community?"[91]

In 1992, Israel badly needed American financial help, in the form of loan guarantees worth $10 billion, in order to settle successfully the hundreds of thousands of immigrants from the former Soviet Union who were then pouring into the country. President George Bush, who had refrained from approving the loan guarantees during the Shamir government in order to extract an Israeli freeze on settlement construction, found Rabin more conciliatory though still unwilling to make a pledge to stop all settlement activities. Nevertheless, with presidential elections approaching, Bush decided to grant the guarantees to the Rabin government; he considered the damage that could be caused by withholding them to be too great.

Despite the success in securing the loan guarantees from Bush and despite the friendship of the Clinton administration, Rabin feared an erosion in the American aid to Israel.[92] This assistance was considered to be of cardinal political, military, and economic value. Therefore, Rabin accepted American leadership on almost any subject. For example, he sought American advice on how to respond to Iraqi overtures to Israel since 1992. Subsequently, he overruled recommendations to start a dialogue with Iraq.[93] Another example occurred during his tour of Japan in December 1994 when he explicitly told his hosts that Israel would vote the same as the United States on the issue of a seat for Japan in the UN Security Council.[94]

In 1993, Rabin expressed his desire for "active American participation in Israel's security."[95] Specifically, he asked the Americans to station, once again, Patriot SAM batteries in Israel and to provide economic assistance in deploying a defense system against missiles.[96] Rabin also expressed interest in the stationing of American troops on the Golan Heights as part of the security arrangements in an Israeli-Syrian peace treaty involving Israeli withdrawal.[97] Rabin wanted a significant American involvement in the peace process to minimize the risks taken by Israel. Such a preference was already evident in the mid-1970s: Rabin had welcomed an American monitoring force in the Sinai as a useful "trip-wire" arrangement for warning of hostile movements and as a mechanism for slowing the transition to war. Furthermore, the presence of American personnel, Rabin believed, would raise the political cost of violating a U.S.-sanctioned status quo. Yet Rabin did not go so far as to demand the formalization of American-Israeli ties into a defense treaty that would commit American military personnel to actively defend Israel.

Rabin also believed that only the United States could lead an international effort to stop nuclear proliferation in the Middle East.[98] Israel relied on the United States to prevent the sale to Tehran of North Korean Nodong (Scud III) missiles, which could place Israeli targets within reach of the Iranians.[99] As soon as Washington indicated displeasure with a discreet Israeli attempt to negotiate independently with North Korea, the bilateral contacts were halted.

A mirror effect of Rabin's pro-American disposition was his anti-Soviet inclination. As noted in the previous chapter, he viewed the Soviet Union encroachment in the Middle East as a dangerous development that played a destructive role in the Arab-Israeli conflict. He continuously objected to the Soviet attempts to reach a recognized partnership with the United States in the region[100] and viewed the dissolution of the Soviet Union at the end of the 1980s as a great strategic bonus for Israel.

As ambassador, Rabin attempted to dissuade Kissinger from reaching an American-Soviet agreement over the contours of an Arab-Israeli agreement.[101] He also strongly recommended that Israel share with the Americans its experience of fighting Soviet equipment, since the United States was facing the same rival.[102] As prime minister, he disliked any forum, such as the Geneva Conference, in which the Soviets were present.[103] In 1975, he was extremely critical of the attempt made by one of his ministers to use the services of a German cabinet member (Egon Bahr) to mediate between Israel and the Soviet Union in order to improve bilateral relations between the two countries.[104] He was angered by Peres's suggestion that Soviet personnel be included in the monitoring force for the American-brokered September 1975 Sinai II Agreement between Egypt and Israel.[105] Similarly, in the mid-1980s, when Peres toyed with the idea of an international ceremony (with a Soviet presence) to open an Arab-Israeli dialogue, Rabin refrained from backing him and was pleased with Shamir's veto of this idea.[106]

THE LIMITS ON U.S.-ISRAELI RELATIONS

Despite his strong American orientation and his desire for strategic coordination with the United States, Rabin believed that Israel should and could maintain a certain measure of freedom of independent action. He did occasionally dare to confront the United States or to hold his own on some important point. He did not hesitate to criticize the Rogers Plan, of December 1969, as not meeting Israeli interests. In fact, he felt that the Foreign Ministry back home was not being adamant in its opposition to the plan and was undermining his efforts to fight it.[107] Even when Israel was extremely isolated in the world community during the 1970s, Rabin rejected the compromise that Secretary of State Kissinger mediated between Egypt and Israel: "I was the prime minister who said to Kissinger no in March 1975, when I came to the conclusion that to say yes would endanger vital Israeli security interests."[108] He did not realize at that time, however, that this move would engender a setback in American-Israeli relations—the reassessment policy announced by the administration of U.S. President Gerald Ford. Yet Rabin weathered this crisis. He was relieved to see the American shipments of military equipment arrive on schedule. Moreover, Rabin realized that in the longer view, Kissinger's Middle East strategy (the step-by-step approach), as well as Rabin's lack of enthusiasm for reconvening the Geneva Conference, where the Soviet Union would be present, and Israeli political leverage in Washington, would bring the crisis to an end and try again to bridge the differences between Egypt and Israel.[109] In addition, Rabin displayed greater territorial flexibility than planned in order to allow Kissinger to succeed in his shuttle diplomacy.

In reaction to the Rabin government's decision to build the settlement of Maale Adumim (a part of greater Jerusalem) in 1976, President Ford sent a message via his ambassador to Israel, Malcolm Toon, calling for a halt in the building of all housing in settlements beyond the Green Line (the 1967 border). Rabin refused to accept the presidential message and insisted on Israel's right to build in the territories.[110] Rabin also did not hesitate to confront the Carter administration when it deviated from the Kissinger step-by-step approach and attempted to implement a new Middle East policy based on a comprehensive approach and a willingness to accept the PLO as the representative of the Palestinians. The meeting between newly elected President Jimmy Carter and Prime Minister Rabin in March 1977 was very tense indeed.[111]

A decade later, in 1987, Rabin did not hesitate to criticize American policy concerning the Iran-Iraq War. The gradual U.S. tilt toward Iraq was viewed quite unfavorably in Jerusalem, and this view was conveyed to Washington through diplomatic channels.[112] Rabin went public in October 1987 (after several American attacks on Iranian military targets), saying that the United States was being manipulated by Iraq into using force against Iran.[113] He added that, unfortunately, the Soviet Union had become the only superpower that could talk to both parties. "The United States cannot do it."[114] These remarks reflected Rabin's traditional Israeli pro-Iran stance and his assessment that Iraq could not be a partner in the peace process, as some of his dovish colleagues in the cabinet thought it could. Rabin's criticism came at a time when he and others were apprehensive about the possibility of a cut in American aid to Israel, but this did not deter him. The American administration was greatly annoyed. President Reagan, in a meeting with Israeli President Chaim Herzog in Washington, was enlisted to convey the American displeasure with Rabin's position.[115]

Despite Rabin's Americophile predisposition and his desire for American support, he never warmed to the idea of a formal U.S.-Israeli defense treaty. Rabin emphasized again and again, particularly to American audiences, that Israel had no intention of asking American soldiers to fight its wars. "Israel has an important principle: It is only Israel that is responsible for our security."[116] In 1987 Defense Minister Rabin reiterated his reluctance to enter into any military pact and said that in his dealings with the United States, he borrowed Winston Churchill's phrase from World War II: "Give us the means and we will do the job."[117] He clarified to the Americans: "In the face of any combination of Arab states fighting together, even with limited Soviet involvement, Israel can defend itself on its own." He expressed his conviction that the Americans were consistently pleased with Israel's position in this regard.[118] In May 1994, in an interview with the

CNN television network, he said that Israelis were proud of their independence: "We have never dragged one foreign soldier to fight our wars."[119] He always wanted self-reliance in Israel's use of force.

He was just as explicit to Israeli audiences. In the 1970s, the American government was willing to consider a defense treaty in exchange for territorial concessions, but Israel under Rabin rejected the idea.[120] He explained that this approach was important for creating sympathy and goodwill for Israel, which could be translated into American assistance.[121] Rabin believed that a defense treaty could undermine the widespread support within the United States for assisting the Jewish state. Israeli demands for direct American participation in the defense of Israel would undermine the Israeli moral right to ask for American matériel aid. Though favorable toward the use of force in promoting American and Israeli interests, a defense treaty could curtail Israel's freedom of action. He pointed out that Germany, a NATO member, could not initiate a surveillance flight without the approval of the NATO commander, usually an American officer.[122] When approving military actions in Lebanon, he occasionally pointed out that a defense treaty with the United States would not have sanctioned such Israeli behavior.[123] Furthermore, Rabin realized that such a treaty could be reached only following a settlement of the Arab-Israeli conflict, and he was concerned that the Americans would consider such a treaty only in the framework of an Israeli withdrawal to the 1967 borders, which he opposed.[124] A formal treaty could also increase the pressures on Israel to make concessions on the nuclear issue.[125]

At the same time, Rabin believed that only understandings with the United States would endow Israel with a measure of freedom of action to use the IDF in accordance with Israel's interests. The unilateral formulation of a set of well-advertised *casi belli*, which he disapproved (see chapter 4), could not be a substitute for American-Israeli understandings that would provide the necessary political backing for Israeli action.[126]

RELATIONS WITH AMERICAN JEWRY

Although Rabin was widely popular and respected in the American Jewish community, he sometimes had a rocky relationship with leaders of U.S. Jewish groups. When he arrived in Washington as ambassador, he preferred to open his own channels to the administration rather than use those of American Jewry. At that time, the activities of the American-Israel

Public Affairs Committee (AIPAC), the "Jewish lobby," were limited, dealing primarily with securing foreign aid on Capitol Hill. Rabin had many disagreements with the group's leaders.[127] Rabin's Zionist perspective, which denied the value of Diaspora Jewish life, made him uncomfortable with what he called "the court Jews," and he preferred that Israel not be dependent on them. His tactless behavior insulted American Jewish leaders more than once.[128] Furthermore, most influential Jews then had liberal inclinations and were critical of the Nixon-Kissinger administration, which Rabin admired. Rabin was also lukewarm about the American Jewish community's support for the Jackson Amendment, which linked most-favored-nation status for the Soviet Union to a more liberal Soviet emigration policy. Kissinger opposed such linkage, and Rabin was willing to help the American administration on this matter. Generally, Rabin felt more comfortable with the more conservative foreign policies of Republican administrations than he did with Democratic foreign policy positions. As noted, he favored Nixon's reelection, and in 1976 he hinted to American Jewish leaders his preference for President Ford.[129] American Jews were upset by such behavior,[130] and these formative experiences influenced Rabin's future attitudes toward American Jewry.

The AIPAC's adamant opposition to sales of American weapons to Arab states and the great political struggles conducted by American Jewry against U.S. administrations on these issues were seen by Rabin as harmful to Israeli interests. The two major battles—over the F-16 warplanes in 1978 and the AWACS (Airborne Warning and Command System) jets in 1981, both sold to Saudi Arabia—did not end with "Jewish" victories. At the time, Rabin held no position in the Israeli government.[131] His pragmatism led him to prefer limiting such deals and attempting to get compensation for Israel. He understood the American rationale for the transfer of arms to Arab countries and shied away from direct confrontation on this issue.[132]

By the time Rabin and the Labor Party returned to power in 1984, he realized that the American Jewish community had become much more influential than it had been in the period when he served as ambassador.[133] Nevertheless, he did not hesitate to boycott the American Jewish Congress for over half a year after its president, Theodor Mann, in January 1988 expressed concern over Israel's response to the Intifada.[134] In August 1992, Rabin belittled the importance of the powerful AIPAC in a closed meeting with its leadership and criticized the organization for seeming to support the previous, Likud-led government. Furthermore, the premier urged the lobby to stop pursuing independent initiatives and to work instead under the guidance of the embassy, on the grounds that the AIPAC's past efforts had "hindered rather than helped." Rabin reportedly said: "You waged battles which were lost in advance, and so you merely caused Israel damage, by generating unnecessary antagonism over issues such as the AWACS plane sales to Saudi Arabia, and the loan guarantees request. You did not manage to bring Israel a single cent."[135]

In addition, Rabin told the Conference of Presidents of the Major American Jewish Organizations that Israel would call its own shots in making decisions during the peace process. His remarks confirmed to members of his audience his reputation of not thinking much of the role that American Jews played in U.S.-Israel negotiations. Alluding to an upcoming sale of American-made F-15 warplanes to Saudi Arabia, Rabin asked the leadership of the American Jewish community to "please try to understand" that the United States had "wider interests" in the Middle East than simply preserving Israel.[136] He wanted to prevent another confrontation with the administration. Rabin's low esteem of American Jewry was reflected also by the fact that he left vacant the position of adviser to the prime minister on Diaspora affairs until American Jewry began to challenge his peace policies through Congress.[137] The improvement in Israel's relations with the international community at the end of the 1980s and in the 1990s also minimized Israel's dependence on American organizations to lobby on its behalf in Washington and in other capitals.

Indeed, in October 1995, at the General Assembly of American Jewish Organizations, the most important American Jewish gathering, he criticized American Jews for not contributing enough to the resettlement efforts for new immigrants to Israel. In addition, Rabin could at times be prickly and curt in dealings with Jewish leaders in the United States, as with others, and was criticized for thinking that they should line up in support of the Israeli government, no matter what policies it pursued. He was particularly vexed when leading members of the American Jewish community criticized the 1993 Israeli deal with the PLO and what they perceived as Rabin's willingness to make territorial concessions to Syria.

Despite his ambivalence toward American Jewry, Rabin met regularly with its leaders to brief them about Israeli policies and to learn about American politics. Yet, in contrast to other Israeli politicians, he never showed much interest in the politics of American Jewry. He refused to get involved in American Jewish affairs even when asked to do so by friends. For example, at the end of 1992 he refused to endorse Robert Lifton, then president of the American Jewish Congress, for the post of president of the

Conference of Presidents of the Major American Jewish Organizations.[138] For Rabin, meeting American Jews was an additional way of updating himself on developments in the American domestic arena. For him, this was one of the most interesting topics on his agenda.

CONCLUSION

Many Israeli political leaders shared Rabin's American orientation concerning the state's foreign policy, as well as his sensitivity to U.S. wishes in the foreign policy decision-making process. Yet more than others, Rabin was identified with this approach, which he articulated quite early in Israel's diplomatic history. He constantly looked to Washington for signs of approval or disapproval in forging Israel's national strategy. Furthermore, he considered himself an expert on American politics.

Rabin's tenure as ambassador in Washington was instrumental in forging a close relationship with the United States. While prime minister in the 1970s, he insisted on strategic coordination with the Americans, a policy he continued to advocate and implement in the posts he held thereafter.

Rabin's prominent position in the Israeli political system and his Americophile disposition were well appreciated by Americans, and his tragic death was mourned in the United States by Jews and non-Jews alike. It was clear to many Americans that in Rabin's strategic analysis, a small country like Israel, which relied on America for its survival, had a great stake in America's prosperity and steadfastness. He was correctly viewed as a staunch American ally.[139] His funeral was attended by an impressive array of American political figures, including President Clinton, former Presidents George Bush and Jimmy Carter, and many other members of the high policy elite in Washington. The U.S. ambassador to Israel, Martin Indyk, lamented Rabin's death as the loss of America's greatest friend in Israel. He even referred to Rabin as an American hero.[140]

CHAPTER THREE

BUILDING A CONVENTIONAL
MILITARY FORCE

The Israel Defense Force (IDF), established immediately after the Declaration of Independence (15 May 1948), has been one of the most important institutions in the sociopolitical history of Israel.[1] David Ben-Gurion, Israel's first premier and defense minister, left a lasting imprint on its structure and philosophy.[2] Chief of Staff Yigal Yadin (1949–52) laid the foundations for the IDF three-tier system of professional army, conscripts, and reserve service.[3] Chief of Staff Moshe Dayan (1953–1958) also left an important mark on the IDF, primarily by emphasizing the IDF's combat spirit and fostering its initiative. In contrast with other new armies that emerged after World War II, the IDF was not trained by foreign officers. The IDF did not adopt an imported model for growth; its evolution was a self-learning process capitalizing on the experience of its own personnel in foreign armies (primarily British and Russian) and in the battles of the War of Independence. The young and austere Israeli army sent officers to study in military academies abroad, and they were expected to adapt their acquired knowledge to Israeli circumstances.

Yitzhak Rabin began his military career in the Palmach. Ben-Gurion disbanded this elite force after the War of Independence, and many of its senior officers left the IDF.[4] Rabin, to whom Ben-Gurion took a liking, stayed in the military. Rabin's relations with several of the early chiefs of staff were not particularly warm. Dayan even tried to make him leave the

IDF in 1958, and on several occasions Rabin felt he was overlooked for promotion to the chief of staff position.[5] His slow move up was due primarily to the fact that he was not considered to be a supporter of Ben-Gurion's Mapai Party.[6] Nevertheless, Rabin liked the military life, and as long as he felt he was making a contribution to the IDF, he stayed there. Stubborn and pragmatic, he persisted in his career until he reached the position of chief of staff at the age of forty-one, when Ben-Gurion, a strict party loyalist, was no longer prime minister.

Rabin was not a member of the IDF's founding generation, but he exerted a profound influence on the way the IDF operated. According to Maj. Gen. (Res.) Israel Tal, Rabin became the highest intellectual authority on military matters many years before he became chief of staff in January 1964.[7] When Rabin reached this position, he was the oldest ever to assume this job (the first above forty), after serving for ten years as a general and a member of the General Staff, longer than any previous supreme commander of the Israeli army. According to Maj. Gen. (Res.) Uzi Narkis, who served under Rabin, the combination of his personal qualities and the many positions he held at the apex of the IDF hierarchy allowed Rabin to wield great influence on the operational and planning modus operandi of the IDF for years to come.[8] Even Maj. Gen. (Res.) Ezer Weizman (later to become minister of defense and president of Israel), whose relations with Rabin were not particularly cordial, praised Rabin's organizational and analytical capabilities and admitted that Rabin was an unchallenged authority within the IDF.[9] Maj. Gen. (Res.) Rehavam Zeevi, in his capacity as the leader of the extreme right-wing Moledet Party, became a vocal and most critical political opponent of Rabin's policies in the late 1980s and the 1990s; yet he concluded, "Rabin's contribution to the IDF was gigantic."[10] Only late in Rabin's military career and, subsequently, when he was part of the political elite did he also have an impact on Israel's national security strategy.

In his military career and later as a decision-maker at the highest national level, Rabin was always extremely concerned with the building of an effective fighting force, which was necessary, he felt, to meet current and future security challenges. In 1948, he was very critical of the shortsightedness of the Jewish community in Palestine, before the outbreak of the War of Independence, for failing to prepare an adequate military force. In his memoirs, Rabin explained that during the War of Independence, he felt tormented by the thought that he was sending into battle men poorly armed, untrained, and frighteningly outnumbered. Therefore, at the end of the War of Independence, he made a personal commitment to dedicate his life to ensure that the state of Israel would never again be militarily unprepared to meet aggression. Building a mighty army was, for Rabin, a moral responsibility he owed to his comrades-in-arms.[11]

In his opinion the IDF was designed to serve a fundamental national objective of paramount importance and commanding a broad national consensus: the continued existence and security of Israel.[12] This evaluation was characteristic of a widely accepted view within Israeli society. According to Rabin's own testimony, the building of an effective military machine was his first priority when he was appointed, in April 1956, to head the Northern Command and later when he was promoted, in May 1959, to serve as chief of the Operations Branch of the General Staff.[13]

RABIN'S EARLY CONTRIBUTION

Rabin's first opportunity to have a serious impact on the IDF concerned the creation in 1949 of a course for battalion commanders. Haim Laskov (a British-trained officer), then commander of the Training Branch, entrusted Rabin, despite his Palmach background, with commanding this course. By then, due to his performance in the War of Independence, Rabin had a reputation for possessing a good mind for careful planning and detail. The course, of a type never before offered, was intended to blend the various backgrounds and traditions of the IDF officers into a unified Israeli military doctrine.[14] It provided a chance for commanders and trainees to develop together the IDF military doctrine and a new professional language (Hebrew, an ancient language that had been newly revived, lacked much of the necessary terminology). Common patterns for staff work emerged, along with models for military evaluations and procedures for going into battle. New problems for the IDF, such as coordinating maneuvers and the use of fire in large military formations, were studied, and a standardized approach and common language were diffused throughout the whole army. Rabin's meticulous approach—dissecting a problem into various parts and systematically dealing with each component on its own and with the synchronization of each component with the other components—occasionally proved exasperating and frustrating for the participants, who were less perfectionist and patient. Nevertheless, they usually gave in to Rabin, realizing that he was creating in the IDF a comprehensive approach for dealing with military problems. Maj. Gen. (Res.) Shlomo (Chich) Lahat, one of the pupils in the course, noted that Rabin radiated excellence: "He projected authority, knowledge, wisdom, and common sense."[15]

This three-month course, which trained sixty senior officers, was extremely challenging intellectually and served as the melting pot for the future command skeleton of the IDF as it blended personnel, including graduates from the Palmach and the British Jewish Brigade.[16] On Rabin's staff at the battalion commanders' course were a number of future generals and chiefs of staff, partially chosen by Rabin personally, such as Asaf Simchoni, Uzi Narkis, Zvi Zamir, Aharon Yariv, Haim Bar-Lev, and David Elazar. Rabin's evaluations of his pupils affected their careers. The success and the importance of the course for battalion commanders was so great that it forced the highest officers of the IDF, the generals, to undergo a similar course to catch up with and to communicate in the same terms as their subordinates.[17] Subsequently, Laskov wanted to allow Rabin to continue his contribution to the training of military cadres with the recently established course for brigade commanders. Though Rabin was moved to another post, he managed to prepare the program for this course too.[18]

Rabin's next post was on one of the units of the General Staff, as head of the Operations Division. He considered this to be his first desk job as a staff officer, though he had performed important staff duties before, while serving under Yigal Allon. His division was responsible for three spheres: operations (operational and future contingency planning), current security,[19] and the organization and mobilization of the reserves.[20] Planning of military operations was guided by the lessons of the War of Independence. Operations Danny (July 1948) and Yoav (October 1948) of that war, both of which Rabin helped plan, served as models for future contingency planning.[21] Rabin and others understood that the Arab armies were more numerous and had greater firepower than the IDF. This led to, inter alia, the adoption of the indirect approach to planning military operations, an approach that shied away from frontal attacks and encouraged maneuvers to outflank and encircle the enemy.[22]

At that time, the IDF implemented plans to organize the reserve units along the Swiss model, which allowed for a large pool of reservists to be used for general military duties. What made the Israeli version unique was that the reserve forces would constitute the bulk of the army and not simply an appendage of its standing forces. This is why Rabin and those who followed him made strenuous efforts to improve the quality of the reserve forces and to reduce the qualitative differential between the units of the standing army and the reserves.

In 1953 Rabin was appointed to command and reorganize the Training Branch, which he headed until 1956. In this capacity, he was promoted to the rank of major general and joined the IDF General Staff. In this position, he made a most significant contribution to the IDF, revising the ways the IDF trained its forces and prepared itself for war. His eye for detail was extremely useful in this job. Under his energetic leadership at the Training Branch, the whole literature on training the troops was standardized and the exercises designed for various types and levels of units were systematically spread throughout the IDF to create an integrated military doctrine. Entirely new sets of detailed doctrine manuals were written for combat and for technical training for each of the various branches of the IDF. Rabin devised a comprehensive, multiyear training program for IDF units and ways to measure their performance. In fact, Rabin founded the military methods for preparing the Israeli army for war.[23]

An example of the new training courses initiated at the end of 1953 was the course designed for the officers in the IDF geographical commands (northern, central, and southern). Taken by officers ranging from company to battalion commanders, the course was intended to enhance their knowledge of military history and doctrine.[24] The specific goals of the two-and-a-half-day course were to acquaint the participants with the geography of their command, with the battles fought in the specific territorial confinement of their command, and with battles fought under similar conditions elsewhere. Each command had to organize four to five courses a year, ensuring continuity in terms of the material learned. Taking into consideration the other duties of the officers, this proved to be a rather demanding enterprise.

Rabin devoted much time to overseeing the implementation of his reforms, and his persistence served him and the IDF well. He insisted on visiting the training bases under his command frequently and on meeting often with his subordinates. The fine details were always of great interest to Rabin. He would listen with the utmost care to the remarks and criticisms of the instructors and trainees in order to make improvements, and his staff at the Training Branch was encouraged to follow his example. It was well-known that Rabin was extremely knowledgeable about myriad aspects of the IDF work and had a phenomenal memory, and his subordinates knew they had to appear at meetings and briefings well prepared.[25]

In the context of the professionalization of the IDF, Rabin was one of the moving forces behind the establishment of the IDF College of Command and Staff in 1954, for the training of midcareer officers. Rabin realized the need for an institution of higher military education to propagate military doctrine within the IDF.[26] Furthermore, Rabin noted: "With the development of military organizations, military tasks become more complicated, requiring a higher intellectual and professional level."[27] His primary goal was to enhance professionalism in the Israeli army.

In his capacity as chief of the Training Branch, Rabin emphasized the importance of training exercises with live fire. He boasted that the IDF had more such exercises than any other military organization. In his opinion, training with live ammunition, particularly in offensive exercises, was necessary not only to create conditions as close as possible to real battle but also to cultivate the necessary spirit for going forward and storming enemy positions.[28] He attributed great importance to troop morale.

Rabin's attention was directed toward the training of junior officers as well. He was instrumental in founding, in October 1953, the military high school associated with the prestigious Hareali High School in Haifa. The graduates of this school became an excellent pool for senior combat officers. Rabin was no intellectual, but he prized intellectual capability as an element that contributed to professionalism within the army. In his greetings to the graduates of a junior officers' course (second lieutenant) in July 1955, Rabin emphasized that the important qualities for an officer were not only discipline, personal initiative, and readiness for sacrifice but also "critical thinking."[29] Rabin understood that the growth of the IDF required a stream of intelligent trainees. (During his term as chief of staff, additional military high schools were established.)

On returning from a study trip with the U.S. military in the fall of 1954, Rabin decided to make a systematic effort to evaluate what could be learned from American training methods. He shared his impressions with senior IDF officers and recommended the emulation of several aspects of American practices.[30] One of these was the requirement that each combat officer pass a paratrooper or commando course as a condition for promotion. For Rabin, paratrooper training was "the apex of willpower, surpassing any physical effort."[31] Indeed, Chief of Staff Dayan and the members of his General Staff, Rabin among them, were the first group of senior officers to undergo paratrooper training.

In April 1956, Rabin was appointed commander of the Northern Command, where he served until May 1959. During this period, he of course became closely acquainted with the security problems on the Syrian front. He missed, however, action against the Egyptians in the Sinai Campaign, which was fought entirely in the south. Following his tour of duty in the Northern

Command, Rabin was promoted by Chief of Staff Laskov (1958–61) to chief of the Operations Branch, the most important position on the General Staff. Beginning in 1961 he also served as deputy to the new chief of staff, Zvi Tzur. As chief of the Operations Branch, Rabin felt, for the first time, that he could deal comprehensively with every facet of the defense forces.[32] Some of the topics were familiar from when he had served as head of the Operations Division (one of the divisions of the Operations Branch) and others from when he had served in other posts, but only as chief of the Operations Branch was he in a position to have an all-encompassing view of the IDF and a chance to offer input into almost every aspect of the army's activities.

In Rabin's opinion, the primary challenge was to build, given the available means, a better military force. This meant formulating an operational doctrine that would determine the preferred force structure, the rate of weapons acquisition, and the training system best suited to deal with future military challenges.[33] Other preoccupations as chief of operations were current security, relations with foreign armies, and political issues, such as contacts with United Nations officers and weapons procurement abroad. Contact with foreign armies and the import of weapons also allowed him to get better acquainted with the U.S. defense establishment—a task to which he attached great importance.

Rabin realized that Israel's Arab neighbors were acquiring not only Soviet-made weapons but also elements of the Soviet military doctrine, which was instilled in the Arab armies by the officers, who were trained either in the Eastern bloc or at home by Soviet instructors. Beginning in 1960, Rabin insisted on intensive intelligence efforts to learn about the Soviet army and its method of waging war.[34] One of Rabin's most important contributions to the IDF was preparing it to fight Soviet-equipped and -trained Arab armies. Under his leadership, and thanks to the efforts of the Training Branch under the command of Maj. Gen. Yeshayahu Gavish (who held this post from 1962 to 1965), the IDF engaged in meticulous planning and military training for a particular type of warfare—countering the Soviet doctrine. Full-scale model Soviet-style defense lines, complete with trenches and fences, were built at IDF training sites, and soldiers practiced day and night methods of attacking and overcoming these awesome fortified positions.[35]

In 1961, Rabin announced that all new officers would also undergo training in the use of armored vehicles. This underscored the changes that had to occur in the IDF, in his opinion, in order to keep abreast of changes in the nature of warfare. "Each officer in the army will learn early on, in the initial stages to think fast, [a skill] which is necessary for managing a battle of movement." The officers would also learn "the command problems of a mobile force, as well as the main elements of maintenance of an armored force."[36] As far back as 1949, Rabin had recognized the crucial importance of armor for ground forces and had asked Allon, his superior, to help him be appointed as commander of Brigade 12, then the only IDF unit that was partially armored. At that time the entire IDF armored force consisted of a single battalion of old Sherman tanks. Understanding their importance required a certain amount of creative vision.[37]

PREPARING THE IDF FOR WAR

Rabin, the first chief of staff to come from a Palmach background, assumed command on the first day of 1964. He had acquired more organizational experience than his predecessors, serving in a variety of command, staff, and training positions throughout the military hierarchy. His slow promotion to the head of the pyramid and his lateral rotation through several senior posts gave Rabin an excellent feel for how to operate a complex machine such as a large military organization. This experience was complemented by his balanced personality. He was less "glamorous" than some of his predecessors, but he was experienced, solid, thoughtful, and original.[38] Rabin inherited the basic IDF structure, which was to remain in place for several decades: a strong air force and, on the ground, an emphasis on swift armored operations that could quickly carry the war into the enemy's territory. Despite this continuity, he left his own clear imprint on the IDF. Capitalizing on his earlier contributions, particularly as chief of operations, Rabin prepared the IDF for its next war.

Rabin had two clear criteria for setting the magnitude of IDF strength.[39] A cautious and pessimistic commander, Rabin believed that he had to build an army for the worst-case scenario: to confront all Arab opponents and their overall force order at once. Meeting a concerted Arab effort required a sizable Israeli army, but Israel could not hope to achieve numerical superiority. Therefore, the second consideration regarded the quality of Israeli manpower and weapons, which had to compensate for the quantitative edge that the Arabs enjoyed. More than other chiefs of staff (with the possible exception of Tzur), Rabin put great emphasis on training and on improving the skills of the troops as the best way to utilize the available tools of war, even at the expense of quantitative and qualitative growth.[40] These two criteria continued to guide his thinking about the IDF until his death.[41]

In the 1960s, making available as much military muscle as possible for offensive operations represented the highest priority. Rabin further reduced the size of the fighting force at the disposal of the "territorial defense" battalions, whose manpower was drawn primarily from the settlements along the border and along the invasion routes into pre-1967 Israel. The mission of these units was essentially static defense.[42]

One of the lessons that Rabin had learned from the 1956 campaign and that he tried to implement later as chief of staff was that Israel must strengthen and better train the reserve units.[43] The average quality of reserve officers sharply improved during the 1960s. Israel had to maintain an army that relied on a swift transition, in an emergency, from a civilian routine to a war footing.[44] Rabin stressed the need to upgrade the quality of the reserve forces, which formed the bulk of the IDF; in contrast, in the military structure of the Arab forces, the reserves played only a secondary role in war-fighting doctrines.

The branches of the IDF that received the most attention and allocations from Rabin, a focus that did not differ from that of previous periods, were the Israel Air Force (IAF) and the Tank Corps because of their roles in swiftly carrying the war into enemy territory and achieving a decisive victory in a short time (Israel's military doctrine is discussed in the next chapter).[45] During Rabin's tenure as chief of staff, the IAF was designed not only to achieve air superiority in a short time but also to participate in the land battle and even to ensure sea control.[46] The IAF increased the number of Mirage-3C warplanes (the first twenty-three arrived in Israel in April 1962) to sixty-five in its order of battle.[47] The IAF trained intensively to destroy airfields and aircraft on the ground and generally to improve its capability for low-altitude attacks. Special munitions were developed for these purposes.[48]

Rabin's four years as chief of staff also saw the crystallization of the Tank Corps into a force of considerable dimensions and quality, even if it was still markedly inferior, in terms of equipment available, to the Arab armies. Immediately after his appointment, Rabin pressed for growth in the tank force, even at the short-term expense of the IAF. In the summer of 1964, he preferred purchasing British Centurion tanks rather than Mirage-4 airplanes.[49] By June 1967, 210 American Patton tanks had been procured by the IDF, in addition to the 160 Centurions added to the Israeli arsenal.[50] Within three years (April 1961–April 1964), the proportion of high-quality tanks almost tripled, from 10.6 to 27.3 percent; the proportion of medium-quality tanks grew from 27.1 to 46.3 percent while the proportion of poor-quality tanks was reduced from 62.4 to 26.4 percent.[51] The use of tanks to destroy the Syrian equipment deployed in the endeavor to divert the Jordan waters (1964–65) precipitated a systematic training effort to improve the marksmanship of Israeli tank gunners.[52] During Rabin's tenure as chief of staff, the Tank Corps was transformed into independent operational entities capable of simultaneous deployment on a larger scale than ever before. Rabin repeatedly called for larger-scale maneuvers. This was a particular Rabin achievement: the IDF's ability to deploy large masses of troops, with all their follow-on maintenance echelons, for fighting that could last a considerable amount of time. This agility in the deployment of large-scale armored formations was in great contrast to the 1956 IDF (led by Dayan), which was primarily an infantry-based army.

Rabin did not neglect the infantry and particularly the paratroopers, which were his third priority after the IAF and the Tank Corps, as they were when he was chief of operations. He believed that the ability of the infantry to capture important points deep in enemy territory was important in demoralizing the enemy and eroding the enemy's will to fight.[53] Indeed, he decided to expand the reserve paratrooper battalions.[54]

Rabin also made a contribution to less glamorous parts of the IDF, such as the Logistics Corps. Under Rabin, Maj. Gen. Matty Peled revolutionized the logistic system in emphasizing that ammunition and gas be "pushed" to the armored combat units rather than be supplied in response to demand. Rabin was fully aware that the fighting effectiveness of modern mechanized armies depended also to a large degree on the quality of their maintenance, repair, and recovery services. Therefore, his drive for managerial and technical improvement was directed not only at the "teeth" of the army but also at its "tail." Under Rabin's leadership, the IDF upgraded support services and introduced new management techniques (including the extensive use of computers), and attempts were also made to streamline the military bureaucracy. After the logistics system was computerized, significant savings in manpower were achieved and organizational channels were shortened, allowing for better command and control. Indeed, the difference in performance between 1956 and 1967 was striking: instead of chronic breakdowns, much of the IDF's far more complex equipment was kept in running order for the duration of the war.[55] The Manpower Branch of the IDF underwent similar computerization and restructuring, allowing for a better utilization of the manpower at the IDF's disposal.[56]

While introducing modern management techniques and planning methods and raising the professional standard of the Officers Corps, Rabin also succeeded in preserving and in spreading the fighting spirit of the paratroopers and the special units.[57] When he was shown research about the importance of higher education for the performance of IDF officers, Rabin nevertheless continued to emphasize the cultivation of fighting spirit as the most important aspect of officer training.[58] During his tenure, the IDF adhered to the practice of job rotation and early retirement for senior officers. He realized that this practice meant that experienced officers left the army early, so he favored slightly extending the service of battalion and brigade commanders. Yet he defended the IDF preference for a continuous influx of young, dynamic commanders. He said, "When it comes to officer commissions for combat units, dynamism is of paramount importance."[59]

Rabin used his position to secure the resources needed for building a well-equipped IDF. Prime Minister and Defense Minister Levi Eshkol was no military expert, and he depended on Rabin for advice on national security affairs and military needs.[60] Eshkol was also politically vulnerable to attack from the opposition, including the charge that he did not care enough about security matters. Therefore, Eshkol complied with most of Rabin's requests for new weapons, in contrast to the previous ministers of defense, who routinely overruled IDF requests for higher budgets.[61] The defense budget grew in the 1964–66 period, when Rabin served as chief of staff, by 28.5 percent (in real terms by 12.1 percent) while defense outlays as a proportion of the gross national product (GNP) grew only slightly, from 10.1 to 10.4 percent.[62] Rabin was sensitive, however, to the needs of the economy. For example, he agreed in 1963 to shorten the period of conscription by four months (to twenty-six months) in order to increase the manpower available to the Israeli economy.[63] He also bowed to the economic constraints of the pre-1967 recession and reduced the number of Mirage fighters, on order from France, from ninety to seventy.[64]

Another budgetary constraint on the quantitative growth was the maintenance costs of the equipment procured. Chief of Staff Rabin was fully aware of the need to balance procurement with maintenance and manpower costs, and he was concerned that present acquisitions of weapon systems could reduce resources for future procurement.[65] Moreover, in 1966 he realized that the expansion of the tank force had not been matched by an increase in ammunition stocks. The tension between quantitative increases in weapon systems and the need to meet ammunition and spare parts requirements from within a fixed budget reinforced his concern for a balanced growth.[66]

In 1965, Rabin approved the plans for a reform of Israel's navy.[67] At that time, the General Staff decided to adopt the navy's plan, formulated in

1963, to purchase fast missile boats and to arm them with Israeli-made Gabriel missiles, which were then still in the development stage. The navy had always been given lower priority in Israeli strategic thinking because control of the sea was viewed as secondary to the outcome of an Arab-Israeli war. It was not, therefore, an easy decision to divert funds for its modernization. Admitting to his own hesitations because of the uncertainties involved, Rabin harbored no illusions about the chances that Israel's larger vessels would have in a naval encounter with the fast Ossa and Komar missile boats provided to Egypt and Syria by the Soviet Union. According to Maj. Gen. (Res.) Shlomo Erell, the former chief of the Israeli navy, Chief of Staff Rabin understood the needs of the navy better than any of his predecessors, and Erell praised Rabin's courage in approving a revolutionary concept.[68] Rabin's main fear was that the funds for modernizing the navy would come at the expense of the air force.[69] Therefore, he opposed an increase in the number of submarines from two to four.[70] The 1965 decision to procure missile boats did not influence the outcome of the limited naval engagements of 1967, but its benefits were reaped in the October 1973 war.

Unquestionably, Rabin's greatest military achievement was preparing the IDF for winning the 1967 war. In this conflict, he had at his disposal an unusually talented group of generals. They probably could have prevailed even had Rabin not been around at the time of the actual test—precisely because of his decisive contribution to building a well-oiled military machine that operated according to the principles of a thoughtful combat doctrine and was imbued with a remarkable esprit de corps. The period of relative quiet along Israel's borders in 1956–67 allowed the IDF to focus on preparing for large-scale warfare rather than having to solve current security problems. Rabin made good use of this time.

RABIN THE CIVILIAN

After leaving the IDF, Rabin continued to be preoccupied with building a strong military machine. As noted in the previous chapter, his first priority as ambassador to the United States was to secure modern weapons for the IDF. Indeed, much of his time was taken up by his efforts to get Phantom combat jets for Israel. U.S. President Lyndon Johnson promised Prime Minister Eshkol, at their meeting in January 1968, to consider the Israeli request for fifty Phantoms. President Johnson announced his approval of the sale on 9 October 1968, only a few weeks before the U.S. presidential elections. This decision followed a congressional resolution in favor of the sale and the realization that American attempts to slow down the arms race in the Middle East were not being reciprocated by the Soviets. Rabin also was successful in resisting American attempts to link the sale to a U.S. presence in Israeli research and development installations.[71] Finally, on 27 December 1968, the U.S. Department of State issued a statement on an American-Israeli deal for the delivery of the fifty Phantoms, worth $200 million.

This was one of the most important decisions in the U.S.-Israel weapon relationship; it opened a new era in ties between the two countries and launched a major IDF buildup. The Americans proved that they were ready to redress the regional military balance in Israel's favor, so that Israel could now demand weapons of quality, better than those found in Arab arsenals. The Phantom was a versatile combat jet with better performance than the Soviet MiG-21, which had been supplied to Egypt and Syria. It could engage in dogfights as well as in ground attacks. Doubling the IAF's range, it could carry a much larger load of ammunition than the MiG. Furthermore, its avionics and weapon systems, such as the Sparrow air-to-air missiles, were more advanced than the Soviet equipment.[72] Rabin wholeheartedly supported the transition of the IDF into an almost fully American-equipped army in the aftermath of the 1967 war.

Rabin's presence in Washington, and particularly his military expertise, were instrumental in changing the American policy toward arms transfers to Israel. Soviet behavior in the Middle East and elsewhere (for example, the August 1968 invasion of Czechoslovakia) and the advent of the Nixon-Kissinger outlook on world politics facilitated the shift in American policies toward Israel. President Richard Nixon had expressed support for the sale of Phantoms to Israel in his 1968 election campaign as part of his commitment to preserve the Arab-Israeli military balance, a commitment he articulated more clearly than his predecessors had. In fact, he went beyond promising to preserve the balance—he said that he would, if elected president, give Israel a military and technological advantage.[73] Practically, the Johnson decision to supply the Phantoms already exemplified this principle.

Despite this support, Nixon decided in 1970 to delay for an indefinite time the approval of a new arms deal with Israel (requested by Golda Meir in September 1969), which included twenty-five additional Phantoms and one hundred Skyhawks.[74] The delay was the result of the new administration's deliberations over the course of its foreign policy toward the Soviet Union and the Middle East. Instead, Nixon suggested to Rabin (and in a

letter to Meir) that IAF losses be replaced ad hoc, without any public an-
nouncements. Later, the administration also approved the sale of two hundred of the latest M-60 tanks and electronic equipment to counter surface-
to-air missiles. Even so, there were now many apprehensions on the Israeli
side about the linkage of arms sales to political developments in the American-Soviet and Middle East arenas, whereas Israel preferred formal commitments in the form of arms sales. Only in December 1971, during a visit
by Meir to Washington, did Nixon announce that the United States would
ensure a continuous delivery of weapons and would commit itself to the
long-range modernization of the IDF.[75] Ambassador Rabin was a key player
in this successful Israeli attempt to put the American arms transfers on a
more permanent basis.

Rabin was also intensively involved in weapons procurement, particularly from the United States, during his first tenure as prime minister. This
was a period of accelerated growth in IDF weapon stocks. Rabin's partner
in these achievements was Defense Minister Shimon Peres, who then articulated more hawkish positions. Under Rabin's government, Israel's immediate goals were to rebuild an effective and confident military force and
to delay any future war with the Arabs until the political circumstances improved and until the IDF was ready militarily for such another encounter.
According to Rabin, a "supreme effort" was urgently needed to strengthen
the IDF.[76] Invariably, Rabin's visits to Washington included discussions of
military procurement. Indeed, at the end of 1974, Israel presented the
United States with an impressive multiyear shopping list, the Matmon-B
plan, which was the basis for further discussions between the two parties.[77]

A major departure from previous military thinking was the determination to establish, as quickly as possible, a much larger army.[78] There were
several reasons for the new quantitative emphasis. First, Israel wanted a
larger army with greater firepower to avoid collapse if the country was surprised again. A small state such as Israel has much more to fear from a surprise offensive because it has little strategic depth. It must stop the enemy
at the outer limits of its vital centers. Therefore, what matters is not military potential but the military power that is immediately available.[79] In the
wake of the 1973 surprise attack and previous experiences, Rabin was extremely skeptical about the ability of the intelligence community to provide adequate warning about an impending war. He was generally suspicious of claims to expertise and superior knowledge by Israeli intelligence
officers and academics, an anti-intellectual residue of Ben-Gurion's well-
known contemptuous attitude toward experts who disagreed with him.[80]

Rabin, during his military career, was twice surprised by Egypt's massive introduction of forces into the Sinai desert, in February 1960 and in May 1967.[81] The IDF was surprised also in October 1973, a mistake for which Israel paid a high price. Therefore, Rabin and others at the helm of security affairs in Israel in the immediate post-1973 period recognized the need to have greater forces to hold the frontiers, as well as the need to have more units on alert.

Second, Rabin realized that the IDF was unable to deter an Arab-initiated war under all circumstances, as the 1967 and 1973 wars demonstrated. Particularly after 1973, Israeli conventional deterrence deteriorated because the Arabs recognized that losing a war did not necessarily mean a political setback. Arab power was not great enough to defeat Israel militarily, but it could be used to change the status quo and create more favorable political conditions to further Arab political and military interests.[82] Indeed, in September 1974 Rabin astutely observed: "Because the Arabs no longer fear a military defeat, it seems to me that it is necessary for us to change our military doctrine and to build the IDF with the aim of decisively subduing the enemy, rather than deterring him."[83] This change of strategy required a larger army.

Third, the 1973 war highlighted the neglect of firepower capacity in the IDF fighting doctrine, an omission that had resulted from the previous Israeli emphasis on mobility. For example, the IDF had a very limited number of artillery pieces. The traditional Arab quantitative advantage, therefore, had to be matched by enhanced IDF firepower. The great expansion of the Arab arsenals after 1973 reinforced this new tendency within the IDF.

Fourth, Israel hoped to establish a force large enough to enable the country to mount a counteroffensive on two fronts simultaneously. Israel desired to accumulate enough military muscle to smash the Arab armies before the superpowers could intervene. Such a victory was also needed to enhance Israel's credible deterrent, which was thought to have been degraded by limited Arab successes in the 1973 war.

Fifth, Israel calculated that in the next Arab-Israeli contest, the Arabs would field larger armies. The neighboring countries' armies were expected to grow and to be joined by significant contingents from more-distant Arab countries. The petrodollars made such growth within easy reach financially, with massive weapons transfers from the West to Arab countries.

Sixth, Israel anticipated a higher attrition rate in the next encounter than had occurred in 1973. The greater destructive power and accuracy of Arab weapons, as well as the expected increase in the size of the opponents' armies, led to this conclusion. Therefore, Israeli leaders wanted to have large-enough stocks of weapons, spare parts, and ammunition to last through a war without needing an American airlift. The American airlift of 1973 underscored Israel's dependence, which of course damaged Israeli interests. Further, Rabin did not expect a recurrence of the political circumstances that had led to the American decision to aid Israel so conspicuously in 1973.[84]

Within three years, the size of the military establishment was considerably expanded. Close to 50,000 men and women were added by tightening service regulations and by drawing on categories that had previously been exempted. In addition, many areas previously limited to men were opened to women in order to divert men to combat assignments. The first Rabin government also successfully executed its weapons procurement plan. By June 1977, Israel had replaced all of its losses in matériel. Its tank force had increased in size by 50 percent, the artillery by 100 percent, armored personnel carriers by 800 percent, and aircraft by 30 percent.[85] Moreover, the United States approved the sale of combat jets of the F-15 and F-16 type, as well as several items of advanced technological nature.[86] This remarkable growth in such a short period created problems in finding suitable officers to command the newly established units, despite efforts to bring senior officers from the reserves into the regular army. The short-range cost of expansion was a less strict promotion system.

In June 1977, Rabin handed over the government to the leader of a different party, marking the first time in Israel's political history that the Labor movement left power. For seven years (1977–1984) Rabin was on the opposition benches in the Israeli parliament, outside the decision-making process on national security matters. Indeed, when appointed defense minister in September 1984, he quickly learned that the circumstances of the late 1970s and the early 1980s had changed completely. The strategic environment had improved considerably because of the peace treaty with Egypt, as well as the Iran-Iraq War (1980–88), which reduced the chances of an eastern front coalescence. Domestically, the picture was less rosy. Budgetary constraints were more stringent, and the general atmosphere was more hostile to diverting resources to security needs.[87] Israel was, in Rabin's opinion, unable to maintain its standard of living and build a strong army without massive financial assistance from the United States.[88]

As defense minister, Rabin was responsible for making sure that the IDF was well equipped and ready for war. Nevertheless, Rabin was willing to accept severe cuts in the defense budget in 1985 to help the Israeli economy recover after several years of mismanagement that had resulted in three-digit hyperinflation. He understood the importance of a healthy economy to national power. The $650 million that Rabin agreed to forgo constituted approximately 15 percent of the defense budget. He fully realized that such deep budgetary cuts would have a severe impact on the IDF order of battle, the level of training, weapons procurement, and research and development and would reduce Israel's margins of security. However, given the favorable strategic environment of that period, he was willing to take the risks.[89] To a great extent, it was a gamble that only Rabin, with his unsurpassed authority within the defense establishment, could take.

The IDF contracted as a result of Rabin's budgetary decision. About seven thousand IDF civilian employees were dismissed. Laying them off was a great emotional burden for Rabin.[90] Many ground units were dismantled, and several formations of the standing army were transformed into reserve units.[91] Generally, units operating the oldest equipment, such as Soviet-made tanks, were decommissioned. By early 1988, the IDF cut the order of battle by three armored divisions and seven tank brigades.[92] This fate also awaited three older missile boats. In addition, Rabin struggled to reduce the size of the IDF and its overall activity in order to save on maintenance costs.[93] A number of headquarters were closed. An important saving was the cut of more than one million reservist days (about 10 percent). Moreover, a new accounting system gave army units an incentive to save on reservist days.[94] Instead of buying new ammunition, the IDF was also allowed to tap ammunition from the emergency depots, which reached unprecedentedly low levels of stocks.[95]

The IAF was hit the hardest, because this was where the most money could be saved. Rabin pointed out that flying an F-15 for one hour cost the same as one year's service for a professional soldier. Training hours for pilots were cut by approximately one-third. Also, reservist pilots were decommissioned—an irreversible step. Over a little more than a year, Rabin retired seventy warplanes, deciding that when new F-16s arrived in the spring of 1987, older Kfirs would be put in storage so that the IAF order of battle would not exceed five hundred active warplanes.[96]

The cuts Rabin forced on the military were not only quantitative but also qualitative. Many "smart weapon" projects were delayed or canceled.[97] Similarly, procurement plans for new weapon systems were trimmed.[98] Nevertheless, Rabin continued to stress the need for an offensive-capable army. His priorities in building the IDF were, as in the past, a strong air force and armored forces, though he agreed to cut the number of the armored divisions.[99] He desired increased armored mobility and hoped also to establish a capability for long-range airborne operations (less than divisional strength).[100] Israeli military planners were increasingly aware that an armored breakthrough of the denser defensive lines was more difficult and costly, particularly in light of the increase in the lethality of the modern battlefield. Moreover, the urbanization process in the neighboring countries (with the exception of the demilitarized Sinai) reduced the open areas for armored outflanking maneuvers along the indirect approach.[101]

In light of the difficulties in using armor, Rabin and the chiefs of staff, Moshe Levy and Dan Shomron, maintained that the upgrading and expanding of infantry and commando units was necessary. Furthermore, the emphasis on the procurement of Precise Guided Munitions (PGM) continued.[102] Rabin was primarily interested in developing the capacity to engage and destroy targets far beyond the contact line between battling armies (15–30 kilometers and possibly farther away). This also required improved intelligence. He wanted to enhance significantly the ability to operate at night or in bad weather conditions in the air and on the ground.[103] Though Rabin had a good grasp of military technology, his approach to new weapon technologies was conservative. An experienced military man, Rabin was not carried away by the evaluations in the 1970s that the age of warplanes was over, and he did not attribute to any newly designed weapon the necessary features "to solve all the problems."[104]

Rabin was led to believe in 1985 that once the Israeli economy improved, the defense budget would be increased; there were thoughts of linking it to the GNP. Despite his growing influence in Israeli politics, this did not happen, and subsequently Rabin opposed cuts in the defense budget.[105] The financial stringencies negatively affected the preparedness of the IDF, that is, the alertness and the magnitude of the present forces.[106] In 1989 in a closed forum, Rabin revealed that the stocks of spare parts in the armored forces were in a "critical" situation.[107] Even when he was both prime minister and defense minister in the 1992–95 period, the defense budget did not increase—to the displeasure of the IDF leadership.

In any case, the financial sources available were, according to Rabin, to be spent on qualitative advancement. Toward the end of the 1980s, he explained to the student body in the National Security College that the quantitative dimension of the IDF's order of battle was satisfactory but that the IDF must improve technologically, particularly in light of the narrowing of the technological gap between Israeli and Arab weapons.[108] One qualitative project that received Rabin's enthusiastic support was the Israeli intelligence satellite program (Ofeq), whose function was to improve and extend the range of real-time surveillance. Rabin decided to divert funds to the Ofeq project and used his weight as defense minister to change priorities in the Israel Aircraft Industry (IAI), which was responsible for its development, in order to speed up the process.[109] The first experimental Ofeq satellite was launched in September 1988.[110]

As defense minister, Rabin looked beyond the horizon at distant enemies. Rabin spoke about "a long arm," which meant extending Israel's reach to thousands of kilometers.[111] This strategic prognosis was partly related to the proliferation of long-range surface-to-surface missiles in the Arab arsenals.[112] For example, in the mid-1980s, the Israeli intelligence community closely followed developments in Iraq and realized that Israel's population centers could soon be in range. Therefore, Rabin decided to put greater emphasis on the emerging missile threat to Israel. In accordance with past military doctrine, he and the IDF preferred developing versatile offensive capabilities for dealing with this threat.[113]

Nevertheless, Rabin decided to go along in the 1980s with the Arrow antitactical ballistic missile (ATBM) program, an active defensive solution. This was primarily because it was 80 percent funded by the United States, which was extremely interested in the Israeli technology.[114] Against the IDF General Staff's recommendation not to invest in such a project, Rabin approved only the development stage, deferring a decision on deployment.[115] Politically, rejecting developing measures for protecting Israeli population centers was also difficult. Yet, the Arrow ATBM program aroused little enthusiasm because of the technological uncertainty surrounding its development and deployment and the projected cost of $3–5 billion.[116] In January 1993 Rabin told the Knesset that Israel was "still too far away from the technological and financial solutions necessary to fully realize" the Arrow ATBM program.[117] In the main, he accepted the military's point of view on the Arrow ATBM program and assigned the system a lower budgetary priority than it had occupied during the tenure of the previous defense minister, Moshe Arens (1990–92). He also stopped the development of an early-warning system for the Arrow ATBM.[118] This left Israel dependent on American satellites for early warning, which was critically important for the movement of Israel's population into sheltered areas in case of missile attacks.

Several of Rabin's decisions concerning the IDF force structure reflected his evaluation of the distant nature of strategic threats posed to Israel. For example, he approved the procurement of American-made Apache attack helicopters in 1989. Their extended range and night-flying capabilities made them more attractive to Rabin and the IAF, whereas the Field Headquarters Command (Mafhash) had recommended the procurement of a large number of cheaper and less sophisticated helicopters (mainly the Cobra, which was already in the service of the IAF).[119] The IAF also wanted the more advanced Apache helicopter and its better weapon systems in order to preserve a qualitative edge.

For similar reasons, Defense Minister Rabin approved ambitious navy plans to build four missile corvettes of the Saar-5 class. This new class of ships was larger and could stay longer at sea than the Saar-4 missile boats, which the Israeli navy then used.[120] Furthermore, despite financial stringencies, Rabin did not accept his chief of staff's recommendation to scrap preparations for buying Dolphin-class submarines in March 1989; he hoped that the money for the expensive procurement plan would eventually be located. Submarines were seen as an offensive strategic weapon system because of their long range and their capacity to launch missiles. In addition, they were considered to have a deterrent value at the nonconventional level.[121] The submarines were, in Rabin's view, more important than the corvettes.[122]

Similarly, Rabin opted in February 1993 (when he was defense and prime minister) for the F-15I rather than cheaper warplanes (F-16s), as Iran was added to the potential missile threat to Israel. Again the IDF, under Rabin's guidance, preferred a more expensive system because it had the qualities necessary to attack distant targets; the F-15I could deliver a large payload of explosives (11 tonnes) of various types of munitions at ranges of over 1,000 miles in all weather conditions. In March 1994, Israel signed an agreement for the purchase of twenty-one F-15Is (the first airplane was to be delivered in 1997).[123] Thus Rabin began providing answers to distant threats by developing capabilities in the air, on the sea, and in space (the Israeli satellite program).

Overall, Rabin tended to accept the judgment of the chief of staff in debates over procurement plans for major weapon systems, multiyear development plans, and allocations of resources among the IDF branches, though on several occasions Rabin sent back the recommendations for further work or rejected them.[124] For example, as noted, Rabin declined to accept Chief of Staff Shomron's recommendation to cancel the navy's submarine program.[125] But in general he preferred the view of the chief of staff to that of the director general of the Defense Ministry because he believed that ultimately, the chief of staff would bear the responsibility for the outcome of the next war.[126] Rabin's own experience as chief of staff in 1967 probably led him to this conclusion. Moreover, when the Agranat Commission, which investigated how the IDF had been surprised in the 1973 war, blamed Chief of Staff Elazar and absolved Minister of Defense Dayan, Rabin became extremely sensitive about the role of the chief of staff.[127] Rabin was unhappy with the recommendations of the Agranat Commission and felt that senior officers were mistreated while the political level was allowed to escape responsibility.[128]

Yet Rabin closely guarded his power to promote senior officers. Because of his close acquaintance with the military, he felt confident enough to intervene frequently, often using his power to delay or make appointments at the general ranks against the chief of staff's initial inclination.[129] His active participation in making appointments went beyond the criteria for military efficiency, but he was also a civilian and a politician. He was sensitive to how such appointments were perceived by the Israeli public at large. For example, he promoted Avigdor Kehalani, of Yemenite origin, to brigadier general.[130]

PROCUREMENT FROM THE ISRAELI DEFENSE INDUSTRIES

Rabin was also the one who formulated the prevalent IDF attitude toward purchases of weapons from the indigenous military industries.[131] He wanted to reach a balance between the import of weapons and the local production of weapons. The golden mean was connected to the distinction that he had introduced, as a senior officer in the IDF, between preparedness (immediate readiness to wage war) and preparation (the process of augmenting future capabilities). Rabin recognized the tension between the two concepts. The preparedness of the IDF required timely purchases, often from abroad, whereas the preparation of the IDF involved the development of Israeli military industries, reducing dependence, enhancing the Israeli technological base, and contributing to the Israeli economy. Rabin preferred emphasizing preparedness. This short-range perspective meant importing available equipment now, instead of diverting scarce resources to local production, because in a worst-case analysis, military conflict could be expected in the immediate future. Furthermore, Rabin insisted that in making decisions concerning local production, the most important perspective was that of the user, that is, the IDF, rather than that of the buyer (the Defense Ministry) or the producer.[132] Moreover, throughout his career, he maintained that it was not the military's duty to take care of the defense industries and that if these industries served nonmilitary goals, the defense budget should not pay for them.[133] Rabin was focused on building a ready military force, despite the fact that he was among those Israeli generals more sensitive to considerations beyond the narrow military realm, such as national economic development.[134] His views usually prevailed when he was in a decision-making position.

Rabin's criteria for developing and/or producing weapons in Israel included the following scenarios:[135]

1. When foreign powers refused to sell critical weapons to Israel
2. When Israeli weapons engineers achieved a technological breakthrough that would allow the IDF to acquire a significant advantage on the battlefield (i.e., missiles, electronic warfare, intelligence equipment)
3. When production in Israel was cheaper than abroad or equaled the price of weapons produced abroad

Rabin recommended that Israeli weapons manufacturers specialize in adapting imported weapons to the specific needs of the IDF and the local theater. Moreover, since he realized that replacement of weapon systems was very expensive, he expected the local industries to extend the life of the systems. For example, in 1959, he suggested equipping Mystere combat airplanes with air-to-air missiles and equipping Centurion and Patton tanks with improved subsystems rather than buying expensive new warplanes and tanks.[136]

The issue of local production put him into direct conflict in the late 1950s and 1960s with several senior officials in the Ministry of Defense, Peres being one of them,[137] but Rabin's preferences became incorporated into policy when he served as chief of staff under Prime Minister and Defense Minister Eshkol. Indeed, in 1966, Rabin rejected the long-range plan prepared by the Ministry of Defense for producing main battle systems (tanks and airplanes) in Israel.[138] Another example of Eshkol's acceptance of Rabin's view on buying abroad concerned the purchase of mobile communications equipment for securing contact between ground and air units. The Defense Ministry's demand that all the necessary equipment be produced indigenously was rejected, and local industry was allowed to produce only a fraction of the systems. Rabin often cited this incident because only the equipment bought abroad was available for the 1967 war.[139]

The criteria developed by Rabin served as guidelines for subsequent Israeli governments as he continued to exert influence on these matters in the

1970s, 1980s, and 1990s. In the post-1973 period, the need to use most financial aid received from the United States to buy American weapons reinforced Rabin's skeptical outlook toward the Israeli military industries. The guidelines, later called Make or Buy (MOB), became the foundation for Israeli procurement policies, although the implementation was, in practice, often determined by bureaucratic infighting. Even Rabin could not always resist the pressures from within the defense establishment. For example, in 1976 he could not prevent allocations to the IAI for a pilot project for developing a new warplane.[140] In the mid-1980s, Defense Minister Rabin allowed his director general, Maj. Gen. (Res.) David Ivri, to establish a discretionary fund of about $35 million for helping the defense industry.[141] One reason for procrastination in ending the Lavi project was the concern about finding alternative employment for many scientists and engineers.

More than other Israeli leaders, Rabin was skeptical about the need to build a large local infrastructure to produce military equipment, as well as about the capabilities of Israeli engineers. This was particularly so in the pre-1967 period, before the great expansion of the Israeli military industries. For example, in 1965, during one of his first visits to RAFAEL (the Weapon Development Authority), Rabin canceled a project to develop an IFF (identify foe-friend) system because he was skeptical about its successful completion.[142]

Indeed, the crucial decisions to develop the Kfir warplane in 1968 and the Merkava tank in 1970, both after Israel had difficulties purchasing these items abroad, were taken when Rabin was in Washington and had limited influence over the decision-making process in this area.[143] These projects fueled the great growth of Israeli industries. In the post-1973 period, there was even greater respect for the capabilities of the local industry and more willingness to invest in new weapon systems. Still, in an interview with the author in 1979, Rabin summed up his experience by stating that the procurement of weapons from Israeli military industries often ended up with a product being more expensive and less effective than planned and delivered later than promised.[144] Indeed, he told Chief of Staff Mordechai Gur to make sure that the equipment needed for battle was in Israel, even if bought abroad, and not to worry about the destiny of the defense industries.[145] Rabin did little justice to the Israeli achievements in arms production. He belittled the originality of the Israeli weapon designers and, in his blunt way, referred to Israeli achievements in the area of arms manufacturing as the product of "copying, imitating or stealing foreign technology."[146] Even when he complimented the technological contribution of the Israeli military industries in 1988, he mentioned its high economic cost.[147]

His clear and consistent preference was to buy completely developed arms with known qualities off the shelves, particularly if they were American. When American-Israeli strategic cooperation began to grow in the late 1980s and there was much more cooperation between the two armed forces, Rabin also preferred American systems in order to ensure interoperability.[148] This feature facilitated common exercises and contingency planning.

Another impediment to the expansion of Israel's military industries was Rabin's attitude toward selling Israeli weapons abroad.[149] Though he understood well the economic and political advantages of exporting arms, he usually agreed with the IDF in constantly preferring to keep Israeli-made systems secret and off the world market for as long as possible. The IDF wanted to minimize the release of information concerning the performance of its latest Israeli-made equipment. For example, in 1984, Rabin was unwilling to override IAF opposition to offering the Americans the Popeye air-to-ground standoff weapon, which was then in the final stages of development. Only a year later, when the IAF had lost interest in the expensive project, was this weapon made available to the U.S. Air Force, which was looking for just such a system.[150]

Rabin, particularly after 1973, believed that the development of the Israeli defense industry was only a marginal addition to Israel's security, whereas he considered coordination with the United States to be absolutely essential. Moreover, the dream of Israeli self-sufficiency in weapons production evaporated after 1973. Therefore, if the United States objected to certain Israeli steps in the direction of a greater and more diverse weapons production, it simply was not worth a fight with the Americans. For example, in March 1977, Rabin publicly declared his refusal to take up the cause of selling Israel-made Kfir airplanes to Ecuador against American opposition. He did not want a confrontation with President Jimmy Carter on a marginal issue at their first meeting.[151] Maintaining strategic coordination was more important than satisfying the defense industry's business interests in producing more airplanes.

Indeed, Rabin, as defense minister, joined the struggle against the Lavi airplane project. His negative position was critical in the 30 August 1987 decision to scrap the project.[152] This reflected his general opposition to the development of high-unit-cost platforms. As early as 1976, Rabin had tried unsuccessfully to prevent the initiation of the Arieh project, the predecessor of the Lavi, by Peres, then defense minister.[153] In 1980, Rabin, as an

MK, voted in the Knesset Committee for Defense and Foreign Affairs against the Lavi project.[154] Before becoming defense minister in 1984, Rabin went publicly on record against this project. Yet once the project was in progress, Rabin hesitated before terminating it. He preferred not to embarrass Israel's friends on Capitol Hill, who had voted for financial aid for the Lavi,[155] and he was reluctant to engage in a difficult domestic political battle, though he continued to fear that the IAF would end up with an airplane whose performance would not be comparable to that of its American competitors. It took over two years for Rabin to recommend to the government that the project be canceled, a move he made in July 1987.[156] This is indicative of, inter alia, the slowness, hesitation, and lack of domestic political acumen in Rabin's decision-making. The growing American opposition to the project was, of course, an important factor in Rabin's canceling the Lavi. Yet only after he was certain that the American administration would continue the $300 million offshore procurement funding (permitting Israel to spend the money at home, not in the United States) and would fund the Lavi termination liabilities did Rabin officially announce his opposition to the project.[157]

In 1988, Rabin was quite proud that he forced the IAI to contract, firing over 5,000 employees within a year; he emphasized that the sales of the company remained the same despite a reduced workforce. Similarly, he demanded a reorganization of RAFAEL, including the firing of 1,200–1,300 of its personnel. He objected to the fact that the losses of RAFAEL and of the Israel Military Industries (IMI) had to be covered by the budget of the Ministry of Defense, leaving less money for the IDF.[158]

In 1992, when Rabin held the portfolio of defense minister and was again in charge of several military industries in financial trouble, he did not hesitate to express in frank terms his minimalist approach: "The military industries are too big for Israel."[159] He also saw the difficulties stemming from the fact that part of the defense industry was government-owned. He favored privatization.[160]

The decline in domestic and international demand for weapons as a result of the end of the cold war also affected the Israeli defense sector.[161] Thus, local weapons purchases by the IDF in 1995 were 23 percent lower than they had been in 1984, constituting only 17 percent of the defense budget—in contrast to 40 percent a decade earlier.[162] In 1994, Rabin reiterated his view that Israeli military industries needed to "adapt to changing circumstances."[163] Indeed, during his last tenure as defense minister, the scope of Israeli defense industries contracted considerably.[164] In the mid-1980s, total manpower in the defense industries reached a peak of

80,000 employees; this fell to some 40,000 in 1990, 24,000 in 1994, and 18,000 by the end of 1996.

CONCLUSION

According to Rabin, a strong IDF was instrumental for the survival of Israel in a hostile environment and was a prerequisite for entering into peace negotiations with its neighbors. The military might also served as the ultimate guarantor of peace agreements. He was committed during his whole life to the building of a strong Israeli military machine. The hallmark of his success was preparing the Israeli army for the June 1967 war. In the post-1973 period, Rabin and his government led the largest military expansion in IDF history. After leaving the defense establishment for seven years, Rabin became defense minister in 1984. One of his first steps was to initiate a $650 million cut in the defense budget. Only Rabin had the necessary authority to reduce so drastically the defense budget, which obviously led to an unprecedented contraction of the IDF. Yet as economic conditions improved, he persisted in building a modern and offense-capable army, considerably extending its strategic reach.

Rabin's record is marred by the IDF's lack of preparation for Intifada-type operations. Instead, he prepared the IDF for a large-scale war, which was more threatening to Israel's existence than the Palestinian uprising. The next chapter shows that despite the strategic surprise, Rabin managed to develop in a short time a coherent strategy to combat the Intifada. The IDF was also inadequately equipped to deal with the missile attacks in the winter of 1991. But in the 1980s Rabin had correctly assessed that Israel's rear was vulnerable to such attacks and had supported the Arrow ATBM program, which was primarily funded by the United States. Israel was the first country in the world to take steps for meeting the missile challenge. Moreover, as was the case with the Intifada, missiles with conventional warheads in 1991 did not pose an existential threat to Israel.[165] Generally, Rabin's conservative inclination precluded drastic changes in the doctrine and structure of the IDF.

In his procurement policies, Rabin preferred weapon systems purchased off American shelves. He was extremely cautious in his dealings with the Israeli defense industries. Typical of Rabin's lifelong preoccupation with strengthening the IDF, his last decision as defense minister, before his assassination in November 1995, was to approve the purchase of four additional F-15Is.[166]

CHAPTER FOUR

THE USE OF MILITARY FORCE

The building and use of military power has preoccupied the Israeli political leadership since the pre-state period. Since its establishment in 1948, Israel has fought six wars: the 1948 War of Independence, the 1956 Sinai Campaign, the 1967 Six-Day War, the 1969–70 War of Attrition, the 1973 Yom Kippur War, and the 1982 Lebanon War. On numerous occasions, Israel has used limited force against neighboring Arab states and also in the West Bank and the Gaza Strip. Indeed, military activities consume a considerable part of Israel's resources and energies, a reality of which the political elite is very much aware. In fact, retired professional soldiers are an important component of this elite. Yitzhak Rabin was already commanding a brigade in 1948, was a major general and commander of the Northern Command in 1956, and of course, was one of those responsible for developing the Israel Defense Force (IDF) into the mighty military machine that achieved the great victory of June 1967, when he was chief of staff. In most of Israel's other wars, he participated in decision-making as a civilian.

This chapter reviews Rabin's attitudes toward the use of force in the Arab-Israeli conflict and the formulation of national strategy. It analyzes Rabin's modus operandi in several areas where force was used or considered by Israel.

THE POLITICAL DIMENSIONS OF
ISRAELI MILITARY FORCE

Rabin deeply appreciated the intricate links between politics and the use of military force. He became sensitized to this linkage early on, when he was senior officer in the War of Independence, and immediately afterward, when he participated in the Israeli delegation to the armistice talks with Egypt in 1949 in Rhodes. Rabin, like David Ben-Gurion and other Israeli leaders, believed that Israeli military strength was a necessary precondition for surviving in the protracted Arab-Israeli conflict. Taking into consideration the Arab aim at politicide, Israel could not afford to lose a war. According to Rabin, even if peace treaties were to be signed with all of Israel's neighbors, they would have to be backed up by Israeli military power. Military might was the most important component in the strategic equation.[1]

Rabin viewed the construction of a military machine not only as a prerequisite for victory on the battlefield, vital for survival, but also as a requirement for negotiations with the Arab neighbors. Israel could reach a negotiated settlement with its neighbors only from a position of strength, he believed.[2] Israeli military superiority was seen as a tool for moderating Arab political expectations in the conflict. Military force was the means for a "diplomacy of violence."[3]

His approach to the use of force was totally instrumental. He never indulged in an expressive use of force, and in contrast to other Israeli leaders, he never mentioned revenge or national honor as a reason for using military force.[4] Despite his temper and his lack of qualms about using force, what counted for Rabin was political results. In 1966, he wrote of the 1956 Sinai Campaign: "Each battle, each campaign and each war is measured primarily by its results. It is not important whether the results were achieved by following the proper rules of conducting war, whether the politico-military circumstances were constant or changing. War is a cruel struggle whose paramount test is success, while all the rest is secondary."[5] He rejected the view of war as a stylized duel writ large. Years later, in 1981, before students at the National Security College, Rabin reiterated this view quite bluntly: "The use of military force is intended to achieve a political goal and it is not a competition in operating airplanes or tanks."[6] His approach was fundamentally that of the Prussian general Karl von Clausewitz, a theorist whom he occasionally praised in military forums as one of the most profound thinkers on war and politics.[7]

Yet he did not believe that the Arab-Israeli conflict could be solved by military means alone. He criticized the tendency, prevalent among some right-wing leaders, to rely only on the use of force to determine the outcome of the Arab-Israeli conflict. In Rabin's view, Israel would never be able to muster enough military power to impose a peace treaty on its neighbors.[8] Even if Israel could devote a few years to building a force able to win a war convincingly against all of its neighbors and to conquer the Arab capitals, the imposition of the Israeli will would still be unlikely. Rabin claimed that international circumstances would not allow Israel to apply military force according to classical Clausewitzian methods: forcing the enemy to comply with the political dictates of the victor. He emphasized that what the United States did at the end of World War II—dictating the terms of the peace to Germany and Japan and even reengineering their societies to fit the democratic model—was simply beyond Israel's means. The circumstances of the Arab-Israeli conflict and the superpowers' involvement in the region precluded this possibility.[9] Moreover, what the great powers had been able to achieve through use of force was no longer possible. In 1988, when the Soviet Union was mired down in Afghanistan, Rabin's assessment was that even such a superpower, a totalitarian country with no organized opposition to its military adventure, was looking for ways to extricate itself, having realized the limits of its use of military force.[10]

Rabin also claimed that Israel could not attain absolute national security. He made the point, in 1985, that as defense minister, he could not promise that no Katyusha rockets would fall on the northern town of Kiryat Shmona or that the IDF could prevent all terrorist attacks.[11] Such declarations stood in contrast to the rhetoric often heard from Likud Party leaders, who had promised "40 years of peace" when justifying the 1982 invasion of Lebanon. Rabin was honest and refused to make promises that he could not keep. He advocated realistic expectations as to what could be achieved through military superiority.

In 1983, in the midst of the Lebanon War, Rabin praised Ben-Gurion for his quick reading of the political reality in the aftermath of the October 1956 Sinai victory. Ben-Gurion had switched, in the space of a few days, from a euphoric declaration about the expansion of Israel's borders to a decision to withdraw from the conquered Sinai Peninsula in light of international pressures.[12] For Rabin, this was a wise move resulting from a sober appraisal of what was attainable under the particular international circumstances of that time. After all, the French and the British had failed to depose the regime of Gamal Abdel Nasser and impose their will. This, Rabin pointed out, demonstrated the limits of the use of force.

Israel has been, since its establishment, a status quo power and has been reluctant to initiate large-scale military operations. Its predilection for pre-emptive and preventive strikes in the 1950s and 1960s was part of a defensive strategy. Rabin's cautious approach to the utility of waging war was in line with the mainstream thinking in Israeli politics, and he became the authoritative spokesman for this school of thought.[13] We can see over time, however, a greater awareness of the limits of the use of force. For example, in 1959, during a General Staff discussion, Major General Rabin reflected the contemporary thinking by including in the objectives of a future war not only destroying the enemy regime but also frustrating its goals and decimating its military.[14] A few years later, in May 1967, as chief of staff, he threatened to overthrow the Syrian regime (so did Prime Minister Levi Eshkol and several members of the cabinet) when Israel was attempting to deter Syria from lending further support to the sabotage raids waged by the Palestine Liberation Organization (PLO) against Israel.[15] Such statements were part of the usual pattern of Israeli warnings that, if unheeded, would have been followed by reprisal actions.

But after 1973, Rabin appeared to be increasingly doubtful about the utility of initiating a large-scale war against the Arabs, because neither territory nor the destruction of the enemy forces warranted the price that would have to be paid in such a war by Israel. He did not see any political goal worth the cost of initiating another war.[16] He also observed that each successive war had precipitated an increase in the military power of the Arab armies beyond Israel's borders.[17] The better use of weapons on the Arab side and the general increase in the lethality of sophisticated weapons of the modern battlefield had made war much more costly in losses and in economic terms. Rabin emphasized that easy victories with few casualties and little damage to the rear in Israel, as achieved in the Israeli-initiated wars of 1956 and 1967, were unlikely to occur in the near future.[18]

Moreover, the military history he knew taught him that 70–80 percent of the wars in the past one hundred years had ended with the failure of the party that had initiated them. The examples he gave were the two world wars and the Iran-Iraq War.[19] This remark was an oblique response to former prime minister Menachem Begin who, having ordered the invasion of Lebanon in 1982, claimed that preemptive and/or preventive initiatives confer great advantages.[20] When forced to reduce drastically the defense budget in 1985, which led to smaller Israeli forces, Rabin rejected the argument that a smaller IDF would have to rely more on preemptive or preventive strikes than on a defensive posture.[21]

During the public debate over the legitimacy of the Lebanon War, Rabin, like many other Israeli politicians, clarified his position on the subject of the use of force. He wrote several pieces in the Israeli press.[22] One of the more lucid Israeli leaders on the subject of war, Rabin distinguished between two types of goals in war: those that relate to the security of Israel's citizens and borders; and those that, though desirable, do not have a *direct* influence on the security of the state.[23] An example of the second type of goals was the establishment of a friendly regime in Lebanon or the imposition of a peace treaty. In contrast with some of his colleagues in the Labor Party, Rabin refused to deny the legitimacy of the second group of war objectives, but he expressed reservations about the effectiveness of the use of force in order to attain them.

In Rabin's opinion, the issue had never been whether Israel's wars were just; of course they were, so long as the Arab countries refused to sign peace treaties. Rather, the cardinal question concerning these wars was whether they were "worthwhile, necessary or desirable."[24] His criticism was never couched in normative language. In contrast to some of his dovish colleagues in the Labor Party, he never labeled the invasion of Lebanon as a "war of choice," which implied that the war had been unjust. He refused to join the growing ranks of those who opposed the war, who denied that Israel had "no choice" but to go to war—a charged term in Israel's political culture.[25] Actually, Rabin explicitly admitted his dislike of the normative term "war of no choice."[26] Moreover, though he was aware of the need to have broad national support when a military campaign was initiated, Rabin maintained that lack of consensus would have little effect on the normative character of the war. It would, however, diminish the stamina required to endure the difficulties involved. The feeling of "no choice" was, therefore, an important asset in waging war but not a normative precondition.[27]

The war in Lebanon was unquestionably legitimate in Rabin's judgment; what he was skeptical about was its necessity and wisdom. He preferred, in other words, a calculus of utility rather than normative deliberations. Although he was not oblivious to the importance of moral factors in waging war, what counted for him was the assessment of what was feasible. This was the typically pragmatic Rabin.

ISRAEL'S NATIONAL STRATEGY

After 1967, Israel's borders were farther from its population centers than ever before. Enjoying strategic depth, Israel could deemphasize the need for preemptive and/or preventive strikes. It could opt for absorbing an Arab strike before going on attack and transferring the war into the enemy's territory.[28] As discussed below, Rabin continued to adhere to this defensive posture even after the October 1973 war.[29] Since Rabin hardly perceived any benefits in initiating large-scale conventional war, he advocated a defensive strategy built primarily around the notion of deterrence. Deterrence had always been one of the main pillars of Israeli strategic thinking, and Rabin was one of the main spokesmen in propagating its importance within the IDF and the public at large.[30] After 1973, Israeli society was more open in discussing security matters, and Rabin, with his military record and reputation, became a sought-after speaker on national security issues.

The deterrent posture was designed to prevent aggression or actions against Israel's cardinal interests. In 1983, Rabin concluded that a retrospective view of the Arab-Israeli conflict revealed that as the Arabs accumulated experience, the Arab political elites, led by Egypt in particular, began to see wars against Israel as very costly. Rabin made a theoretical distinction between general and specific deterrence. In his opinion, Israel was generally successful in persuading the Arabs not to initiate war against Israel, though specific deterrence was not always achieved.[31] Rabin, like other makers of Israeli strategy, spoke about cumulative deterrence as being a function of success in delaying wars and in winning decisively those forced upon Israel.[32]

The skeptical Rabin realized, of course, that deterrence could not be foolproof. As chief of staff in the 1960s, he said: "The IDF's job is to deter the enemy; if that fails it is to achieve its total defeat."[33] Even after the great 1967 victory, Rabin observed: "Our deterrent power was not sufficient to prevent war."[34] The 1973 war further sensitized Rabin and the Israeli defense establishment to the notion that the IDF could not deter an Arab-initiated war under all circumstances. Rabin also understood that Arab rivals might resort to violence even if the chances of invading Israel were low, because achievements in the diplomatic sphere do not always correspond to results on the battlefield. The Arabs recognized that losing a war did not necessarily signify a political disaster.[35]

The Israeli reluctance to go to war and its deterrence requirements led in the post-1973 period to efforts to improve the defensive capabilities of the

IDF—deterrence by denial. A good defense could deny the Arabs an achievement of their military and political goals. The IDF expansion in the mid-1970s, reviewed in the previous chapter, was accompanied by an unprecedented effort to augment the military's capabilities to withstand a defensive battle in case of an Arab invasion and to exact a high price from the aggressor when on defense. Even offense-minded generals did not see a defensive battle as a terrible constraint. Actually, the lessons of the battles with the Syrians in 1973, when a considerable part of the Syrian armor was decimated by the IDF in a defensive deployment, led to the conclusion that it is much easier to annihilate the enemy when an army, well prepared and ready for the coming attack, is on the defensive.[36] This reasoning was also grounded in the theory of the "superiority of the defense"—the idea that the defender enjoys an advantage because the attacker has to expose himself and, ceteris paribus, requires several times as many men and resources.[37]

Indeed, an intensive fortification effort designed to improve the Israeli capability of absorbing an Arab attack was implemented after 1973. The failure of the Bar-Lev Line to prevent the initial Egyptian successes in 1973 was attributed to the deficiencies in manning the strongholds, to faulty deployment of the armored forces in the rear, and to poor defensive tactics.[38] Fortifications were still seen as a good option to raise the cost of an attack, though they had to be integrated into a comprehensive framework of defensive strategy.[39] Wherever possible, the fortifications in the post-1973 period were incorporated into the territorial defense infrastructure, which regained prominence after the neglect of the 1967–73 period.[40] The emergence of efficient Precise Guided Munitions (PGM), used extensively for the first time in the October 1973 war, also seemed to enhance defensive capabilities, although Israeli military planners and Rabin himself doubted whether the PGM, or any single type of weapon, could be a panacea for halting a well-planned and executed offensive and for winning a war.[41] Finally, Rabin and others preferred a defensive posture because of growing concerns about the increasing costs, in casualties and in matériel, of an offensive against a well-fortified and defended line.[42]

Yet defensive capabilities, according to Rabin, were "categorically" not enough to ensure deterrence.[43] As early as September 1974, Rabin had concluded that Israeli conventional deterrence had become problematic and had to be enhanced by a capacity for subduing the enemy in a decisive way.[44] Rabin advocated a strong deterrent that could also achieve a decisive victory if war broke out: "I considered the prevention of war as the test of our security policy, in addition to being able to rapidly and forcefully end any war forced upon us."[45] Only an army capable of inflicting an un-equivocal defeat could have a deterrent value. Moreover, such an army was also needed to achieve a swift decisive victory in case of deterrence failure. Such offensive and threatening capabilities were necessary to enhance deterrence and to exact a high price from an enemy who initiated war against Israel. A strong air force was crucial for such missions. In 1986, Rabin was still arguing that a good defense, which could decimate the invading forces, and the achievement of air supremacy were preconditions for administering a decisive blow to the enemy in a devastating counterattack.[46] Yet he rejected suggestions that IDF military doctrine be revised to rely mainly on defensive capabilities.[47]

At the same time, Rabin did not share the evaluation that the 1991 Gulf War—in which a Western army, well equipped with highly sophisticated weapons, easily vanquished an Arab force—was an entirely valid model for technologically advanced Israel. Rabin claimed that Israel did not have the logistical and the political leeway that the United States had possessed in that war.[48] Rabin represented the typically cautious Israeli attitude toward the so-called Revolution in Military Affairs (RMA).[49]

Rabin also represented the school of thought that believed that after the 1973 war, Israel could still repel Arab aggression by conventional means and win a conventional war if deterrence should fail.[50] In his first government (1974–77), influential figures who shared such views were Foreign Minister Yigal Allon and Minister without Portfolio Israel Galili. The chief of staff at that time, Lt. Gen. Mordechai Gur (1974–78), also supported the conventional perspective. The subsequent chiefs of staff—Rafael Eitan (1978–83), Moshe Levy (1983–87), Dan Shomron (1987–91), and Ehud Barak (1992–1995)—shared the same view. In accordance with this school of thought, Rabin advocated building a force that could achieve a decisive victory within a minimum of time and with as few casualties as possible if a war was forced on Israel.[51] For him, victory meant making the opponent ask as quickly as possible for a cease-fire, after a major part of the enemy's fighting force had been destroyed or the enemy's country badly damaged. The war was to end with some territorial gains, but the rival's capital was not to be conquered.[52] Taking an Arab capital was seen as an unnecessary escalation. It required the IDF to fight in an urban setting, which was costly in casualties. In addition, humiliating the enemy by occupying his capital was politically unwise. The time factor was a lesson learned in the War of Independence, when foreign political intervention to end hostilities had interfered with military operations. Then the operational timetable in the field had not always been synchronized with the moves in the political arena, leading to failures in achieving military objectives of political value. Since the War of Independence, the IDF contingency planning had, according to Rabin, been more sensitive to the need to preempt political moves, even at the expense of the principle of conservation of forces.[53]

Preemption had always been a central tenet of Israeli military doctrine. In the waiting period before the 1967 war, Rabin advocated preemption. Yet in the immediate post-1973 period, Rabin downplayed the importance of preemptive strikes as long as the IDF was deployed along the defensible post-1967 borders and as long as it was well equipped.[54] Rabin's government was not interested in fostering the image of an "aggressive" Israel. His intention of lowering the offensive profile of the IDF corresponded with the perceived growing isolation of Israel in the 1970s and the foreseeable diplomatic repercussions that Israeli-initiated attacks could induce. U.S. Secretary of State Henry Kissinger's opposition to preemptive strikes was of particular importance to Rabin. Therefore, Rabin expressed his displeasure with Chief of Staff Gur's June 1974 statement in favor of preemptive strikes.[55] One additional reason for his reluctance to rely on preemptive strikes was Rabin's skepticism about the ability of Israeli intelligence to provide an adequate warning of the enemy's aggressive plans and intentions. Rabin, a pessimist by nature, had a very low opinion of the quality of the estimates that the Israeli intelligence community had supplied to policy-makers.[56] Thus he refused to base Israel's national strategy on preemptive strikes, and this remained his position to the end of his life.[57]

Preemption was, to be sure, still on the menu of choices, though its profile was lowered. In 1983, Rabin still favored preemption only in those cases in which Israel faced going to war.[58] In 1988, he did not preclude a preemptive strike against Arab armies if a war was "imminent."[59] Yet even then, this was not an automatic response. When the threat of surface-to-surface missiles started looming in the 1980s (see the discussion in the next chapter), Rabin considered the mobilization of the IDF without interference from such missiles, which could be fired as a result of Israeli preemption, to be more important than obstructing the imminent attack of the opponent through a preemptive strike.[60] Such a mobilization could also serve as a last-minute enhancement of Israeli deterrence, which was preferable to preemption.[61]

Rabin the pragmatist did not like the concept of casus belli, or "red lines," that had developed in Israel's strategic parlance. These committed Israel to use force in situations it defined in advance as unbearable.[62] In

1967 he supported a military riposte to Egyptian provocations because they created an unbearable political-military equation. He played down the alleged casus belli of the 1967 war, the Egyptian blocking of the Tiran Straits at Sharm al-Sheikh, which was in his opinion more of a symbol than the real cause of the war. Similarly, in 1976, when Chief of Staff Gur asked Prime Minister Rabin what the casus belli would be, Rabin refused to enumerate any. His response was that the IDF must plan and be ready for all contingencies and that the political leadership would decide when and how to use the IDF.[63] Rabin pointed out that there are limitations to the ability to forecast contingencies and that the political leadership must retain its freedom of action. Automatic responses were not always wise, he counseled, and he refused to term a serious Egyptian violation of the demilitarization agreement in Sinai as a casus belli. For Rabin, only a massive attack on Israel constituted a clear casus belli, requiring a parallel Israeli military reaction.[64] In 1986, he refused to consider what had been a casus belli in the past—an Arab concentration of forces along Israel's borders—as warranting immediate Israeli action, because of the costly nature of the modern battlefield.[65] It is not clear whether Rabin was aware of the possible contribution of a set of enunciated casus belli to the enhancement of deterrence, which he emphasized so much.

Rabin was willing, however, to sanction the use of force to attain limited goals. Moreover, the occasional use of force was seen by Rabin as useful in signaling determination and in restoring and/or enhancing Israeli deterrence, though it was never clear for how long the effect would last. Rabin learned this lesson from the 7 April 1967 air duel, which ended with six Syrian MiGs being shot down. He had believed that this demonstration of superiority by the Israel Air Force (IAF) would provide a long respite, but only a month later war broke out. Taking into consideration the hectic conditions of the Middle East, the always cautious Rabin expected war at any moment.[66]

THE MODUS OPERANDI OF THE USE OF FORCE

Rabin's IDF military experience is of great interest partly because of the disparate nature of the military contingencies involved. In general, Rabin preferred a measured use of force and was always cognizant of the political ramifications of military action. A review of Rabin's experience conducting large-scale operations and of his reactions to the Syrian attempts to divert the

Jordan waters in the 1964–66 period, to Palestinian terrorism, to the Intifada (1987–90), and to the situation in Lebanon (1975–77, 1984–90, 1992–95) shows that although he supported relatively limited applications of military force, he always subordinated military policy to political considerations.

Large-Scale Operations

As Allon's deputy and in other positions, Rabin planned military operations during the War of Independence. He understood that Arab advantages in numbers and firepower made frontal assaults inadvisable. Like Chief of Staff Yigael Yadin (1949–52), Rabin pointed out the similarity between Israeli military practice and the theory of the "indirect approach" evolved by the British military thinker Sir Basil Liddell-Hart.[67] Generally, this approach advocated avoiding frontal attacks on the enemy's forces and instead aimed at disrupting the enemy's defenses by attacking the "line of least expectation." As noted in the previous chapter, the planning of military operations in the IDF at an early stage, when Rabin was in charge of the Operations Division in the General Staff, closely followed this indirect approach, which was practiced by Rabin (and others) intuitively during the War of Independence. Rabin suggested that Operations Danny and Yoav of that war become models for IDF operational planning.[68]

In June 1967, Rabin was once again responsible for directing the large-scale use of force, though he could never be described as trigger-happy. During the first days of this crisis, in mid-May, he advocated using diplomatic means to defuse it, since he and others saw in it a version of the 1960 Rotem scenario. However, against the advice of his intelligence officers, the cautious Rabin decided to move forces to the south and to make preparations for calling up two reserve brigades.[69] When, on 22 May, Egypt closed the Tiran Straits, Rabin realized that this act had greater significance than just cutting off shipping to Israel's southern port of Eilat. It was a challenge to Israel's deterrence and survival and required a military response. Furthermore, he shared the views of all his generals that a delay in attacking the Egyptian forces in the Sinai would only improve Egyptian defensive capabilities and thus exact higher casualties from the IDF.[70] Rabin sided, however, with the more moderate group in the General Staff and did not demand immediate action. One cabinet minister reported: "The chief of staff never called expressly for war. He pointed out all the possibilities to us, the comparative strength of forces, and he did say we could win—but he never put pressure on us to open hostilities."[71] This was also because of Rabin's cautiousness and skepticism. Even though he knew that the IDF was well prepared, he was not sure and he could definitely envision pessimistic scenarios. His physical collapse a few days before the war reflected the weight of the responsibility he felt as the authority of Premier and Defense Minister Eshkol eroded, as well as his eternal skepticism and pessimism.[72]

On 4 June 1967, the Israeli government decided to go to war. Under Rabin's command, the IDF functioned in accordance with the basic strategic thinking that had "always guided the IDF's organization and operation."[73] Facing an Egyptian-Jordanian-Syrian military coalition, Israel gave first priority in the allocation of forces to smashing Egypt's military might, while on the other fronts the IDF was deployed primarily in a defensive mode (with attack options). Only Egypt was strong enough to stand up alone against the IDF, and according to the prevalent thinking, the main body of the enemy force had to be dealt a crushing blow first. This was achieved, first through a daring preemptive air strike against the Arab air forces in order to gain air supremacy and second through a lightning-fast use of armored forces to decimate the Egyptian forces in the Sinai Peninsula. Speed was important in order to shatter the enemy's fighting spirit and to account for uncertainty regarding the amount of time available for military operations.[74] Because of Jordan's control of the West Bank, which lay perilously close to Israel's population centers and airbases, Jordan was given priority over Syria, which was dealt with last.

The transfer of the war to enemy territory was also in accordance with Israeli military doctrine. In the conduct of the war in the south, the main political decisions—such as whether to reach the Suez Canal—were made by Rabin. On the other fronts, the important decisions—such as whether to conquer Jerusalem and when and where to stop fighting on the Golan Heights—were made by the recently appointed minister of defense, Moshe Dayan.[75] This appointment reduced Rabin's influence on strategic matters during the war and immediately afterward.

The Battle over the Jordan Waters

Toward the end of 1964, Syria began implementing the Arab summit decision of January 1964 to divert the waters of the tributaries of the Jordan to thwart the construction of the Israeli National Water Carrier. The Israeli government regarded the diversion plan as a casus belli. Some within the Israeli political elite (MK Dayan in particular) advocated a military campaign to capture the Syrian territory where diversion was under way.[76]

Rabin, then IDF chief of staff, opposed the idea because of its potential to lead to full-scale war with Syria. If the diversion could not be stopped by diplomatic pressure, he insisted on a limited use of force and explained that not every military action necessarily leads to all-out war.[77] Rabin suggested that Israel hit the Syrian engineering equipment by tank and/or artillery fire without crossing the border and that it make sure that the IDF could perform this task successfully.[78] Premier and Defense Minister Eshkol accepted the cautious approach of his trusted chief of staff.

Rabin also preferred to obstruct the diversion efforts by capitalizing on "incidents" at the Syrian border. He took advantage of Syrian-Israeli artillery duels, begun by the Syrian army, to respond in the area where the diversion efforts were taking place rather than initiating an exchange with the diversion equipment as the main target. Long-range fire and several commando operations in Syria and Lebanon, considered "low-profile" military measures, ended the Arab water-diversion plan.

Yet in response to Syrian heavy shelling of Israeli civilian targets, Rabin also sanctioned the use of airpower to overcome the Syrian topographic advantage. At that time, this was viewed by the parties to the conflict as an escalatory step. Rabin secured in November 1964 the approval of Prime Minister Eshkol to use the IAF to suppress Syrian artillery fire coming from the Golan Heights and directed against Israeli kibbutzim. The Israeli-Syrian air duels that followed were the precursor to the 1967 Six-Day War, as they climbed to a higher rung in the ladder of violence between the protagonists.[79]

It is noteworthy that before Israel decided to use limited strikes against the Syrian engineering equipment, Rabin cautiously tested the proposition by explaining the situation to two high-level American officials—Averell Harriman (a roving ambassador) and Robert Komer (of the National Security Council). Visiting in early 1965, the two men were taken by Rabin on a tour of the northern border. They did not respond negatively to Rabin's exposition of Israeli military options, and Rabin and Eshkol took this to indicate tacit American approval.[80] The need to secure this approval of Israeli military action formed a constant feature of Rabin's policies.

Palestinian Terrorism

According to Rabin, "Terrorism has attended the Jewish settlement in the Land of Israel for the past 100 years."[81] He understood that whereas the intimidation of Israelis was a goal in and of itself for the terrorists, they also intended to interfere with the economic development of the Jewish state by creating an atmosphere of fear and uncertainty. Another terrorist aim was to discourage immigration, since immigration was an important Zionist goal. Furthermore, Rabin realized that terrorist organizations calculated that their acts and the expected Israeli countermeasures could bring about an escalation in Arab-Israeli relations and even a large-scale military confrontation with an Arab state.[82]

Nevertheless, Rabin classified terrorism as a "current security" issue— that is, it disrupted routine and affected the quality of life, but it was not going to defeat Israel: "It hurts, it annoys, it disrupts, but it does not constitute an existential threat to the state."[83] He minimized the importance of the cumulative impact of terrorist activities. The increasing size and sophistication of the Arab armies was always, for him, the gravest threat to Israel.[84] In strategic terms, terrorism was merely a nuisance. Budgetarily, it also demanded only limited resources in comparison with the building of a modern air force or armored divisions. Speaking at the IDF National Security College in 1985, Rabin explicitly excluded terrorism from his discussion of national security challenges on the grounds that it was "a secondary problem."[85] In 1988, he pointed out that the annual number of casualties (seven to nine Israelis) from terrorism in the previous five years was equal to the number of Israelis killed in road accidents in a single week.[86] Rabin's approach to terrorism was in line with mainstream Israeli thinking, which he himself shaped. It deviated, however, from the approach of the Israeli right wing, which attributed great strategic significance to the cumulative impact of terrorism and consequently to counterterrorist activities.[87]

Rabin had no illusions about Israel's ability to eradicate terrorism completely. His 1988 statement was typical of his long-held realistic attitude: "We cannot uproot terrorism once and for all by military means alone. As long as Arab countries support Palestinian terror groups and Islamic countries support Shiite terror groups, it will be impossible to end terrorism militarily."[88] The battle against terrorism was additionally complicated by the financial, territorial, and diplomatic support provided by sovereign states. Rabin was careful in confronting these states: "I propose that we use the utmost caution before considering a large-scale operation against an Arab state which helps terrorists or is involved indirectly in acts of terrorism against Israel."[89] He suggested that ways be found to deal with terrorism in order to achieve two goals: "to minimize the damage inflicted on Israel, while maximizing the damage we inflict on them [the terrorists]."[90]

That Rabin assigned lesser significance to terrorism in his national security priorities did not mean he was fatalist or passive. Rabin advocated an
unceasing campaign against terrorism, a policy conducted even before he
assumed a decision-making post within the Israeli defense establishment.
He adhered to the determined Israeli strategy of continuously searching
for the perpetrators of terrorist acts and punishing them, no matter how
distant the targets. According to his wife, Leah: "Yitzhak had little hesitation about reprisals when Jewish lives had been taken."[91]

In the 1950s and 1960s, the Israeli policy of retaliation was a strategy of
deterrence by punishment.[92] Rabin realized, however, that deterrence is
problematic when it comes to terrorism.[93] Therefore, the offensive policy
also occasionally served a preventive function by obstructing preparations
for attacks on Israel. It was also attritional, forcing the PLO to devote resources to defense and lowering PLO morale. The timing and the character of the counterterrorist operations were often linked to larger political
goals. Yet Rabin also advocated defensive efforts to prevent terrorists from
entering Israel. He often praised the Israeli navy's successes, in the late
1970s and the 1980s, in intercepting, through active and passive defense,
all attempts to attack Israeli targets from the sea.

Rabin saw the Israeli struggle against terrorism as reflecting its national
security predicament: "Our ability to prevent terrorism on our northern
border and inside Israel depends on Israel alone. We cannot count on outside assistance."[94] Despite the fact that many countries in the world suffered from terrorism, Rabin concluded in 1986 that "very little" had been
achieved "in terms of willingness on the part of the international community to join hands politically, economically and militarily against terrorists
and countries supporting them."[95]

After 1965, Israel was subjected to waves of terrorist attacks from
Palestinian armed groups, usually affiliated with the PLO (established in
1964). Similar acts in the 1950s had elicited many retaliatory raids.[96] Rabin
disclosed, however, that he was never enthusiastic about the Israeli policy
of retaliation as practiced in the 1950s. He questioned the efficacy of retaliation raids and their price in casualties. He doubted whether they
achieved their political goal of pressuring the neighboring governments
(particularly the Jordanians) into making greater efforts to stop infiltration
into Israel.[97]

Rabin suggested that the counterterrorist policy should differentiate between available options in the various theaters of operation. Since the terrorism originating from Syria was fully controlled and directed by the

Damascus government, it made strategic sense to attack governmental targets, such as military or police installations.[98] In contrast, the Jordanian and Lebanese arenas were suitable for a new type of coercive diplomacy in terms of targets and operational style. Rabin preferred raids against the actual perpetrators of terrorist attacks, or against the civilians who lent support to them, rather than against governmental targets. Furthermore, he advocated military operations during daylight, using relatively large, well-armed forces, often including armored formations, to keep casualties to a minimum. The attack against the Jordanian village of Samoa on 13 November 1966 was an example of this type of operation.[99] While ambassador in Washington, Rabin also supported the March 1968 large-scale raid on the village of Karameh, which served as the headquarters for much of the PLO command structure. This attack was fought along the same lines as the Samoa raid, though Rabin realized that the Karameh foray had negative consequences, since it promoted the public relations campaign of the PLO. But he believed that the politico-military advantages of weakening the military arm of the PLO outweighed the political costs.[100] Rabin seemed to have regarded the political repercussions involved in large-scale operations as temporary and of lesser consequence than continuing to administer strong military blows on the opponent.

In the mid-1970s, Lebanon continued to serve as a base for frequent terrorist attacks in which Israeli civilians were brutally murdered. The PLO gradually gained greater and greater freedom of action in Lebanon, which had a weak central government that collapsed completely as a result of the civil war that began in 1975. Maj. Gen. (Res.) Rehavam Zeevi, who served as the prime minister's adviser on counterterrorism during Rabin's first term, and Maj. Gen. Yitzhak Hofi, the head of the Mossad at that time, have pointed out that Rabin approved, almost without exception, all operations suggested to him by the various security agencies. This was definitely not a green light to do whatever they wanted, because Rabin used to review pedantically every detail of the operations; knowing this, the planners in advance took into consideration Rabin's great cautiousness, sensitivity to political factors, and fear of casualties.[101]

Rabin took a number of concrete steps to fight terrorism. The IDF sealed the northern border almost hermetically, forcing the Palestinian terrorist organizations to use the sea to penetrate Israel. He also established a Civil Guard, which used volunteers to patrol Jewish neighborhoods. Furthermore, Rabin assigned his adviser for counterterrorism to devise a better division of labor between the police and the IDF.[102]

In Lebanon, the IDF continued its regular counterterrorist activities, which included commando raids and the use of its superior firepower (artillery, naval, and air). Because of the risk of high casualties in ground operations, the battle against terrorism in the 1970s relied more on airpower. However, in the absence of a suitable doctrine for deploying warplanes in low-intensity conflict, the IAF sorties into Lebanon were a rather ineffective use of force. On several occasions they inflicted a large number of civilian casualties (as a result of the PLO's practice of locating its bases with refugee camps) and caused bad press for Israel. For example, the *New York Times* quoted an estimate of the civilian casualties of the 2 December 1975 air raids at 75 killed and 120 wounded.[103] These specific air raids had a clear political message. The IDF spokesman stated: "Israeli planes bombed suspected terrorist bases in Lebanon as a warning to the Palestinians not to be encouraged by UN developments into staging further attacks on Israel."[104] The strike was made days after the United Nations (UN) resolution equating Zionism with racism, and it stood as a defiant demonstration of national will in light of the hostile international environment. Indeed, the Rabin government continued these air raids against Palestinian targets despite increasing criticism at home.

In several incidents, the Palestinian terrorists succeeded in taking hostages, but Rabin usually favored attacking the terrorists rather than giving in to their demands. Despite the casualties resulting from military action, he adhered to the slogan: "No surrender to terrorism."[105] Rabin was, however, not dogmatic about refusing to negotiate with terrorists. Israel's policy had always been flexible, he claimed; in fact, the precedent of negotiating with terrorists was set in 1968 when, in exchange for releasing a hijacked El Al airplane and its Israeli passengers, Israel freed several terrorists.[106] Indeed, Rabin voted with the majority of the ministers in the Israeli cabinet to negotiate with Palestinian terrorists who, in May 1974, took nearly one hundred high-school teenagers as hostages in the town of Maalot, near the Lebanese border. He did not want to risk the lives of a large number of students.[107] In March 1975, however, a similar situation that involved a limited number of hostages triggered a military response. The timing of the terrorist attack, just before Kissinger landed in Israel for a round of difficult negotiations, required, Rabin believed, a strong riposte signaling toughness and resolution.[108]

This was the preferred policy if the terrorists were in Israel or could be reached by IDF units. The outstanding example came in June 1976, when an Air France passenger jet was hijacked to Entebbe in Uganda by a Palestinian terrorist organization (a splinter group of the PLO). In the absence of a ready military action plan, Rabin decided to deviate from his non-negotiation policy, and he sent his adviser Zeevi to Paris to hold indirect talks with the kidnappers. Yet as soon as a rescue plan was presented to Rabin and he became convinced of its feasibility, the IDF was sent to release the hostages in a much-admired airborne operation.[109] In May 1985, Rabin again made a deal with a terrorist organization (Ahmad Jibril's PFLP-General Command) when he released 1,150 jailed terrorists in exchange for only three IDF soldiers, who had been held as prisoners since 1982. The price was extremely high; about six hundred of the detainees were allowed to stay in the territories, and most later became activists in the Intifada.[110]

After the 1982 Israeli invasion of Lebanon, the PLO was weak. It was only during 1984 that it increased its level of activities against Israelis within Israel and abroad, eliciting a military response primarily against Palestinian targets in Lebanon. A daring and impressive air raid took place in October 1985 against the PLO headquarters in Tunis, 2,000 kilometers from Israel. Rabin, then defense minister, claimed that there had been a dramatic increase in PLO terrorism and asserted: "We decided the time was right to deliver a blow to the headquarters of those who make the decisions, [those who] plan and carry out terrorist activities."[111] The raid was a direct response to the killing of three Israelis on a yacht in Cyprus on 25 September. Rabin opted for hitting a high-value target for maximum retaliation effect. The method of response—an air strike—was chosen because it could be implemented shortly after the provocation and put at risk only a few Israelis.

Yet the long-range air raid was a military measure with clear escalatory potential. Tunisia was one of the more moderate Arab countries; it had agreed to host the PLO headquarters following the forced PLO evacuation from Beirut in 1982 only under heavy pressure from other Arab states and the United States. At the time of the raid, Israel was engaged in delicate negotiations with Egypt over the destiny of the small Taba area near Eilat, and contacts with Jordan seemed to be yielding some progress. These negotiations did not restrain Rabin. He believed that these two countries had little sympathy for the PLO and that their current policies toward Israel accorded with their national interests, which would be affected only marginally by Israel's military actions against the Palestinians. On the Israeli political map, such an outlook was considered hawkish, since it minimized the importance of the Palestinian issue in the Arab-Israeli conflict. In fact, the raid was also meant to be a warning to King Hussein not to allow a free hand to the PLO military presence on his territory, a presence that had been reestablished as a result of the February 1985 Jordan-PLO agreement.[112] Furthermore, Rabin capitalized on the spectacular long-range air strike against Tunis to issue warnings to Syria (the evening after the raid) not to engage in any military adventure against Israel. While the right and center in Israel applauded Rabin's actions, the leftist parties accused Rabin of military adventurism and of playing irresponsible power politics.

Another spectacular military feat approved by Rabin was the April 1987 assassination of PLO leader Abu Jihad in Tunisia.[113] Abu Jihad had been responsible for many terrorist operations against Israelis. The assassination of PLO terrorists was not a new Israeli policy—figures connected with the 1972 Munich massacre of Israeli Olympic athletes had been hunted down and killed. In that case, as in this one, Israel did not acknowledge responsibility—in order to minimize criticism abroad. Rabin did not, however, escape criticism at home. This type of action was no longer "politically correct" in Israeli leftist circles and even in the dovish wing of his own party.[114] Whereas reservations about the use of force in general were one factor in the doves' opposition, they were also disturbed by the choice of target. Doves were now calling for an open dialogue with the PLO and therefore opposed eliminating senior PLO personnel, even those who had engaged in terrorism.

Rabin's tough stance on terrorism was in line with the preferences of a large majority of the Israeli public, which continuously supported violent but limited measures against Palestinian terrorist organizations.[115] This fact contributed to Rabin's popularity. It was only during his second tenure as prime minister that Rabin revised his evaluation of the impact of terrorism and, to some extent, also of the calculus of using force against it. (This is discussed further in chapter 6.)

The Intifada

The Palestinian uprising that began in November 1987, the Intifada, was a strategic surprise for Israel.[116] Moreover, it was a novel tactical challenge for the IDF.[117] The Intifada featured many nonviolent methods of struggle, such as commercial shutdowns, economic boycotts, labor strikes, demonstrative funerals, the hoisting of Palestinian flags, the resignations of policemen and tax collectors, and the development of self-reliant educational, economic, and political institutions. These activities were accompanied by low levels of violence, such as throwing stones and gasoline bombs, as well as by internal terrorism, in which many Palestinians suspected of cooperation with Israel were murdered. Only about 5 percent of Palestinian activities included the use of firearms and Molotov cocktails.[118] The Intifada was a rather unusual mixture of nonviolent civil disobedience and subconventional uses of force. In essence, it was neither a guerrilla war nor a terrorist campaign. Despite experience with low-intensity operations, Israel had to develop a different response and to wage what the British termed "small war."[119]

Rabin was defense minister at the time. The political constellation of the 1980s allowed him to be the final arbiter in affairs pertaining to the IDF, and to the use of the IDF inside and outside the territories, with little interference from other cabinet members. The Likud prime minister, Yitzhak Shamir, had full confidence in Rabin and shared his analysis of the situation.[120] So did the chief of staff, Lieutenant General Shomron.[121] Rabin's perception of the situation and his prescriptions, therefore, constituted the most influential input in forming the Israeli response to the Intifada.

Rabin eventually convened in his office a special forum with representatives from the IDF, the police, several civilian ministries, and the security services. He called this the territories forum, and it met regularly to take stock of the situation and deliberate about the future. This is where the tactical decisions were made. Rabin, a man of details, personally involved himself in the campaign against the uprising—admitting, with typical frankness, that Israel's responses were essentially "trial and error," a process quite typical of Israeli decision-making.[122]

The strategic dimensions of the armed struggle against the Palestinians, however, were not discussed in this forum or probably in any other.[123] Rabin was usually oriented toward problem solving and shied away from discussions of grand strategy. Though he definitely was not arrogant, he seemed to be confident that his own analytical capabilities served him best in assessing the long-range implications of an impending situation. The absence of a civilian long-range planning unit in the Ministry of Defense also contributed to the lack of grand strategy discussions.

Initially, Rabin assumed that the riots would quickly decrease in intensity; therefore, he decided to go for a working visit to the United States in December 1987, as originally planned. Before he left, he ordered a massive IDF military presence in the territories and the arrest of Palestinian inciters, coupled with orders to the military to minimize contact with rioters and to refrain from shooting live ammunition unless directly threatened. Nevertheless, Rabin preferred a tough riposte for deterrence purposes. In an interview on NBC's *Meet the Press,* Rabin emphatically asserted: "What we have to drive [in]to the minds, the hearts of the people of the Arab countries, their leaders, [and] the Palestinians—[is] that by wars, threats of wars, terror, and public disorder in a violent way, they'll achieve nothing."[124] He projected confidence: "I believe that basically the situation can be controlled and will be controlled."[125] He conceded that the tough Israeli tactics might be damaging his country's image but that Israel has learned "the hard way" not to give in "to the use of force and the use of terror."[126]

Later, in January 1988, Rabin ordered a stronger response: forceful confrontations with the demonstrators and a policy of beatings. The new policy was rooted in (1) Rabin's realization that the Intifada had far-reaching political objectives (Israeli withdrawal from the territories and the establishment of a Palestinian state) that had to be denied, and (2) his rejection of methods that might lead to a bloodbath.[127] Rabin was impressed with the ability of the Border Police to restore order with clubs, so he equipped other units with clubs as well. Soldiers were ordered to use the clubs and, as much as possible, to avoid using live ammunition. This was the context of Rabin's infamous remark: "Nobody dies of a beating." Through the use of measured force, he sought to restore some of the deterrent power lost by the IDF. Though a reduction in casualties was quickly achieved, the policy of beatings failed to accomplish its main goal of ending the mass demonstrations. Furthermore, Rabin learned that beaten Palestinians were even hotter news than dead ones.[128] The political implications of the international attention, in particular the repercussions in the United States, coupled with soldiers' distress at having to beat civilians led in March 1988, four months after the eruption of the Intifada, to a reassessment and to the adoption of a new policy, which remained in effect during the following years.

In this reassessment, Rabin applied his outlook on the use of force in the Arab-Israeli dispute to the particular violent opposition that Israel faced in the territories. The Intifada was regarded as another facet of the protracted Arab-Israeli conflict, where the use of military force was no longer sufficient to eliminate the problem: "While we cannot solve it by military means only, they cannot solve it by violence or terror or wars."[129] Rabin, with the support of Prime Minister Shamir, devised a politico-military strategy to deal with the issue. He initiated a policy of attrition against the Palestinian population through military and administrative measures, emphasizing that Palestinian violence would be met with severe Israeli countermeasures.[130] Referring to Palestinian demonstrators, he said: "They will have to learn that more violence will bring more suffering to them."[131]

Rabin advocated a patient, three-part approach to grinding down the Intifada: first, limited use of military force to prevent violence; second, judicial means such as incarceration, administrative detention, and selective deportation; and third, administrative and economic pressures in the form of a carrot-and-stick policy, which would also increase the dependence of the Palestinian population on the Israeli authorities.[132]

A strong response to the Intifada in order to reduce its political impact was also needed to prevent diversion of international attention to the Palestinian issue, which was not central to Rabin's political agenda. His state-centered approach to the Arab-Israeli conflict dictated minimizing the significance of the Palestinian dimension. The use of force, if necessary, was needed to push the Palestinians toward his preferred solution, which required the involvement of neighboring Arab states.[133]

Notwithstanding the harsh nature of Rabin's approach, which evoked criticism within his own party and in leftist circles outside of it, he was not interested in pushing the Palestinian population to despair and to further opposition: "We have to strike a balance between actions that could bring on terrible economic distress and a situation in which they have nothing to lose, and measures which bind them to the Israeli administration and thus prevent civil disobedience."[134] This understanding constituted a moderating factor in the fine-tuning of the implementation of Israeli policy in the territories. Tactical solutions, such as restrictions on the use of live ammunition and the introduction of plastic bullets and gravel throwers, were adopted to reduce the lethality of Israeli countermeasures. The possible effects that Israeli policies toward the Palestinians could have on the government's public relations in Israel and abroad formed an additional constraint.[135] Yet even the hawkish Prime Minister Shamir had to curb Rabin's combative mood on a few occasions, and some of the suggestions for action recommended by the defense minister were not authorized.[136]

Moreover, Rabin insisted that his attritional approach, which emphasized Israeli determination not to succumb to the Palestinian use of force, had to be complemented by political measures. Despite the emphasis on a limited-power contest, the search for a political avenue to satisfy some of the Palestinian aspirations was an imperative for Rabin. He believed that the Intifada had created a situation in which, for the first time, the residents of the territories themselves were leading the Palestinian struggle. These local leaders, he thought, might serve as suitable partners for negotiations.[137] Rabin expressed the hope that local leaders, though paying lip service to the PLO, would be "strong enough to be the masters of their own fate," that they would "realize that through violence they will achieve nothing," and that they would be "ready to negotiate."[138]

Whereas in the past, Rabin had been skeptical about elections in the Israeli-ruled territories, he became convinced by his Labor colleagues that since the PLO was not the right partner for negotiations, elections were the only feasible mechanism for selecting a Palestinian delegation with any mantle of legitimacy. Therefore, he and Shimon Peres proposed an election plan in the territories so that the Palestinians could select representatives who would then negotiate with Israel for peace. The elections were to be held only after the territories had three to six months of calm. Rabin envisioned that after the elections, "the Palestinians would receive expanded autonomy or an administration for self-rule which would conduct their daily affairs."[139]

Yet in early 1989, when the Israeli government offered a political avenue to the Palestinians (the May 1989 peace initiative) to deal with the conflict, Rabin did not hesitate to escalate slightly the level of force used against the Palestinians. Rabin's orders liberalized the army's use of purportedly nonlethal ammunition, such as plastic bullets and the newly introduced rubber-coated, rounded steel bullets. He authorized several tougher measures, including allowing a greater number of soldiers to fire on demonstrators, sealing or destroying the homes of stone throwers, expanding the policy of fining the parents of children caught throwing stones, and confiscating the cars or other property of those taking part in uprisings. He also closed several schools whose students had repeatedly participated in stone throwing. In January 1989 Rabin told the Knesset: "As long as the residents of the territories are not ready to sit down at the negotiating table, as long as they respond with violence, rocks and bottles, they will not make us run away, they will not make us surrender. They will suffer."[140] In May 1989, Rabin warned the Palestinians that if they did not accept Israel's offer for elections, he would order the military to deal more harshly with the Palestinian uprising: "We will use whatever is needed, more force, to put down the violence, and with much greater justification."[141]

The attritional approach implemented by Rabin scored several successes. By mid-1988 mass demonstrations had practically ended, and there was only minor interference on most travel routes. The attempt to organize a "popular army" in the Palestinian villages that declared "independence" during the summer of 1988 also failed.[142] The hunt for Intifada activists, who were often armed, ended on many occasions in their elimination or capture by special Israeli units. Indeed, the IDF was much better suited to this type of assignment than to quelling mass demonstrations. Such encounters were obviously less problematic for Israeli public opinion. Moreover, after more than two years of the Intifada, Rabin pointed out that coping with it consumed only 4 percent of the defense budget, in contrast to the 8 percent allocated to patrolling the borders.[143] Rabin had come to see the Intifada as a manageable "current security" problem that Israelis could live with. It was stressed that an important element in low-intensity conflict strategy was the development of societal tolerance for ambiguous and indeterminate conflict.[144] Israeli society has generally been successful in routinizing conflict.[145] Although Rabin's approach in trying to crush Palestinian violence was uncompromising, even often brutal, this use of force can only be described as measured. Moreover, he simultaneously showed great flexibility in his approach to negotiations for peace. This approach made Rabin popular at home.

Lebanon

A final example of Rabin's approach to armed conflict is the Lebanese arena. Until the civil war of 1975–76, Jerusalem's main concern was the Palestinian armed presence in Lebanon. Rabin's government occasionally retaliated against Palestinian raids, primarily by bombing Palestinian targets from the air—a rather blunt counterinsurgency technique and a source of friction with the United States. The inability of the Beirut authorities to extend Lebanese sovereignty over the Palestinian organizations led to the destabilization of the fragile political system. This, and additional domestic factors, led to the civil war.[146]

Escalation of the Lebanese civil war from January 1976 onward, along with the American presidential campaign, put a temporary halt to the U.S. search for an Israeli-Syrian agreement and additional Israeli territorial concessions. This was good news for Rabin in light of improvements in American-Syrian relations and his unwillingness to make more than minimal concessions on the Golan Heights. Actually, the United States was at that time becoming more responsive to Israeli interests because of the growing realization that the turmoil in Lebanon and the Syrian military encroachment provided Israel an opportunity to adopt a more militant stance and increase regional tensions. Moreover, the logic of the war in Lebanon elevated Israel in American eyes to the status of a potentially valuable ally. For all their differences, Israel shared with the United States an interest in preventing the radicalization of hitherto pro-Western Lebanon and/or its annexation by Syria. Israel was in a position both to deter the Syrians and to help the Christians. Nevertheless, Israel's role, from the American perspective, was to set limits to the level of Syrian involvement, not to interfere with it. This suited Rabin, especially since this role implied serving American interests.[147]

As much as Rabin would have wanted to deter a Syrian invasion, he was unwilling to go to war with Syria in defense of the Christian community, especially since the latter was concentrated in the northern part of Lebanon. He adamantly refused to commit any Israeli troops north of the Litani River to help the Christians, although Israel did provide other forms of military assistance.[148] He stated his motto for relations with the Christians: "Israel should help them, so they will be able to help themselves." This was reminiscent of the Nixon Doctrine, which he held in great esteem. He and his colleagues (Allon, Peres, and Galili) calculated the military and political risks of such a war as too high, especially in view of the prospect that other Arab countries might come to Syria's defense. Furthermore, Rabin was reluctant to commit the IDF in advance to a specific course of action in Lebanon, particularly one that the United States would not condone.[149] Therefore, Israeli warnings were cautiously phrased. Interviewed by the BBC in January 1976, Rabin said that Israel would not tolerate foreign involvement in Lebanon, but he declined to say under what specific circumstances Israel would go to war.[150]

Rabin was more outspoken about Israel's aims in Lebanon during his visit to Washington in the same month. To all his audiences, he emphasized Israel's solidarity with Middle Eastern minorities and its intention to help the Christians. In addition, Rabin stressed that in the event of a Syrian invasion, Israel would oppose the extension of Syrian control to *southern Lebanon*.[151] In closed discussions with the Americans, he admitted that irrespective of all the firm words in Israeli public declarations, a Syrian invasion would not necessarily be regarded as a casus belli. This alleviated American (and subsequently Syrian) fears of an active Israeli response to the Syrian military presence in Lebanon. Rabin may very well have intended his statement as a concession to be made to the United States in exchange for tacit American recognition of Israel's strategic interests south of the Litani River.

Perceiving Syria as a stabilizing factor, and aware of what Israel's limited objectives were in Lebanon, the United States seized the opportunity to demonstrate to the Arab world that it could exercise leverage on Israel. Indeed, it coordinated the Syrian invasion.[152] Using Washington as an intermediary, Rabin did communicate to Syria President Hafez al-Assad his concept of the "red line" beyond which Syria was to refrain from any intervention. The "red line," a notion Rabin did not like to use, was primarily a device to contain a Syrian invasion of Lebanon rather than a casus belli. The "red line" ran from Jezin to Zahrani, 25 kilometers north of the Litani River, that is, still south of Sidon.[153] Israel insisted, however, that the line was to be interpreted with flexibility, depending on such factors as the depth of the Syrian penetration, the strength of the invading force, and the deployment of Palestinian terrorists. Furthermore, Rabin regarded a ban on Syrian naval operations on the Lebanese coast, on air activity, and on the deployment of surface-to-air missiles in Lebanon as vital Israeli interests. Rabin succeeded, via the United States, in acquiring Syrian acquiescence to these Israeli terms in exchange for a pledge of Israeli noninterference (military intervention was never really entertained) in the 1976 Syrian invasion of Lebanon.

A first test of the Syrian commitment to respect the understandings with Israel occurred in November 1976, when a non-Syrian unit of the Arab Peace-Keeping Force (the cover name chosen at the October 1976 conferences in Riyadh and Cairo for what was actually the Syrian invasion force) was ordered to move into southern Lebanon. Stern Israeli warnings conveyed through the Americans nipped this move in the bud. In January 1977 the Syrians tried again to erode the "red line" by sending a battalion south of it to a position in Nabatiyah. Rabin resisted the prodding of Peres, his minister of defense, to allow the IDF to deal with the new situation; Rabin chose to use first the good offices of the United States to deliver a warning to the Syrians, before considering the use of force.[154] And indeed, in February, the Syrian unit withdrew.

Ironically, Israel's "red line" created in southern Lebanon a haven for Palestinian terrorists (who were fleeing from the advancing Syrian army). Although Rabin anticipated this consequence, he considered it a lesser evil than allowing the Syrian army to approach the Israeli border and police the area. For him, Palestinian terrorism represented merely a military nuisance, preferable to the "basic security" challenge of an enhanced Syrian military presence close to Israel's borders. In March 1977, Rabin even rejected President Jimmy Carter's idea to station UN forces on the Lebanese border.[155] He did not believe that UN forces could adequately substitute for the friendly Lebanese militia in the south, and he also feared that the UN presence might limit Israel's options.

During this period Rabin's government, capitalizing on the willingness of several Lebanese officers to defend their villages against armed Palestinian organizations, established the "good fence" policy (involving economic and military assistance to friendly militias). This policy was the forerunner of the "security zone" established north of the Israeli border in 1978.

All in all, Rabin succeeded, through the use of credible military threats, in preventing the Syrians or any other Arab power from establishing a presence in southern Lebanon, and in this endeavor he had America's blessing. Moreover, the diversion of Syrian troops and their protracted engagement in Lebanon had an adverse impact on Syria's readiness to fight Israel. Finally, the list of Israeli achievements in Lebanon during this period include the establishment of a buffer zone patrolled by friendly forces. The risk to northern Israel increased as a result of these developments in Lebanon, but Rabin's main concern was to gain time. The Lebanese crisis gave Israel a respite from further pressures for territorial concessions in other sectors.

Over the next few years, however, the security situation in Lebanon deteriorated, aggravating Israeli threat perception and eventually leading to the 1982 invasion of Lebanon.[156] As noted, Rabin questioned the wisdom of the Lebanon War and its far-reaching political goals. But even though he was a member of the opposition, his criticism was muted. Rabin and other Laborites were initially reluctant to oppose what seemed to be a military intervention backed by the United States.[157] The pragmatic Rabin realized, however, that once the war started, there would be some benefits to be reaped. He believed that the IDF should take advantage of the progress of troops toward Beirut to weaken the PLO. According to Leah Rabin, "Yitzhak could not sit idly by without offering his advice."[158] In a meeting with Prime Minister Begin on 4 July 1982, he supported Defense Minister Ariel Sharon's plan to tighten the siege of Beirut by shutting off the city water supply.[159] Moreover, Rabin said: "In the midst of fighting there is no place for public debate."[160] As a soldier, Rabin was intensely concerned about negatively affecting the morale of the troops fighting at the front. Nevertheless, he expressed reservations about the effectiveness of using force to attain the government's goals in Lebanon.

The military recognized the futility of the extended stay in Lebanon after realizing that the American-brokered May 1983 Israel-Lebanon agreement was doomed to failure. Subsequently, it advocated a large-scale withdrawal, although the exact scope was debated within the military.[161] This led only to a redeployment along the Awali River (in southern Lebanon) in September 1983, since the Likud-led government was unwilling to withdraw further without securing any political gains.

When Rabin again became an influential decision-maker (as defense minister in the national unity government of 1984), he decided to extricate the IDF from the Lebanese quagmire.[162] Peres, then prime minister, wholeheartedly supported this move, but Rabin's efforts and his political stature were central to the decision to withdraw unilaterally from Lebanon and to maintain the security zone in southern Lebanon.[163] The Israeli cabinet voted (19–6) on 14 January 1985 in favor of a plan to leave Lebanon in stages. Rabin then commented: "After two and a half years in Lebanon, we have learned the hard way that Israel should not become the policeman of Lebanon."[164] In July 1985, he proudly told the students of the National Security College that his policy had led to a reduction of the Israeli presence in Lebanon from 13,000–14,000 soldiers to 600–700.[165]

Gradually, the armed Palestinian presence was weakened, and the main enemy in Lebanon became armed extremist Islamic Shiite groups aided by Iran. On the whole, Israel's military operations, with the support of the South Lebanese Army (SLA), were effective both in containing the level of activity by Palestinian and Lebanese armed groups and in limiting their geographical scope to southern Lebanon. Yet as the Shiite Hizballah pressures on the SLA grew during 1987, and as Katyusha attacks on Israeli settlements increased, Israel doubled its military presence in the security zone and increased the recruiting, equipping, and training of SLA troops.[166] On 21 April 1987, Rabin warned that increased IDF activity in southern Lebanon would follow if these attacks continued.[167]

Indeed, the IDF carried out a major two-day incursion into southern Lebanon in May 1988 in an effort to clean out areas from which infiltration efforts were emanating. On the second day of the preemptive action, the Israelis engaged Hizballah fighters in the village of Maidun, which was totally destroyed. Maidun became for the Hizballah what Karameh had become in Palestinian historiography—a great victory against the Zionists. Counter-Hizballah operations escalated in July 1989 when Israeli commandos kidnapped Sheik Obeid, one of the Hizballah leaders, primarily to increase Israel's leverage in a prisoner exchange.

The price for holding on to the security zone in southern Lebanon gradually increased, but the Rabin government of 1992–95 limited its response to the Hizballah attacks from Lebanon. This reluctance to use force was prompted by the desire to prevent escalation that might interfere with the peace negotiations with Syria and to prevent damage to Israeli villages along Israel's northern border. The aversion to the use of force was strengthened by the presence of the extremely dovish ministers of the Meretz Party in Rabin's government. It was only after many months of restraint, and following repeated Katyusha attacks on Israeli settlements, that Rabin succeeded in gaining approval for a large-scale military operation in July 1993.

Operation Accountability used massive firepower to scare the population of southern Lebanon, force the residents to move, and thereby create a refugee problem in Beirut; Israel suffered no casualties. The refugee wave—Rabin and his chief of staff, Barak, believed—would lead to pressure on Damascus in order to engender greater Syrian constraints on the Hizballah's freedom of action. At the same time, Rabin emphasized his desire to avoid any further escalation. This was hardly the stuff to move the person in control of Lebanon—Syria's Assad. Not surprisingly, his capacity to withstand pressure was great, particularly when the price was being paid by Lebanese civilians. The pictures of the poor refugees were actually having the unintended effect of arousing world pressure on Israel to curb its military activities. Although Operation Accountability led to vague understandings between the Hizballah and the IDF on leaving civilians out of the armed struggle, understandings that were later violated, it left Assad as the final arbiter of what the Hizballah could or could not do in Lebanon.[168]

Indeed, Rabin seemed to develop second thoughts about military activism in southern Lebanon. In December 1994, Rabin publicly criticized the new Northern Front commander, Maj. Gen. Amiram Levine, for calling for a more offensive mind-set in dealing with stepped-up Hizballah attacks in southern Lebanon. He said: "If anybody thinks he has a military formula to solve the problem, he is wrong. We were successful during the year of 1994 with two military strikes against the Hizballah and its environment— the hijacking of Mustafa Dirani and the air strike at Ain Dardara. The response was in Buenos Aires and London."[169] He pointed out the Hizballah terrorist potential to hit Israeli and Jewish targets overseas and seemed to indicate that Israel should not provoke this organization too much.

Rabin exercised restraint in southern Lebanon and continued to believe, to his last day, in the value of the security zone and the need to fight there until a political solution to the ongoing conflict emerged. In 1994, he rejected the recommendations of a specially appointed committee of civilian security experts (appointed by his deputy in the Ministry of Defense, Lieutenant General Gur) to withdraw from the security zone and to defend the Israeli villages in the north by redeploying the IDF along the international border.[170]

CONCLUSION

Rabin epitomized the Israeli power-politics perspective on the Arab-Israeli conflict. The use of force was part of the dialogue between the protagonists and was for many years its most frequent and important expression. Military might was a precondition for survival in the hostile and extremely volatile Mideastern environment. Yet Rabin generally displayed caution in applying force. Particularly after 1973, he could not see any worthy goal to be achieved through war and, therefore, favored a defensive strategy, minimizing the need for preemptive or preventive strikes. He hoped to defend the status quo and to use a strong deterrent to force Arab neighbors to come to the negotiating table. He understood, however, that only a mighty offensive force could serve such a deterrent function and that only such an army could win a war convincingly in case of the failure of deterrence.

Rabin was essentially a military man whose expertise was the management of violence. Because he was thoroughly acquainted with the IDF, he could immerse himself in every operational detail. This was a source of great pleasure for him and often astonished his subordinates. Rabin often used force in a very measured way, ensuring subservience to his immediate political goals. His policies regarding the use of force reflected his risk aversion in military planning, his growing sensitivity to casualties, and his insistence on firm political control of military operations.

Rabin's perceived toughness and his willingness to use force if necessary were valued by most Israelis. These aspects of his personality and of his policies evoked much admiration, gaining him great popularity. At the same time, however, he became the target for harsh criticism from leftist circles in Israeli politics during the 1980s and early 1990s.

CHAPTER FIVE

WEAPONS OF MASS DESTRUCTION

Israel's nuclear program and strategy have always been secret, and public discussion of nuclear matters has been consciously restrained, particularly during the first three decades of the state's existence. Behind the scenes, however, a debate about the utility of nuclear weapons in the Arab-Israeli conflict has taken place. This debate has often crossed party lines and political camps holding differing views on how to deal with the Arab-Israeli conflict. One school of thought, once associated with Shimon Peres, has attributed great importance to nuclear weapons, particularly in light of the asymmetries in the military balance between the few Israelis and the many Arabs. Nuclear weapons, the advocates of this view have maintained, could compensate Israel for the greater Arab conventional potential and could eventually freeze the conflict.[1]

Another school of thought, primarily associated with Yigal Allon and others (including Yitzhak Rabin) in the Achdut Haavodah faction of the Labor movement, has argued that Israel can realistically expect to maintain a conventional military balance well into the future.[2] As long as Israel enjoys conventional superiority, it has no reason to rely on nuclear weapons for its national survival. Furthermore, this school has claimed, an Israeli public nuclear posture could accelerate the acquisition of such weapons by the Arabs, a development not conducive to Israeli interests. This camp has also been skeptical about the possibility of establishing in the Arab-Israeli arena a stable balance of terror like the one that existed between the superpowers. Despite the reluctance to develop openly a nuclear deterrent force and a doctrine for its use, members of the conventional school of thought have not opposed the development of an Israeli nuclear infrastructure that could make nuclear weapons available if needed.

Israel's first prime minister, David Ben-Gurion, accepted in 1962 the logic of the second school of thought. He opted for reliance on conventional power while developing Israel's nuclear option but also laid the foundation for Israel's nuclear ambiguity.[3] Levi Eshkol, Ben-Gurion's successor as prime minister, perfected Israeli nuclear opaqueness by introducing in 1965 the formula: "Israel is not a nuclear country and will not be the first state to introduce nuclear weapons into the Middle East." This somewhat obscure formula has served all Israeli governments ever since and remains the Israeli official position on nuclear weapons to this day. Israel has also refrained from signing the 1968 Nuclear Non-Proliferation Treaty (NPT). Israel first claimed that the treaty was under scrutiny and consideration, but it later announced its reluctance to join the NPT. From Israel's point of view, the NPT was deficient in several respects. First, Israel claimed that the inspections of the International Atomic Energy Agency (IAEA) were unreliable and could not verify the true and full nature of the inspected nuclear programs. Second, the treaty allowed for developing a full nuclear cycle and stockpiling large quantities of fissionable material as long as the stockpiles and facilities were subjected to periodic inspections by the IAEA. Finally, Israel, in the absence of comprehensive peace with its neighbors, preferred not to give up its nuclear option.[4]

This chapter presents the strategic rationale underlying Rabin's position on nuclear weapons and the nuclear policy he participated in shaping. It concludes with an analysis of Rabin's evaluation of the threats involved in the proliferation of long-range missiles and other weapons of mass destruction and in the ways to cope with the emerging nonconventional challenges to Israel's national security.

RABIN'S SKEPTICISM OF NUCLEAR WEAPONS

Rabin was skeptical about the usefulness of nuclear weapons. In 1962, he supported the policy of relying on conventional military power, a policy that Ben-Gurion eventually adopted.[5] Rabin's coolness to the efforts to develop military technologies in Israel also affected his approach to nuclear weapons.[6] His initial thinking was probably reinforced by the fact that it was Peres, his rival, who was identified with the building of the Dimona reactor and who favored the development of nuclear weapons as Israel's main deterrent force.

In a rare public statement on nuclear weapons, in 1976 Rabin said: "Conventional power suffices to guarantee Israel's security in the near future. Attempts to rely on mystical weapons are negative trends."[7] Like others within the Israeli political elite in the 1970s, he preferred to use euphemisms such as "mystical weapons" rather than to utter the word "nuclear." He was, however, more specific later, in closed forums. For example, he advised the 1981 class at the National Security College not to believe that nuclearization of the Middle East would freeze the Arab-Israeli conflict and would contain security dangers to Israel.[8]

Rabin became well acquainted with the American debates over nuclear weapons. He rejected the Dulles doctrine of massive retaliation, which relied on nuclear weapons to stave off aggression. In 1981, looking back at the 1962 Cuban Missile Crisis, Rabin concluded that it was American conventional superiority in the Caribbean theater that won the day, rather than its more advanced nuclear force.[9] Similarly, Rabin pointed out in December 1990 that the American nuclear arsenal had no relevance to the Gulf crisis following Iraq's conquest of Kuwait, despite the fact that an American strike with tactical nuclear weapons against the Iraqi forces in the desert would not affect the civilian population.[10]

In Rabin's view, nuclear weapons had limited utility. Such weapons could not, he explained, constitute an adequate response, for example, to an Egyptian conventional thrust to cut off the southern part of Israel, the Negev.[11] In 1983, Rabin was skeptical whether the rumors of Israeli nuclear warheads had any effect on the behavior of its neighbors. "I do not think Syria gives a damn whether Israel possesses nuclear weapons because it is sure that as long as it operates on the conventional level there are Soviet missiles to neutralize any nuclear threat against Syria."[12] Ten years later, when the Soviet Union was no longer around, he asserted that Israel's nuclear image in Damascus could not prevent a limited Syrian conventional attack that would not threaten Haifa or Tel Aviv.[13] He obviously realized that nuclear weapons were not useful for dealing with the whole gamut of threats to Israel's national security but rather could help only in very few extreme contingencies. Therefore, relying on nuclear weapons instead of continuing to develop Israel's conventional power in order to confront the growing Arab conventional armies would be "disastrous for Israel,"[14] or a "historic mistake."[15]

In 1985, under grave economic constraints, Defense Minister Rabin rejected the hypothetical option of adopting a public nuclear posture instead of continuing to build a strong conventional force. An Israeli announcement on a nuclear posture would also have led, in all probability, to the Soviet extension of a nuclear umbrella over the Arab countries, which could have negated the advantages of Israeli nuclear bombs.[16] Furthermore, Rabin did not believe that the delicate balance of terror between the superpowers, which was based on the existence of a reliable second-strike capability, could be emulated in the Middle East.[17] He pointed out that it was not at all clear whether all Arab leaders who practiced brinkmanship could necessarily learn the rules of the nuclear game.[18] One important rule, according to Rabin, was "not to push one into a corner" but to leave the enemy a path of retreat. This is defined by the strategic studies literature as the "last clear chance."[19] He also questioned the rationality of future Arab leaders: "Maybe somebody will go crazy and will think: it is worthwhile to lose 30 million Arabs in order to eliminate 1.5 million Jews."[20] Nuclear deterrence is, after all, based on the assumption of mutual rational decision-making.

Rabin did not advocate a public nuclear posture despite his characteristically pessimist evaluation that nuclearization of the Middle East was inevitable. He had no illusion that, in the long run, nuclear weapons technology could be denied to the Arab states. In 1980 he expressed great concern about Iraqi nuclear activity and accused European countries of behaving in a totally irresponsible manner.[21] In April 1981 he singled out France as a country ready to sell such technology to Israel's rivals or to be of significant assistance on their nuclear path. At that time, he estimated that an Arab country could build a nuclear warhead within five to fifteen years.[22] Although he confessed that the introduction of nuclear weapons into Arab arsenals would make him sleepless at night, he refused to regard an acquisition of a nuclear bomb by Arab states as constituting the "end of Israel."[23] Nuclear weapons in hostile countries were a serious threat, but he seemed to think that Israel would have to think of ways to survive in a nuclear neighborhood.

Therefore Rabin, like his mentor Allon, insisted that Israel would have to be ready to precede any Middle Eastern country in going nuclear.[24] Rabin emphasized that Israel could not afford to be the second country to acquire nuclear weapons in the Middle East. What this meant in terms of the Israeli nuclear program is not entirely clear, though perhaps it implied an advanced stage of weaponization. In any case, nuclear proliferation in the region was not something to which Rabin looked forward. He preferred to postpone this development for as long as possible. "The longer it takes it the better it will be for the Jews and for the whole world."[25] Rabin always preferred to play for time and to put off difficult choices, all the more so when it came to nuclear issues.

RABIN'S EARLY NUCLEAR ENCOUNTERS

Rabin was sensitized to the nuclear issue while serving as a senior officer in the Israel Defense Force (IDF). He noticed in 1954 the U.S. Army doctrine of fighting a nonconventional war.[26] He also realized the potential for tensions between the United States and Israel because of the American stand against the spread of nuclear weapons.[27] Rabin, who was appointed chief of staff by Eshkol in 1964, became Eshkol's senior security adviser and had input into devising the ambiguous nuclear formula.[28] He also realized the intricate linkage between the nuclear issue and the supply of American conventional weapons to Israel. In 1965 he participated in the attempt to persuade the United States to deliver M-48 tanks to Israel, and he supported the arrangements reached with the Americans concerning their supervisory visits to the Dimona reactor.

Rabin also dealt with the nuclear issue while he was ambassador in Washington. At the end of 1968, the administration of President Lyndon Johnson tried to link the supply of the Phantom airplanes to supervision of Israeli nuclear installations, a proposal that Rabin rejected.[29] He was instrumental in the American change of policy toward Israel's nuclear program. Rabin met Henry Kissinger in December 1968 (Kissinger was then slated to be national security adviser in the incoming administration of President Richard Nixon) and was led to believe that the new U.S. foreign policy team would be more understanding of Israel's position on the nuclear issue than the previous administration had been.[30] Indeed, Nixon and Kissinger were not adamant, as previous administrations had been, on controlling the Israeli nuclear program and bringing Israel under the NPT regime.[31] Nevertheless, Rabin recounted in his *Memoirs* several high-level American attempts to assess the state of the Israeli nuclear program and to secure an Israeli promise to join the NPT during the summer of 1969.

In response to these attempts, Rabin suggested dealing separately with the two questions involved: (1) the meaning of the Israeli commitment not to be the first to introduce nuclear weapons; and (2) membership in the

NPT.[32] Israel promised to curtail its nuclear program and not to pass the testing threshold. Rabin was the channel for clarifying the Israeli position to the United States.[33] Without a test, Israelis could continue to maintain nuclear innocence while the Americans were willing to turn a blind eye to the Israeli nuclear option. Moreover, as the Israelis attempted to marginalize the effect of the U.S. supervisory visits to the Dimona reactor, the Americans stopped asking in 1969 for a periodic American presence in the Israeli reactor. The U.S. decision to end the visits to Dimona was a result of Nixon's great respect for the embattled American ally and for its prime minister, Golda Meir, as well as of his evaluation that Israel was a country still facing existential threats. In addition, the decision also reflected a realization that cosmetic visits would not make that much difference.[34]

THE POST-1973 PERIOD

The October 1973 war and the subsequent visible dependency on the United States shook Israel's confidence, and fundamental assumptions of national security became subject to public soul-searching. The nuclear path attracted greater support than it had before the war. More voices were calling for an Israeli nuclear force, on the grounds that conventional military power had become too expensive for Israel. Given the regional arms race, Israel could not muster enough conventional weapons to protect itself, they argued. They therefore advocated disclosing Israel's nuclear deterrent or openly adopting a nuclear posture. The debate became more heated and caught international attention in 1976 as the renowned Moshe Dayan, at that time outside the government, made several statements in favor of going nuclear.[35]

Immediately after the 1973 war, at a little-noticed academic symposium, Prime Minister Rabin expressed his assessment, in response to a question, that conventional weapons would continue to be decisive in a future Middle East war. He belittled the role of nuclear weapons.[36] In 1974 he told a BBC interviewer that Israel was not a nuclear power in a military sense.[37] In 1975, when questioned in an ABC interview about Israel's willingness to use the ultimate weapon, Rabin said, "No doubt that Israel is ready to [do] the ultimate for its defense, but we believe that we live in an era in which we can do it [defend Israel] with conventional weapons."[38]

The press reported that at a cabinet meeting Rabin expressed reservations about Dayan's nuclear statements. In response to a question from a member of the cabinet (Yitzhak Rafael of the National Religious Party), Rabin maintained that Dayan's remarks were not coordinated with the government and that he welcomed the opportunity to state unequivocally that Israel's nuclear policy remained unchanged.[39] Perhaps hoping to prevent further discussion of the nuclear deterrent or fearing the effects of Dayan's views on internal and foreign affairs, Rabin decided to clarify his position further and to speak to the Israeli public. In a speech to the Tzavta Club in Tel Aviv, he reiterated that the official nuclear policy had not changed. He added, "Conventional power suffices to guarantee Israel's security in the near future."[40]

Prime Minister Rabin did not institute a reassessment of Israel's nuclear policy, as demanded by the pronuclear faction in Israeli politics. Yet Israeli policies were rarely researched and formulated in a systematic fashion.[41] In the 1970s, Israeli nuclear declaratory policy did not change significantly while Rabin was prime minister. Substantively, however, Israel's nuclear program progressed as Rabin approved several important steps in the weaponization process. By then he was less skeptical about the Israeli technological ability in this field.[42] In light of the continuing conflict with the Arabs, Rabin and his government (1974–77) wanted to preserve Israel's option for nuclear weapons. Yet Rabin, together with his foreign minister Allon, intuitively and on an ad hoc basis emphasized Israel's preference for a conventional deterrent and hoped to lower Israel's nuclear profile.

An analysis of events relating to Israel's nuclear status during Rabin's first term as prime minister does not reveal any intention to become a formal nuclear power; on the contrary, Israel took pains to refute such accusations. The first "nuclear event" was Nixon's offer, while visiting Cairo in June 1974, to sell a nuclear power reactor to Egypt, a proposal that took Israel by surprise. Rabin admonished the Knesset not to foment panic, since in the long run it was not possible to prevent the introduction of nuclear power reactors in the Arab countries.[43] Moreover, he expressed his preference for an American reactor to one of another origin (French or Russian).[44] Despite the widespread concern within Israel about the American-Egyptian nuclear deal, the government's reaction was consistently low-key and very cautious. Rabin did not believe that any opposition would be productive, and he took care not to spoil Nixon's visit to the region.[45] Obviously, Rabin's government wanted to minimize internal and international attention to the nuclear issue, which could have caused difficulties in Washington at a time when U.S.-Israeli relations were considered to be of paramount importance. Only later did the government realize that the deal could be delayed or killed in Congress without Israel's having to oppose publicly the American administration.[46]

The disclosure in September 1975 that Israel was asking for long-range Pershing missiles again focused attention on Israel's nuclear potential, for observers deduced that Israel wanted a carrier for nuclear weapons. Yet the Pershing mentioned in the September 1975 memorandum of understanding (MOU) between Israel and the United States was a new model, a very accurate surface-to-surface missile designed to carry conventional warheads only, and was not yet in production. The interest in this model was actually a clear indication of Israeli conventional preferences.[47] Nevertheless, seeing that a link was being made between the new model of the Pershing and nuclear weapons, and concerned about potential friction with the United States, Rabin quickly decided on a tactical retreat. In October 1975, in a meeting with the media at a symposium in Jerusalem, Rabin said that he did not consider the Pershing ground-to-ground missile to be a critical weapon in Israel's defense and that Israelis should realize that whenever Israel had put in a request for a certain type of weapon in the past, there had been a lapse of several years before the weapon was received. Rabin also emphasized that the acquisition of the Pershing missiles was not a test case for relations between the United States and Israel.[48]

A most significant "nuclear event" occurred on 30 September 1975. In a speech to the United Nations (UN) General Assembly, Foreign Minister Allon announced Israel's support for consultations with all states in the region toward the creation of a Nuclear Weapons Free Zone (NWFZ) in the Middle East.[49] Israel's 1975 willingness to accept an NWFZ without conventional arms control was definitely a change in its declared policy. Israel had previously maintained that any arms control measures should include both conventional and unconventional weapons.[50]

Thus, this was the first time that Israel had openly supported a regional NWFZ with no conventional strings attached. Allon succeeded in persuading Rabin (over the telephone!) to support the Iranian proposal at the UN for a regional NWFZ, though Rabin was to insist on direct intergovernmental consultations.[51] Allon's argument that Israel should try to please Iran, at that time Israel's main source of oil and a regional ally, appealed to Rabin's power-politics orientation. Rabin and others in the government were somewhat concerned about a possible change in Iran's policy toward Israel as Tehran improved its relations with Cairo.[52]

Rabin's first government also clarified to the Americans, several times, that Israel's nuclear ambiguity meant that in the absence of an Arab nuclear bomb, Israel would not cross the threshold of exploding a nuclear device.[53] On the NPT, however, Rabin held to Israel's established position.

At the end of the 1970s, while serving in the opposition, Rabin remained skeptical whether the next decade would see the introduction of nuclear weapons in the Middle East, and he continued to maintain that conventional weaponry would be the decisive factor in the Arab-Israeli region. Furthermore, refuting Dayan's argument that Israel lacked enough manpower to sustain an arms race, Rabin wrote in a 1979 *Maarachot* article: "The factor that had constrained the power of the IDF in the past and which will continue to do so in the future is weapon systems rather than manpower. What I mean is that the supply of weapons, in quantitative and qualitative terms, will act as a brake on building the might of the IDF and not the number of people at its disposal."[54]

The nuclear issue attracted much attention immediately after the June 1981 Israeli air strike that destroyed the Iraqi nuclear reactor near Baghdad.[55] Peres and Rabin, Labor's leaders in the opposition, commended the IAF for its fabulous achievement but refrained from praising Menachem Begin's Likud-led government.[56] Playing down the government's role in successful military operations was typical of Israeli politicians in opposition.[57] All Laborites, including Rabin, charged that the timing of the air strike (a few weeks before the general elections) was an election ploy. Their main concern was the question of whether Israel had exhausted all other options before sending its warplanes to deal with an indeed threatening situation.[58] Yet Rabin and other hawkish Laborites were very restrained in their criticism, whereas the more dovish politicians in Labor and outside the party even attacked the government for adventurism.[59]

Publicly lukewarm toward the June raid, Rabin nevertheless supported, in principle, any action, including the use of force, against the nuclear infrastructure of hostile Arab countries. He said in 1981: "Israel must do everything to prevent an Arab state [from] reaching a serious potential for building a nuclear bomb or acquiring one. Israel must first exhaust all diplomatic means and covert operations. Yet, if these measures fail, I do not preclude Israeli direct military action designed to obstruct or to delay the realization of a nuclear option (its elimination once and for all is impossible), particularly in a country whose leaders are of the Saddam Hussein or Muammar Qaddafi kind."[60] Despite the fact that Rabin did not declare nuclearization of an Arab country to be a casus belli, he continued to believe to the very end that it was Israel's duty to do everything in its power to prevent, or at least to postpone, the introduction of nuclear weapons to the Middle East.

Rabin pointed out in 1981 that the Israeli attack on the Iraqi reactor had far-reaching military and political implications. Achieving surprise and total destruction despite the long distance to the target and the evasion of a variety of surface-to-air missiles (SAM-2, -3, and -6) and antiaircraft guns was, according to Rabin, a demonstration of excellence on the part of the Israeli pilots and their American warplanes. He suggested that the Israeli action—an important precedent—might deter Arab countries from attempting to go nuclear, as well as the Europeans from selling sensitive nuclear equipment and installations. Although many foreign governments sharply criticized the Israeli attack, Rabin believed that in time they might come to appreciate its utility. He also correctly assessed that American-Israel relations would remain unaffected in the long run.[61]

The destruction of the Iraqi nuclear reactor delayed the development of a nuclear threat in the Arab world and reduced threat perception on this issue in Israel. In 1987, Rabin, by then defense minister, remained sanguine about the threat of nuclear weapons: "I hope that the Middle East will not go nuclear. We have proposed that, instead of signing the Non-Proliferation Treaty, all countries in the Middle East should sign a regional agreement preventing the nuclearization of the region. However, the Arab countries refuse to sign such an agreement. Nevertheless, I believe that in the next ten years, at least, the Middle East will not go nuclear. Beyond that I dare not predict."[62]

A reevaluation of the nuclear threat took place only after the 1991 Gulf War. The Israeli defense establishment, including Rabin, was no less surprised than the rest of the world when the full dimension of the nuclear progress made by Iraq was revealed.[63] In that respect this war and the destruction of a large part of the Iraqi nuclear infrastructure were a great relief to Israelis, but according to Rabin, this was just a temporary respite because nuclear proliferation in the Middle East was likely to happen within a period of five to fifteen years.[64]

The dissolution of the Soviet empire, a strategic development welcomed by Rabin, had negative ramifications for nuclear proliferation. Rabin realized that the loss of central control in the former Soviet Union facilitated the seepage of nuclear technology and fissionable materials to the Middle East. Moreover, cash-strapped China and North Korea could be tempted to provide nuclear services.[65] True to his character, he was pessimistic about the ability of the international community to prevent the nuclearization of the Middle East. The best Israel could hope for in the 1990s was to slow down the process.[66]

The fears that Iraq would acquire a nuclear arsenal were soon augmented by increasing apprehensions of the reemerging Iranian nuclear program.[67] In 1992–93, American and Israeli officials estimated that Iran might be able to produce nuclear weapons within eight to ten years. By January 1995, Rabin and U.S. Defense Secretary William Perry seemed to have somewhat revised their evaluation: "That seven to fifteen years was a 'reasonable' estimate of how long it will take Iran [to obtain nuclear weapons] at its present pace."[68] The Iranian nuclear program attracted much of Rabin's attention, particularly as Iran became, for Rabin, the arch-enemy of the Jewish state in the 1990s. To a great extent, the nuclear progress of countries in the region served as a catalyst for Rabin's efforts to conclude peace treaties with Israel's neighbors. (This is discussed further in the next chapter.)

MISSILES AND CHEMICAL WEAPONS

Through the end of the 1980s, there was no increase in the threat perception concerning the spread of nuclear weapons; however, this decade saw the introduction of long-range ballistic missiles and chemical weapons. The IDF and Rabin's attention had already been attracted to this development in the mid-1980s as a result of the intelligence reports surveying Iraqi progress in missile technology and production.[69] Moreover, intelligence reports indicated that Arab leaders, such as Hafez al-Assad, viewed the surface-to-surface missiles as the main weapon to be used in the next Arab-Israeli war.[70]

Rabin regarded the Arab efforts to acquire long-range surface-to-surface missiles as a continuation of their past attempts to overcome the IAF's air supremacy.[71] He argued that, after 1967, the Arabs had initiated an intensive procurement of SAMs in order to deny the IAF freedom of action in the battlefield and in the Arab rear. The SAMs were largely successful in achieving this goal in 1973. In June 1982, however, the IAF proved that it had finally learned to adapt to the presence of SAMs and was able to suppress successfully the Syrian SAM system.

The emphasis on long-range ballistic missiles in Arab procurement programs constituted a response to the Israeli capacity to hit almost any Arab target from the air. The ballistic missiles arsenal largely put an end to the Israeli escalation dominance (i.e., the advantage of escalating beyond the enemy's capability).[72] The ballistic missiles also represented a credible deterrent against Israeli countervalue threats.[73] Since 1967, Israeli population centers had actually been immune to attacks from the air because the IAF had been able to provide almost foolproof protection for the Israeli rear. With the advent of ballistic missiles, this situation changed. Moreover, Rabin recognized the asymmetry in sensitivity to civilian casualties, which put Israel at a disadvantage. The missiles exposed the Achilles' heel of Israeli society.[74]

Indeed, in 1986, Rabin warned the Israeli public that surface-to-surface missiles could land on Israeli population centers in a future Arab-Israeli military encounter, giving war a hitherto unknown character.[75] Rabin envisioned the Arab use of missiles in a countercity mode in order to terrorize and demoralize the civilian population.[76] He was not sure how resilient the Israeli rear would be after repeated missile attacks. Moreover, he was apprehensive that many civilian casualties could exacerbate the political divisions in Israeli society and negatively affect the esprit de corps of the IDF. Rabin explicitly included the social dimension of the conflict as an important factor in the formulation of Israeli defense policy.[77] The government needed to educate the Israeli civilian population about the difficult tests that might arise in the future, but without causing panic by bringing up the issue.[78] Indeed, in many instances of protracted conflict, the protagonists have been worn out by their dispute, and the outcome of the conflict has thus been determined not only by superior military strength but also by perseverance and the ability to suffer pain.[79]

A second anticipated use of Arab missiles, particularly the more accurate ones, such as the SS-21, was purely military in a counterforce mode: against airbases and the staging areas for mobilizing the reserves.[80] A selective use of missiles against Israeli military targets could hinder a strong and effective Israeli response in the critical early stages of an Arab-initiated war. Israel also envisioned an attrition war (characterized by a static exchange of fire with a zero invasion ratio) in which missile exchanges played the major role.[81]

The missile threat became, according to a Rabin speech in February 1988, a great priority in Israel's national security policy. Rabin mentioned the Iran-Iraqi exchanges of long-range surface-to-surface missile attacks and clarified to his audience that Tel Aviv and other cities in Israel were also within the range of Iraq's improved Scud-B missiles. This allowed Iraq and other countries to harm Israel without having to send expeditionary forces to fight the IDF.[82] A concerned Rabin stated: "We see a reality where the world, by inaction, awards legitimacy to the indiscriminate use of missiles against population centers in the capitals of the two countries."[83]

Threat perception of missiles was high. It was heightened further by the possibility, which emerged in the 1980s, of equipping long-range missiles with chemical warheads. Israel had had apprehensions about the Arab use of chemical weapons as early as the 1960s, when Egypt had used chemical warheads in its intervention in the civil war in Yemen.[84] The Syrian chemical weapons effort, the most advanced in the Middle East, also elicited concern in the 1980s.[85] Still, Israel was much more alarmed by Iraq's use of gas toward the end of its war against Islamic Iran, and by the absence of serious condemnation of this action by the rest of the world. At that time, Rabin sadly concluded: "We see already legitimacy to chemical warfare, which uses the most advanced chemical agents in the world."[86] In a radio interview in July 1988, Rabin declared: "One of our fears is that the Arab world and its leaders might be deluded to believe that the lack of international reaction to the use of missiles and gases [during the Iran-Iraq War] gives them some kind of legitimization to use them."[87]

With Rabin at the helm as minister of defense from 1984, the IDF increased its efforts to prepare its troops for surviving and fighting in a chemically affected battleground. Beginning in the late 1980s, the civilian population was similarly trained on how to behave in case of attacks by chemical warheads. In March 1990, Chief of Staff Lt. Gen. Dan Shomron disclosed that a decision had been reached to provide gas masks to the entire population in case of an emergency.[88] The procedure and its publication were undoubtedly cleared with Minister of Defense Rabin. However effective, these passive defensive measures, intended to minimize the impact of chemical attacks, obviously would not be sufficient to prevent a great number of civilian casualties. The Israeli ability to use active defensive measures (interception of incoming missiles) was likewise limited.

The Israeli defensive measures intended to protect the population from chemical attacks may well have been counterproductive in terms of deterrence; they signaled to Arab leaders that the use of chemical agents was not unthinkable and therefore not out of the question.[89] Rabin seemed not to have been persuaded by such logic, since he sanctioned the development of a defensive posture in the area of chemical weapons. Nevertheless, he complemented the policy with deterrence. On several occasions, he threatened terrible consequences for those daring to use chemical weapons against

Israel, but he refrained from explicitly mentioning preemptive attacks or chemical or nuclear retaliation. In June 1988, Defense Minister Rabin threatened that if Iraq used chemical weapons, Israel would retaliate "tenfold."[90] A month later, in a radio interview, Rabin made it clear that Iraq should not draw inferences from others' reactions to chemical weapons: "It is a whole different ballgame when it comes to us. God forbid, they should know we will hit them back 100 times harder."[91] When Sadam Hussein threatened, on 2 April 1990, to use binary chemical weapons that would "consume half of Israel" in case Iraq was attacked, Rabin responded: "We have the means for a devastating response, many times greater than Saddam Hussein's threats."[92]

Because of his Jewish prism, Rabin was adamant that Israel would not accept being subject to an attack with chemical weapons: "As a Jewish state, Israel cannot tolerate the use of poison gas against Jews a second time in this century."[93] The memory of the Jewish Holocaust in World War II, when many Jews were gassed to death in Nazi camps, dictated a strong response. The Israelis were not fully informed about the Iraqi chemical ability, but what they knew of it and of Hussein was enough to cause some concern in Jerusalem, even though an unprovoked nonconventional attack on Israeli cities seemed unlikely.

Rabin appeared to address these new threats with increased deterrence through escalation dominance rather than through coercive diplomacy. He explicitly downgraded the possibility of a preemptive strike on the missile launchers. Like other Israeli leaders, Rabin refrained from issuing any explicit nuclear threats but used loaded language that could be construed as referring to Israel's nonconventional capabilities. The attempt by Rabin and other Israeli leaders to lower the Israeli nuclear profile was, however, problematic in terms of deterrence, particularly at a time when missiles and weapons of mass destruction had spread into the Middle East and when the Iraqis had even used chemical weapons in their war against Iran.

According to Rabin, an additional layer of Israel's posture versus the missiles was an active defense. He reminded his audiences that Israel had been the first country to join the 1986 Strategic Defense Initiative, and he showed an interest in purchasing Patriot SAMs, though these missiles did not constitute an entirely adequate answer to the challenge of the ballistic missiles. The Arrow antitactical ballistic missile (ATBM) program, initiated in the 1980s when Rabin was defense minister, promised to provide at least a partial defense against incoming missiles. Finally, Rabin suggested that an effective response to the missile challenge required also upgrading

Israel's offensive capabilities in armored warfare and in air battles. Only a quick, decisive victory could eliminate the threat of missiles.[94] This underscored Rabin's preference for remaining within the conventional realm if possible. The mix suggested by Rabin for dealing with the threat of missiles remained, for the time being, untested.

Despite his emphasis on deterrence, which required a threatening image, Rabin remained cautious. As the Gulf crisis evolved, Rabin did not join Yitzhak Shamir and the Likud-led government in issuing counterthreats against Iraq. Rabin warned: "In case of Iraqi missiles landing in Israel, we should not respond automatically, but should rather carefully weigh the options available and refrain from falling into the trap Saddam Hussein is preparing for us."[95] He thought that a chemical attack on Israel was unlikely and feared a military entanglement with more than one Arab state. He was glad that Israel was not part of the coalition against Iraq.[96] Typically, Rabin advocated that Israel follow a cautious and sober policy, rather than trying to improve deterrence by issuing threats that Israel might not be able to carry out.

Indeed, Rabin supported the policy of restraint exercised by Prime Minister Shamir in response to Iraqi missile attacks in the winter of 1991. He shared the belief that the continuation of Israeli noninvolvement in the Iraqi theater best suited Israeli interests as long as several initial conditions remained constant: a bearable number of missiles with conventional warheads falling on Israel; and no agreement with the United States on the coordination of Israeli military action.[97] He seemed to suggest a reevaluation of Israeli restraint only if these conditions changed.

In August 1992, two months after again becoming prime minister, Rabin reacted cautiously to renewed fears of Iraqi missile attacks in the wake of clashes over UN inspectors and the American forceful imposition of the "no fly zone" in southern Iraq. Rabin said then that if Iraq used missiles or chemical weapons, Israel had "a broad choice of responses."[98] He refused to go into details in public but added: "We will not accept a situation in which the Jewish state will be traumatized by the use of gas against her."[99] He hoped such statements would enhance deterrence.[100]

A SHIFT FROM SELF-RELIANCE

Rabin, as well as others in the defense establishment, gradually realized that some of the impending regional threats—missiles and weapons of mass destruction—could not be dealt with unilaterally.[101] In 1981, Israel eliminated the Iraqi nuclear threat for some time, but the question arose as to whether Israel could repeat such a feat single-handedly. Iran is farther from Israel than is Iraq. The limited success of the American strikes against Iraqi nuclear installations and the U.S. hesitations to use force against North Korea showed that in the 1990s, even a superpower had difficulties in destroying key components of a country's nuclear infrastructure. Rabin was fully aware of Israel's limitations and looked for international cooperation to meet the new challenge. He felt that the proliferation of such weapons meant trouble not only for Israel but also for the West. According to Rabin, only the United States was in the position to lead an international campaign to stop nuclear proliferation in the Middle East.[102] Rabin also relied on U.S. diplomacy, rather than Israeli diplomatic efforts, to prevent the sale of North Korean Nodong missiles to Iran.[103]

Rabin tried to complement deterrence with some measure of arms control in the area of weapons of mass destruction, a rather new feature in Israeli national security policies.[104] Yet he advocated a regional approach that would provide mutual verification by the regional actors, rather than adhering to international regimes with dubious verification mechanisms.[105] In January 1989, when the specter of chemical weapons in the Middle East was very visible, Rabin, in a lecture to a delegation of the European Parliament, proposed the inclusion of chemical weapons in an arms control treaty.[106]

Therefore, in September 1992, Rabin's government decided to sign the Chemical Weapons Convention (CWC), relinquishing Israel's previous insistence on prior signature from its Arab neighbors. This was not a regional arrangement but an international regime. The intrusive character of the CWC, which was initially considered as improving verification capabilities, later constituted a problem for Israel, which feared continuous indiscriminate inspections of its military installations. Indeed, in 1997 Israel declined ratification of the CWC.[107]

Rabin also approved Israel's willingness to adhere to the Comprehensive Test Ban Treaty (CTBT), which was put on the international arms control agenda in 1993.[108] Subsequently, an Israeli delegation was sent to the preparatory meetings in Geneva for drafting the treaty to safeguard Israeli interests.[109] Israel tried to find a balance between a reliable verification regime, which was germane to the effectiveness of the treaty, and a minimalization of unwarranted intrusiveness of inspections, which could expose Israel to espionage or to harassment by hostile powers. Israel wanted to establish an independent verification agency for this treaty, rather than trust the existing NPT/IAEA monitoring system. Israel's signature on the CTBT in 1995 was a formalization of the earlier Israeli pledge to the United States not to cross the testing threshold.

Before the NPT review conference in April 1995, the pressures, especially from Egypt, on Rabin's government to sign the NPT were mounting up. Yet Rabin, who realized that the United States had no intention of putting the NPT on the agenda in the bilateral relationship, resisted these pressures. Meanwhile the conference considered and eventually approved the treaty's indefinite extension.[110] Egypt tried to link the extension to changes in Israeli nuclear policies and attempted to organize a group of states to support its positions. Egypt also used the Arms Control and Regional Security (ACRS) multilateral forum, established in the aftermath of the 1991 Madrid Peace Conference, as a vehicle for this goal. Yet for Rabin, like most other Israelis, the post–Gulf War revelations about the advanced stage of the nuclear program in Iraq, which was a party to the NPT, vindicated their reservations about the NPT regime. Rabin's basic skepticism toward the NPT remained unchanged, and he continued to suggest instead a Middle Eastern NWFZ based on bilateral agreements and inspections.[111]

Rabin's government nevertheless hinted that its position on the NPT was no longer an uncompromising and categorical "no." The Israeli delegation to the ACRS suggested in December 1994 that the preamble to the ACRS statement indicate the willingness of all of the region's countries to consider becoming a part of the NPT and other international arms control regimes after the establishment of peace and a Weapons of Mass Destruction Free Zone. This formula, which was primarily intended to please the Egyptians, was approved by Rabin.[112] The Egyptians were not satisfied with the new Israeli language, but the Americans were, causing a strain in the American-Egyptian relations. Rabin succeeded in securing the American understanding that Israel held on to its last-resort weapon, while he displayed a willingness to take security risks in the peace process.[113]

Despite suggestions by Peres that Israel commit to a specific timetable for negotiating a Middle East NWFZ—an additional step to placate the Egyptians—Rabin preferred to stick to the traditional position, which linked such an arrangement to comprehensive peace in the region.[114] Rabin also opposed any plans for freezing the production of fissionable materials, such as the 1991 initiative of President George Bush and the 1993 initiative of President Bill Clinton, which were discussed at the highest policy echelons.[115] The "cut-off" proposals were termed by Rabin as "unworkable."[116] Though Rabin was ready to lower the nuclear profile, he wanted to keep Israel's nuclear option alive as long as possible.

In the 1990s, Israel under Rabin was, more than ever before, willing to experiment with collaborative security measures, primarily to delay the introduction of weapons of mass destruction into the Middle East.[117] This willingness extended also to the conventional arena. By November 1993, Israel under Rabin had begun to comply with international demands to report its arms sales to the UN arms registrar, and in May 1994, Israel agreed to an American request to ban the export of antipersonnel mines.

CONCLUSION

Rabin belonged to the conventional Israeli school of thought, which minimized the role of nuclear weapons in Israel's national security predicament. According to this strategic thinking, a conventional environment was preferable for Israel. Moreover, until the late 1980s and early 1990s, the general perception of this school of thought was that nuclearization of the Middle East was not an immediate problem. However, every effort had to be exercised to delay such a development for as long as possible.

Rabin seemed to have a good grasp of the intricacies of nuclear strategy. He realized that nuclear weapons were useful only in a very limited number of scenarios—when the very existence of the state or its most vital interests were in jeopardy. In any case, there is no evidence that Rabin initiated any organizational or doctrinal preparations in the IDF, or elsewhere, for the establishment of a nuclear second-strike force. It is not clear what preparations were made in Israel, under Rabin, for living among a nuclear-armed crowd.

Rabin was sensitized to the nuclear issue early in his military career, and while he was ambassador to the United States, he negotiated this issue with the Americans in order to minimize the tensions between the two countries. While he was prime minister in the 1970s, he and his colleagues made efforts to lower Israel's nuclear profile. Such a policy was continued by Rabin at the end of the 1980s and particularly in the 1990s.

The missile threat became quite real in the latter half of the 1980s, and the marriage between missiles and chemical weapons was frightening. In dealing with the threats posed by the proliferation of missiles and chemical weapons, Rabin preferred to emphasize deterrence over preemption. This was also in accordance with the national defensive strategy, analyzed in the previous chapter.

The specter of weapons of mass destruction in the Middle East was most apparent during and after the 1991 Gulf War. Rabin's second government was thus very concerned about the spread of weapons of mass destruction to the Middle East. Rabin hoped that the United States could alleviate some of the new security challenges. Moreover, his government displayed a greater willingness than had any of its predecessors to engage in arms control schemes. It signed the CWC and the CTBT. Nevertheless, Rabin zealously guarded Israel's nuclear option from any erosion, in spite of the pressures, at home and abroad, to limit the nuclear program.

CHAPTER SIX

RABIN OF THE 1990s:
THE CHANGING STRATEGIC
ASSESSMENT

The previous chapters have dealt primarily with Yitzhak Rabin the military man, who focused his attention almost exclusively on defense matters. Yet Rabin never forgot that the political atmosphere was an important variable in the national security equation. The political climate, he knew, was critical to the transition from dormant war to engaging in actual war or, conversely, to making peace possible. Indeed, the last chapter in Rabin's career was characterized by his attempts to conclude peace treaties between Israel and its neighbors.

In 1992, Rabin succeeded in wresting the leadership of the Labor Party from his longtime rival Shimon Peres, and that June he led the party to its first clear-cut electoral victory since 1973. Subsequently, Rabin formed a government committed to ensuring security and to pursuing peace with Israel's neighbors. His coalition did not include any hawkish parties, and it planned to capitalize on the peace process launched at the October 1991 Madrid Conference. This process grew out of the new political atmosphere in the Middle East, resulting primarily from the victory of the American-led coalition in the 1991 Gulf War.

In the last years of Rabin's life, during the early 1990s, he developed a new diagnosis of Israel's strategic predicament.[1] As a result of his new evaluation of the strategic equation, he changed some of his views on key issues and departed from positions that he had held for many years. This was, of course, translated into Israeli policies once he assumed the posts of premier and defense minister in July 1992. Israel under Rabin indicated its readiness to make a significant withdrawal on the Golan Heights and handed over parts of the West Bank and Gaza Strip (the Land of Israel) to the Palestinians. Many Israelis were surprised by the magnitude of Israel's concessions. The domestic controversy over the government's policies and the opposition within Israel to the steps taken by Rabin's government gradually intensified, and the political discourse became increasingly strident. The growing tension and acrimony over the peace process created an atmosphere in which a young, right-wing extremist assassinated Rabin.

This chapter analyzes Rabin's evaluation of the strategic environment of the 1990s and his positions on the Syrian, Palestinian, and Jordanian tracks of the peace negotiations. It evaluates the continuity and change in Rabin's views on the Arab-Israeli conflict and concludes with an attempt to understand the "old-new" Rabin.

THE NEW STRATEGIC DIAGNOSIS

Rabin always paid close attention to the international scene and to the linkages between global developments and Middle East regional dynamics. In the 1990s he concluded that Israel faced a much better strategic environment than ever before. At the global level, he viewed the Soviet Union's collapse as a dramatic, positive change, creating an entirely new international reality. He credited this development in part with opening the door to the Middle East peace process. Israel's adversaries had lost their "Soviet umbrella," a political-military relationship that was an important factor in the Arab ability to confront Israel.[2] Concomitantly, the United States, Israel's traditional ally, emerged as the hegemonic power in the international arena. The new unipolar moment in world politics was seen as having a largely stabilizing impact on the Middle East and particularly on the Arab-Israeli conflict.[3]

Also new was Rabin's evaluation of Israel's international status. In the past, Rabin had seen Israel as an isolated state that could rely only on itself. He sensed this acutely as chief of staff on the eve of the 1967 war. In the period immediately after the 1973 war, at the peak of Israel's isolation in world politics, he had a similar experience as prime minister. But later, in his seventh decade, Rabin began to notice that attitudes toward the Jewish state were changing, and this mitigated his fears and suspicions of the gentile world. The Eastern European countries, once in the Soviet orbit, renewed the diplomatic relations with Israel that they had severed in 1967. The former Soviet republics, even the Moslem ones, opened diplomatic legations. Similarly, following the Madrid Conference, several Third World countries, including China and India, established full diplomatic relations with Israel. In a 1992 speech, Rabin emphasized the change in Israel's diplomatic history: "Israel is no longer 'a people that dwells alone.' "[4]

Known for his realpolitik approach to regional and world politics, Rabin also began to speak in terms he had never used before, terms that surprised many of those who closely followed his views and policies.[5] In his 1992 inaugural address to the Knesset, Rabin spoke of an emerging "new world" and of his government's duty to investigate the risks as well as the opportunities for making peace. Quite uncharacteristically, he lectured about the need "to join the campaign of peace, reconciliation and international cooperation spreading all over the globe."[6] This terminology had been used since the 1980s by Peres and other left-of-center political leaders, but it was entirely new for Rabin.

At the regional level, Rabin also identified several international developments that were positive from Israel's perspective. One important event that Rabin regarded as conducive to Israel's security was the defeat of Iraq by the U.S.-led coalition.[7] Iraq, a bitter enemy of Israel, had great military potential, so its defeat was in Israel's interest. Furthermore, Rabin believed that the American intervention in the Persian Gulf had had a positive effect on the American extended deterrence (deterrence against an attack on a third party) in the case of Israel, whose informal alliance with the United States would now more forcefully discourage an Arab attack. The American display of political will and its stunning military performance strengthened Israel's deterrence against a possible Arab military challenge.[8]

An additional development that considerably strengthened Israel was the immigration of over half a million people from the former Soviet Union.[9] The influx of such a large number of people, many of whom were highly skilled professionals, expanded the economy. Little Israel started acquiring the necessary demographic critical mass that it considered sufficient to force the Arabs to come to terms with Israel and to realize that their dream of destroying the Jewish state was unrealistic. In concluding his overall assessment of the regional environment in 1992, Rabin said: "We live today in a period in which the threat to the very existence of Israel has been reduced."[10] His traditional existential fears were "reduced" (but not eliminated), and he displayed a much lower threat perception.

In 1993, in front of his favorite audience, a gathering of the most senior Israel Defense Force (IDF) officers, Rabin emphasized: "The world is *no longer* against us. . . . States that never stretched their hand out to us, states that condemned us, that assisted our bitterest enemies . . . regard us today as a worthy and respectable address. . . . This is a new reality."[11] He then added: "We must think differently, look at things in a different way. Peace requires a world of new concepts, new definitions."[12] Such language was very new for Rabin and reflected his assessment of a much improved strategic situation.

Rabin's second tenure as prime minister was also characterized by a perception that the Middle East was ripe for an Arab-Israeli rapprochement. He sensed a change in Arab positions vis-à-vis Israel. Indeed the attainment of peace agreements with all Israel's Arab neighbors was regarded by Rabin to be within reach. From Rabin's perspective, the strategic equation allowed for negotiations from a position of strength, a sine qua non for progress toward regional acceptance of Israel. Syria and the Palestinians were weak. Syria had lost its superpower ally, and the Palestine Liberation Organization (PLO) had foolishly sided with Saddam Hussein, the losing side in the 1991 Gulf War. Moreover, by then the Intifada had lost much of its energy and had withered. Both Syria and the PLO were forced by the United States to come to Madrid and negotiate with Israel on its terms. Indeed, the terms of reference for the Madrid Conference were in accordance with Israel's demands: direct negotiations and no preconditions on an Israeli withdrawal from territories taken in 1967. The Palestinians also agreed to negotiate first an interim agreement, without an Israeli commitment to a Palestinian state in the future. In Israel, direct negotiations were always seen as facilitating the conclusion of agreements.

In July 1992, Rabin expressed his belief that due to the new international circumstances, Israel faced "a great hour, a special opportunity."[13] As early as 1990, Rabin had estimated that the Palestinians could be brought into a meaningful political dialogue with Israel. This was his impression from the contacts he had with Egyptian President Hosni Mubarak.[14] In early 1992, he still believed that an agreement with the Palestinians over autonomy was a real possibility if a "sane" policy was pursued.[15] So, in September 1993, he and the PLO leader Yasir Arafat signed the Declaration of Principles, which led to two additional accords on implementing the interim agreement between Israel and the Palestinian Authority (PA). Concerning Syria, the IDF Intelligence Branch had, since 1991, estimated that Hafez al-Assad had changed his strategy and was ready for reaching a peace agreement (on his terms) with Israel.[16] Using this intelligence evaluation, Rabin remarked in 1994 that even Syria wanted peace with Israel, though it was not doing what was "necessary to truthfully demonstrate to the Israeli people" that it had "genuinely turned toward peace."[17] Israel under Rabin was also successful in concluding a peace treaty with Hashemite Jordan in October 1994.

Rabin also succeeded in restoring good relations with the United States after a short period of strain caused by the settlement policies of Yitzhak Shamir's right-wing government (1990–92). During Rabin's August 1992 visit to the United States, he reestablished "strategic coordination" with Washington. Rabin convinced President George Bush that he was serious about making progress in the peace process and reordering Israel's priorities in such a way as to minimize construction beyond the Green Line. In exchange, the Bush administration approved $10 billion in loan guarantees intended to help Israel absorb the immigrants from the former Soviet Union, money that had been denied to the Shamir government. However, Rabin was aware that with the end of the cold war, the importance of small allies, such as Israel, for the United States was reduced, since their contribution in the containment of the Soviet Union was no longer needed. Indeed, in his relations with Washington, Rabin was very careful to preserve American diplomatic and financial support for Israel.[18] The benign regional environment and a strong relationship with America were the main ingredients that allowed for progress on the Arab-Israeli front.

Yet Rabin was a sober analyst and did not engage in utopian deliberations about a new Middle East, as did his colleague Peres.[19] In November 1993, Rabin said that although Israel welcomed peace, he had no illusions that it could be achieved overnight: "One hand will reach out for peace, the other we will keep poised on the trigger . . . the danger has not passed . . . in time of need we will pull that trigger."[20] In October 1994, Rabin said to the Knesset: "Peace is not blinding us. We are keeping our eyes open and closely examining what is happening around us. . . . We have not for a moment stopped training and increasing the IDF's capability in various spheres."[21] Rabin viewed the peace process as a lengthy historic development that left Israel and its neighbors in a state of armed peace—absence of aggression because of a military balance rather than because of the existence of a cordial relationship.

Rabin believed that Israel still faced serious military challenges. However, the nature and source of the danger had shifted in his thinking. Although the peace process *reduced* threats from Israel's immediate neighbors, Israel was *increasingly* threatened by "second-tier" countries such as Iraq and Iran. According to Rabin, the peace process had influenced the *probability* of the use of Arab force against Israel but not the Arab *capability* to harm Israel. The latter had actually been augmented.[22] Because of missiles and chemical and biological weapons, and because of efforts in the region to acquire nuclear weapons, Rabin warned that a future war could entail a large number of civilian casualties.[23] Like others, Rabin was very surprised, after the 1991 Gulf War, by the revelations about the great progress the Iraqis had made in the area of nonconventional weapons.

Similarly threatening was the growing appeal of Islamic radicalism in the region.[24] Rabin attributed great importance to this threat, and from the Knesset podium he called on all nations to devote greater attention to the danger of Islamic fundamentalism. This was, in his opinion, one of the main threats to the world in the near future. He pointed out that just as Israel had been the first to issue a warning about the Iraqi nuclear threat, it was now in the vanguard against radical Islam.[25] Rabin warned that Iranian-backed Islamic fundamentalism could spill out beyond the Arab world, especially to countries with Moslem communities.[26] In an interview with NBC on 26 July 1994, Rabin pointed to the existence of a wave of extreme Islamic terrorist movements linked to Iran and called on the world "to wake up and to realize the tremendous danger not only to Israel, not only to the peace between the Arab countries and people and Israel, but also the danger to moderate Arab regimes and Muslim regimes . . . [to] European, American, Latin American countries."[27]

Israeli fears of nuclear proliferation and Islamic extremism converged on Iran. This strong regional power was distant, 1,000 kilometers away, but was engaged in acquiring a nuclear bomb and in sponsoring Islamic terrorism and subversion throughout the Middle East. Therefore, Iran became the major enemy of Rabin's second government. This emphasis on the dangers from Iran was new for Rabin. Only a few years previously, when he had served as defense minister, Israel had sought an opening with the Islamic regime in Tehran. In October 1987 Rabin had criticized American support for Iraq in the war it waged against Iran, though he had acknowledged that Iran under Ayatollah Ruhollah Khomeini was a bitter enemy of Israel and that without a change in the regime, the Iranian anti-Israeli policy would continue. Nevertheless, he had added: "At the same time, allow me to say that for 28 out of 38 years [since the end of the War of Independence] Iran was a friend of Israel. If it could work for 28 years . . . why couldn't it happen again once this crazy idea of Shiite fundamentalism is gone?"[28] Following David Ben-Gurion's analysis, Rabin's geopolitical instincts told him that non-Arab Iran, which had historically been in conflict with the Arabs, was a potential Israeli ally. Rabin, like his predecessor Shamir, was unwilling to see Iran as a perpetual enemy and wanted to keep the option of Iranian realignment open.[29] In 1990, he still regarded the American tilt toward Iraq and against Iran as a historic mistake that had led to the Iraqi invasion of Kuwait,[30] but he later seemed to have come around to a belief that a change in Iranian policy toward Israel had become extremely unlikely. Moreover, a nuclear-armed Iran could become a formidable enemy. Rabin even contemplated whether officially to designate Iran as an "enemy state."[31]

Rabin's new strategic diagnosis blended an uncharacteristic optimism, based on an evaluation of several positive international and regional developments, with a very pessimistic assessment of the potential existential dangers to Israel, stemming primarily from the proliferation of missiles and weapons of mass destruction.

NATIONAL STRATEGY

Rabin's reevaluation of the strategic environment, particularly the new threats, led to a significant change in his strategy toward the Arab-Israeli conflict. This change centered on the time vector. In contrast to his long-held view that time was on Israel's side, he came to believe that Israel no longer had much time at its disposal. Starting in the late 1980s, Rabin advocated greater activism than before in the search for peace. In the last years of his life, there was a sense of unprecedented urgency in Rabin's statements, an urgency typical of Israeli doves.[32] The global and regional developments were seen by Rabin as providing a "window of opportunity" for reaching agreements between Israel and its neighbors.[33] This new term was American, imported into Israeli political language, and Rabin liked it very much.[34] It implied that there was a certain urgency in taking advantage of propitious conditions before the window closed. In August 1992, Rabin estimated that Israel had about five years to strengthen itself economically and to make peace with its neighbors before the threat of war became real.[35] For example, he said in 1994: "If Israel fails to reach a peace treaty with Syria in two to three years, I will suggest changing Israel's budgetary priorities in order to channel huge amounts of money to the IDF to allow preparations for a possible war with Syria."[36]

In addition to a conventional war, Rabin feared the proliferation of nuclear weapons. The nuclear progress of Iraq and Iran was extremely threatening and was an important factor in the evaluation of whether time was on Israel's side. As noted in the previous chapter, Rabin hoped to mobilize the assistance of the United States in curbing proliferation. Moreover, he accepted the prognosis of his rival Peres that the eventual nuclearization of the Middle East must be preceded by an Arab-Israeli détente in order to mitigate the consequences. One way to deal with this development was the attempt to complete the peace process begun with Egypt in the 1970s. Rabin wrote in 1992: "I believe that if we succeed within five to seven years to conclude peace, or almost peace, with the Palestinians, Jordan and afterwards with Syria, we will largely limit the motivation for a [nonconventional] arms race."[37] In his opinion, an attack by a second-tier country, even if ruled by an Islamic fundamentalist elite, was unlikely if Israel lived in peace with its immediate neighbors.[38]

Therefore, Rabin tried to capitalize on the available window of opportunity to make peace quickly. Rabin and his government assiduously attempted to conclude peace agreements with the first-tier countries around Israel. Portraying Iran, a second-tier country, as a formidable archenemy of Israel also helped to market the peace process to the Israeli public.[39] Rabin adopted a most determined attitude in bringing peace. For him, the quest for peace was similar to the determination to win a war, and he often referred to himself as a soldier in the battle for peace. He defined his responsibility as prime minister: "to do whatever can be done to exploit the unique opportunities that lie ahead of us to move towards peace."[40]

A secondary factor leading to the unprecedented urgency was the delicate domestic political situation. Rabin failed in 1992 to establish a government with a large majority in parliament. He headed a fragile coalition and feared that his government might lose its majority. This concern led Rabin to expedite the negotiations with the Palestinians, implying a greater willingness to make concessions.[41] Initially, Rabin refused to rely on the Arab parties' support in the Knesset for maintaining a parliamentary majority for his policies, preferring to rule with a "Jewish majority." He changed his mind, however, after the defection from the ruling coalition of the six MKs from the Shas Party and of two hawkish Labor MKs who opposed substantive territorial concessions to Syria.

Militarily, Rabin remained committed to the defensive strategy outlined in chapter 4. The benign strategic environment facilitated the maintenance of a defensive posture and reduced temptations to emphasize preemptive and preventive strikes. Deterrence remained the pillar of Israel's strategic doctrine under Rabin. The development of the long reach of the IDF, reviewed in chapter 3, came in response to the threats emanating from the second-tier countries. Rabin envisioned a constant military presence by the F-15I and the Saar-5 far from Israel to enhance conventional deterrence.[42] Moreover, as seen in the previous chapter, Rabin, in contrast to Peres, was unwilling to relinquish the nuclear option, which was needed, Rabin thought, to complement Israel's deterrent power in the area of weapons of mass destruction.

Rabin's tendency to use military force judiciously was also reinforced by the peace process, since Israel desired to project an image of restraint and moderation in order to encourage Arab elements interested in coexistence. In addition, Israeli decisions to use force have become tied to a more complex matrix of costs and benefits than when there was unanimous Arab support for Israel's destruction. For example, Israel refrained from hitting the Hizballah in southern Lebanon with greater force and more often in order not to cause an escalation that could have hindered the negotiations with Syria. Rabin had difficulties in persuading his dovish cabinet to escalate the struggle against the Hizballah, and it was only in July 1993 that Operation Accountability took place. Yet the IDF did not attack Syrian targets in Lebanon, even though Damascus controlled the logistical pipeline of the Hizballah, as well as its training and staging areas.

However, the peace process entails the dilemma that restraint meant to reassure the Arabs of Israeli moderation could be misunderstood as weakness or lack of resolve. Furthermore, Rabin preferred not to emphasize preemptive strikes against the security challenges stemming from the second-tier countries. The self-imposed restraint on the country's freedom of action was thus problematic for deterrence. The reputation for striking back when challenged is essential for maintaining deterrent power.[43] It is not clear whether Rabin was aware of this inherent contradiction of any political process designed to reduce tensions between rivals.

A significant change occurred in Rabin's assessment of the importance of terrorist activities. In the past, terrorism had been considered as basically a military nuisance with only marginal influence on Israel's existence. Israel under Rabin had fought terrorism with great determination, but this had always been a secondary arena. In 1993, Rabin still belittled the importance of Palestinian terrorist organizations and even that of the Hizballah, which had superior weaponry. "The PLO and other terrorist organizations are not an existential threat to the state of Israel and it would be an insult to the IDF were I to consider the Hamas and the Hizballah as a serious threat to Israel," he said.[44]

He was not oblivious, however, to the implications of terrorist acts for the domestic political arena.[45] The timing of such acts affected the outcome of the 1988 as well as the 1992 elections. He also realized the great public impact of terrorism and the political reverberations of such acts. In 1995 he complained to the editors of Israel's newspapers that they were giving too much coverage to such activities: "Look, one non-fatal stabbing and it appears in letters twice as big as those announcing the outbreak of the Six-Day War."[46] He admitted that the editors sensitized him to the fact that terrorist acts sell newspapers. The attraction of the media and the public to terrorist acts was politically significant.

Indeed, Rabin started regarding terrorist activities by Islamic fanatics as a serious factor in the peace process. This political evaluation was reinforced by a strategic reassessment. Reacting to the April 1994 suicide attack in Afula, Rabin finally recognized that terrorist activities by Hamas and other Islamic radicals were "a form of terrorism . . . different from what we once knew from the PLO terrorist organizations." Their mode of operation was reminiscent of the Hizballah tactics in southern Lebanon, which had caused "considerable harm and cost many lives."[47] Rabin admitted that there was no "hermetic" solution available to protect Israeli citizens against such terrorist attacks and that the only way to deal with them was through "a combination of a political solution and military action."[48] In the aftermath of the Tel Aviv suicide terrorist bombing on 19 October 1994, Rabin reiterated a similar analysis.[49]

By January 1995, following several suicide bombs attacks perpetrated by Hamas and resulting in many casualties and huge publicity, Rabin came to a conclusion: "Islamic terror is strategically significant."[50] He realized that terrorist attacks provided excellent ammunition for the opposition to the government to become more vocal and effective. He also understood that such incidents intensified the domestic pressure to freeze the Palestinian track of the peace process. Islamic terrorism thus initially contributed to the pressure for accelerating the negotiations on his part.[51]

Notably, his new evaluation of the great impact of the terrorist threat was more in consonance with the Likud's position of attributing great political importance to terrorism. (Indeed, the left-wing parliamentarian Shulamit Aloni, whose party was part of Rabin's coalition, attacked him for this.)[52] Furthermore, the Islamic terrorism in the territories or in South Lebanon was not "local" but was connected to a powerful transnational phenomenon. This terrorism was preserving the friction between Israel and the Arab and Islamic world. It was also dragging Israel into a conflict with Iran, a regional power that supported terrorism.[53]

Paradoxically, the Palestinian peace process, which was beneficial to Israel in overall strategic terms, was problematic in terms of counterterrorism.[54] Israeli security services lost intelligence and preventive capabilities by turning over territory to the PA. Despite the new evaluation of the importance of suppressing terrorist activities, Rabin did not divert greater resources to the organizations responsible for counterterrorism.

THE SYRIAN TRACK

After assuming office in 1992, Rabin zigzagged between giving priority to the Syrian and to the Palestinian tracks.[55] There were apprehensions that Assad could block progress on the Palestinian track, but Rabin was not averse to the notion of playing Syria and the Palestinians against each other. Neither, Rabin conjectured, would want to be the last Arab actor negotiating a peace agreement with Israel, because that would leave it with reduced leverage. The pragmatic Rabin was willing to proceed with any partner who promised progress. On the one hand, the Palestinian track was attractive because it was premised on a step-by-step approach, aiming first for an interim agreement. Rabin had always favored a gradual approach to progress in the Arab-Israeli conflict. Incremental progress was the premise for the Sinai 2 Agreement that U.S. Secretary of State Henry Kissinger had mediated between Rabin and Egyptian President Anwar Sadat in 1975 and that, in the 1980s, became Rabin's guiding principle in dealing with the Palestinian problem. On the other hand, dealing first with Syria, the strongest remaining military foe among the first-tier countries, appealed to the power-oriented Rabin. According to his state-centered prism of the Arab-Israeli conflict, removing states from the circle of enmity was most important. President Assad of Syria was a more respected rival than Arafat or any other Palestinian leader. Furthermore, the dispute with Syria seemed to be less complicated than the Israeli-Palestinian rivalry.

A clear inhibiting factor was Rabin's initial reluctance to make substantial territorial concessions on the Golan Heights, which he considered a great strategic asset. In fact, in June 1992, during the election campaign, Rabin had promised voters: "We will not leave the Golan Heights, not even in exchange for a peace treaty. We will be ready for a limited compromise and it does not have to include territorial terms."[56] He flirted with the idea of leasing the plateau from the Syrians.[57] After 1967 Rabin supported settling Jews on the Golan, and most of the settlers were connected politically to the Labor Party. Indeed, he told the settlers before the 1992 elections that he was proud that Qazrin, the Golan's main Jewish town, was founded during his first term as prime minister, and he promised that his future government would continue to invest in the Golan Heights. He added: "Descending from the Heights means the abandonment of Israel's security."[58]

In the past, Rabin had been willing to consider only what he termed "cosmetic" changes in Israel's deployment on the Golan, which included the dismantlement of a few settlements.[59] His reservations about reaching a deal with Syria by granting significant territorial concessions on the Golan reflected the overwhelming public sentiment against any withdrawal.[60] Yet Rabin understood well that Assad was unlikely to settle for less than Sadat had in 1979, and this is precisely why Rabin hesitated to emphasize the Syrian track. The Egyptian precedent, in which Israel withdrew to the international border in exchange for a peace treaty, was compelling.[61] Rabin was not sure he would be able to evade this historic rationale.

At the time Rabin came to power, not much progress had been made in the bilateral talks that had started after the Madrid Conference.[62] The Israeli unwillingness to discuss any withdrawal before the Syrians specified the substance of peace (i.e., the type of diplomatic relations and the nature of other interactions), Syria's refusal to do so and insistence on dealing with the territorial issue first, and the American evaluation that any intervention at this stage of the negotiations was premature led to an impasse at the Washington talks.

Rabin wanted to break the impasse and appeared to adopt a new position on the strategic importance of territory, including the Golan Heights. First, his newly appointed envoy to Washington and head of the delegation to the talks with Syria, Professor Itamar Rabinovich, accepted on 24 August 1992 the principle of implementing United Nations Resolution 242 (which included a withdrawal clause) regarding the Golan, a clear departure from the Shamir government's position. Taking into consideration the Labor Party's platform, which also advocated "territorial compromise" with Syria, and Rabin's own willingness to consider a limited withdrawal on the Golan, Israel's new flexibility was not so surprising.[63] Indeed, Rabin announced from the Knesset podium in September that Israel would be ready to give up some territory on the Golan Heights in exchange for peace.[64] Presumably in exchange, Assad spoke in public of the possibility of the "peace of the brave" with Israel, although he was reluctant to clarify what he meant by the term.[65] These developments caused a stir, with Israel's foreign minister, Peres, commenting that progress was "almost sensational."[66] Rabin instructed Rabinovich to find out whether Syria was indeed ready to sign a peace treaty without any linkage to the Palestinian or Jordanian negotiations. He was adamant in his refusal to accept the Syrian condition of linkage between progress on the Syrian track and a comprehensive agreement on all outstanding issues of the Arab-Israeli conflict.

Although Rabin (like his predecessor Shamir) refused to specify the extent of a possible Israeli withdrawal, or to enter discussions on security arrangements without prior knowledge of what kind of peace Syria had in mind, dovish members of the Rabin government, such as Shulamit Aloni, Yossi Sarid, and Uzi Baram, expressed their view that a full withdrawal had to be considered. In December 1992, Rabin thought that the Syrians were reluctant to make peace in the Israeli sense of the term (full diplomatic relations and free movement of goods and people) and were also unwilling to decouple the issue of bilateral relations from other issues in the Arab-Israeli conflict.[67] Despite the improved atmosphere at the negotiations, the Israeli and Syrian positions reached a deadlock, with each side waiting for the other to make a conciliatory move. Rabin's expulsion of a large group of Hamas activists to Lebanon in December 1992 provided an excuse for slowing the peace process. Furthermore, all sides looked to the new administration in Washington, under President Bill Clinton, to provide renewed impetus once it shaped its own Middle East policy.

The renewed American involvement in the process and Rabin's commitment to pursue seriously the chance of peace with Syria led to a reassessment in his thinking. In contrast to his past statements in favor of holding on to the Golan Heights, Rabin began contemplating full withdrawal from the strategic plateau. By the beginning of 1993, Rabin had formulated a new slogan for negotiations with the Syrians: "The depth of the withdrawal will correspond to the depth of the peace."[68] This position was welcomed and embraced by the Israeli left, which understood it to constitute a willingness to part with all the Golan plateau in exchange for a peace treaty along the lines of the Egyptian precedent. Although Rabin would have preferred less than a full withdrawal, he continued to express his doubts about whether, given the precedent of the return of the entire Sinai to Egypt, the Syrians would accept anything less.[69] Moreover, he juxtaposed the security risk involved in the withdrawal from the Golan Heights with the risks taken in the withdrawal from the Sinai. Though he still regarded the Golan as a piece of real estate with military importance, Rabin now noted: "The importance of peace is extraordinary."[70]

Surprisingly, on 3 August 1993, Rabin crossed the Rubicon on the issue of withdrawal. In response to a hypothetical question posed by U.S. Secretary of State Warren Christopher, who was then visiting the region, Rabin replied that if Syria would agree to the security arrangements and the type of peaceful relations demanded by Israel, Israel might fully withdraw from the Golan Heights.[71] Rabinovich confirmed the reports that Rabin had deposited with Christopher a verbal agreement in principle to discuss Syria's demands for a withdrawal to the 1967 lines. This deposit, however, was conditional on Syria's acceptance of Israel's peace package, including security arrangements and the full-fledged peace that Israel envisaged.[72] Rabin was skeptical about Assad's willingness to accept the package.[73] Moreover, in accordance with his American orientation, Rabin seemed to prefer a situation in which the United States could not blame Israel for lack of progress, despite the fact that there was no American pressure on Israel.[74] Subsequently, Christopher was unsuccessful in securing approval for the hypothetical deal from Assad. The cultural differences between Rabin and Assad were probably also a contributing factor in the unsuccessful negotiations.[75]

As a result of the impasse with Syria, Rabin decided to progress on the Palestinian track via the clandestine contacts then taking place in Oslo.[76] The two strategic decisions during the summer of 1993 on the Syrian and the Palestinian tracks were taken by Rabin himself, without any consultations with his advisers. Even the IDF top brass was kept in the dark. In fact, the General Staff's proposal for an IDF withdrawal line on the Golan Heights included a recommendation against total withdrawal, even in times of peace.[77] Rabin seems to have relied on his own intuition and rich experience rather than on staff work and consultation with his colleagues.

Although Rabin faced increased domestic opposition to the concessions made to the Palestinians, as well as a more organized resistance to a potential withdrawal from the Golan Heights, he nevertheless persisted in his attempts to reach an agreement with Syria. In May 1994, the *New York Times* reported that the Rabin government had offered to withdraw from the Golan Heights in three phases over a five-to-eight-year period in return for peace and normal relations with Syria.[78] On 18 July 1994, Rabin even indicated to the American mediators his willingness to consider accepting Assad's ultimatum demanding Israeli withdrawal to the line of 6 June 1967.[79] During the summer of 1994, the Israeli offer for full withdrawal became more explicit. Peres declared, "Israel has accepted Syrian sovereignty on the Golan Heights on many occasions."[80] No denial or rebuttal came from the prime minister's office. Actually, a few days later the information was leaked that the Egyptian-Israeli peace treaty was to be the model for the Syrian track.[81] This meant, inter alia, that a full withdrawal could take place within three years. Indeed, the chief of IDF intelligence, Maj. Gen. Uri Sagui, told the Knesset Committee for Foreign and Security Affairs on 9 August 1994 that if he were the Syrian intelligence chief, he would have concluded, on the basis of the statements coming from Israel, that the Israeli government was ready to give up all of the Golan Heights.[82]

Other issues over which negotiations were taking place were the scope of the security arrangements,[83] the extent and timing of the withdrawal stages, and the linkage between these stages and the normalization of relations. Rabin's guiding principle in the negotiations was indeed the Egyptian precedent, whereas Assad seemed to offer less than the Egyptians had on all issues but expected to get more than the Israelis had conceded to Egypt in 1979.[84] It is worth noting that the Rabin government no longer demanded the evacuation of Syrian forces from Lebanon but instead insisted on a Syrian guarantee to prevent a war of attrition from southern Lebanon, which implied an Israeli recognition of the Syrian occupation of that country. In December 1994, the two sides decided to send military experts to Washington to deal in detail with the security arrangements, and the two chiefs of staff even met there on 21 December 1994, but there was no real progress.[85] During 1995, Syria accepted the principle of asymmetry in the size of demilitarization zones in exchange for symmetry in the reduction of the regular forces. However, Rabin's repeated calls for a summit meeting with Assad, or at least an upgrading of the diplomatic level of the negotiations, remained unanswered. Finally, Rabin, with his eye on the polls, became increasingly skeptical about the electoral wisdom of concluding a deal with Syria before the 1996 elections; such a deal could cost him many votes and could decrease his chances to retain power after the elections. The Oslo agreements were themselves encountering much domestic resistance, which would only be intensified by a decision to withdraw from the Golan Heights as well.[86]

Nevertheless, Rabin continued to prepare the Israeli public for the territorial concessions entailed in a peace treaty with Syria. On 18 January 1994, four days after the Clinton-Assad Geneva summit, Rabin instructed his deputy at the Defense Ministry, Mordechai Gur, to suggest a national referendum to approve a treaty with Syria if the territorial price would be substantial. The referendum proposal was not the result of any detailed staff work but was Rabin's own idea, and it surprised everybody at home and abroad. Rabin believed he had no mandate from the electorate for a withdrawal from the Golan Heights, and he felt the need to get the approval of the people for such a drastic move.[87] The referendum, an unprecedented measure in Israeli political culture, may also have served as a signal to Assad that Rabin's own bargaining freedom was limited, since any negotiated settlement required convincing a majority of the Israelis of its value.

Rabin indicated several times during 1994 that he was considering withdrawal from the Golan plateau. In April 1994, at the Labor-linked TAKAM kibbutz movement convention (including representatives of the Golan kibbutzim), Rabin declared: "Peace with Syria would provide more security than a few settlements on the Golan."[88] Rabin's devaluation of the "security contribution" of settlements was closely linked to the assessment, prevalent in dovish circles, that territories had diminished strategic value. In October, Rabin justified his plea for changing long-held security views; he stated to personal friends living on the Golan Heights: "The world has changed, and the Arab countries too, though not all."[89] Emphasizing his own responsibility for pursuing every opportunity to make peace, he added that it was also the responsibility of the Golan settlers to take into account the benefits that peace would bring to all of Israel. Speaking from the Knesset rostrum, Rabin asked the Golan settlers: "Shouldn't we try to make an effort to reach peace? Can we reject out of hand the possibility of putting an end to all wars?"[90]

In September 1994, Rabin tried to dissuade six Labor MKs from submitting a private bill intended to strengthen Israel's constitutional hold on the Golan Heights and accused them of "destroying the peace process."[91] At a party caucus in February 1995, he again opposed this legislative initiative and demanded freedom of action for his government's negotiations with Syria.[92] Rabin's confidence was based in part on indications from his pollsters that he could carry the day in a referendum on a Syrian peace treaty that involved full withdrawal from the Golan Heights.[93]

In his negotiations with Syria, Rabin was greatly disappointed with President Assad, who failed, in his opinion, to reciprocate Israel's tremendous concessions.[94] In February 1994, on Israeli television, Rabin said: "Regretfully, even if I believe that Syria wants peace, according to its behavior Syria is not doing what is necessary to truthfully demonstrate to the Israeli people that it has genuinely turned toward peace. . . . I do not expect that Assad will dare to do what President Sadat did during his visit to Jerusalem, but there is still much to be done in order to demonstrate the

Syrian government's desire for peace."[95] Although he appreciated the fact that Syrian television broadcast the meetings between Rabin and King Hussein of Jordan, he complained that Assad was unwilling to emulate the small covert or public steps taken by Egypt and Jordan before concluding peace with Israel. Rabin suggested several possible confidence-building measures, such as mutual visits of journalists or the acceptance by Damascus of a delegation of parents of soldiers missing in action.[96] But in January 1995, Assad rejected Rabin's call for a summit between the two in order to bridge the differences.[97]

One week before his death, Rabin again probed Assad's intentions as he approved an American mediating effort and submitted a "non-paper" on the security arrangements between the two sides.[98] The skeptical Rabin remained unconvinced that Assad was ready to join other Arab actors in signing a peace treaty with Israel and in starting a process of reconciliation with the Jewish state. As far as Rabin was concerned, he could do no more to bring about an Israeli-Syrian peace. Many others in the Israeli leadership, even reputed doves such as Yossi Beilin, shared the evaluation that Assad had not risen to the occasion and was probably not very keen on reaching a peace treaty with Israel.[99] Similarly, U.S. Secretary of State Christopher blamed Assad for missing a historic opportunity to conclude a peace agreement with a Rabin-led Israel.[100]

THE PALESTINIAN TRACK

Rabin did not believe that the protracted conflict with the Palestinians could be easily resolved. Therefore, he continued to adhere to an incremental approach to this problem, as designed in the Camp David Accords and the Madrid Conference. At the same time, he identified a "window of opportunity" and was determined to keep his election campaign promise to reach an interim agreement with the Palestinians within six to nine months. Yet the Washington talks did not progress well, and Rabin increasingly realized that the PLO could not be circumvented. In March 1993, he even agreed to permit Faisal Husseini, a resident of Jerusalem and a prominent Palestinian leader with close ties to the PLO, to join the Palestinian negotiating team in Washington, but no substantial change occurred.[101]

The disillusionment with the Washington talks was the main reason why Rabin agreed to open several other channels to the Palestinians.[102] He also agreed to continue the clandestine Israeli-PLO dialogue in Oslo, started by

Yossi Beilin and sponsored by Peres.[103] Rabin was informed about the contacts with the PLO almost from the beginning and decided to keep the talks secret from the officials in the two ministries under his control. Initially, Rabin did not attribute great importance to the Oslo channel.[104] He allowed the low-profile meetings to continue as long as secrecy was maintained and the Washington talks continued.[105] Nonetheless, he became personally involved in directing the Israeli team and in upgrading its membership when the secret negotiations turned more serious.

Much to his surprise, the PLO showed some flexibility, which allowed for reaching an agreement. In Washington, on 13 September 1993, Israel and the PLO signed a breakthrough Declaration of Principles (DOP) on Palestinian interim self-government.[106] This historic accord was followed by two additional agreements specifying the implementation of the interim stage. Both were negotiated by Rabin. The first, signed in Cairo on 4 May 1994, handed over the Gaza Strip and the Jericho area to the nascent PA.[107] According to the second agreement, signed on 24 September 1995 in Taba, Israel would withdraw from six major Palestinian cities in the West Bank, giving them the same status as Gaza and Jericho, and would extend full civilian authority of the PA (including internal security) to all the Palestinians in the West Bank. The agreement also stipulated three additional redeployments of the IDF (from areas B and C), which would leave under Israel's control only the Jewish settlements and unspecified "military locations."[108] Rabin always emphasized that the agreements with the Palestinians did not constitute a peace treaty but were only a first phase toward the permanent solution of the Israeli-Palestinian conflict.[109]

Rabin deviated from his past preferences on an important issue—his firm opposition to any dealings with the PLO (see chapter 1). Even after the PLO finally accepted a two-state solution (Israeli and Palestinian) at the end of 1988, Rabin still termed the group a "murderous terrorist organization."[110] Rabin said that a dialogue with the Palestinian inhabitants of the Israeli-ruled territories might possibly lead to coexistence; in contrast, talks with the PLO meant discussing the establishment of a Palestinian state, the division of Jerusalem, and the "right of return" for Palestinian refugees. Rabin firmly opposed even putting these issues on the agenda. As late as March 1993, Rabin refused to accept an American suggestion to negotiate with the PLO, despite his growing realization that the Palestinians within the territories did not have the political leeway to reach an agreement without PLO approval. He took this position precisely because he did not want to meet the PLO's demand for a Palestinian state with Jerusalem as its capital.[111] (At that time, the Oslo back channel for Israeli-PLO negotiations was operating, but Rabin was skeptical about its chances for success.)

In retrospect, the change in Rabin's position toward the PLO is not that surprising. His pragmatism enabled him to accommodate revisions in his stance on the negotiating partner. If convinced that a change was necessary or expedient, Rabin could adjust his views to new circumstances and accept the PLO as an interlocutor.[112] As discussed in the first chapter, he had tested the PLO's intentions in the past. Moreover, Rabin believed that he had achieved his main goals in the negotiations with the Palestinians. The DOP was a bilateral agreement not linked to progress with any other Arab state. The PLO recognized Israel and promised to amend the PLO Covenant; it renounced the use of terrorism and other acts of violence.[113] Generally, the DOP clauses met Rabin's approval because they were in accordance with his basic requirements: the final disposition of the political nature of the emerging Palestinian entity and its borders was delayed to a second phase, designed to deal with permanent status issues; all the settlements remained under Israeli control; Jerusalem was not included in the area under the jurisdiction of the Palestinians during the interim agreement; Israel reserved overall responsibility for the security of all the Israelis in the Israeli-ruled territories; and the IDF maintained responsibility for external security.[114]

Moreover, Rabin believed that the DOP clause stating that the outcome of the permanent status negotiations would not be prejudiced by interim agreements; Article V.4 indeed kept all options open.[115] Immediately after the deal with the PLO, Rabin felt that the agreement did not entail grave security risks to the state of Israel and that it was not dangerous even in terms of personal security for the Israelis.[116] In his evaluation, Israel's superior power sufficed to preserve its vital interests, and the concessions made could be revoked in case of a serious violation of the agreement on the part of the Palestinians.[117] The suggestion that most concessions were reversible seemed somewhat incongruous with the pragmatic nature of Rabin, who understood very well that facts on the ground have an impact on determining the future. The timing of the agreement was also important for Rabin, because the Mideast was, in his opinion, "in the midst of a wave of Khomeinism in the Arab and Muslim world."[118]

Yet the entrenchment of Palestinian rule in parts of the territories brought them nearer to the goal of a Palestinian state, which Rabin opposed. He realized that the self-rule granted to the Palestinians within the framework of the proposed Gaza-Jericho interim arrangement could lead to a Palestinian state.[119] Actually, in 1995 Rabin was willing to accept a

Palestinian state limited to the Gaza Strip.[120] Rabin agreed also to the September 1995 Oslo II Agreement, which constituted an important step toward a Palestinian state by extending the authority of the PA to all Palestinian cities in the West Bank.[121] Indeed, the agreements reached with the PLO treated all territories as an indivisible political unit, reducing the chances for revisions in Israel's eastern border along the lines of the Allon Plan—which Rabin had supported in the past. The September 1995 Oslo II Agreement even eroded the Allon Plan map (see chapter 1). It extended Palestinian rule to villages that controlled the two highways to Jerusalem, the Jordan Rift roads, and the access to the Etzion Bloc. Under the Allon Plan, all these areas were to be annexed by Israel.

Despite his qualms during the negotiations with Arafat, Rabin did not regret his historic decisions that led to the repartitioning of the Land of Israel. He followed the historic willingness of mainstream Zionism to reach a territorial compromise with the Arabs living in Palestine. He always emphasized that he did not belong to the Greater Israel camp. Separation—a new term in Israeli political parlance that denoted the partition of the Land of Israel between Arabs and Jews, as well as a reduction in the contact and the friction between the two populations—became Rabin's operative goal on the Palestinian track. This is why, in March 1993, he imposed a closure on the territories in response to a wave of terrorist acts.[122] Separation was repeatedly put forward by Rabin as a political and ideological choice. He was interested in "a political solution" that would not "blur the demarcation lines between Jews and Israelis on one side, and Palestinians on the other side."[123] Thus he favored a withdrawal from the Palestinian cities and areas heavily populated by Arabs.

Interestingly, Rabin did not hold even one session in the cabinet or elsewhere to discuss the long-range implications of the Oslo agreements. He was a loner and kept all his deliberations to himself. He admitted to his strategic adviser, Haim Assa: "I do not know what to do with advisers."[124] He often did not explain his decisions, either to his subordinates or to his colleagues in the government. Even his closest advisers did not know where he was heading. As a matter of fact, Rabin communicated to his entourage considerable ambiguity regarding the agreements with the Palestinians. For example, in the spring of 1994, when Assa devised a solution to overcome one impasse in the negotiations, Rabin's closest advisers, Eitan Haber and Shimon Sheves, reproached Assa because they were not sure that the boss was really interested in overcoming that hurdle at that particular time.[125]

The only thing Rabin continued to insist on was his reluctance to rule over a large number of Arabs, which could lead to a binational state. If he had any additional strategic goals or any clear vision of where the Oslo process should go, he did not share it with others. According to Beilin, the architect of the Oslo agreements, Rabin refrained from dealing with final status issues and suppressed any thoughts about them.[126] The hawks in his party, such as cabinet member Shimon Shitreet, also criticized the government's lack of clarity concerning the goals for the future. Shitreet prodded Rabin several times to discuss the long-range plans of the government, particularly Israel's future borders, but to no avail.[127] Rabin the arch-pragmatist preferred to deal with the present rather than speculate about the future. He was particularly averse to engaging in such speculation with his fellow politicians, whom he held in low esteem.

The reluctance to present the premises and specify the objectives of his policy was also politically motivated. Rabin believed ambiguity to be useful in reducing the opposition to the concessions he had in mind for the future.[128] This may also have been Rabin's way of dealing with the inevitability of a Palestinian state, a scenario he did not like at all. Instead of analyzing the situation together with his colleagues and reaching conclusions about where the process was going, he deferred the analysis. Though far from enthusiastic about the prospect, he seems to have reconciled himself in private to the emergence of a Palestinian state. His analytical abilities simply could not lead him to another conclusion.[129]

He remained, however, ambivalent about the road he had chosen. Initially, it was clear to all who observed him that he could not stand the presence of PLO Chairman Arafat. Rabin's body language betrayed his true feelings. In public he confessed to how difficult it was for him to shake Arafat's hand: "Of all the hands in the world, this was the one I never wanted or even dreamed of touching."[130] Yet Arafat succeeded in changing Rabin's attitudes. He learned how Rabin operated, noting in particular Rabin's penchant for details, and adapted himself to the Israeli leader's style. Arafat was a skilled negotiator, and more than once he was able to end up with much more than Rabin had originally been willing to bargain away.[131] According to Rabin's wife, Leah: "As his relationship with Arafat matured, Yitzhak's comments to me reflected his increasing respect for the veteran Palestinian leader as a strong and intelligent man who was nevertheless not easy to work with."[132]

From the beginning, however, Rabin doubted whether Arafat was the right partner. The IDF, under Chief of Staff Ehud Barak, was critical about the security aspects of the Oslo Agreement, which reinforced Rabin's suspicions, whereas Peres tried to persuade him not to pay attention to "minor details."[133] Initially, Rabin considered the PA struggle against terrorism and its ability to successfully manage local Palestinian affairs as the two litmus tests for evaluating the success of the Oslo Agreement.[134] Yet Arafat's negotiating tactics, the inefficient takeover of Gaza, and Arafat's resistance to accountability or transparency in administering the funds being donated to the PA by foreign countries exasperated the Israelis.[135] Rabin, as well as other Israeli leaders, found Arafat's May 1994 call for Jihad to liberate Jerusalem totally unacceptable and a breach of the agreement.[136] Israeli protests did not prevent Arafat from repeating such inflammatory language.[137] The suicide terrorist attacks in October 1994 and in January 1995, which originated from the territory under Arafat's rule, further undermined Israeli confidence in Arafat's intentions and/or capability to deliver what he promised. Israel's continuous demand that the PA combat terrorism stemmed not only from a desire to minimize its human losses. Israeli insistence on cooperation against terrorism was a continuous test of Arafat's determination to confront the enemies of reconciliation with Israel within Palestinian society.[138]

Rabin appreciated the fact that Arafat stopped, for all intents, all acts of violence by the Fatah group (the largest PLO component),[139] but several times he publicly questioned Arafat's commitment to deliver on what Rabin considered to be the main part of the deal—the struggle against terrorism. Rabin told the Labor Knesset faction on 31 August 1994: "We cannot bear for long a situation where the PA does not act against the terror perpetrated by the Hamas. If the PLO does not combat terror, it will negatively affect the peace process."[140] He explained that he did not expect the PA to be able to totally eradicate terrorist activities but that he did expect a greater effort. He also reported that Israel would not transfer several civilian functions to the PA, as required by the agreement with the Palestinians, before he was convinced that the PA could fulfill these responsibilities.[141]

At the end of 1994, Rabin was very pessimistic about Arafat's performance. He admitted that the PA had taken certain actions to prevent terrorism or to capture its perpetrators, but he added: "We do not feel that enough has been done. . . . The results up until now have been far from satisfactory—to use an understatement."[142] Indeed, the chief of intelligence, Major General Sagui, in his periodic report to the government, gave very low grades to Arafat in three critical areas of activity: security, administration, and economics.[143] Nevertheless, under Rabin's instructions, the IDF continued preparing plans for evacuating the Palestinian cities, for conducting the Palestinian elections, and for providing better access to settlements by building bypass roads.[144] In April 1995, in an interview on ABC television, Rabin said that he did not believe that Arafat was serious in maintaining law and order in Gaza and Jericho. Although he emphasized that there was no alternative to negotiations with Arafat, who was despite everything a partner willing to make peace, the fulfillment of Israeli commitments was conditioned on Arafat's ability to combat the terrorism originating in the areas under his rule.[145]

Even at the time that Rabin approved the September 1995 Taba agreement, which transferred additional territory to the PA jurisdiction, Rabin stated unequivocally: "They have to show more determination to cope with terror." He complained about Palestinian violations of previously made pledges, such as the extradition of terrorists and the annulment of the offensive clauses in the Palestinian Covenant.[146]

Rabin's disappointment with the policy, which was not initiated by him but for which he was ultimately responsible, became more and more evident with the passage of time and reflected the public's wary mood toward the peace process.[147] Although Rabin's faith in cooperative security arrangements with the PA eroded, and his skeptical nature increasingly questioned whether Arafat was the right partner, he remained committed to the idea that the peace process with the Palestinians should continue unabated. He even said: "We have passed the point of no return."[148] This is why he eventually signed the September 1995 agreement, but it does not provide a satisfactory explanation of the magnitude of the concessions made.

Rabin believed that despite the losses caused by Palestinian terrorism and the concessions made to the PA, the chances for creating a new political reality—one markedly more beneficial for Israel—were greater than the risks involved. He often mentioned that Israel was already reaping the fruits of peace. He was elated by the expansion of Israeli ties with Arab countries in North Africa and the Persian Gulf.[149] Moreover, Rabin's concessions to Arafat were heavily influenced by Israel's perceived need to enhance Arafat's status versus that of his opposition. The paradox of having to negotiate with Arafat while at the same time trying to support him weakened Israel's bargaining position.

Despite Rabin's decisions and the political efforts to gather public support for them, he did not hide his doubts about the government's policy. Candid as usual, he remarked in February 1995: "I am torn between two problems. On the one hand implementing the agreement and, on the other hand, Israel's security."[150] He definitely stressed his commitment to security, which—Rabin maintained—was even more important than peace, since peace could be meaningful only if security was provided to the citizens of Israel.[151] Moreover, he did not exclude the possibility that the Oslo agreements might not lead to reconciliation. He was not sure that an agreement on final status issues with the Palestinians could be reached. Yet he believed that Israel would be ahead even if the process stalled. Israel had transferred the authority over most of the Palestinians to the PA, minimizing Israel's unpleasant need to police the areas heavily populated by Arabs.[152] Rabin also understood that there was a political imperative for making progress. Identified with the peace process in the 1990s, he wanted it to succeed and wanted to be reelected in 1996. On the other hand, his instincts led him to prefer an incremental approach with the Palestinians, allowing him to assess each stage and wait for a proper time, for a "window of opportunity," to move to the next phase. "Let us wait and see what happens" was one of his favorite expressions, but he was caught in the dynamics of a process no longer fully under his control.

Peacemaking with the Palestinians pointed out Rabin's weaknesses as a politician, a subject beyond the scope of this book. When the DOP was put to a vote in the Knesset in September 1993, his Shas coalition partner abstained, but Rabin was luckily able to win the vote by a 61-to-50 margin due to the surprise abstentions of three MKs from the Likud opposition party.[153] By October 1995 the parliamentary opposition was much stiffer, and Rabin managed only at the last moment to secure the support of 61 MKs over 59 opponents to the Taba agreement.[154] Rabin's behavior also estranged segments of the public that were apprehensive about his policies but that had in the past been willing to give him the benefit of doubt. This was reflected in the growing public support for the opposition. By the beginning of 1995, the Likud leader Benjamin Netanyahu was ahead in the polls.[155] It was only Rabin's authority and integrity that enabled him to continue to mobilize the necessary support in the Knesset for the Oslo agreements and to minimize the opposition to the road taken by his government.

THE JORDANIAN TRACK

In several aspects, the easiest Arab country with which to make peace was Jordan.[156] It had a long history of cooperation with Israel in many areas, and over the years King Hussein had held many secret meetings with most

Israeli leaders. Moreover, Israel became the tacit guarantor of Jordan's independence. King Hussein gradually lost his influence over the West Bank Arabs and reduced his involvement in their affairs, particularly after the outbreak of the Intifada. This minimized the area of Jordanian conflict with Israel, although Israel would have preferred Jordan to the PLO as the representative of Palestinian interests.

At the Madrid Conference, on Israel's insistence, there was a joint Jordanian-Palestinian delegation. After Israel agreed to talk in Washington to a separate Palestinian delegation, Israeli-Jordanian negotiations were largely limited to bilateral relations. These included the delineation of the border between the two countries, water rights, and Jerusalem.

The turning point came on 28 October 1992, when the two delegations in Washington agreed to include in the agenda a clause about reaching a peace treaty.[157] The agenda was not formally signed, however, until 14 September 1993 in a modest ceremony. Rabin, as well as Peres, wanted to balance the PLO-Israeli DOP with a similar Jordanian-Israeli document and ceremony.[158] Although Rabin shared the conventional wisdom that the DOP with the Palestinians paved the way for the peace treaty with Jordan, he was aware that the DOP was not welcomed by King Hussein. The king feared the development of a Palestinian orientation in Israeli foreign policy, which several of the doves in Israeli politics had long advocated. The doves had always attributed great importance to the Palestinian issue, claiming that its resolution would bring an end to the Arab-Israeli conflict. Indeed the DOP precipitated the treaty with Jordan by granting additional legitimacy to a separate Arab-Israeli deal. Yet its main effect was not in the sphere of legitimacy but on the Israeli-Jordanian-Palestinian triangular relationship. King Hussein had to outdo the Palestinians in good relations with Israel in order to prevent a Palestinian orientation in Israel's foreign policy, which could be very dangerous to the Hashemite regime. It is not clear whether Rabin fully understood the dynamics of the triangular relationship, although he obviously preferred the company of Hussein to that of Arafat. Rabin compared the Jordanian track and the negotiations with the Palestinians: "It is easier for us to deal with Jordan. Jordan is a state, a moderate state . . . there is a king that leads his people, and therefore it was much easier to make a deal with a state that we believe wants peace."[159]

Rabin devoted much time to the Jordanian channel, including several meetings with King Hussein, while his two emissaries Elyakim Rubinstein and Efraim Halevy tried to hammer out an agreement over a Declaration of Principles. The two sides became closer to such an agreement when Rabin clarified to Hussein, in their meeting in London (28 May 1994), that Israel was willing to grant Jordan a preferential status with regard to the Moslem holy sites in Jerusalem. Moreover, Rabin promised to recommend to the United States that it cancel Jordan's debt. Then King Hussein agreed to go to Washington with Rabin for the issuing of a Declaration of Principles, which would include Israel's promise on Jerusalem, along with an Israeli commitment for border revisions and for a reallocation of the water quotas.[160]

The negotiations intensified and led to the 25 July 1994 Washington Declaration, which also included an announcement on the end of belligerency between the two countries and was the venue for the first public Hussein-Rabin meeting.[161] Once the king broke the taboo on public events with Israelis, many ceremonies followed, such as the opening of a direct telephone line and the inauguration of the Arava crossing point between the two countries. Consequently, the negotiations on a peace treaty became more concrete. Hussein agreed to an exchange of land in the Arava, to Israeli leasing of farmland, and to free access for Israelis to areas to be handed over to Jordanian sovereignty. These concessions were necessary to prevent dismantlement of several Israeli settlements. For Rabin, the exchange of land and the leasing arrangements were extremely important because they provided an alternative to the Egyptian precedent of full withdrawal to the international border. In return, Rabin agreed to increase Jordan's share in Israel's water resources (against the advice of Israeli water specialists).[162]

The impressive ceremony of signing the peace treaty took place on 26 October 1994 in the Arava and was attended by President Clinton and representatives from many other countries. This treaty was most welcome in Israel and was approved by a huge majority in the Knesset (105 in favor, with 3 opposing and 6 abstaining). The warm personality of King Hussein and the excellent rapport he had with Rabin won the hearts of the Israeli public. Moreover, Jordan was seemingly willing to develop, in a short time, good relations with Israel in many fields.[163] It offered Israel a "warm peace," which Israelis longed for and had been denied by Egypt.[164]

THE OLD-NEW RABIN

For many Israelis, Rabin in his last years was a changed Rabin, willing to takes steps he had strongly opposed in the past and speaking a new language. The contemplated withdrawal from the Golan Heights constituted a greater change in Rabin than the Oslo agreements, because the withdrawal concerned a change in his core security outlook. In contrast, on the Palestinian issue, he had always been ready for a renewed partition of the Land of Israel, to which Oslo led. Moreover, despite his abhorrence of the PLO, he had been willing to test its behavior as early as the 1970s. In the last years of his life, however, he seemed to display a different self.[165]

Rabin did not publicly admit that he was considering withdrawal from the Golan Heights, nor did he provide an elaborate explanation of his moves toward the Palestinians. Rabin had excellent analytical qualities but was never a good communicator. We will probably never get a definitive explanation of what brought about this transformation. His comrades-in-arms Maj. Gens. (Res.) Amos Horev, Zvi Zamir, and Yitzhak Hofi remained perplexed by Rabin's change of position on the Golan Heights.[166] Beilin, the architect of the Oslo agreements, admitted he could not understand the sudden change in Rabin's negative attitude in June 1993 to the Oslo venue and why he approved its continuation.[167]

After the first Oslo Agreement, Rabin started using language previously foreign to him, such as seeking to avoid having "to rule over a foreign people" and criticizing the desire of some Israelis for "a deluxe occupation" of the Palestinians at a minimal price, when such a policy actually "costs blood."[168] In his calculus of utility, the costs of Israel's presence in the West Bank and Gaza had started to outweigh the benefits that Israel had derived there in the past. Furthermore, the military occupation of the territories inhabited by Palestinians was a contributing factor to the erosion in the staying power of Israeli society.[169] In 1994, he even started referring to the Palestinian problem as "the heart of the conflict."[170] In the last years of his life, Rabin seemed to have adopted the dovish diagnosis of the Arab-Israeli conflict, as well as much dovish terminology. The new language was meant to lend legitimacy to his policies vis-à-vis the Palestinians and was partly the result of the polarization in the political discourse in the country.[171]

Similarly, the greater weight given by Rabin to economic factors at the expense of military power was closer to the dovish perceptions of the conflict. In his midterm report (published in June 1994) Rabin, like his colleague Peres, underscored the importance of economic factors. "Steps toward a rapprochement between Israel and the Arab states create a process that turns economics into a moving force that shapes the regional relations instead of nationalist interests that were dominant in the past."[172] Addressing the Islamic threat, Rabin pointed out: "Practically the only way to dry the swamp of radical Islam is through economic development and an

improved standard of living."[173] In his last years, Rabin was more interested in economic issues than before and was closely involved in many
economic decisions. He also became closer to Israeli industrialists.[174] The
greater attention to economic factors in the strategic equation also contributed to a reduced threat perception, since Israel's economic situation
in the early 1990s was much better than that of any of its neighbors.

Also new was his emphasis on the psychological aspects of the Arab-
Israeli conflict, in contrast to his usual stress on calculating interests. In an
interview with the journalist Marvin Kalb, Rabin spoke not only about the
differences concerning the tangibles but also about "the hatred, the psychological walls" that had been built "all through the Arab-Israeli conflict."[175]
Specifically in reference to the dispute with the PLO, Rabin mentioned "the
great emotional barriers, the prejudice and suspicion."[176] Rabin expressed
his interest in focusing on "how to bring down the psychological walls,"
claiming that changing attitudes was no less important than addressing
practical issues.[177] This alluded to the possibility of reducing any real conflict of interests and of using a softer approach to the Arab-Israeli conflict.

Rabin also agreed to put the issue of Jerusalem on the negotiating
agenda for the final status issues, in contrast to his past preferences. Moreover, he agreed to allow Peres to send a secret letter to the Norwegian foreign minister, Johan Jorgen Holst, acknowledging an unspecified Palestinian role in the affairs of the Moslem and Christian Arab inhabitants of
Jerusalem.[178] He even tolerated the presence of the PLO's security organs
in the Arab neighborhoods of Jerusalem.[179] Moreover, in May 1995, Rabin
shied away from supporting a congressional initiative calling on the United
States to move its embassy from Tel Aviv to Jerusalem because the move
would have complicated the already strained peace talks with Arafat.[180]

Jerusalem, however, was one issue on which Rabin was willing to specify his long-term goals. He remained fully committed to the traditional
Israeli position that the city should remain undivided under Israeli sovereignty. On Jerusalem, Rabin was emotional and no longer the cool analyst.
In 1948, it was his brigade that was unable to hold on to the Jewish Quar-
ter in the Old City, and he was the chief of staff in 1967 when the eastern
city was liberated. This achievement was a great joy to him.[181] To the Knesset he said in May 1995: "There is only one Jerusalem; from our point of
view Jerusalem is not subject to compromise; Jerusalem was ours, will be
ours, it is ours and so it will be forever and ever."[182] Rabin was willing to
accommodate the interests of other religions in the city but refused to contemplate any political presence, particularly if it had any implications for

sovereignty. For example, Rabin refused to allow the countries contributing funds to the PA to channel any investments into Jerusalem.[183] Despite the fact that Jerusalem was supposed to be, according to the Oslo Agreement, an issue to be dealt with only at a later stage, when negotiations over the final status issues were to take place, the struggle with the PA over Jerusalem started immediately after Arafat set foot in Gaza. This development confirmed Rabin's initial judgment about the negative consequences of a deal with the PLO. Yet from what we know about his concessions to the Palestinians and the Syrians, we can never be sure that Rabin would have stuck firmly to his initial position on Jerusalem.

Some explanations for the changes in Rabin's positions have been mentioned already: his strategic assessment of the dynamics of international, regional, and domestic political factors; the urgency he felt in bringing peace to his country; and his general evaluation that the advantages of making peace were greater than the security risks involved. In addition, several other reasons, of a less rigorous nature, can be enumerated to understand better the new image of Rabin. First, Rabin, as well as other political leaders, realized that Israeli society increasingly displayed signs of fatigue and was becoming clearly more reluctant to pay the price of protracted conflict with the Arabs. As early as 1985, in a lecture to the students of the National Security College, he had analyzed the troubling changes in public attitudes toward national security issues.[184] He sensed that the Israeli public was disappointed with the IDF, which had not been very successful in the 1973 and 1982 wars. This feeling stemmed, according to Rabin, partly from unrealistic expectations. Military successes such as the ones achieved in 1956 and in 1967 could not easily be repeated. Furthermore, the peace treaty with Egypt and the long Iran-Iraq War created a feeling that Israel's security problems were less severe. These developments had pushed "the pendulum of the public mood from total support for the security complex to the other pole," which Rabin described as an extremely dangerous situation and one that he could not have imagined ever happening in Israel.[185] He lamented the thirst for a better economic life and the lack of social support for bearing the costs of providing security. He emphasized that in a democratic country, national security needs cannot be met without national willingness to make sacrifices.

In another public address, a few years later, Rabin compared the behavior of Israelis when bombed from the air by the Egyptians in 1948 with what happened during the missile attacks of 1991. In 1948, over thirty civilian casualties left no imprint on daily life in Tel Aviv. In 1991, however, the city and its suburbs were deserted by tens of thousands of residents, who moved to safer places in the country or even fled Israel entirely. He concluded the comparison by saying: "We have changed."[186] Rabin implied that Israelis had lost some of their perseverance and determination. He was indeed shocked by the behavior of the Israelis during the 1991 Gulf War. Pictures of Israelis abroad "confessing shamelessly" that they had decided to leave the country for safer places were, in his opinion, "unprecedented."[187] On another public occasion, he explicitly stated his assessment that the staying power of Israeli society and its willingness to pay a painful price, an important element in Israeli national power, had somewhat eroded.[188] Rabin said that the Israeli public was spoiled and that it panicked easily. He was afraid that in case of war, there would be much pressure to end the war quickly, denying the IDF the time needed to attain its goals.[189]

Eitan Haber, Rabin's close adviser, regarded the evaluation of growing weakness within Israeli society as the central factor in the prime minister's strategic prognosis. Ariel Sharon, who was very close to Rabin and had regular tête-à-tête meetings with him despite their political differences, also testified to the importance of this factor in Rabin's sense of urgency in attempting to conclude peace with Israel's neighbors. He quoted Rabin as saying, while explaining to him the government's policies: "The people are weak. . . . The people will have difficulties withstanding an additional war . . . this is why we have to make concessions."[190] Maj. Gen. (Res.) Israel Tal, who was also close to Rabin, testified that the prime minister was particularly worried about the corrosive effects of the Intifada on the staying power and morale of the Israelis. In general, Rabin felt that the Arabs could better withstand the attrition involved in a protracted conflict.[191] Rabin was afraid that a missile war would cause great panic and that Israel's freedom of action would be limited by public pressure. Rabin's assessment that Israeli society had "softened" served as a catalyst, in his strategic evaluation, for speeding the peace negotiations and adopting more flexible positions in the bargaining with the Arab interlocutors.

Furthermore, in private meetings Rabin defended his decisions to make concessions to the Palestinians and to the Syrians, going so far as to question the ability of the IDF to meet successfully the military challenges posed by the Arab armies.[192] Rabin regarded parts of the IDF as a large and somewhat cumbersome military bureaucracy.[193] He often questioned the operational ability of IDF units to perform as claimed by the top brass.[194] As noted, Rabin was very concerned about the IDF's ability to separate itself from negative trends within Israeli society. In August 1989, he told the graduates of the IDF College for Staff and Command: "I refuse to accept the view that what happens in the IDF is a reflection of what is happening in Israeli society, both positively and negatively."[195] Yet he was not oblivious to the notion that the IDF was no longer an elite ready for sacrifices. The off-the-record Rabin expressed a great measure of pessimism about the direction of Israeli society and the capacity of the IDF to meet the security challenges facing Israel. This aspect remained hidden, however, from the public at large.

Interestingly, the IDF was not consulted before two strategic decisions—withdrawal from the Golan Heights and the Oslo Agreement—were made. Possibly Rabin wanted to insulate the army from controversial political decisions. The IDF was brought into the picture only to negotiate the details of implementing the Oslo Agreement. It was also asked to prepare the staff work for a future withdrawal from the Golan Heights only after the possibility of such a move was conveyed to the Americans in August 1993.

The American factor probably also played a role in the mellowing of Rabin. The United States was somewhat surprised by Rabin's concessions, but it was clearly pleased with his peace policy. For the Clinton administration, the evolving peace process in the Middle East provided numerous opportunities to demonstrate foreign policy successes while other areas of the world, such as Bosnia and Somalia, were increasingly problematic. Therefore, the American administration embraced the process and buttressed U.S. relations with the Jewish state. This was extremely important for Rabin, who continued to regard the American involvement in the process and U.S. support for Israel as vital for Israeli interests. The American praise and even admiration for Rabin also seemed to provide some comfort in his domestic struggles.

Finally, it seems that Rabin could not resist the temptation to be registered in history as the person who successfully concluded the peace process. In the last years of his life, he spoke more and more approvingly of Likud leader and Prime Minister Menachem Begin, whose record included the 1979 peace treaty with Egypt—even if that record also included the ill-advised Lebanon War, a weakness in running the government, and a disposition for acerbic attacks on his political opponents. Rabin often cited him as a great leader, and there had been mutual respect between the two men.[196] In October 1994, Rabin in the Knesset said: "This government has decided that, under certain conditions, peace is preferable to Sharm al-Sheikh—just as the Likud government, headed by Menachem Begin, bravely decided."[197] He claimed that his government was "the first since that of [the] late Menachem Begin which has advanced peace."[198] In September 1995, Rabin praised Begin for being one of the great prime ministers who displayed courage and imagination: "Let's face it, the real breakthrough in the relationship between Israel and the Arab peoples was the peace treaty with Egypt. Nobody can take this credit away from him."[199]

The compliments to Begin were obviously designed to prepare the people of Israel for additional territorial concessions, as well as to gain greater legitimacy in the bitter domestic debate. Yet heaping praise on Begin was also a genuine evaluation of the place the former leader occupied in the history of the country and was a sign of Rabin's appreciation of Begin's ability to revise his positions and take risky decisions. Rabin had similar admiration for the Nixon-Kissinger team, which changed American policy toward China and created a new strategic landscape. Rabin probably yearned for a similar status. Rabin was not immune to thoughts about his role in Israeli history. Moreover, he was aware that his first tenure as prime minister (1974–77) was not considered in Israel to be a particularly successful one.[200] He had the personality of a classic achiever, and in the 1990s, he seemed to be bent on leaving a better mark on history.[201] Bringing peace to Israel, as he had promised, would obviously be an achievement of which he could be proud and one that could overshadow his poor performance in the 1970s.

Rabin's advanced age was probably also a contributing factor to his change of views. Like other aging political leaders, he viewed the younger generation with skepticism. Just as Israel's leaders of 1967 dismissively referred to the youth of that time as "the espresso generation," Rabin in the 1990s was concerned with the quality of the new generation of Israelis. Furthermore, he was not sure that the next, more liberal generation in his own party would be able to manage the negotiations with the Arabs satisfactorily.[202]

The mere fact that he had a grandson who started serving in 1992 as a combat soldier in the IDF seemed to have an effect on him. Rabin, known for his shyness and for being an introvert who never spoke publicly about family and personal matters, now kept reminding people that he was a grandfather. Rabin's daughter observed: "My dad hoped in the past that we, his children, would not have to go to fight, and the moment his grandson put on a uniform and went to the same wars—I believe it did something to him."[203] In October 1995, when visiting soldiers wounded in Lebanon, he told the audience that his grandson had also served in southern Lebanon. He noted: "I feel like any grandfather. I have overall responsibility for the life of each one serving there, but naturally I have greater sensitivity to my own grandson."[204] In his last public speech (4 November 1995), at the rally convened to demonstrate support for his government policies in the peace process, he did not fail to mention being a grandfather. Minutes before his assassination he said: "It is better to make peace than to wage war. I say it to you as a soldier and as a defense minister that sees the pain of the bereaved families of the fallen soldiers of the IDF. For them, for our children and in my case for our grandchildren, I want my government to exploit every opportunity to promote and reach a comprehensive peace."[205]

From 1992 on, then, Israel was led by a somewhat different Rabin—an enigmatic mixture of old dispositions and new language and positions. Rabin was indeed determined to continue the course he had chosen. Despite the fact that he was very cautious and risk-averse, Rabin regarded peace as worth taking considerable risks. He ended his 1979 autobiography with the statement: "There is no doubt whatsoever in my mind that the risks of peace are preferable by far to the grim certainties that await every nation in war." But even when many around him celebrated and were bursting with optimism, he remained the eternal skeptic and pessimist. Only rarely did he project enthusiasm and elation about his political path. Unlike Peres, he never outlined a clear strategic vision of a better tomorrow. More often than not, Rabin expressed his doubts, his qualms about an uncertain future. He perceived an improved strategic environment containing less chances for existential dangers, but he knew that such military challenges still existed. He was unmoved in the belief that an armed peace was the best to which Israel could aspire in the near future. In an interview a month and a half before his assassination, Rabin said that for at least the next thirty years, Israel would have to maintain its military strength and not cut the defense budget.[206] Like the majority of Israelis, he was willing to take risks and to give the peace process a chance, but he remained suspicious of his partners and skeptical about the outcome. He also underestimated the extent of domestic opposition to the risks he considered plausible.

CONCLUSION

This chapter has presented the Rabin of the 1990s—the leader intent on making peace with Israel's immediate neighbors. In his opinion, the international circumstances of the 1990s were most propitious, offering Israel a window of opportunity for improving its relations with the Arab world. At the same time, the specter of weapons of mass destruction and the appeal of Islamic radicalism in the Middle East created a sense of urgency in making good use of the window of opportunity. The peace treaty that Rabin succeeded in signing with Jordan was unanimously praised in Israel; the progress made on the Palestinian track, however, was more controversial. Yet the repartitioning of the Land of Israel, the consequence of the reluctant deal he made with the Palestinians, was his strategic goal. His efforts to conclude an agreement with Syria were foiled despite his willingness to part with the Golan Heights. Israel also improved relations with several Arab countries not in its immediate vicinity—in the Maghreb and in the Gulf. Generally, Israel's international status had never been better.

Rabin remained a skeptical realist, projecting ambivalence toward segments of the peace process. But he was determined to pursue peace, even at great risk, and to accomplish this, Rabin deviated from some positions and convictions he had held for many years. Unfortunately, he was not very good at explaining the changes he introduced in Israel's policies, and this cost him much domestic support.

CONCLUSION

Yitzhak Rabin played key roles in Israel's military establishment at significant junctures in the state's history. He served in important military positions and contributed to making the Israel Defense Force (IDF) into a mighty military organization. As chief of staff from 1964 to 1967, he commanded the army in the Six-Day War, and he served as prime minister after the Yom Kippur War (1974–77), presiding over the army's recovery process. During his 1984–90 tenure as defense minister, he oversaw a major restructuring of the army, the withdrawal of Israeli troops from Lebanon, and the IDF handling of the Intifada. He served again as prime minister and defense minister in 1992–95, signing several interim agreements with the Palestinians and the peace treaty with Jordan.

Rabin fought for Israel's independence in 1948, and the army he prepared for war achieved a stunning victory in 1967. He also was the first Israeli-born prime minister, leading a generational change in Israeli politics. After he died, the generation that had participated in the 1948 War of Independence was practically gone, and a younger generation of leaders was ushered in.

From an early age, Rabin adopted a realpolitik outlook on international affairs. This was the result of the particular circumstances in which he grew up: the prevalent attitude of the Jewish community in Palestine to what was then called the "Arab problem"; and his lifelong preoccupation with the violent aspects of the Arab-Israeli conflict. His emphasis on military power as the most important element in world politics and in Arab-Israeli relations remained unchanged. Furthermore, his pessimism and suspicious nature reinforced his conservative approach.

Rabin was one of the chief builders of the American-Israeli alliance. He was an early advocate of the American orientation in Israeli foreign policy and chose to serve as Israel's ambassador to the United States. He lived to see a web of complex military and strategic ties developing into solid cooperation between the two countries. He showed keen interest in American politics and considered himself to be an expert on the United States and its foreign policy. Nevertheless, he remained cautious toward the United States and feared a possible deterioration in the bilateral relations. Even though he attributed paramount importance to Israeli relations with Washington, he was averse to transforming the relationship into a formal alliance.

As a lesson of the War of Independence, Rabin dedicated his life to building a strong military machine. This was his undisputed greatest achievement. Early in his IDF career, he distinguished himself by a systematic and profound treatment of military problems. His meticulous penchant for detail served him well in planning training and military operations. Israel Tal, Ezer Weizman, and Rehavam Zeevi, generals of diverse temperaments and political views, said that Rabin's contribution to the development of the IDF was being "the greatest teacher of all." As a civilian, the job he liked most was the post of minister of defense, which allowed him to immerse himself in building a modern fighting force. Only he had the authority to make cuts in the defense budget and in the IDF's order of battle. Rabin also liked the job of defense minister because he was surrounded by people in military uniform, and he clearly preferred their company to that of fellow politicians.

According to his realpolitik outlook on international affairs, Rabin was not averse to the use of military force. He was exposed early on to the political ramifications of the use of force, and he discussed military matters with David Ben-Gurion during the War of Independence. The protocols of the Knesset Committee for Defense and Foreign Affairs show that as early as 1951, Rabin was invited to present the IDF's views to the legislators. Rabin was generally cautious in the use of military force, however, being cognizant of its limits and of its linkages to political goals.

Gradually, the proliferation of missiles and weapons of mass destruction in the Middle East became a greater problem for Israel's national security.

Rabin continued to adhere to Israel's nuclear ambiguity and resisted the temptation to adopt a public nuclear posture. His preferred response was deterrence, and he hoped that the United States and other international players would help in addressing this challenge. It is not clear whether Rabin-led Israel made the adjustments necessary for moving into an era in which the country could be attacked by weapons of mass destruction.

Toward the end of his illustrious career, Rabin led a partial shift in Israel's strategic thinking, predicated on a new mixture of optimism and pessimism. On the one hand, Rabin had a more optimistic evaluation of the regional environment and accepted part of the strategic argument of dovish circles in Israel. On the other hand, he displayed greater pessimism about the looming existential threats and the ability of the Israeli society to withstand the security challenges ahead. Rabin capitalized on the more benign strategic circumstances and made significant progress in the peace process with the Arab world.

Rabin was first and foremost a military man. Peace was primarily a means to buttress security. During the last years of his life, peace seemed to become an important goal for him, one that was within reach. Yet until the end, Rabin believed that the transition to peaceful relations between Israel and its neighbors, relations like the interactions among West European countries, would take decades.

The transition to the role of peacemaker was not easy for Rabin. He obviously had the courage to make difficult decisions, but this was not enough. The qualities needed for the new task were probably different from the ones required to face armed hostility and to mobilize popular support for protracted struggle. His greatest difficulty—and failure—lay in explaining to the people of Israel why it was worth taking the risks he took in the peace process. He failed to instill the Israeli public with faith in the correctness of his intuition. He himself was not sure of the path chosen. Nevertheless, considering his popularity and his credibility as an honest leader in the 1980s and early 1990s, his inability to secure greater domestic support for his policies was somewhat surprising.

This failure was connected to his limitations as a politician. Despite his power-oriented outlook on international relations and his understanding of strategic affairs, Rabin was no strategic thinker. He did not articulate a coherent strategic vision for Israel. He did not even outline his long-term goals and his ideas about how to achieve them. As usual, he was immersed in the details, and his pragmatism led him to look for ad hoc solutions to emerging problems.

In addition, Rabin was to a great extent a loner, and his decision-making style reflected his introverted and skeptical nature. He did not have much use for advisers. He opposed the creation of a civilian body for strategic and defense planning in the prime minister's office. Despite his appreciation of good staff work and his admiration for the American political system, he refused to adopt a decision-making structure along the lines of the U.S. National Security Council. He preferred to work either alone, revealing his lack of respect for his colleagues of political life, or directly with military planning staff units. His cautiousness, or hesitations, led him to react slowly, delaying reaching conclusions. His huge influence after 1973 meant his preferences generally won out, and this created a serious impediment in Israeli decision-making in the area of national security.

Yet his common sense, his rich experience, and his hard-nosed approach to strategic affairs appealed to most Israelis. He had a tremendous influence on the public at large and on high-ranking army officers in particular. His authority on military matters was unchallenged. He was often invited to speak on various subjects at the College for Command and Staff and the National Security College, the highest institution of learning in the IDF. He liked these opportunities immensely and appeared before the colleges anytime his schedule permitted. His analyses influenced generations of officers.

Rabin's most important contribution to Israel's national security was preparing the IDF for the 1967 war. On this there is consensus. His second greatest contribution was more controversial: the repartitioning of the Land of Israel through the Oslo agreements. Though it was not his initiative, Rabin defended this achievement proudly. A corollary of this move was the entrenchment of the Palestine Liberation Organization in the West Bank and Gaza and the establishment of the infrastructure for a Palestinian state. On this matter, Rabin was less clear and displayed much ambivalence. He probably reconciled himself to this development because it was, in his opinion, the only option available to Israel in order to rid itself of the heavily Arab-populated areas of the Land of Israel. At the time of this writing, in the late 1990s, a Palestinian state, which Rabin opposed, seems to be a fait accompli. The risks of Palestinian statehood will be dealt with by regional leaders in a post-Rabin era. The largest party opposing Rabin's policies, the Likud, came to power in 1996, but it accepted the Land of Israel partition created by Rabin's policies. To a great extent the grip of the Oslo agreements will dictate the future course of Israeli policies vis-à-vis the Palestinians. The ideology of Greater Israel has vanished as a realistic and respectable policy option in Israeli politics. These important political facts are Rabin's doing.

Many political and strategic questions remain unanswered. Rabin will be judged by outcomes he unfortunately could not influence, since his political career was ended by the bullets of an assassin. The assassin deprived him of the chance to face the Israeli electorate again and to ask for its support for the path he had chosen. It remains to be seen whether the course taken by Rabin will indeed correspond to the emergence of a more benign Middle East.

The circumstances of Rabin's tragic death provide the materials for the creation of a myth. Indeed, many in Israel speak now in the name of Rabin's legacy. Yet Rabin did not leave any writings that deal systematically with the Arab-Israeli conflict and the peace process. The bits and pieces he did write reflect his pragmatic, ad hoc approach and his reluctance to commit himself to a specific future scenario. It is, therefore, important to set the historical record straight. Rabin was a complex personality, and some of his views changed over time, but the centrality of the national security of Israel in his thinking remained basically unchanged. This is the best prism for understanding the late prime minister, and this book has, I hope, contributed to a better understanding of Rabin's strategic legacy.

The mythology on Rabin is still in the making, and we do not yet know what shape it will take. Although he was murdered because his deeds aroused much opposition, Rabin's figure could well become a unifying myth for the divided Israeli society. Various aspects of his complex personality could become foci of identification for different people within Israel. His personal traits were admirable: he was an Israeli patriot who unselfishly dedicated his life to enhance the security of the Jewish state; he had an impressive mind; he was an honest and unpolished Israeli; he was courageous; he was "Mr. Security." His achievements were no less impressive: he built the IDF into a mighty military machine and led it to the victory of 1967; he liberated Jerusalem; he rebuilt the IDF in the post-1973 period; he extricated Israel from the Lebanese quagmire; he managed to fight the Intifada without leaving too many scars in the IDF and Israeli society; he partitioned the Land of Israel in a quest for peace; and he reached a formal peace treaty with Jordan. These are the materials to be used for drawing the psycho-historical picture of Rabin as an Israeli leader. It remains to be seen how the next generation of Israelis will complete the painting of that portrait.

AFTER THE GULF WAR: ISRAELI DEFENSE AND ITS SECURITY POLICY

(Address by Yitzhak Rabin at the Begin-Sadat Center for Strategic Studies, Bar-Ilan University, 10 June 1991)

I wish to speak about the directions that Israel ought [to] take in security and defense policy, not about security doctrine. Specifically, I wish to relate to the role of the Israel Defense Force (IDF) in fulfilling the objectives of a defined security policy.

It is true that a significant change has occurred in the international arena; the Gulf War is a prime example. We would never have believed, one year ago, that the scenario for the next Middle East war would involve: the military force of one of the two countries most hostile to Israel being crippled by a foreign power; advance warning of five months time; and Israel suffering only negligible damage, without a spilt drop of IDF blood. I assume that if someone had predicted this he would have been told to "go sleep-it-off," or sent to a sanitarium. Israeli security policy never has been designed to take into account such a scenario; nor was the IDF built for such an eventuality. Nor is this the scenario for which Israel must prepare and adopt a security policy.

In determining security policy, one should ask: against what and for what? What are the likely threats? What is required? Beyond the response to menace, one should ask: what can be gained via Israel's military power?

Translated and edited by David M. Weinberg. This speech is typical of Rabin's presentations on Israel's strategic thinking in the 1980s and 1990s. At the time of delivery, Rabin was not a cabinet member and could speak more freely.

Threats as a whole, today and in other periods, may be divided into two types. On one level is the existential threat—that imperils the very existence of the State of Israel. Such peril might be posed by the armies of Arab states, led by leaders such as Saddam Hussein, Hafez al-Assad, or other figures that might confront us in [the] future. Arab armies are our major security concern.

A second level of "threat" is that known in the IDF as "current security," involving challenges to the daily life of Israelis. In [the] past, this term referred to border clashes with Arab armies, incidents which are mostly a thing of the past. Today, "current security" relates to Palestinian terrorist incursions aimed at targets in Israel (and at Israeli and Jewish targets worldwide), and to fundamentalist Islamic terrorism and the *Intifada*.

These two types of terrorism are no more than a nuisance. Despite the pain and the continuous assaults, terrorist attacks have never been, are not, and never will constitute an existential threat to the State of Israel. Terrorism always has been, remains, and shall ever be the weapon of the weak.

Therefore, when speaking of security policy today, one should focus on the existential dangers and not on "current security." It is noteworthy that about 90 percent of our military budget is allocated to defense against "existential" threat. I will therefore address Israeli security policy vis-à-vis the existential threats posed to Israel.

I still remember such discussions during the first years of the IDF in 1955, and they should be held today as well. The primary question in the formulation of Israeli security policy is this: under the given situation of Arab-Israeli conflict, is it possible for the State of Israel to adopt a security policy that seeks one great war that shall be "the end of all wars," and in this way realize the Clausewitzian axiom that war is the continuation of diplomacy by other means?

When one's objective is to destroy the enemy's forces, one must ask "for what purpose?" In order to impose your political will! A case in point was World War II. The Allies defined the war's objective as the unconditional surrender of Nazi Germany, Fascist Italy, and Imperialist Japan—and they attained this objective. They then implemented radical reforms: MacArthur implemented social reform in Japan, the Allies divided Germany, and West Germany underwent a transformation, as did Italy.

The first question that requires a clear-cut answer in the formulation of the Israeli security policy: is the result attained by the Allies a feasible alternative in the Arab-Israeli conflict? Realistically, can we undergo five years of economic austerity and devote the national budget to an IDF military buildup—and then conquer the Middle East? Are we capable of bringing Arab nations to a state of affairs comparable to that of the Axis powers at the end of World War II? This question must be answered before a security policy can be formulated.

We must strive to defend the state and attain a solution to the conflict with our neighbors, but there are great differences in the international situation pertaining in World War II and the international situation today of Israel. I once said that between the Allies, the Axis, and the "Almighty," there wasn't any entity that could have restricted the actions of the Allies. In the case of the Arab-Israeli conflict, there are superpowers and international actors that stand between the Arab countries at war with Israel and the "Almighty."

Furthermore, in the situation that exists today Israel cannot formulate a security policy involving the imposition of preferred peace arrangements following upon the defeat or conquest of Arab countries. This is not a pleasant situation—but it is a given! I repeat and further emphasize: without agreeing on an approach in this regard, a security policy cannot be fashioned. And therefore, we cannot set for ourselves far-reaching political goals such as the *imposition* of peace as a security policy.

I ask myself a second question: is there any territorial target that justifies the initiation of war? I am speaking of a preemptive attack, of a war that is planned several months in advance, a year or two years in advance—a deliberate attack aimed at achieving a territorial goal. I believe that we have more than enough land, and we assuredly have no need of any more land—no territorial needs that could justify a war initiative.

The third possible objective for an Israeli-initiated war might be the destruction of an Arab military force when it appears that its military buildup constitutes a danger to us. Perhaps, then, war is worthwhile—to destroy the adversary's military power and thus prevent the risk of a future war.

We have learned the hard way from previous wars—irrespective of their origins—that Arab armies undergo a rapid refurbishing of their military. To date, experience has shown that following each war, Arab countries have obtained armaments in greater quantities and improved quality. I cannot remember a war where the country defeated by us did not subsequently improve the quantity and quality of its arms.

Thus, Israel has no reason to adopt a policy that involves the initiation of war, whether for far-reaching political and territorial objectives, nor for the destruction of enemy forces. And if we can identify no significant objective in initiation of war, then the best course for Israel is the prevention of war.

It's worth remembering that there are no more "Six-Day Wars," neither in duration nor in casualties—nor, in my opinion, in political results. Today's quantities of Mideast arms, and their destructive power and range—all will make future military conflict painfully expensive and costly. Therefore, as Minister of Defense, I considered the prevention of war as the test of our security policy, in addition to being able to rapidly and forcefully end any war forced upon us. What does it mean to be "able to rapidly and forcefully end any war"? I will deal with this later.

The bottom line is that this is a defensive strategy. The question is how to prevent war—conventional war—between Arab countries and ourselves. Simply put, we are speaking of deterrent power. Has Israel's deterrence policy succeeded? The fact that wars have occurred shows that it did not succeed completely, for if this were so, we would have prevented each war. In my opinion, no complete and guaranteed deterrence of conventional wars is possible. We can only strive for the most convincing decisive victory should deterrence fail. How can the Arab ruler of a country such as Syria be deterred? Can we always deter him? I think not.

Deterrence is not attainable if the Syrian ruler (who is the major threat today) believes that the worst that might happen to him in war is that he will fail to attain his objectives. Yet, several wars with Syria have already shown that deterrence *is* possible within the conventional war framework. If this same Arab ruler learns to fear the starting of war because he knows that his armies will be crushed, that he will suffer significant collateral damage, and that his own strategic installations will be threatened—he will think twice before starting armed conflict.

In other words, defensive capabilities are not a deterrent factor in the Arab-Israeli conflict. Only the power to defeat an enemy's forces and to thwart his strategic objectives, to the point where his regime is at risk, makes deterrence possible. If this is the case, and if we mean to prevent war, we have no objectives that justify an Israeli war initiative!

We are aware of the terrible price that war entails, and therefore deterrence is preferable. Concurrently, however, we must keep in mind that successful deterrence is not assured; thus we require the power that can secure a decisive victory. What is victory in the context of Arab-Israeli conflict? Victory requires the defeat of the attacking power to the point that it requests a cease-fire on the spot, whereby the enemy has not conquered any of our lands, and where we have conquered lands that were under enemy control, and thereby we constitute a strategic threat to the enemy.

I am aware that such a "mathematical" equation cannot easily be applied in every situation, along territorial lines; but this is our problem—there are no easy solutions. A situation where the enemy requests a cease-fire on the spot, where most of his army is destroyed, and where we hold the lands or threaten the enemy's capital city—this is an Israeli victory.

How can this be attained? Israel maintains a defensive strategy designed to deter. If this fails, decisive victory is required (in the manner I have defined). This defeat can be attained by an army that is powerfully offensive in character and is capable of reversing the war from defensive to offensive action, transferring the fighting to the enemy's territory, and attaining his decisive defeat as quickly as possible. We require a powerful tactical air force, armored forces, sophisticated weapons, supporting units to secure the naval arena, and additional forces to secure other arenas. An offensive military force fulfills two missions: it serves as both a deterrent force and as a force to attain decisive victory in the event that deterrence fails.

I also believe that the IDF plays a part in the promotion of peace. Through military power, Arab rulers can be persuaded that they are incapable of attaining their goals by way of military force. The IDF is called upon to propel Arab-Israeli conflict from the battlefield to the negotiating table, under conditions that are favorable to Israel. In my opinion, no Arab ruler seriously will consider the peace process as long as he still can toy with the idea of achieving more by way of violence.

As for the Gulf War: when I was last in the US, I was asked to explain the differences in U.S. and Israeli combat styles. Israel and the IDF care deeply for the lives of Israeli soldiers and citizens. The American army conducted a remarkable war in the Gulf. The air force was utilized to the utmost, resulting in the decisive defeat of the enormous Iraqi force with minimum casualties—something we never managed to achieve in any of our wars. This is indeed true.

Israel has paid a price in its wars and may be forced to absorb high costs of war in future, because of two factors:

- Limited time at our disposal to attain military objectives. Under the conditions of the Middle East, we cannot be certain of implementing a fighting strategy that requires time—45 days, for example. The fighting could be halted on the seventh day without our having attained any of our key objectives.
- Limited logistic infrastructure. We cannot compare ourselves, a small country, to the American superpower. Israel and the IDF

boast outstanding logistic abilities, but these do not compare with those of a superpower.

These two factors force us [to] aim for rapid victory, for which we pay in equipment and, bluntly speaking, in blood.

Consider, for example, the American air attacks in the Gulf—45 days of bombing. I have heard some people in the air force and in other corps discussing the inaccuracy of these bombing raids. One must understand that the U.S. has its own methods, working gradually—from limited to greater accuracy, while saving equipment and human life. According to my calculations, more than 1,000 U.S. fighter jets were involved in the attacks. The U.S. lost close to 40 planes, which is about 3.5 percent of their air force, within 45 days. During the Six-Day War, we lost about 12 percent of our jet fighters. During the Yom Kippur War, which lasted 18 days, we lost about 100 planes, equaling approximately one-third of our air force. Israel is forced to live with such differentials.

Yet another reality recently driven home to Israelis—which we've known about for more than a decade—is the missile issue. The Arab countries have learned a few lessons of their own. Following the Six-Day War, Arab leaders reached the conclusion that they had little chance of attaining air superiority against the Israeli air force, neither in aerial combat nor in tactical battlefield support. Our first indications of this came during the War of Attrition, and even more so during the Yom Kippur War, when Arab armies extensively employed surface-to-air missile batteries. To be frank, we did not emerge victorious in these missile-versus-air force engagements. In addition to the utility of surface-to-air missiles, Arab states reached the conclusion after the Yom Kippur War that they ought to develop surface-to-surface missiles too. They understood the advantage of hitting the Israeli home front, with its multifold targets.

In the late 1970s we picked up evidence that Arab countries were seeking to develop surface-to-surface missiles capabilities. Today, we know that hostile Arab states intend to attack us, in the next war, on three fronts simultaneously: on the battlefield, at our rear logistical and support bases, and at our civilian population centers.

I remember a discussion held in 1955 in the IDF General Staff, during a presentation to David Ben-Gurion, then prime minister and minister of defense. He asked about the issue of home-front defenses. Army officers replied, as they are prone to, that it wouldn't be the end of the world if several bombs (today—several missiles) were to fall on civilian targets. Ben-

Gurion angrily responded: "You weren't in the Blitz on London. I was! I do not want the Israeli home front exposed, in any degree, to that which the British home front endured." He never explained why.

Ben-Gurion conditioned Israel's participation in the British-French action against Egypt in 1956 on the arrival of two French squadrons to defend Israeli airspace. Ben-Gurion was not dissuaded by the protests of Israeli air force commanders, who considered this a vote of no-confidence in their abilities, as did many of us in the General Staff. He insisted that without the two French squadrons—pilots, planes, and all—our battalions would not parachute into the Mitla Pass in Sinai. He also demanded that antiaircraft air defense units be stationed in Tel Aviv and Haifa.

I do not wish in public forum to dwell on the vulnerability of the Israeli home front—as it emerges from the 45 days of the Gulf War. I do not wish to address the question [of] whether things might have been different. Was the correct policy adopted? Did the entire country have to be paralyzed for 45 days because of the missile threat? The fact that surface-to-surface missiles with conventional warheads, possibly tipped with chemical warheads (I shall not mention other possibilities), can be fired against us requires a basic examination of the nature of Arab-Israeli war.

The Iraq-U.S. confrontation has little relevance for, or can teach us little about, the Arab-Israeli conflict. I do not believe that Israel's deterrent ability was harmed. Is there any relevance in what Israel might have done to Saddam Hussein, during a conflict between Hussein and the USA and its allies?!

These are the basic issues I have attempted to define: the IDF's purpose, the outlines of Israeli security policy, what this policy is meant to prevent, and for what we should prepare in the event that war is imposed on Israel. The army should be offensive in character. As for the home front, the issues should be examined anew.

POLICY STATEMENT BY PRIME MINISTER YITZHAK RABIN TO THE KNESSET, 3 OCTOBER 1994

Mr. President, Mr. Speaker, Honorable Knesset,

A blessed new year is upon us, and on behalf of the Government, I want to wish Knesset members and their families, IDF soldiers and members of the security branches who stand on guard, and all citizens of Israel, a good year. A good year of continuity and prosperity, a year of peace, a year of security—in which we see the realization of the words: "And I will give peace in the land, and you shall rest and not be afraid. And I will make evil beasts extinct from the land, and no sword shall pass through your land."

We are entering the gates of the new year stronger than ever, more just than ever—and, on the threshold of 5755, we hope, pray and say that this be a year of peace with the Arab states and with the Palestinians. In Gaza and Jericho, in Amman, Damascus, and Beirut, and in Cairo and Jerusalem, people will speak peace to each other.

Members of Knesset: Year after year, speech after speech, Prime Ministers of Israel have stood at this podium. The late David Ben-Gurion and Moshe Sharett, Levi Eshkol and Golda Meir, Menachem Begin—as well as Shimon Peres and Yitzhak Shamir—addressed Arab rulers from this dais, called for peace, and invited them to this House, to be partners in the journey to peace.

We believe that the Knesset in Jerusalem, which has for generations heard our voices calling for peace, which has seen our hands extended for peace, this House that has seen our greatest hours and our most painful moments will host—perhaps this year—the King of Jordan, the President of Syria, and the Prime Minister of Lebanon, and others, who will come through the gates of Jerusalem, the city of peace.

Members of Knesset: The holiday atmosphere that envelops every Jewish home each year during the month of Tishrei has also been accompanied by much sorrow over the past twenty-one years. Twenty-one years have passed since that Yom Kippur. We have experienced much since then, both good and bad.

A generation has gone and a generation has come. We have forgotten a great many snapshots of our lives, they have been erased from memory—but we do not forget the images of that day, we do not forget the voices resounding in our ears as if it were yesterday. We recall every moment of that day, everything we did and said, the holiday atmosphere and the quiet in the streets, the masses of worshipers praying in the synagogue, the military vehicles violating the sanctity of the holiday, the questions we asked and for which there were no answers, and the alarm siren at two o'clock in the afternoon.

History does not recognize the term "what if," but—within the bitter memory of that Yom Kippur—we cannot free ourselves of the thought: What would have happened if . . . ?

Egyptian President Anwar Sadat said: "I am prepared to sacrifice the lives of one and one-half million Egyptian soldiers to liberate the lands."

Defense Minister Moshe Dayan said: "We are waiting for a telephone call from the Arabs." He also said: "I prefer Sharm al-Sheikh over peace, rather than peace without Sharm al-Sheikh."

We responded to the words of the Egyptian president with mockery and arrogance—and the words of Moshe Dayan expressed the opinion of many and reflected the thoughts that were felt in the hearts of a large, broad public in Israel.

It required a bloody war with Egypt and Syria—it required thousands of casualties among the IDF soldiers so dear to us, and among the soldiers of the armies of Egypt and Syria—in order for those in Cairo to reach the correct conclusion that peace is preferable to war and for those in Jerusalem to reach the correct conclusion that peace is preferable to Sharm al-Sheikh.

Members of Knesset: The current government has decided to do everything that is necessary and possible to save us from wars, bloodshed, and tears. This government has decided to pick up the telephone receiver to the Arab states because it is ringing. And this government has decided that, under certain conditions, peace is preferable to Sharm al-Sheikh—just as the Likud government, headed by Menachem Begin, bravely decided.

The telephone rang in Cairo years ago, and it is now ringing in Gaza and Jericho, in Amman, in Damascus, and in Beirut. And we, gentlemen, are lifting up the receiver—and there is someone saying hello on the other side of the line.

Members of Knesset: For a generation, we have known how to assault enemy outposts, to seize control of enemy cities, to strike hard and lethally. We were the best at war. We are now exercising this same determination in another battle. We are again charging—this time, to be the best at peace.

We are prepared for any dialogue with the Arab states and with the Palestinians—under conditions of real partnership for peace and security. But at the same time, our eyes have not been blinded—and we do not intend to be an innocent lamb in a world of wolves. We have no intention, for even one moment, to cease strengthening the IDF and increasing its power, but to keep our eyes open and to be prepared. We are prepared for peace. We are also prepared for war, should it be forced upon us.

Members of Knesset: We have already encountered, ad nauseam, the expression "window of opportunity"—but what can we do? This is the correct expression for these times. In recent years, we have witnessed conflicting trends around the world. On the one hand, a spirit of conciliation and peace has overtaken the world due to, and maybe primarily because of, the collapse of the Soviet empire.

But on the other hand, there also exists a countertrend—an ugly wave of radical, fanatic Islam that is attempting to engulf many countries. Extremist Islamic terrorist organizations are operating in a number of directions: Hamas and Islamic Jihad are carrying out most of the terrorist attacks against Israelis in Israel and in Judea, Samaria, and Gaza. Hizballah, part of the same wave, is carrying out most of the attacks against IDF and SLA soldiers in Lebanon. International terrorism, which is also part of the same wave, harms Israelis, Jews, and others the world over. There is no need to recall what happened in Buenos Aires and London, and what occurred in 1992 in Buenos Aires and in Istanbul. The extremist Islamic terrorist organizations are trying to strike at moderate Arab regimes that are prepared for peace with Israel.

In recent years, Iranian assistance—direct and indirect—to this terrorism has been prominent. Iranian involvement has found expression in attacks carried out by radical Islamic terrorist elements, in the Middle East and throughout the world. As members of the Jewish people, we respect the beliefs of all other religions. As Jews, we are sensitive to freedom of worship for members of all religions. We will confront and struggle against "Khomeinism without Khomeini," which is the central element characterizing the radical-terrorist wave of Islam.

We welcome the trends of peace, and view with concern the ugly wave of extremist Islam. Never has comprehensive peace been closer to us, and at the same time, the danger of extremist Islam hovers above it as a shadow that will not pass.

Many of the Arab states neighboring us are partner to this great fear of the extremist danger—and they say, and know, that practically the only way to dry the swamp of radical Islam is through economic development and an improved standard of living. Poverty and deprivation are the stepping-stone of this dangerous wave—and only economic growth, and I stress this, growth and improvements in the societies in Egypt and Syria, in Jordan and Lebanon, and among the Palestinians will strike at these radicals. Such improvements, such economic development, can only be implemented when peace will reign throughout the entire Middle East.

We view ourselves as partners in this important task, and we perceive comprehensive peace as one of the vital tools in helping Arab states to help themselves—whereby we will also help ourselves to achieve peace.

Members of Knesset: The past year, 5754, was marked by the beginning of a settlement with the Palestinians, by peace negotiations with Jordan, and by the very beginnings of peace negotiations with Syria and Lebanon.

The current government adopted the Madrid formula, as initiated by the previous government under Yitzhak Shamir, and yet—when it became clear to us that the principle was correct, but the method was leading us to an impasse—we chose to alter the method and we began separate talks. I never supported the idea of an international peace conference. We succeeded in turning the Madrid Conference into a bilateral conference in the fullest sense of the word. And indeed, this path bore fruit.

Last year, the Government signed a Declaration of Principles with the Palestinians, the Gaza-Jericho First Agreement, and the early transfer of authority in other spheres. In the coming days, negotiations on the next phases will begin.

It is not with an easy heart that we approached the signing with the Palestinians. Bitter memories of the 100 years of bloody conflict weighed, and still weigh, heavy upon complete reconciliation. And yet, we said that we have to make this attempt. We said: We must do this for the generations to come. We said we would try to begin a new chapter in the history of relations between the Palestinians and the State of Israel.

One year ago, after the holiday season, the Palestinian leadership stood before the harsh reality in Gaza in Jabalya and Khan Yunis. The poverty and the hunger—the hatcheries of radical terrorist activities—were, and are today, the Palestinian leadership's enemies. In our opinion, they will be tested by [their ability to] improve the economic situation and welfare of the residents. This, in large measure, will determine whether or not peace with the Palestinians will indeed succeed.

After the first completely erroneous steps—at least from our point of view—after embarrassments and inconsistencies, we are now seeing the first buds of authority and governance. Many countries have mobilized to render economic assistance to the Palestinians, and we are encouraging this in every way because it is also our interest—from the point of view of security and otherwise—that the residents of Gaza and Jericho achieve prosperity and a better life.

But we will not conceal and we will not deny: Palestinian terrorism still continues and claims victims among us. Since the Declaration of Principles was signed in Washington, one year ago, sixty-two IDF soldiers and civilians have been murdered and killed by terrorists in Israel and the territories, most of whom were from the Hamas and Islamic Jihad. Many have been injured. On your behalf as well, I wish to express that the Government shares the grief of the families and wishes a speedy recovery to the wounded.

Members of Knesset: We will not tire from stating, and emphasizing, that security is the foremost of our concerns and that peace will not come to this country without security. Therefore, we view terrorist activity with the utmost severity. Indeed, it has not escaped us that the Palestinian Authority has made some efforts to prevent terrorism and capture its perpetrators, but we do not feel that enough has been done. From our point of view, results are the sole test, and the results up until now have been far from satisfactory—to use an understatement.

In my meetings with the Chairman of the PLO, especially the most recent one, I have made it known—as forcefully as possible—to him and to the members of the Palestinian Authority—that continued progress on the road to peace is very much contingent on his ability, and the ability of his people, to eliminate terrorism emanating from the area under their control. If terrorism continues, it will be difficult for us to continue the peace process with the Palestinians.

Members of Knesset: The signing of the Declaration of Principles with the Palestinians paved the way to negotiations with King Hussein I of the Hashemite Kingdom. During the year, peace negotiations were begun between Israel and Jordan. They are currently in full swing. In recent weeks, Israeli and Jordanian representatives have been meeting daily until late at night, in an attempt to find just solutions to the problems that Jerusalem and Amman have raised.

The major achievement is already behind us. In Washington, we took a big and symbolic step forward, agreeing to put an end to the state of belligerency. An even larger achievement is still before us. In my meeting with them last Thursday in Aqaba, the King and the Crown Prince made it clear that they soon intend to sign a full peace treaty between Israel and the Hashemite Kingdom of Jordan. According to the King, he intends to create a "warm peace" between Israel and Jordan. He told me: "In our peace, the border between Israel and Jordan will be completely insignificant."

Several problems—regarding borders, water, and security—still await solution. Soon, our delegates will sit around the negotiating table with Jordanian representatives in order to bring about the signing of another peace treaty for the State of Israel. Therefore, it is with satisfaction, joy, and also pride, that I can say to you today, Members of Knesset, that—according to my best estimation—it is possible that the signing of a full peace treaty between Israel and the Kingdom of Jordan will take place soon, before the end of this calendar year.

I know that everything I have said is like a dream and that perhaps you are smiling. But this week, while reading the newspaper, among usual advertisements for discounts at hotels in Tiberias and offers to sell apartments, I also saw an advertisement for trips from Israel to Petra, Amman, and Jerash, and nobody in Israel gets excited anymore. There it was, an advertisement on page three of a newspaper.

Members of Knesset: More than twenty-seven years ago, when a sharp sword was held over our necks, the IDF went to war to defend our lives. The great victory found us on the banks of the Suez Canal and the banks of the Jordan River, and on the Golan Heights, which were then called "the Syrian Heights." In the twenty-seven years that have passed since the Six-Day War, the Golan Heights have been transformed from a land of boulders into a flourishing garden. On the black basalt rocks, families were established, homes were built, and children were raised.

The State of Israel and Israeli governments—all Israeli governments— sent the best people to the Golan. There are none better: the pioneers, visionaries, and the fighters who built an honorable and admirable enterprise.

It is no coincidence that the admiration for the people of the Golan Heights crosses party lines and is shared by the broad public. All that is beautiful and good, that we desired and hoped to see in the State of Israel and in its children, is evident in Drora and Yehuda of Merom Golan, in Sami of Katzrin, and in Deganit of Kfar Haruv: the people of the Golan.

We were not mistaken when we sent them to the Golan. We were not mistaken when we encouraged them to build homes, raise children, plant vineyards, and pick fruit. This was the right thing, at the right time, in the right place. With all the respect that we have for the settling of the Golan— and I have respect for it—this was never the main object. More than anything said here, the Golan Heights are important to the security of the State of Israel, with or without settlements.

Permit me a few personal words. I have spent a large part of my adult life in the IDF. For part of my military service, I served as Commanding Officer of the Northern Command. I know every corner in the north, every community, every stone. It was during my service in the north that the serious incidents with the Syrians began, and names that have been almost forgotten—Durijat, Jalbinah, Tewfik, and Tel Azaziat—were my daily bread. I witnessed and joined in the suffering of the communities, which determinedly and heroically withstood the shelling. Important scenes in my life are the destroyed children's rooms in Gadot, the blazing dairies of Tel Katzir, the burning fields at Hulata, Gonen, and Lehavot Habashan.

We did not ascend the Golan Heights, and we did not occupy them during the Six-Day War, so that these scenes would return—and no force in the world will move us on the Golan so much as one centimeter, if there will not be full peace, a true peace, peace with complete security arrangements. Yes, a peace of the brave between Syria and Israel. Only true peace will make us ready for change.

Members of Knesset: For twenty-seven years, we have held fast to our political and security opinions and have not changed them—because the world had not changed and the Arab countries had not changed. But one would have to be an ostrich in order not to distinguish that something has happened in recent years: the world has changed, and the Arab countries too, though not all.

Members of Knesset: As long as Syria did not recognize Israel's right to live in peace, there was no room for negotiation. As long as Damascus rejected our outstretched hand, we held tight our military and civilian grasp on the Golan, several dozen kilometers from Damascus. Syria took the first step towards the possibility of peace—when the Likud Government headed by Yitzhak Shamir was in power—when it agreed to, and participated in, the Madrid Conference. We welcomed this—and continued on the difficult journey toward peace.

Gentlemen, the situation has changed. In recent weeks, we have discerned indications of Syria's willingness to be a partner in the effort for peace. The road is still long; there is much work yet to do. Peace with Syria is distant—but we have no intention of ignoring these signs. We will not return to the days of "there is no one to talk to," we will not return to the days of "we are waiting for a phone call," and we will not return to the days of "the world is against us." Gentlemen, we will not return to those days. We are going forward.

And this is what I have to say to the people of the Golan Heights today: I have accompanied you for many years, during the good times and the painful moments. I have seen you flourish and I have been a loyal partner on your journey. I have always told you my opinions, honestly and faithfully. My opinion was, and is today, that there is a large measure of security risks in any territorial concession to Syria. We are putting much in the balance—both peace and security—but we will sign no peace agreement with Damascus if we are not convinced that our security is assured. Maximum security—as much as it is possible to achieve it.

I appeal to you Drora, to you Yehuda of Merom Hagolan, to you Amitai and Roni of Mevo Hama, to you Sami of Katzrin and Uri of Ortal, residents of the Golan, and say to you: my supreme obligation as Prime Minister, our obligation as a government to the people of Israel, our obligation is to examine every possibility for peace.

For years we have searched for every crack. We have sought peace. We have pursued peace. And now, for the first time since the establishment of the State of Israel, there is a chance for peace with Syria. Peace with Syria is, to a great extent, the key to comprehensive peace. I would like to ask you, my friends on the Golan Heights: What must we do? Not try? Not make an effort to reach peace? Reject out of hand the possibility of putting an end to all the wars?

It is not only I who owe this answer to all citizens of the State of Israel, including the residents of the Golan Heights. You on the Golan, you too, owe an answer. Remember, you know that the Golan is not only the valley of apple orchards. On the Golan Heights there is also the valley of tears, and perhaps your son, Drora, the son about whom you spoke so movingly on television, the son whom you said might have to fight again on the Golan Heights, perhaps your son and thousands of other sons will never have to fight again. Do we have the right to forgo this "maybe"? My decision, our decision in the Government, is to give peace with Syria a chance—a chance that never existed before.

If moving towards peace is a change in position, then yes—I have changed my position. However, we will not—God forbid—abandon the security of the State of Israel. We will add peace to it.

Members of Knesset: What is the current situation of the negotiations with the Syrians? In contrast to the good relations that we have with the Palestinians and the Jordanians, we do not have a good dialogue with the Syrians. The contact between Jerusalem and Damascus is being maintained devotedly, loyally, and diligently by our friends the Americans, and this is an opportunity for us to thank the United States, the President of the United States, the Secretary of State, and the peace team for their efforts, for the hand that they are extending.

Our intention is to reach the signing of a full peace treaty with Syria. In order to reach a peace treaty with Syria, we must reach agreement with it on four components at the same time and we must not make any distinction between them: it is all or nothing.

The first component is the peace border in the peace treaty. As of today, there is no agreement between the Syrians and us about the location of this border.

The second component is the timetable for implementing the components of the peace treaty. In other words, how many years will it take to carry out the withdrawal to the peace border, the stages of withdrawal, the complete implementation of normalization, and the implementation of the security arrangements?

The third component is the test of complete normalization, following the first stage of an extremely limited withdrawal, which will not necessitate the dismantling of settlements on the Golan Heights. The intention is that complete implementation of normalization will be tested over a three-year period, during which we will hold onto most of the Golan Heights area.

Behind the word "normalization" lies an entire realm. That is life itself. This is the peace that we have dreamed of, peace in its daily embodiment: an Israeli embassy in Damascus, a Syrian embassy in Israel; an Egged bus that travels to Aleppo, Israeli tourists in Homs, Israeli ships in Tartus, El Al planes, commercial and cultural ties. Everything—and of course this would work the other way around as well.

The fourth, but not least, component—the most important in any peace treaty with Syria—is security: by this I mean the security arrangements. Here too, this dry term includes a whole range of aspects: beginning with a mutual reduction of regular forces, demilitarizing areas on a geographical asymmetrical basis, deploying multinational forces in a manner like the one that currently exists in the Sinai Desert. More than 1,000 U.S. soldiers have for the past fifteen and one-half years been located in the Sinai. Their mission there is to observe—not within the framework of a UN resolution, but as the result of a Egyptian-Israeli-American decision. In the first stage, there were over 1,000. Today, 980 American soldiers are stationed in Sinai to oversee the military annex of the peace treaty between Egypt and Israel. We will ask nothing else of the Americans when we achieve a peace agreement with Syria on the Golan Heights—the same thing. It will also include early-warning stations, periodic inspections, and the like. I would like to emphasize this once again: only security arrangements that we find to be reasonable will enable us to undertake the risk that a withdrawal on the Golan contains.

Members of Knesset: I must say to you again that, at this stage, in all four of the components that I have outlined to you, there exists today a dispute between Israel and Syria; wide and deep rifts still exist. I am aware of the accusations against us: they say "This is not what you told us before the elections." They say: "We did not think that it would be like this." In the Labor Party platform for the elections to the current Knesset, we explicitly stated that we favor territorial compromise for peace, including with Syria, and therefore a withdrawal on the Golan Heights is part of the Government's declared policy. Despite this, in the event of any significant withdrawal, we are firm in our determination to bring the decision on this subject to a referendum. What is more democratic than that? What is fairer than a referendum?

I repeat my promise that in any event in which we need to pay for a peace treaty by making a significant withdrawal, which would be acceptable to the Government, we will then present it, in all of its details, to every citizen of Israel and ask for the people's decision: Are you for this peace or not? We will not sign a peace treaty with Syria before asking the will of the people in a referendum.

Members of Knesset: Even before comprehensive peace, still in the midst of discussions and agreements, we are witnessing a new wind blowing throughout the world regarding in its relationship with the State of Israel: the claim that the "whole world is against us" has dissipated in the spirit of peace. The world is not against us. The world is with us.

Even now, we are reaping the fruits of peace: dozens of important personages are coming to us and want our friendship. Yesterday, we hosted the Prime Minister of Lithuania; today, the Defense Minister of Chile. Tomorrow, the Vice-Premier of China. Thirty high-level guests will arrive in Israel in the coming weeks, and this is only the beginning.

The gates of hostile countries have opened wide: today, Israelis wander through Oman and Qatar, in Amman and Tunis. Citizens of hostile Arab states are coming to us, establishing initial contacts, economic, commercial, and cultural ties—and this is just the beginning.

Only recently we announced the opening of a liaison office in Morocco, and this week began with a further announcement: the opening of an interest section in Tunis. And thanks to the efforts of Foreign Minister Shimon Peres and the people in his ministry, we will hopefully see more and more such offices being opened in the near future.

And just as all of this is happening, this week the Gulf states—led by Saudi Arabia—announced the end of the decades-long secondary and tertiary Arab boycott of Israel, thereby blazing a new path, a new world for Israel's economic and trade ties. This gives me an opportunity to thank the United States, and the Secretary of State, for their decisive contribution to this important political achievement.

Peace is not blinding us. We are keeping our eyes open and closely examining what is happening around us. We know that, along with the readiness for peace, Arab armies, including that of Syria, are building up their strength. We have not for a moment stopped training and increasing the IDF's capability in various spheres.

American aid has not stopped for a moment, and the past year witnessed the regular continuation of defense aid from the United States, to the tune of $1.8 billion—of which $500 million are actively utilized by the defense industries and research institutes.

In the framework of the American aid, huge contracts were signed this year: more than twenty F-15I aircraft were procured, at a cost of about $2 billion. Artillery rocket launchers were procured, and the first of three Saar-5 boats arrived, in the framework of our efforts to increase the navy's capabilities.

The American administration, under Bill Clinton's presidency, has understood that Israel must be strengthened militarily in order to ensure peace—as we are convinced. The United States has placed at our disposal 24 Apache helicopters, 10 Blackhawk helicopters, 50 F-16 aircraft, antiaircraft missiles, sea-to-sea missiles and sophisticated air-to-surface bombs. All this is new; it was a contribution made by Clinton in talks with me.

Members of Knesset: This is the political situation as is appears today, with all of its shadows and lights—and there are many lights, many more than there are shadows. We are continuing on the journey to peace so that during next year's holiday month, we will be able to come before you, the representatives of the people of Israel, and the entire people of Israel, and say: "Hevaynu Shalom Aleichem" [We bring peace unto you].

Thank you.

Israel Information Service Gopher (ask@israel-info.gov.il) Information Division, Israel Foreign Ministry, Jerusalem.

NOTES

INTRODUCTION

1. See Yehuda Ben-Meir, *National Security Decision-making: The Israeli Case* (Boulder, Colo.: Westview Press, for the Jaffee Center for Strategic Studies, Tel Aviv University, 1986); Yoram Peri, *Between Battles and Ballots: Israeli Military in Politics* (Cambridge: Cambridge University Press, 1983).

2. Leah Rabin, *Rabin: Our Life, His Legacy* (New York: G. P. Putnam, 1997), 190.

3. This was also the view of Israel's president at that time, Chaim Herzog. See Chaim Herzog, *Living History* (Hebrew) (Tel Aviv: Miskal, 1997), 433, 444.

4. For his active role in military appointments, see Yehuda Ben-Meir, *Civil-Military Relations in Israel* (New York: Columbia University Press, 1995), 125.

5. For a discussion of this term and for the importance of strategic cultures, see Stephen P. Rosen, "Military Effectiveness: Why Society Matters," *International Security* 19 (spring 1995): 5–31, and Alastair Iain Johnston, "Thinking about Strategic Culture," *International Security* 19 (spring 1995): 32–64.

6. For the decline of Rabin's rule in the 1974–77 period, see Shlomo Aronson, *Conflict and Bargaining in the Middle East* (Baltimore: Johns Hopkins University Press, 1978), 320–30. For the decline of the hegemony of the Labor Party in Israeli politics, see Asher Arian, "The Passing of Dominance," *Jerusalem Quarterly* 5 (fall 1977): 20–32.

7. The bank account in Washington—which, according to Israeli law, was supposed to have been closed on their return to Israel—was in the name of both;

Yitzhak Rabin was administratively fined because of his passive role in the account, whereas his wife was taken to court, which imposed on her an even higher fine. Rabin's resignation, which was not inevitable, was largely perceived as a sign of honesty on his part, since he could have claimed that he was really not in charge of the bank acount.

8. Efraim Inbar, "Israel," in *Middle East Contemporary Survey,* vol. 16, ed. Ami Ayalon (Boulder, Colo.: Westview Press, 1995), 511–13.

9. For the struggles in the Labor Party over national security positions, see Efraim Inbar, *War and Peace in Israeli Politics: Labor Party Positions on National Security* (Boulder, Colo.: Lynne Rienner, 1991).

10. For a psycho-political portrait of Rabin as a political leader, see Yehudit Auerbach, "Yitzhak Rabin: Portrait of a Leader," in *Israel at the Polls, 1992,* ed. Daniel Elazar and Shmuel Sandler (Lanham, Md.: Rowman and Littlefield Publishers, 1995), 283–317. For a most negative analysis, see Neta Cohen Dor-Shav, "Yitzhak Rabin: A Leader with a Fateful Deficiency: A Clinical Profile," *Nativ* 2 (1994): 14–18.

11. Interview with Maj. Gen. (Res.) Menachem Maron, 1 June 1997. Maron served as director general of the Ministry of Defense from 1983 to 1986.

12. Interview with Eitan Haber, 26 June 1997.

13. Several of Rabin's articles in *Maarachot* were collected in a special issue of the journal (Nos. 344–45, December 1995–January 1996). His newspaper op-eds about the Lebanon War were also collected and published as Yitzhak Rabin, *The War in Lebanon* (Hebrew) (Tel Aviv: Am Oved, 1983).

14. Yitzhak Rabin with Dov Goldstein, *Pinkas Sherut* (Hebrew) (Tel Aviv: Maariv, 1979).

15. Yitzhak Rabin, *Pursuing Peace: The Peace Speeches of Prime Minister Yitzhak Rabin* (Hebrew) (Tel Aviv: Zmora-Bitan, 1995).

16. Yitzhak Rabin, Lecture at the National Security College, 28 July 1986, Library of the National Security College, transcript 6539, p. 2.

17. Ibid. See also Yitzhak Rabin, Lecture at the National Security College, 18 July 1985, Library of the National Security College, transcript 6940, p. 7.

CHAPTER I

1. Dan Horowitz, *Israel's Concept of National Security: Continuity and Change in Israeli Strategic Thinking* (Hebrew) (Jerusalem: Levi Eshkol Institute, 1973), 2–3. For works that analyze Israel's foreign policy assuming a realpolitik perpective of its leadership, see Nadav Safran, *Israel: The Embattled Ally* (Cambridge: Belknap Press of Harvard University, 1978); Avner Yaniv, *Deterrence without the Bomb: The Politics of Israeli Strategy* (Lexington, Mass.: Lexington Books, 1987); Aharon S. Klieman, *Israel and the World after Forty Years* (Washington, D.C.: Pergamon-

Brassey's, 1990); Shmuel Sandler, *The State of Israel, the Land of Israel: The Statist and Ethnonational Dimensions of Foreign Policy* (Westport, Conn.: Greenwood Press, 1993).

2. The main assumptions of political realism are (1) anarchy is the defining characteristic of world politics, in which states are the central actors, (2) states have a military capability to hurt each other, (3) states live in uncertainty as to the intentions of other actors and ultimately rely only on themselves to survive or to pursue other interests, and (4) states think and behave strategically, attempting to maximize power to ensure survival. For an early formulation, see Hans Morgenthau, *Politics among Nations: The Struggle for Power and Peace* (New York: Alfred A. Knopf, 1948); for a later formulation, known as neorealism, see Kenneth Waltz, *Theory of International Politics* (Reading, Mass.: Addison-Wesley Publishing, 1983); for the ongoing debate beween realism and other schools of thought, see John Mearsheimer, "The False Promise of International Institutions," *International Security* 19 (winter 1994/95): 5–49. See also David A. Baldwin, ed., *Neorealism and Neoliberalism* (New York: Columbia University Press, 1993).

3. Yitzhak Rabin, *The House of My Father* (Hebrew) (Tel Aviv: Hakibbutz Hameuchad, n.d.), 21.

4. Yitzhak Rabin, with Dov Goldstein, *Pinkas Sherut* (Hebrew) (Tel Aviv: Maariv, 1979), 18–19, cited hereafter as Rabin, *Memoirs*. Rabin was born into an active Zionist family. His mother was politically involved in Yishuv politics. Moreover, the Kadouri agricultural high school served as a formative experience for a number of Israeli leaders. From childhood, Rabin was exposed to the Zionist leadership in Palestine, whose ethos emphasized pioneering and sacrifice for the national cause.

5. Michael Brecher, *The Foreign Policy System of Israel* (London: Oxford University Press, 1972), 229–44; Efraim Inbar, "Jews, Jewishness, and Israel's Foreign Policy," *Jewish Political Studies Review* 2 (fall 1990): 165–83.

6. For example, he could not hide his anger and disgust when he was served bacon at a luncheon with Defense Secretary Robert McNamara shortly after his arrival in Washington to take up the post of ambassador (Interview with Yossi Ben-Aharon, 6 June 1997).

7. For the "evoked set," see Robert Jervis, *Perception and Misperception in International Politics* (Princeton: Princeton University Press, 1976), 213–16.

8. Rabin, *Memoirs*, 24.

9. *Maariv*, 2 June 1972.

10. *Maariv*, 25 September 1974. For Israel's isolation in the post-1973 period, see Efraim Inbar, *Outcast Countries in the World Community* (Denver: University of Denver Press, 1985).

11. Shlomo Nakdimon, *A Hopeless Hope: The Rise and Fall of the Israeli Kurdish Alliance, 1963–1975* (Hebrew) (Tel Aviv: Yediot Aharonot, 1996), 9. Israel complied with the Iran-Iraq agreement on the demarcation of the border between them

and on putting an end to the assistance to the Kurds because of Israel's good relations with Iran. In Rabin's view, this amounted to "a desertion of the Kurds" (quoted in ibid., 10). In 1965, Rabin, in his capacity as chief of staff, was part of the small informal group that decided to give priority to aiding the Kurds (quoted in ibid., 94).

12. Doron Rosenblum, "The 1,000 Days of Rabin," *Haaretz*, 6 May 1977.

13. *Maariv*, 3 February 1988.

14. *Davar*, 2 February 1973, p. 13.

15. *Maariv*, 3 October 1976.

16. Interview with Yitzhak Shamir, 16 June 1997.

17. Rabin, *Memoirs*, 470.

18. "Interview with Yitzhak Rabin," *Bamahane*, 28 December 1965, p. 4.

19. *Maariv*, 13 October 1975.

20. Lecture at the National Security College, 1 April 1981, Library of the National Security College, transcript 6412, p. 6.

21. Ibid., 14.

22. *Bamahane*, 18 April 1986, pp. 10–11.

23. For the difference between the activist school and the Sharett school of thinking, see Brecher, *The Foreign Policy System of Israel*, 251–90; Gabriel Sheffer, *Resolution vs. Management of the Middle East Conflict*, Jerusalem Papers on Peace Problems No. 32 (Jerusalem: Leonard Davis Institute for International Relations, Hebrew University, 1980).

24. In Israeli political parlance, the terms *left* and *right, doves* and *hawks,* are almost synonymous and refer to the difference in opinion on how to deal with the various aspects of the Arab-Israeli dispute, such as the future of territories, the Palestinian question, and the use of force. For the move of the Israeli elite toward the left, see Efraim Inbar and Giora Goldberg, "Is Israel's Political Elite Becoming More Hawkish?" *International Journal* 45 (summer 1990): 631–60; for the move of the Labor Party toward greater dovishness, see Efraim Inbar, *War and Peace in Israeli Politics: Labor Party Positions on National Security* (Boulder, Colo.: Lynne Rienner, 1991).

25. *Haaretz*, 2 July 1974, p. 1.

26. Razi Guterman and Zisi Stavi, "Special Interview with the Prime Minister," in *Journalists' Yearbook 1994–95* (Hebrew) (Tel Aviv: Journalists' Association, 1996), 15.

27. Ibid. See also Marvin Kalb, "The Promise and Problems of the Israeli Press" (interview with Yitzhak Rabin), *Press/Politics* 1 (winter 1996): 110–11.

28. *Haaretz*, 23 September 1975, p. 3.

29. "Interview with Yitzhak Rabin," *Bamahane*, 28 December 1965, p. 4.

30. "Interview with Chief of Staff Yitzhak Rabin," *Bamahane*, 26 December 1967, p. 5. For Soviet involvement in the Middle East, see Galia Golan, *Soviet Policies in the Middle East: From World War II to Gorbachev* (Cambridge: Cambridge University Press, 1990); Alvin Z. Rubinstein, *Red Star on the Nile* (Princeton:

Princeton University Press, 1976); Robert O. Freedman, *Soviet Policy toward the Middle East since 1970* (New York: Praeger, 1975).

31. "Interview with Chief of Staff Yitzhak Rabin," *Bamahane,* 26 December 1967, p. 6.

32. Ibid.

33. Israel Landers, "Special Interview with Ambassador Yitzhak Rabin," *Davar,* 4 June 1971, p. 9.

34. Motta (Mordechai) Gur, *From the North and from the West* (Hebrew) (Tel Aviv: Maarachot 1998), 186. Gur served as military attaché in Washington while Rabin was ambassador. Such an evaluation served well Rabin's efforts to minimize the dangers of escalation of a military eruption of the Arab-Israeli conflict in order to thwart an American-Soviet solution imposed on Israel.

35. *Davar,* 8 September 1975, p. 1.

36. Lecture at the National Security College, 1 April 1981, Library of the National Security College, transcript 6412, p. 7.

37. For the attitudinal prism of Ben-Gurion, see Brecher, *The Foreign Policy System of Israel,* 253–69.

38. The term *politicide* was coined by Yehoshafat Harkabi See his *Fedayeen Action and Arab Strategy,* Adelphi Papers No. 53 (London: International Institute for Strategic Studies, 1969), 1.

39. The exceptions facing politicide were Taiwan, South Korea, South Vietnam, and West Germany. In the Middle East, the Arab countries subjected to a politicide campaign have been Kuwait and Lebanon.

40. "Interview with Yitzhak Rabin," *Bamahane,* 9 January 1965, p. 4.

41. "Interview with Yitzhak Rabin," *Bamahane,* 28 December 1965, p. 4.

42. "Interview with the Chief of Staff, Yitzhak Rabin," *Bamahane,* 9 January 1964, p. 4. For the importance of the Negev (southern Israel) in the foreign policy considerations of Egypt, Israel, and the Western powers, see Ilan Asia, *The Core of the Conflict: The Struggle for the Negev, 1947–1956* (Hebrew) (Jerusalem: Yad Ben Tzvi Press and Ben Gurion University Press, 1994).

43. "Interview with the Chief of Staff," *Bamahane,* 9 January 1964, p. 4.

44. See Yitzhak Rabin, "Why We Won the War," *Jerusalem Post, Rosh Hashana Magazine,* 10 October 1967, p. 4.

45. Interview with the Chief of Staff," *Bamahane,* 9 January 1964, p. 4.

46. Rabin, "Why We Won the War," 4.

47. Horowitz, *Israel's Concept of National Security,* 9–10.

48. "Interview with Chief of Staff Yitzhak Rabin," *Bamahane,* 26 December 1967, p. 5.

49. Yitzhak Rabin, "The Test of Deterrence in Israel's Wars," *Safra Vesayfa* 4 (November 1981): 28. Rabin regarded the 1956 Suez Campaign as a possible exception to this rule.

50. Yitzhak Rabin, "Eshkol, My Defense Minister," *Bamahane,* 14 February 1973, p. 14.

51. Robert Slater, *Rabin of Israel* (London: Robson Books, 1977) (paperback ed., 1996), 88.

52. *Bamahane,* 9 January 1964, p. 4.

53. *Bamahane,* 4 February 1976, p. 7.

54. Appendix A: Yitzhak Rabin, "After the Gulf War: Israeli Defense and Its Security Policy."

55. Ibid.

56. *Yediot Aharonot,* 8 December 1995.

57. *Maariv,* 20 January 1989; see also *Davar,* 1 September 1989.

58. Landers, "Special Interview with Ambassador Yitzhak Rabin."

59. Chaim Izak, "Interview with Rabin," *Davar,* 27 October 1979.

60. Yitzhak Rabin, "The National Security Problems of Israel in the 1980s," *Maarachot,* nos. 270–71 (October 1979).

61. Yitzhak Rabin, "The Quality That Guarantees Power," in *Israeli Security in the Next Decade* (Hebrew) (Efal: Yad Tabenkin, 1988), 35.

62. Yitzhak Rabin, Lecture at the National Security College, 30 June 1983, Library of the National Security College, transcript 7038, p. 8.

63. Bezalel Amikam, "An Evaluation with No Illusions: In the Aftermath of a Meeting with Yitzhak Rabin," *Al Hamishmar,* 22 February 1980.

64. Yitzhak Rabin, "Middle East Chess: King's Move," *Spectrum* 1 (April–May 1983): 7; see also his statement to *Maariv,* 3 August 1986.

65. Yitzhak Rabin, "The Challenge: To Be the Leader," *IDF Journal* 19 (winter 1990): 3 (adapted from a speech delivered to graduates of the IDF Staff College, August 1989).

66. For the Brookings Institution Middle East Report and the Carter administration, see Steven L. Spiegel, *The Other Arab-Israeli Conflict: Making America's Middle East Policy, from Truman to Reagan* (Chicago: University of Chicago Press, 1985), 323–24.

67. For the Allon Plan, see Yerucham Cohen, *The Allon Plan* (Hebrew) (Tel Aviv: Hakibbutz Hameuchad, 1973); see also Yigal Allon, "Israel: The Case for Defensible Borders," *Foreign Affairs* 55 (October 1976): 38–53.

68. Yosef Harif, "Rabin Suggests a Waiting Period," *Maariv,* 19 October 1988.

69. *Bamahane,* 16 April 1986, p. 10. See also Appendix B.

70. Yitzhak Rabin, "Arafat Is Not the Partner," *Yediot Aharonot,* 30 April 1987, p. 18.

71. See Amos Elon, *The Israelis: Founders and Sons* (London: Weidenfeld and Nicholson, 1971), chap. 9.

72. Rabin, *Memoirs,* 97.

73. Yitzhak Rabin, "The Lessons of Sinai," *Maarachot,* nos. 344–45 (December 1995–January 1996): 16–17, originally published in *Maarachot,* nos. 178–79 (October 1966).

74. Ibid., 18.

75. Ibid.

76. Yitzhak Rabin, "The Six-Day War: Characteristics and Achievements," *Maarachot* nos. 344–45 (December 1995–January 1996): 35, originally published in *Maarachot,* no. 256 (June 1977).

77. Yitzhak Rabin, "Israel Should Have Attacked on May 30, 1967," *Maariv,* 2 June 1972, p. 15.

78. Rabin, "Eshkol, My Defense Minister."

79. Rabin, "The Six-Day War," 35.

80. Asher Maniv, "A Conversation with Yitzhak Rabin," *Migvan* 46 (April 1980): 4.

81. *Haaretz,* 8 August 1984; *Maariv,* 24 April 1975; *Haaretz,* 5 September 1975; *Maariv,* 26 February 1976.

82. Yitzhak Rabin, "Struggling for Peace," *Mibifnim* 40 (March 1978): 9; see also Yitzhak Rabin, "A Peace Plan," *Migvan* 28 (July 1978): 3. The acceptance of UN Resolution 242 by Egypt in 1970 was only an oblique acceptance of Israel.

83. Rabin, "Struggling for Peace," 12.

84. Ibid., 10. For this agreement, see Bernard Reich, *Quest for Peace* (New Brunswick, N.J.: Transaction Books, 1977), 295–347; Safran, *Israel,* 535–60; Saadia Touval, *The Peace Brokers: Mediators in the Arab-Israeli Conflict, 1948–1979* (Princeton: Princeton University Press, 1982), 259–83.

85. Efraim Inbar, "Problems of Pariah States: The National Security Policy of the Rabin Government, 1974–77" (Ph.D. diss., University of Chicago, 1981), part two.

86. See Yitzhak Rabin, "The Israeli-Egyptian Relationship: Whereto? An Israeli Perspective," *Dapei Elazar* 9 (1986): 106; and Yitzhak Rabin, *The Israeli Labor Party* (Hebrew) 10 (December 1986): 11. This was part of a speech given to the party Central Council on 7 June 1986.

87. *Israeli Labor Party,* 10.

88. Yitzhak Rabin, "War, Terror, and Peace," *Bama,* 1 February 1986. (This is an occasional publication of the Labor Party in Jerusalem.)

89. *Haaretz,* 8 March 1990.

90. Rabin, "The Quality That Guarantees Power," 32–33.

91. Yitzhak Rabin, Lecture at the National Security College, 18 July 1985, Library of the National Security College, transcript 6940, p. 13.

92. Rabin, "The Quality That Guarantees Power," 32.

93. Ibid., 33.

94. Ibid., 34. For the missile exchanges, see Philip A. G. Sabin and Efraim Karsh, "Escalation in the Iran-Iraq War," *Survival* 31 (May/June 1989): 241–54. For an analysis of the missile threats to Israel, see Aharon Levran, "Threats Facing Israel from Surface-to-Surface Missiles," *IDF Journal* 19 (winter 1990): 37–44.

95. Rabin, "The Challenge," 2 (emphasis in the original).

96. Ibid., 3.

97. Interview with Maj. Gen. (Res.) Uzi Narkis, 19 January 1997. Narkis served in the General Staff commanded by Rabin. On the Palestinian national movement,

see Yehoshua Porat, *The Emergence of the Palestinian Arab National Movement, 1918–1929* (London: Frank Cass, 1977), and *The Emergence of the Palestinian National Movement, 1929–1939* (London: Frank Cass, 1977); Shmuel Sandler and Hillel Frisch, *Israel, the Palestinians, and the West Bank: A Study in Intercommunal Conflict* (Lexington, Mass.: Lexington Books, 1984); Helena Cobban, *The Palestinian Liberation Organization: People, Power, and Politics* (Cambridge: Cambridge University Press, 1984); Barry Rubin, *Revolution until Victory? The Politics and History of the PLO* (Cambridge: Harvard University Press, 1994).

98. For the interstate and the intercommunal dimensions of the Arab-Israeli conflict, see Shmuel Sandler, "The Protracted Arab-Israeli Conflict," *Jerusalem Journal of International Relations* 10 (December 1988): 54–78. For a psychological treatment of Rabin's views on the Palestinians, see Yehudit Auerbach and Hemda Ben-Yehuda Agid, "Attitudes to an Existence Conflict: Rabin and Sharon on the Palestinian Issue, 1967–87," in *Conflict and Social Psychology*, ed. Knud S. Larsen (London: Sage Publications for PRIO, 1993), 144–67. For a somewhat flawed sketch of the evolution in Rabin's positions toward the Palestinians, see Hemda Ben-Yehuda, "Attitude Change and Policy Transformation: Yitzhak Rabin and the Palestinian Question, 1967–95," *Israel Affairs* 3 (spring/summer 1997): 202–24.

99. "Interview with Yitzhak Rabin," *Bamahane*, 28 December 1965, p. 5.

100. Ibid.

101. Ibid.

102. For excerpts, see *Bamahane*, 4 February 1976, p. 4.

103. Ibid.

104. Rabin, "Middle East Chess," 8.

105. Yitzhak Rabin, "Learning from History," *Spectrum* 6 (May 1988): 10.

106. Ibid.

107. *Bamahane*, 4 February 1976, p. 7.

108. *Davar*, 12 December 1975, p. 2.

109. Rabin, "Struggling for Peace," 13.

110. For the growing struggle between the supporters of the Jordanian orientation and the backers of the Palestinian orientation within the Labor Party, see Inbar, *War and Peace in Israeli Politics*, 58–66. Since the 1970s, it has been the hawks in the party who have opted for the Hashemites.

111. Reuven Pedatzur, "Closing a Circle: Back to the Palestinian Option," *Medina Umimshal Veyachasim Beinleumiim* 40 (summer 1995): 42. For the initial Israeli policy toward the territories, see Shlomo Gazit, *The Stick and the Carrot: The Israeli Administration in Judea and Samaria* (Hebrew) (Tel Aviv: Zmora-Bitan, 1985).

112. For Israeli-Jordanian relations, see Dan Shueftan, *A Jordanian Option* (Hebrew) (Tel Aviv: Yad Tabenkin, 1986); Moshe Zak, *King Hussein Makes Peace* (Hebrew) (Ramat Gan: Bar-Ilan University Press and BESA Center for Strategic Studies, 1996); Aharon S. Klieman, "The Israel-Jordan Tacit Security Regime," in

Regional Security Regimes: Israel and Its Neighbors, ed. Efraim Inbar (Albany: State University of New York Press, 1995), 127–50.

113. Rabin, *Memoirs,* 435; Rabin, "A Peace Plan," 4–6. See also Rabin, "Struggling for Peace," 14.

114. Interviews with Yigal Allon (4 June 1979), Israel Galili (28 August 1979), and Peter W. Rodman (13 August 1996). Already in January 1974, Golda Meir suggested the Jericho Plan to King Hussein, who rejected it. See Zak, *King Hussein Makes Peace,* 163–65.

115. *Maariv,* 16 October 1974.

116. *Davar,* 30 January 1976, p. 2.

117. Auerbach and Ben-Yehuda Agid, "Attitudes to an Existence Conflict," 149.

118. *Knesset Minutes,* 21 October 1985, p. 75.

119. *Bamahane,* 4 February 1976, p. 4. For an analysis of the Palestinian National Covenant, see Yehoshafat Harkabi, *Palestinians and Israel* (Jerusalem: Keter, 1974), 49–69.

120. *Jerusalem Post,* 11 June 1976, p. 12.

121. Rabin, *Memoirs,* 120.

122. Ibid., 542–43.

123. Interview with Maj. Gen. (Res.) Shlomo Gazit, 26 February 1998. The dialogue was approved also by Prime Minister Yitzhak Shamir, and the cover story, in the event that the meetings became public knowledge, was Israel's desire to get information about the MIAs in Lebanon.

124. Rabin, "Struggling for Peace," 13.

125. Rabin, "A Peace Plan," 4–6.

126. *Yediot Aharonot,* 30 October 1980.

127. *Maariv,* 28 April 1987.

128. Ibid.

129. Yitzhak Rabin, interview on Israeli television, transcript, 13 January 1988, *Journal of Palestine Studies* 17 (spring 1988): 153. See also a similar statement in *Haaretz,* 1 June 1988.

130. For the peace initiative, see Menachem Shalev and David Makovsky, "Cabinet to Approve Election Plan Today," *Jerusalem Post,* 14 May 1989, p. 1; Eytan Bentsur, *The Road to Peace Crosses Madrid* (Hebrew) (Tel Aviv: Miskal, 1997), 36–48. For the developments within the Labor Party before the peace initiative, see Yossi Beilin, *Touching Peace* (Hebrew) (Tel Aviv: Miskal, 1997), 35–37.

131. *Haaretz,* 4 August 1988, A4.

132. *Knesset Minutes,* 21 October 1985, p. 77, 10 June 1987, p. 2985.

133. *Jerusalem Post,* 23 August 1985.

134. Rabin, "Struggling for Peace."

135. Harif, "Rabin Suggests a Waiting Period."

136. Amnon Abramovitch, "Interview with Rabin," *Maariv,* 10 February 1989.

137. David Makovsky, "Rabin: Let's Talk about Success, Not Failure," *Jerusalem Post*, 6 October 1996, p. 7.

138. Yitzhak Rabin, "My Jerusalem," *Maarachot*, no. 325 (June–July 1992): 2–3. This is the text of his address at the rally commemorating twenty-five years since the liberation of the city. See also *Knesset Minutes*, 29 May 1995.

139. For this concept, see Dan Horowitz, *Israel's Concept of Defensible Borders*, Jerusalem Papers on Peace Problems No. 16 (Jerusalem: Leonard Davis Institute for International Relations, Hebrew University, 1975), 9.

140. For details, see Yehiel Admoni, *A Decade of Discretion: Settlement Policy in the Territories, 1967–77* (Hebrew) (Tel Aviv: Hakibbutz Hameuchad, 1992).

141. Interview with Prof. Shlomo Avineri (who served then as director general of the Foreign Ministry), 17 April 1997. Rabin reluctantly accepted in 1975 the recommendation of his influential cabinet member, Israel Galili, to build a few settlements east of the Green Line (the 1967 border) in Samaria in order to solidify Israel's control of the coastal aquifer. Rabin's political weakness at that time and his rivalry with Peres were used by the Gush Emunim movement to establish two settlements outside the Allon Plan: Kedumim and Ofra. (See Admoni, *A Decade of Discretion*, 148, 178–80.)

142. Rabin, "Struggling for Peace," 13.

143. The explicit Allon Plan was formally adopted by the Labor Party in 1977, but in the 1990s only the hawks in the party still adhered to it in its entirety. See Inbar, *War and Peace in Israeli Politics*, 88.

144. Rabin, "Middle East Chess," 8. Southern Gaza was also a security zone delineated in the Allon Plan as a buffer between Egypt and the Gaza Strip.

145. "Rabin's Plan," *Jerusalem Post*, 11 March 1988.

146. Ibid. After 1967, the Palestinians in the West Bank retained their Jordanian citizenship.

147. See Rabin, "Arafat Is Not the Partner."

148. Ibid.

149. Rabin, *Memoirs*, 496.

150. Admoni, *A Decade of Discretion*, 168.

CHAPTER 2

1. Aharon S. Klieman, "Israeli Diplomacy in the Thirtieth Year of Statehood: Some Constants and Discontinuities," in *Israel: A Developing Society*, ed. Asher Arian (Assen: Van Gorgum, 1990), 43–49.

2. For the Israeli nonalignment policy and its early efforts to find an ally, see Uri Bialer, *Between East and West: Israel's Foreign Policy Orientation, 1948–1956* (Cambridge: Cambridge University Press, 1990); and Avner Yaniv, *Deterrence without the Bomb: The Politics of Israeli Strategy* (Lexington, Mass.: Lexington Books, 1987), 48–55.

3. For accounts of American-Israeli relations, see Nadav Safran, *Israel: The Embattled Ally* (Cambridge: Belknap Press of Harvard University, 1978); Steven L. Spiegel, *The Other Arab-Israeli Conflict: Making America's Middle East Policy, from Truman to Reagan* (Chicago: University of Chicago University Press, 1985); Avraham Ben-Zvi, *The United States and Israel: The Limits of the Special Relationship* (New York: Columbia University Press, 1993).

4. For the French-Israeli relations, see Shimon Peres, *David's Sling* (Hebrew) (Jerusalem: Weidenfeld and Nicholson, 1970); Yaakov Tzur, *The Diplomatic Campaign in France, 1953–56* (Hebrew) (Tel Aviv: Am Oved, 1968); Michael Bar-Zohar, *A Bridge over the Mediterranean: The France-Israel Relationship, 1947–1963* (Hebrew) (Tel Aviv: Am Hasefer, 1964); Sylvia K. Crosbie, *A Tacit Alliance: France and Israel from the Suez to the Six-Day War* (Princeton: Princeton University Press, 1974).

5. Abba Eban, *An Autobiography* (London: Futura Publications, 1977), 233.

6. Yitzhak Rabin, with Dov Goldstein, *Pinkas Sherut* (Hebrew) (Tel Aviv: Maariv, 1979), 108–9, 114, cited hereafter as Rabin, *Memoirs*. See also Moshe Zak, "A Bridge across the Atlantic," *Jerusalem Post*, 10 November 1995.

7. Other issues of dispute during this formative period in the relationship between the two were the role of the IDF versus the Ministry of Defense in weapons procurement policy, the amount and type of weapons to be purchased from Israeli military industries, and the role of nuclear weapons in Israel's national strategy. At that time, Peres was serving as deputy minister of defense under David Ben-Gurion. Rabin exaggerated the magnitude of the support for the French orientation. Even Peres, who definitely felt more at home in Europe than in America, did not object to bolstering relations with the United States. The French orientation also helped build Israel's nuclear option.

8. Rabin, *Memoirs*, 108–9.

9. Interview with Maj. Gen. (Res.) Uzi Narkis (who served as Israel's military attaché in Paris for the 1959–62 period), 19 January 1997.

10. Yitzhak Rabin, "From the Battles over the Water to the Six-Day War," in *The IDF: An Encyclopaedia of Army and Security* (Hebrew) (Ramat Gan: Revivim, 1981), 187–89. See also Lecture at the National Security College, 1 April 1981, Library of the National Security College, transcript 6412, p. 14.

11. Yitzhak Rabin, "Eshkol, My Defense Minister," *Bamahane*, 14 February 1973, p. 14. See also Ezer Weizman, *On Eagles' Wings* (New York: Macmillan, 1979), 252–54.

12. Rabin, *Memoirs*, 114.

13. For the rise of Eshkol as Ben Gurion's successor, see Shlomo Aronson, *Conflict and Bargaining in the Middle East* (Baltimore: Johns Hopkins University Press, 1978), 30–56.

14. Rabin, *Memoirs*, 105.

15. Ibid.

16. Haggay Levy, "The Hawks," *IAF Organ,* no. 106 (December 1995): 35. According to Rabin, the Eisenhower administration ended the weapons embargo imposed on Israel and sold "defensive" weapon systems, such as antitank 106-mm recoilless guns (1958), and approved the sale of a radar station in 1960. After the 1958 successes of the radical pan-Arab tide in the Middle East (the January establishment of the United Arab Republic, the July 1958 Kassem overthrow of the Hashemite regime in Iraq, and the attempts to destabilize the pro-Western regimes in Jordan and Lebanon), it was easier to overcome American resistance to selling weapons to Israel because the Americans started seeing the Middle East as an arena of superpower conflict. (See Rabin, "From the Battles over the Water to the Six-Day War," 188.) See also Mordechai Gazit, *Israel's Weapons Procurement from the United States* (Hebrew), Policy Papers No. 8 (Jerusalem: Leonard Davis Institute for International Relations, Hebrew University, 1983), 23. Most studies ignore these very modest arms transfers by the Eisenhower administration and credit the Kennedy administration with the first sale of weapons to Israel.

17. For the change in the American policy toward Israel and the Hawk missile sale, see Mordechai Gazit, *President Kennedy's Policy toward the Arab States and Israel* (Tel Aviv: Shiloach Center, Tel Aviv University, 1983); Spiegel, *The Other Arab-Israeli Conflict,* 106–17.

18. Gazit, *President Kennedy's Policy toward the Arab States and Israel,* 45. In the first such meeting, which took place in July 1962, Aharon Yariv, Israel's military attaché to Washington, presented the Israeli military evaluation.

19. Eitan Haber, *Today War Will Break Out: The Reminiscences of Brig. Gen. Israel Lior, Aide-de-Camp to Prime Ministers Levi Eshkol and Golda Meir* (Hebrew) (Tel Aviv: Edanim, 1987), 69.

20. Moshe Zak, *King Hussein Makes Peace* (Hebrew) (Ramat Gan: Bar-Ilan University Press and BESA Center for Strategic Studies, 1996), 71.

21. Rabin, *Memoirs,* 213–14.

22. Interview with Yossi Ben-Aharon, 6 June 1997. Ben-Aharon, then a junior diplomat, worked with Rabin at the Israeli embassy in Washington.

23. Rabin, *Memoirs,* 14.

24. Robert Slater, *Rabin of Israel* (London: Robson Books, 1977), 172.

25. David Horovitz, ed., *Yitzhak Rabin: Soldier of Peace* (London: Peter Halban, 1996), 48.

26. Uzi Narkis, *Soldier of Jerusalem* (Hebrew) (Tel Aviv: Ministry of Defense Publishing House, 1991), 304–5.

27. Rabin, *Memoirs,* 215.

28. Henry Kissinger, *The White House Years* (Boston: Little, Brown and Co., 1979), 355, 1006; Interview with Peter W. Rodman, 13 August 1996.

29. Rabin, *Memoirs,* 464. Rabin wrote that it was too early to disclose the full nature of this contribution, alluding probably to the Israeli nuclear program.

30. Ibid., 223. Nixon also appreciated Rabin, whose analytical skills and personality made a strong impression on the American president. They were both shy and awkward. Interviews with Rodman and with Joseph Sisco (13 August 1996).

31. *Washington Post,* 11 June 1972, A1.

32. *Washington Post,* 15 June 1972, A18.

33. Slater, *Rabin of Israel,* 185.

34. *Yitzhak Rabin Talks with Leaders and Heads of State* (Hebrew) (Givataim: Revivim, 1984), 63.

35. Walter Laqueur, *The Struggle for the Middle East: The Soviet Union and the Middle East* (Harmondsworth: Penguin Books, 1972), 84–86.

36. Aryeh Brown, *Moshe Dayan and the Six-Day War* (Hebrew) (Tel Aviv: Yediot Aharonot, 1997), 222–26.

37. Ibid.

38. Rabin, *Memoirs,* 395.

39. Ibid., 376; Kissinger, *The White House Years,* 1289; Henry Kissinger, *Years of Upheaval* (Boston: Little, Brown and Co., 1982), 22.

40. Eban, *An Autobiography,* 465.

41. For his influence on Golda Meir and other members of the cabinet, see Dan Margalit, *A Message from the White House* (Hebrew) (Tel Aviv: Otpaz, 1971).

42. Interview with Sisco. Maj. Gen. (Res.) Ezer Weizman, then Minister of Transportation in the national unity government, also shared Rabin's evaluation. (See his *On Eagles' Wings,* 273.)

43. Rabin, *Memoirs,* 253–55, 261.

44. Ibid., 313. For an American perspective on these events, see Adam Garfinkle, "U.S. Decision-Making in the Jordan Crisis: Correcting the Record," *Political Science Quarterly* 100 (spring 1985): 117–38.

45. Aronson, *Conflict and Bargaining in the Middle East,* 94.

46. Interview with Ben-Aharon.

47. Ibid.; Rabin, *Memoirs,* 247–48. For a review of American-Israeli relations in that period, see Safran, *Israel,* 414–74.

48. For the details, see Margalit, *A Message from the White House,* 134–35. For the difference between the Rogers Plan of December 1969 and the Rogers Initiative of July 1970, see Aronson, *Conflict and Bargaining in the Middle East,* 120–21.

49. For an argument that the change in the American position toward Israel was primarily a result of strategic considerations, see A. F. K. Organsky, *The $36 Billion Bargain: Strategy and Politics in U.S. Assistance to Israel* (New York: Columbia University Press, 1990).

50. The figures have been taken from Table 6.3 in Organsky, *The $36 Billion Bargain,* 143.

51. For the details of this change in American policy, see *The Other Arab-Israeli Conflict,* 203–15. Egypt, under the new leadership of Anwar Sadat, as well as Israel,

preferred to negotiate an interim agreement. For Rabin's positive attitude toward interim agreements, see his interview with *Davar*, 2 February 1973, p. 13.

52. Spiegel, *The Other Arab-Israeli Conflict*, 178.

53. "Five Stars of Embassy Row," *Newsweek*, 12 December 1972, pp. 50–56.

54. Regarding Israel's isolation, see Efraim Inbar, *Outcast Countries in the World Community* (Denver: University of Denver Press, 1985).

55. Quoted in Slater, *Rabin of Israel*, 204.

56. *Haaretz*, 6 November 1974, A9.

57. Interview with Yitzhak Rabin, 25 April 1979.

58. Slater, *Rabin of Israel*, 156–69.

59. *Maariv*, 3 October 1976.

60. *Maariv*, 18 June 1976.

61. *Haaretz*, 3 December 1974.

62. *Haaretz*, 22 September 1974.

63. *Haaretz*, 1 August 1974.

64. For the text of the MOU, see *Washington Post*, 16 September 1975, and *New York Times*, 18 September 1975. For the Sinai II Agreement, see also Bernard Reich, *Quest for Peace* (New Brunswick, N.J.: Transaction Books, 1977), and Edward Sheehan, "Step By Step in the Middle East," *Foreign Policy* 22 (spring 1976): 3–70.

65. These figures have been taken from Table 6.3 in Organsky, *The $36 Billion Bargain*, 143.

66. Avraham Tamir, *A Soldier in Search of Peace* (Hebrew) (Tel Aviv: Edanim, 1988), 347–48. Maj. Gen. (Res.) Avraham Tamir served then in an IDF planning unit.

67. Yuval Neeman, "Why I Resigned from the Ministry of Defense," *Haaretz*, 6 February 1976. Inadequate Israeli staff work also contributed to this neglect. See Efraim Inbar, "Problems of Pariah States: The National Security Policy of the Rabin Government" (Ph.D. diss., University of Chicago, 1981), 146–47.

68. *Washington Post*, 16 September 1975.

69. Interview with Yitzak Rabin, 18 November 1979.

70. *Newsweek*, 1 January 1979; see also Dov Goldstein, "Interview of the Week with Yitzhak Rabin," *Maariv*, 16 March 1979.

71. Interview with Rabin, 18 November 1979. See also Chaim Izak, "Special Interview with Yitzhak Rabin," *Davar*, 27 October 1978.

72. Interview with Rabin, 25 April 1979.

73. See *Department of State Bulletin*, 23 February 1976, pp. 222, 226, 228. (Rabin's official visit took place on 26 January through 5 February 1976).

74. Yitzhak Rabin, Lecture at the National Security College, 28 July 1986, Library of the National Security College, transcript 6539, p. 18.

75. Interview with Yitzhak Shamir, 16 June 1997.

76. See Shai Feldman, *The Future of U.S.-Israel Strategic Cooperation* (Washington, D.C.: Washington Institute for Near East Policy, 1996), 12–13; Karen Puschel, *U.S.-Israel Strategic Cooperation in the Post-Cold War Era: An American Perspective*, JCSS Study No. 20 (Boulder, Colo.: Westview Press, 1992). For the legal aspects of

the growing cooperation, see Elyakim Rubinstein, *Paths of Peace* (Hebrew) (Tel Aviv: Ministry of Defense Publishing House, 1992), 167–72.

77. Interview with Maj. Gen. (Res.) David Ivri, 8 July 1997. For an analysis of the benefits conferred on Israel by joining the SDI initiative, see Charles D. Brooks, "S.D.I.: A New Dimension for Israel," *Journal of Social, Political, and Economic Studies* 11, no. 4 (1986): 341–48.

78. *New York Times,* 9 March 1986.

79. *New York Times,* 25 October 1988, A10. The agreement was reached in December 1987. In the 1990s, the proportion of American support for the Arrrow was slightly reduced, to 72 percent.

80. Interview with Shamir. Reservations were occasionally voiced by Yitzhak Navon, Haim Bar-Lev, and Chief of Staff Lt. Gen. Moshe Levy.

81. For the political context and the ramifications of this development, see Dore Gold, *Israel as an American Non-NATO Ally: Parameters of Defense-Industrial Cooperation,* JCSS Study No. 19 (Boulder, Colo.: Westview Press, 1992).

82. Puschel, *U.S.-Israel Strategic Cooperation,* 106.

83. "Interview with the Minister of Defense," *IDF Journal* 15 (summer 1988): 7.

84. Ibid. For the valuable contribution of Israel, see Steven L. Spiegel, "U.S. Relations with Israel: The Military Benefits," *Orbis* 30 (fall 1986): 475–97.

85. See James A. Baker III, *The Politics of Diplomacy* (New York: Putnam, 1995), 126, 555–56; George P. Schultz, *Turmoil and Triumph* (New York: Scribner's, 1993), 51, 203n, 654. President Chaim Herzog also felt that by 1991 the Bush-Baker administration already preferred to see Rabin lead Israel, rather than Shamir. See Chaim Herzog, *Living History* (Hebrew) (Tel Aviv: Miskal, 1997), 485.

86. Interview with Maj. Gen. (Res.) Menachem Maron, 1 June 1997.

87. Interview with Shamir. The promotion was made over Rabin's initial opposition. He agreed to the appointment only after long debates with the chief of staff and the IAF's commander.

88. *Washington Post,* 16 February 1987, A1, 32.

89. Interview with Dov Zakheim, 7 March 1997. See also Dov Zakheim, *Flight of the Lavi: Inside a U.S.-Israeli Crisis* (Washington, D.C.: Brassey's, 1996).

90. Rubinstein, *Paths of Peace,* 171. Following the collapse of the Soviet Union, the United States canceled the project.

91. *Jerusalem Post,* 9 August 1992, p. 1.

92. Interview with Imri Tov, 15 January 1998.

93. Interview with Moshe Shahal, Israeli television, 2 February 1998. Shahal served as minister of internal security under Rabin.

94. Aluf Ben, "The Price of Dependency," *Haaretz,* 27 December 1994, A1.

95. *Yediot Aharonot,* 21 January 1993.

96. *Yediot Aharonot,* 16 November 1993, A1.

97. *Haaretz,* 13 September 1994, A5; William Safire, "A Dinner Party," *New York Times,* 24 November 1994, A33.

98. *Davar,* 17 January 1992, p. 18.

99. *Haaretz,* 1 November 1994, A4.

100. For Soviet-Israeli relations, see Avigdor Dagan, *Moscow and Jerusalem* (New York: Abelard-Schuman, 1970); Moshe Zak, *Israel and the Soviet Union: A Forty-Year Dialogue* (Hebrew) (Tel Aviv: Maariv, 1988).

101. Rabin, *Memoirs,* 356–61.

102. Ibid., 402.

103. Ibid., 472.

104. Ibid., 469. Peres and Allon were involved in this initiative. (Interview with Moshe Zak, 19 June 1997.)

105. Interview with Moshe Zak, 19 June 1997.

106. Ibid.; Interview with Shamir. See also Herzog, *Living History,* 415.

107. Rabin, *Memoirs,* 274.

108. "Remarks by Yitzhak Rabin to the United Jewish Appeal Luncheon," Washington Hilton, Washington D.C., Federal News Service, 17 March 1992.

109. Interview with Yitzhak Rabin, 15 April 1979. See also Ben-Zvi, *The United States and Israel,* 89–102.

110. "Remarks by Yitzhak Rabin to the United Jewish Appeal Luncheon."

111. See Jimmy Carter, *Keeping Faith* (New York: Bantam Books, 1982), 279–80; Cyrus Vance, *Hard Choices* (New York: Simon and Schuster, 1983), 171, 173; Zbigniew K. Brzezinski, *Power and Principle* (London: Weidenfeld and Nicolson, 1983), 90–91; Rabin, *Memoirs,* 508–17.

112. Interview with Shamir. For the American policy in this period, see Barry Rubin, *Cauldron of Turmoil: America in the Middle East* (New York: Harcourt, Brace, Jovanovich, 1992).

113. American helicopters set fire to an Iranian mine-laying ship on 21 September 1987 and sunk three Iranian gunboats on 8 October. U.S. forces also destroyed, on 17 October, an oil ring used by the Iranian military as a communication post. These activities were part of the American military effort to provide defense to Kuwaiti oil tankers. See Rubin, *Cauldron of Turmoil,* 106.

114. *Washington Post,* 29 October 1987, A33.

115. Herzog, *Living History,* 418–19.

116. In an address to both Houses of Congress (January 1976). See Rabin, *Memoirs,* 603.

117. Yitzhak Rabin, "War and Peace," *Spectrum* 5 (September 1987): 7–8.

118. Ibid., p. 8. For a critical analysis of an American-Israeli defense treaty, see Yair Evron, "Some Political and Strategic Implications of an American-Israeli Defense Treaty," in *The Middle East and the United States,* ed. Haim Shaked and Itamar Rabinovitch (New Brunswick, N.J.: Transaction Books, 1980), 371–94.

119. "Interview with PM Yitzhak Rabin," *CNN World International Report,* 2 May 1994, Israel Information Service Gopher.

120. Michael Mandelbaum, *Fate of Nations: The Search for National Security in the Nineteenth and Twentieth Centuries* (Cambridge: Cambridge University Press, 1988), 283.

121. Yitzhak Rabin, "No to a Defense Treaty," *Bamahane,* 21 December 1983, p. 10.

122. Ibid.

123. Zeev Schiff, *Whether an Israeli-U.S. Defense Treaty* (Jerusalem: American Jewish Committee, 1996), 12.

124. Lecture at the National Security College, 1 April 1981, Library of the National Security College, transcript 6412, p. 12.

125. Interview with Eitan Haber, 26 June 1997.

126. Lecture at the National Security College, 30 June 1983, Library of the National Security College, transcript 7038, p. 12.

127. I. L. Kenen, *Israel's Defense Line: Her Friends and Foes in Washington* (Buffalo, N.Y.: Prometheus Books, 1981), 219. This book is an account of the AIPAC's history. Kenen was one of the AIPAC founders in 1951 and its chairman from 1974 to 1976.

128. Interview with Ben-Aharon.

129. Dan Margalit, *I Have Seen Them All* (Hebrew) (Tel Aviv: Zmora-Bitan, 1997), 13.

130. Max Kampelman, *Entering New Worlds* (New York: Harper Collins, 1991), 193.

131. For these episodes, see Spiegel, *The Other Arab-Israeli Conflict,* 346–49, 398, 408–9.

132. Interview with Leonard Davis, 13 June 1997.

133. Ibid.

134. Interview with David Clayman, 7 July 1997.

135. *Jerusalem Post,* 17 August 1992, p. 1.

136. *Jerusalem Post,* 16 August 1992, p. 2. A year later, Rabin again rebuked leaders of American Jewish lobbying groups for acting against the interests of the Israeli government. (*New York Times,* 30 September 1993, A1, 4.)

137. Jonathan Rhynold, "Labor, Likud, the 'Special Relationship,' and the Peace Process, 1988–96," *Israel Affairs* 3 (spring/summer 1997): 251.

138. Interview with Clayman.

139. See "Death of a Soldier," *National Review,* 27 November 1995.

140. Martin Indyk's Address at the BESA Center for Strategic Studies, Bar-Ilan University, 31 January 1996. For its Hebrew version, see *In Memoriam: Yitzhak Rabin and Israel's National Security* (Hebrew) (Ramat Gan: BESA Center for Strategic Studies, Bar-Ilan University, 1996), 10.

CHAPTER 3

1. For the importance of preparations for war in the nation state–building of Israel, see Michael N. Barnett, *Confronting the Costs of War: Military Power, State, and Society in Egypt and Israel* (Princeton: Princeton University Press, 1992). For a general argument about the importance of war to the emergence of the modern

state, see Charles Tilly, *Coercion, Capital, and the European States, AD 990–1990* (Oxford: Basil Blackwell, 1990); and Bruce D. Porter, *War and the Rise of the State: The Military Foundations of Modern Politics* (New York: Free Press, 1994). For the IDF status in Israel, see Amos Perlmutter, *Military and Politics in Israel* (London: Frank Cass, 1969); for the changes in the centrality of the IDF in Israeli society, see Stuart A. Cohen, "The Israel Defense Force (IDF): From a 'People's Army' to a 'Professional Military'—Causes and Implications," *Armed Forces and Society* 21 (winter 1995): 237–54.

2. For the transition from the Haganah underground to the IDF, see Zehava Ostfeld, *An Army Is Born* (Hebrew) (Tel Aviv: Ministry of Defense Publishing House, 1994); Meir Pail, *The Emergence of Zahal (IDF)* (Hebrew) (Tel Aviv: Zmora, Bitan, Modan, 1979).

3. Edward Luttwak and Dan Horowitz, *The Israeli Army* (London: Allen Lane, 1975), 76–77.

4. For the disbanding of the Palmach, see Anita Shapira, *The Army Controversy, 1948: Ben Gurion's Struggle for Control* (Hebrew) (Tel Aviv: Hakibbutz Hameuchad, 1985). Ben-Gurion, the leader of the Mapai Party, encouraged the officers identified with the Mapam Party to leave the army.

5. Yitzhak Rabin, with Dov Goldstein, *Pinkas Sherut* (Hebrew) (Tel Aviv: Maariv, 1979), 99, 109, 111, cited hereafter as Rabin, *Memoirs*. See also Leah Rabin, *Rabin: Our Life, His Legacy* (New York: G. P. Putnam, 1997), 103.

6. Lutwak and Horowitz, *The Israeli Army,* 177. For civilian-military relations in the Ben-Gurion era, see Yoram Peri, *Between Battles and Ballots: Israeli Military in Politics* (Cambridge: Cambridge University Press, 1983), 38–69.

7. Interview with Maj. Gen. (Res.) Israel Tal, 5 August 1996.

8. Interview with Maj. Gen. (Res.) Uzi Narkis, 19 January 1997.

9. Ezer Weizman, *On Eagles' Wings* (New York: Macmillan, 1979), 194–95. Similar praise was voiced by Maj. Gen. (Res.) Avraham (Abrasha) Tamir, one of the best planners in the IDF, who served for many years in advisory positions to ministers of defense. See Avraham Tamir, *A Soldier in Search of Peace* (Hebrew) (Tel Aviv: Edanim, 1988), 299.

10. Interview with Maj. Gen. Rehavam Zeevi, 2 September 1997. Zeevi specifically mentioned three primary contributions: the battalion commander's course, the period when Rabin commanded the Training Branch, and the period when Rabin served as chief of the Operations Branch and deputy chief of staff. See also his eulogy: Rehavam Zeevi, "A Friend and Opponent," *Moledet* 88–89 (November-December 1995): 1, 2.

11. Rabin, *Memoirs,* 83–84.

12. Yitzhak Rabin, "The Challenge: To Be the Leader," *IDF Journal* 19 (winter 1990): 2 (adapted from a speech delivered to graduates of the IDF Staff College, August 1989).

13. Rabin, *Memoirs,* 96, 101.

14. Uzi Narkis, *Soldier of Jerusalem* (Hebrew) (Tel Aviv: Ministry of Defense Publishing House, 1991), 137–38. Interview with Zeevi. Zeevi was one of the pupils in this course. The first course was commanded by Laskov himself. See also Rabin, *Memoirs,* 87. For an extremely critical and unbalanced account of Rabin's record in the War of Independence, see Uri Milstein, *Rabin File: How the Myth Swelled* (Hebrew) (Ramat Efal: Yaron Golan, 1995), 143–323.

15. *Bamahane,* 10 November 1995, p. 20.

16. Interview with Zeevi. The Jewish Brigade was formed in 1944 as a separate unit in the British army and attracted many Jewish volunteers from Palestine. Many British-trained officers in the IDF served with the Jewish Brigade.

17. Narkis, *Soldier of Jerusalem,* 138–39.

18. Interview with Zeevi.

19. "Current security" in Israeli strategic parlance refers to challenges to the routine life of Israelis, such as infiltration and terror, whereas "basic security" refers to challenges to the existence of the state and its territorial integrity.

20. Rabin, *Memoirs,* 88–89.

21. Operation Danny captured the towns of Lod and Ramla from the Arab Legion and relieved pressure from the Tel Aviv area. Operation Yoav opened the road to the isolated Negev and destroyed considerable Egyptian forces that had occupied parts of the Negev. For the two operations, see Netanel Lorch, *The Edge of the Sword: Israel's War of Independence,* 2d rev. ed. (Jerusalem: Masada Press, 1968), 333–47, 401–34. For the new rationale underlying these two operations, see Yitzhak Rabin, "Yigal Allon: Commander and Strategist in the War of Independence," *Maarachot* 272 (1980): 1, 54.

22. Interview with Yuval Neeman (who served under Rabin), 23 June 1996. For the implementation of the indirect approach after the War of Independence, see the next chapter.

23. Interviews with Tal and with Zeevi. See also Rabin's Training Branch working plan of 26 September 1954, IDF Archives, File 435/56-7.

24. IDF Archives, File 696/60-145.

25. Interview with Zeevi.

26. Rabin, *Memoirs,* 93.

27. *Bamahane,* 7 January 1965, p. 5.

28. Yitzhak Rabin, "Goals of Training," *Maarachot,* no. 140 (December 1961).

29. *Bamahane,* 27 July 1955, p. 10.

30. *Bamahane,* 28 October 1954, p. 5.

31. *Bamahane,* 6 January 1955, p. 11. See also Rabin, *Memoirs,* 94. Chaim Herzog attributes the decision to make paratrooper training mandatory for officers to Chief of Staff Moshe Dayan, who accompanied Rabin on his trip to the United States. See Chaim Herzog, *Living History* (Hebrew) (Tel Aviv: Miskal, 1997), 160.

32. Rabin, *Memoirs,* 101.

33. Ibid.

34. Yaakov Erez and Ilan Kfir, eds., *The IDF: An Encyclopedia for Army and Security* (Hebrew) (Ramat Gan: Revivim, 1981), 6:65. By 1962, the IDF Intelligence Branch had produced a two-volume comprehensive study on Soviet doctrine and its implementation in the Egyptian army. (Ibid.)

35. Lutwak and Horowitz, *The Israeli Army*, 212–13; Rabin, *Memoirs*, 106.

36. Rabin, "Goals of Training."

37. Rabin, *Memoirs*, 84.

38. Yuval Neeman, *Maariv*, 18 June 1967, in his *The Clairvoyant Policy* (Hebrew) (Ramat Gan: Revivim, 1984), 20.

39. Yitzhak Rabin, "The Lessons of Sinai," *Maarachot*, nos. 344–45 (December 1995–January 1996): 18, originally published in *Maarachot*, nos. 178–79 (October 1966).

40. Yitzhak Greenberg, *Defense Budgets and Military Power: The Case of Israel, 1957–1967* (Hebrew) (Tel Aviv: Ministry of Defense Publishing House, 1997), 101.

41. Interview with Eitan Haber, 26 June 1997.

42. Yitzhak Rabin, "From the Battles over the Water to the Six-Day War," in *The IDF: An Encyclopedia for Army and Security*, 186. The rationale for territorial defense was indeed freeing first-grade manpower for offensive operations, since well-fortified settlements could be defended by older men, women, and youngsters. Israeli strategists, such as Allon, considered territorial defense as the creation of artificial strategic depth. See Yigal Allon, *A Curtain of Sand* (Hebrew) (Tel Aviv: Hakibbutz Hameuchad, 1968), 65–68. For the organizational structure and command line of the territorial defense, see Zeev Schiff and Eitan Haber, *Israel, Army, and Defense: A Dictionary* (Hebrew) (Tel Aviv: Zmora, Bitan, Modan, 1976), 158.

43. Rabin, "From the Battles over the Water to the Six-Day War," 187.

44. Rabin, "The Lessons of Sinai," 19; Luttwak and Horowitz, *The Israeli Army*, 181.

45. As chief of operations, Rabin had recommended these priorities in the preparation of the *Hashmonaim* multiyear procurement program (1961–65). See Greenberg, *Defense Budgets and Military Power*, 104–5.

46. Rabin, "From the Battles over the Water to the Six-Day War," 187. Most credit for the building of the IAF and its 1967 performance deserves to go to Maj. Gen. (Res.) Ezer Weizman, who served as its commander from 1958 to 1966. For his account, see Weizman, *On Eagles' Wings*, 165–90.

47. Greenberg, *Defense Budgets and Military Power*, 194, table 21.

48. Ibid., 189. See also Lutwak and Horowitz, *The Israeli Army*, 193–201.

49. Greenberg, *Defense Budgets and Military Power*, 107. Rabin's temporary emphasis on purchasing tanks was also influenced by the fact that the United States was willing to sell Pattons and by the good financial terms of the deal, whereas the IAF was deliberating over which combat jet for which to opt. (Ibid., 108.)

50. Ibid., 196, table 22.

51. Ibid., 199, table 24.

52. Rabin, *Memoirs*, 122–24. For a more detailed account, see Yoseph Argaman, "Then Talik Shot," *Bamahane*, 1 December 1995.

53. Greenberg, *Defense Budgets and Military Power,* 104. Chief of Staff Haim Laskov (1958–61) delineated these priorities in the *Bnai Yaakov* multiyear procurement plan (1958–61). (Ibid.)

54. Rabin, "From the Battles over the Water to the Six-Day War," 187.

55. Luttwak and Horowitz, *The Israeli Army,* 177–79.

56. Rabin, "From the Battles over the Water to the Six-Day War," 190.

57. Luttwak and Horowitz, *The Israeli Army,* 181.

58. Interview with Dr. Yehuda Ben-Meir, 26 June 1997. Though better known for his political career, Ben-Meir served as psychologist in the IDF.

59. "Interview with Yitzhak Rabin," *Bamahane,* 7 January 1964, p. 5.

60. Greenberg, *Defense Budgets and Military Power,* 155; Eitan Haber, *Today War Will Break Out: The Reminiscences of Brig. Gen. Israel Lior, Aide-de-Camp to Prime Ministers Levi Eshkol and Golda Meir* (Hebrew) (Tel Aviv: Edanim, 1987), 42.

61. Perlmutter, *Military and Politics in Israel,* 106.

62. See Greenberg, *Defense Budgets and Military Power,* 173, table 7.

63. Yitzhak Greenberg, "The 1963 Decision to Shorten the Conscription Period in the IDF: Security Considerations and Socioeconomic Aspects," *Medina Umimshal Veyachasim Beinleumiim* 40 (summer 1995): 75.

64. Yitzhak Rabin, Lecture at the National Security College, 18 July 1985, Library of the National Security College, transcript 6940, p. 26.

65. Greenberg, *Defense Budgets and Military Power,* 95–96.

66. Ibid., 100.

67. Rabin, *Memoirs,* 125. For the development of the Israeli navy, see Efraim Inbar, "The Israeli Navy," *Naval War College Review* 43 (winter 1990): 100–112.

68. *Bamahane,* 10 November 1995. For the development of the missile boat concept, see Shlomo Erell, *Facing the Sea: The Story of a Fighting Sailor and Commander* (Hebrew) (Tel Aviv: Ministry of Defense, 1988), 210–56.

69. Amir Oren, "Another Battle over the Perpendicular," *Haaretz,* 27 June 1997, B5.

70. Greenberg, *Defense Budgets and Military Power,* 96, 110–11. Ben-Gurion and Eshkol did not accept Rabin's recommendation and settled for three submarines. The compromise was suggested by Peres. (Ibid., 111.)

71. Mordechai Gazit, *Israel's Weapons Procurement from the United States* (Hebrew), Policy Papers No. 8 (Jerusalem: Leonard Davis Institute for International Relations, Hebrew University, 1983), 42–43; Rabin, *Memoirs,* 236, 423.

72. Gazit, *Israel's Weapons Procurement from the United States,* 44.

73. Ibid., 45–46.

74. Ibid., 46–48.

75. Ibid., 52–54. See also William B. Quandt, *Decade of Decisions: The American Policy toward the Arab-Israeli Conflict, 1967–1976* (Los Angeles: University of California Press, 1977), 146–47.

76. Rabin, *Memoirs,* 423. See also Yitzhak Navon, "The Changes in the Israeli Position on the Arab-Israeli Conflict," in *Between War and Settlements* (Hebrew),

ed. Alouph Hareven and Yehiam Padan (Tel Aviv: Zmora-Bitan, 1977), 158. M.K. Navon served in 1974–77 as chair of the Parliamentary Committee for Security and Foreign Affairs.

77. Anthony H. Cordesman, "How Much Is Too Much?," *Armed Forces Journal,* October 1977, pp. 36–37. Shimon Peres confirmed the accuracy of the figures in this report. See Shimon Peres and Haggay Eshed, *Tomorrow Is Now* (Hebrew) (Jerusalem: Keter, 1978), 229.

78. Efraim Inbar, "Israel's Strategic Thinking after 1973," *Journal of Strategic Studies* 6 (March 1983): 42–43. For accounts of the political and military aspects of this war, see Chaim Herzog, *The War of Atonement, October 1973* (Boston: Little, Brown and Co., 1975); Avi Kober, *Military Decision in the Arab-Israeli Wars, 1948–1982* (Hebrew) (Tel Aviv: Maarachot, 1995), 327–98.

79. David Vital, *The Inequality of States* (Oxford: Clarendon Press, 1967), 60–61.

80. Interview with Haber, 26 June 1997.

81. In 1960, Rabin was chief of operations. For the Israeli response to the February 1960 events (code-named Operation Rotem), see Rabin, *Memoirs,* 107–8. For Rabin's 1967 surprise, see ibid., 134–35. For an analysis of the Rotem scenario and its impact on later strategic thinking, see Uri Bar-Joseph, "Rotem: The Forgotten Crisis on the Road to the 1967 War," *Journal of Contemporary History* 31 (July 1996): 547–66.

82. Shimon Shamir, "Arab Military Lessons from the October War," in *Military Aspects of the Israeli-Arab Conflict,* ed. Louis Williams (Tel Aviv: University Publishing Projects, 1975), 175; Bernard Lewis, "Settling the Arab-Israeli Conflict," *Commentary* 63 (June 1977): 53.

83. Dov Goldstein, "Interview with Rabin," *Maariv,* 25 September 1974.

84. The American airlift was primarily a response to the Soviet airlift to the Arab states. See Henry Kissinger, *Years of Upheaval* (Boston: Little Brown and Co., 1982), 468, 483, 497, 507–8; Yishai Cordova, *The Policy of the United States in the Yom Kippur War* (Hebrew) (Tel Aviv: Maarachot, 1987), 181–86.

85. Rabin, *Memoirs,* 505.

86. Gazit, *Israel's Weapons Procurement from the United States,* 64.

87. Yitzhak Rabin, Lecture at the National Security College, 18 July 1985, Library of the National Security College, transcript 6940, p. 16.

88. Ibid., 15.

89. Yitzhak Rabin, Lecture at the National Security College, 11 March 1986, Library of the National Security College, transcript 6536, p. 8.

90. Interviews with Maj. Gen. (Res.) David Ivri, 8 July 1997, and with Lt. Gen. (Res.) Moshe Levy, 5 July 1997. Generally, Rabin was extremely reluctant to remove people from their jobs, even if by keeping them, effectiveness was impaired. Rabin lacked the temerity to look somebody in the eye and tell him that he did not perform well. (Interview with Zeevi.)

91. Interview with Lt. Gen. (Res.) Dan Shomron, 1 July 1997.

92. Yitzhak Rabin, Lecture at the National Security College, 14 March 1988, Library of the National Security College, transcript 5732, p. 2.

93. Yitzhak Rabin, Lecture at the National Security College, 11 March 1986, Library of the National Security College, transcript 6536, p. 9.

94. Interview with Ivri.

95. Interview with Haber, 26 June 1997.

96. Yitzhak Rabin, Lecture at the National Security College, 11 March 1986, Library of the National Security College, transcript 6536, p. 8.

97. Ibid., 20.

98. Interview with Levy.

99. Interview with Ivri.

100. Yitzhak Rabin, Lecture at the National Security College, 11 March 1986, Library of the National Security College, transcript 6536, p. 5. The cautious Rabin envisioned only a tactical airborne operation because sending thousands of soldiers far away was too risky a proposition in the political-military circumstances of the 1980s. See Yitzhak Rabin, Lecture at the National Security College, 28 July 1986, Library of the National Security College, transcript 6539, p. 7.

101. Interview with Dr. Zeev Bonen, 31 March 1997. See also Yitzhak Rabin, Lecture at the National Security College, 14 March 1988, Library of the National Security College, transcript 5732, p. 9.

102. Interviews with Ivri, Levy, and Shomron.

103. Lecture at the National Security College, 14 March 1988, Library of the National Security College, transcript 5732, pp. 8–9.

104. Yitzhak Rabin, Lecture at the National Security College, 11 March 1986, Library of the National Security Council, transcript 6536, p. 20. For the Israeli conservative approach to the impact of technological change on warfare, see Eliot A. Cohen, Michael J. Eisenstadt, and Andrew J. Bacevich, "Israel's Revolution in Security Affairs," *Survival* 40 (spring 1998); Zeev Bonen, "Sophisticated Conventional War," in *Advanced Technology and Future Warfare*, Mideast Security and Policy Studies No. 28 (Ramat Gan: BESA Center for Strategic Studies, Bar-Ilan University, 1996).

105. Interview with Ivri.

106. For the distinction between preparedness and preparation, which was made by Rabin, see the discussion later in the chapter.

107. Yitzhak Rabin, Lecture at the National Security College, 3 August 1989, Library of the National Security College, transcript 5393, p. 5.

108. Yitzahk Rabin, Lecture at the National Security College, 5 August 1988, Library of the National Security Council, transcript 5749, p. 4. See also Yitzhak Rabin, Lecture at the National Security College, 3 August 1989, Library of the National Security Council, transcript 5393, pp. 2, 5.

109. Interview with Neeman, 23 June 1996. Neeman founded the Israeli Space Agency in 1983 and served in the 1980s as its chairman. In 1976, Rabin ridiculed the

Ministry of Defense request for an intelligence satellite from the United States (introduced by Neeman, who served then as adviser to Peres). See Rabin, *Memoirs,* 497–98. It may be that Rabin's rivalry with Peres affected his judgment in the 1970s on this matter. When prime minister again in the 1990s, Rabin was helpful in securing for the Israeli space industry greater access to the American civilian space market. See Gerald Steinberg, "Space, Our Final Frontier," *Jerusalem Post,* 21 January 1994, p. 38.

110. An improved model was launched in April 1990, and the more sophisticated Ofeq-3 was launched in April 1995. For an analysis of the satellite program, see James Bruce, "Israel's Space and Missile Projects," *Jane's Intelligence Review* 7 (August 1995): 352–54.

111. Interview with Haber, 26 June 1997.

112. For missile proliferation in the Middle East, see Mark A. Heller, "Coping with Missile Proliferation in the Middle East," *Orbis* 35/1 (winter 1991): 15–28; Martin Navias, *Going Ballistic: The Build-up of Missiles in the Middle East* (London: Brassey's 1993); Aaron Karp, "Ballistic Missiles in the Middle East: Realities, Omens, and Arms Control Options," in *Middle Eastern Security: Prospects for an Arms Control Regime,* ed. Efraim Inbar and Shmuel Sandler, BESA Studies in International Security (London: Frank Cass, 1995), 111–29.

113. Interview with Shomron. For the traditional offensive predilection, see Ariel Levite, *Offense and Defense in Israeli Military Doctrine,* JCSS Study No. 12 (Boulder, Colo.: Westview Press, 1989), 25–62.

114. Interview with Shomron.

115. Yitzhak Rabin, Lecture at the National Security College, 14 March 1988, Library of the National Security College, transcript 5732, p. 6.

116. For a critical analysis, see Reuven Pedatzur, *The Arrow System and the Active Defense against Ballistic Missiles,* Memorandum No. 42 (Tel Aviv: Jaffee Center for Strategic Studies, Tel Aviv University, 1993).

117. *Haaretz,* 21 January 1993, p. 3.

118. *Haaretz,* 30 April 1993, p. 2.

119. Yehuda Ben-Meir, *Civil-Military Relations in Israel* (New York: Columbia University Press, 1995), 157.

120. Inbar, "The Israeli Navy."

121. Interview with Shomron.

122. Yitzhak Rabin, Lecture at the National Security College, 14 March 1988, Library of the National Security Council, transcript 5732, p. 10. Interview with Ivri.

123. In February 1993, Rabin convened a meeting with Chief of Staff Lt. Gen. Ehud Barak, his deputy Maj. Gen. Amnon Shahak, IAF's commander Maj. Gen. Herzel Bodinger, and Director General of the Ministry of Defense Maj. Gen. (Res.) David Ivri. There was a unanimity of opinions on the need to purchase the F-15I from the United States. Rabin took up this subject at his first meeting in March 1993 with President Bill Clinton, who approved the sale. (Amnon Barzilai, "The Next F," *Haaretz,* 13 August 1997, B2.)

124. Ben-Meir, *Civil-Military Relations in Israel,* 157.

125. Interview with Shomron. See also *Maariv,* 22 March 1989, p. 2.

126. Interview with Maj. Gen. (Res.) Menachem Maron, 1 June 1997. In 1967, Rabin felt that the responsibility for the outcome of the war was on his shoulders, particularly since he served also as the senior military adviser to the government and de facto as minister of defense.

127. Interview with Haber, 26 June 1997; Interview with Shomron.

128. For Rabin's negative attitude toward the Agranat Report, see Rabin, *Memoirs,* 413–16.

129. Interview with Shomron. See also Ben-Meir, *Civil-Military Relations in Israel,* 125.

130. Interview with Shomron.

131. For the development of the defense industries in Israel, see Aharon S. Klieman, *The Global Reach: Arms Sales as Diplomacy* (Washington, D.C.: Pergamon-Brassey's, 1985), and Stewart Reiser, *The Israeli Arms Industry: Foreign Policy, Arms Transfers, and Military Doctrine of a Small State* (New York: Holmes and Meier, 1989).

132. Rabin, *Memoirs,* 111.

133. Interview with Maron.

134. Even Moshe Dayan praised Rabin (and Zvi Tzur) to Ben-Gurion, in 1956, for having sensitivity to economic issues. In 1963, Rabin agreed to reduce the length of the military service from 30 to 26 months because this was considered to be a contribution to the manpower market in the Israeli economy. See Greenberg, *Defense Budgets and Military Power,* 74, 76–77.

135. Interview with Tal.

136. Greenberg, *Defense Budgets and Military Power,* 98–99.

137. In contrast to Rabin, Peres attributed great political weight to self-sufficiency in the area of weapons production and regarded the military industries as the spearhead for technological advancement in Israel. Therefore, he believed, the defense establishment had to foster the industries. As a civilian, he had a somewhat different perspective on the role of the Ministry of Defense and did not share Rabin's preoccupation with preparedness. See Shimon Peres, *David's Sling* (Hebrew) (Jerusalem: Weidenfeld and Nicholson, 1970), 87–112; Greenberg, *Defense Budgets and Military Power,* 151–53.

138. Greenberg, *Defense Budgets and Military Power,* 78–79.

139. Rabin, "From the Battles over the Water to the Six-Day War," 189.

140. Efraim Inbar, "The American Arms Transfer to Israel," *Middle East Review* 15 (winter 1982/83): 46–47.

141. Interview with Shomron.

142. Interview with Bonen.

143. Rabin actually attempted to dissuade the Israeli government from approving the Kfir project. See Reiser, *The Israeli Arms Industry,* 103.

144. Interview with Rabin, 18 November 1979.

145. Motta (Mordechai) Gur, *Chief of the General Staff (1974–1978)* (Hebrew) (Tel Aviv: Maarachot, 1998), 206.

146. Interview with Ben-Meir.

147. Yitzhak Rabin, Lecture at the National Security College, 5 August 1988, Library of the National Security College, transcript 5749, p. 5.

148. Interview with Maron.

149. For Israeli weapon sales, see Klieman, *The Global Reach.*

150. Interview with Bonen.

151. *Maariv,* 6 March 1977.

152. See Dov S. Zakheim, *Flight of the Lavi: Inside a U.S.-Israeli Crisis* (Washington, D.C.: Brassey's, 1996).

153. Inbar, "The American Arms Transfer to Israel," 46–47.

154. Yitzhak Rabin, Lecture at the National Security College, 11 March 1986, Library of the National Security Council, transcript 6536, p. 5.

155. Ibid., 6–7.

156. Interview with Haber, 26 June 1997.

157. Interview with Shomron. See also Zakheim, *Flight of the Lavi,* 246–47.

158. Yitzhak Rabin, Lecture at the National Security College, 14 March 1988, Library of the National Security Council, transcript 5732, p. 10.

159. *Haaretz,* 20 November 1992, A2.

160. Interview with Ivri.

161. For a review of the international market in the early 1990s, see Ian Anthony, "Politics and Economics of Defense Industries in a Changing World," in *The Politics and Economics of Defense Industries,* ed. Efraim Inbar and Benzion Zilberfarb, BESA Studies in International Security (London: Frank Cass, 1998).

162. *Haaretz,* 16 January 1996.

163. *Haaretz,* 8 February 1994, A4.

164. Sharon Sadeh, "The Rehabilitation Process of the Defense Industries," in *The Defense Industries in Israel* (Hebrew) (Ramat Gan: BESA Center for Strategic Studies, Bar-Ilan University, August 1995), 15–29; Aharon S. Klieman, "Adapting to a Shrinking Market: The Israeli Case," in Inbar and Zilberfarb, *The Politics and Economics of Defense Industries.*

165. For an argument that the IDF must concentrate on the missile threat and low-intensity activities, see Stuart A. Cohen, "Israel's Changing Military Commitments, 1981–1991," *Journal of Strategic Studies* 15 (September 1992): 330–50.

166. *IAF Organ,* no. 106 (December 1995): 6.

CHAPTER 4

1. Interview with Eitan Haber, 11 August 1997.

2. See appendix A: Yitzhak Rabin, "After the Gulf War: Israeli Defense and Its Security Policy."

3. See Thomas C. Schelling, *Arms and Influence* (New Haven: Yale University Press, 1966), chap. 1.

4. For a study of the Israeli leadership's approach to the use of force, see Efraim Inbar, "Attitudes toward War in the Israeli Political Elite," *Middle East Journal* 44 (summer 1990): 431–45. For the difference between instrumentality and expressivity in the use of force, see Yehoshafat Harkabi, *Israel's Fateful Decisions* (London: I. B. Tauris, 1988), 72.

5. Yitzhak Rabin, "The Lessons of Sinai," *Maarachot,* nos. 344–45 (December 1995–January 1996): 16–17, originally published in *Maarachot,* nos. 178–79 (October 1966).

6. Yitzhak Rabin, Lecture at the National Security College, 1 April 1981, Library of the National Security College, transcript 6412, pp. 7–8.

7. Rabin was not a well-read person and probably never read Clausewitz, though it is clear from his references to the Prussian general that he was acquainted with what the author of *On War* stood for.

8. See appendix A: Rabin, "After the Gulf War," and Efraim Inbar, *War and Peace in Israeli Politics: Labor Party Positions on National Security* (Boulder, Colo.: Lynne Rienner, 1991), chap. 6.

9. Yitzhak Rabin, Lecture at the National Security College, 30 June 1983, Library of the National Security College, transcript 7038, pp. 2–3.

10. Yitzhak Rabin, Lecture at the National Security College, 14 March 1988, Library of the National Security College, transcript 5732, p. 14.

11. Yitzhak Rabin, Lecture at the National Security College, 18 July 1985, Library of the National Security College, transcript 6940, pp. 12–13. See also Yitzhak Rabin, Lecture at the National Security College, 28 July 1986, Library of the National Security College, transcript 6539, p. 14.

12. Yitzhak Rabin, Lecture at the National Security College, 30 June 1983, Library of the National Security College, transcript 7038, p. 8. For Ben-Gurion's quick change of mind, see Mordechai Bar-On, *The Gates of Gaza: The Foreign and National Security Policy of Israel, 1955–57* (Hebrew) (Tel Aviv: Am Oved, 1992), 318–26.

13. For a simplistic dichotomous presentation of two schools of thought in Israel concerning waging war—the "Clausewitzian" and the "denial" approaches—see Zvi Lanir, "Political Aims and Military Objectives," in *Israeli Security Planning in the 1980s: Its Politics and Economics,* ed. Zvi Lanir (New York: Praeger, for the Jaffee Center for Strategic Studies, 1984), 14–49. The attitudes toward use of force represent one aspect of the multidimensional hawkish-dovish continuum in Israeli politics. Only in the late 1980s and early 1990s can we detect a growing aversion to the use of force in the Arab-Israeli conflict, primarily in the Labor Party. See Inbar, *War and Peace in Israeli Politics,* 12–15, 121–48; Efraim Inbar, "Contours of Israel's New Strategic Thinking," *Political Science Quarterly* 111 (spring 1996): 51–57.

14. Quoted in Yitzhak Greenberg, *Defense Budgets and Military Power: The Case of Israel, 1957–1967* (Hebrew) (Tel Aviv: Ministry of Defense Publishing House, 1997), 103.

15. See Michael Brecher, *Decisions in Israel's Foreign Policy* (London: Oxford University Press, 1974), 359–61.

16. Yitzhak Rabin, "The Quality That Guarantees Power," in *Israeli Security in the Next Decade* (Hebrew) (Efal: Yad Tabenkin, 1988), 40.

17. Yitzhak Rabin, Lecture at the National Security College, 18 July 1985, Library of the National Security College, transcript 6940, p. 4.

18. Yitzhak Rabin, Lecture at the National Security College, 28 July 1986, Library of the National Security College, transcript 6539, p. 4.

19. Yitzhak Rabin, Lectures at the National Security College: 18 July 1985, Library of the National Security College, transcript 6940, p. 8; 11 March 1986, Library of the National Security College, transcript 6536, p. 17; 28 July 1986, Library of the National Security College, transcript 6539, p. 6.

20. For an analysis of the political leadership's views in the public debate over the Lebanon War, see Efraim Inbar, "The 'No Choice War' Debate in Israel," *Journal of Strategic Studies* 12 (March 1989): 22–37.

21. Yitzhak Rabin, Lecture at the National Security College, 11 March 1986, Library of the National Security College, transcript 6536, p. 4.

22. These were collected in a book: Yitzhak Rabin, *The War in Lebanon* (Hebrew) (Tel Aviv: Am Oved, 1983).

23. Ibid., 45.

24. Ibid.

25. For the domestic debate, see Inbar, "The 'No Choice War' Debate in Israel."

26. "Interview with Rabin," *Migvan* 72 (August 1982): 3.

27. Rabin, *The War in Lebanon*, 45.

28. This was the thinking in the IDF during the first years after the establishment of the state in 1948, before adopting a posture relying on preemptive strikes. Avner Yaniv, *Deterrrence without the Bomb: The Politics of Israeli Strategy* (Lexington, Mass.: Lexington Books, 1987), 57–58. In 1951, when Rabin served as head of the Operations Division, he agreed with the defensive strategy, since it served the premise for a position paper he had submitted for a discussion on the structure of the IDF. See Greenberg, *Defense Budgets and Military Power*, 36.

29. Efraim Inbar, "Israel's Strategic Thinking after 1973," *Journal of Strategic Studies* 6 (March 1983): 38–40.

30. For works analyzing the role of deterrence in Israel's strategic thinking, see Michael Handel, "Israel's Political-Military Doctrine" (Harvard University Occasional Papers, Harvard University, Cambridge, July 1973); Israel Tal, "Israel's Doctrine of National Security: Background and Dynamics," *Jerusalem Quarterly* 4 (summer 1977); Yoav Ben-Horin and Barry Posen, *Israel's Strategic Doctrine*, Paper R-2845-NA (Santa Monica: Rand Corporation, 1981); Dan Horowitz, "The Constant and the Changing in Israeli Strategic Thinking," in *War by Choice* (Hebrew), ed. Joseph Alpher (Tel Aviv: Hakibbutz Hameuchad, 1985), 58–77; Ariel Levite, *Offense and Defense in Israeli Military Doctrine*, JCSS Study No. 12 (Boulder, Colo.: Westview Press, 1989); Inbar, "Israel's Strategic Thinking after 1973," 36–59; Yaniv,

Deterrence without the Bomb; Jonathan Shimshoni, *Israel and Conventional Deterrence: Border Warfare from 1953 to 1970* (Ithaca, N.Y.: Cornell University Press, 1988); Efraim Inbar and Shmuel Sandler, "Israel's Deterrence Strategy Revisited," *Security Studies* 3 (winter 1993/94): 330–58.

31. Yitzhak Rabin, Lecture at the National Security College, 30 June 1983, Library of the National Security College, transcript 7038, pp. 3–4.

32. Yitzhak Rabin, Lecture at the National Security College, 18 July 1985, Library of the National Security College, transcript 6940, pp. 5–6. See also David Ben-Gurion, *Uniqueness and Mission* (Hebrew) (Tel Aviv: Am Oved, 1975), 367; Yigal Allon, *A Curtain of Sand* (Hebrew) (Tel Aviv: Hakibbutz Hameuchad, 1968), 363–64; Shimon Peres, *The Next Phase* (Hebrew) (Tel Aviv: Am Hasefer, 1965), 216.

33. Quoted in Lanir, "Political Aims and Military Objectives," 36.

34. Yitzhak Rabin, "Why We Won the War," *Jerusalem Post, Rosh Hashana Magazine,* 10 October 1967, p. 5.

35. See appendix A: Rabin, "After the Gulf War." See also Inbar and Sandler, "Israel's Deterrence Strategy Revisited," 342. For a study of the decisive victory, see Avi Kober, *Military Decision in the Arab-Israeli Wars, 1948–1982* (Hebrew) (Tel Aviv: Maarachot, 1995).

36. Yitzhak Rabin, Lecture at the National Security College, 14 March 1986, Library of the National Security College, transcript 5732, p. 10. This was argued also by Chief of Staff Lt. Gen. Rafael Eitan (1978–1983). See Dov Goldstein, "Interview with Rafael Eitan," *Maariv,* 16 April 1976. In 1976, Eitan served as chief of the Northern Command.

37. It was Clausewitz's conviction that defense was the "stronger form" of war. See Karl von Clausewitz, *On War,* ed. and trans. Michael Howard and Peter Paret (Princeton: Princeton University Press, 1976), 357–66. Henry Kissinger also observed that conventional war favors the defense. See his "Limited War: Conventional or Nuclear," *Daedalus* 90 (fall 1960): 809. For a historical sketch of favorable ratios of defense, see Basil H. Liddell-Hart, *Deterrence or Defense* (London: Stevens and Sons, 1960), 97–110.

38. See the discussion of the Agranat Commision of Inquiry established after the 1973 war to investigate the reasons for the intial failures in the battlefield. *Commission of Inquiry: The Yom Kippur War—A Partial Report* (Hebrew) (Tel Aviv: Am Oved, 1975), 40–41. For the debate within the Israeli defense establishment over the Bar-Lev Line between the static and the mobile defense advocates, and for a discussion of its poltical rationale, see Yaakov Bar-Siman-Tov, "The Bar-Lev Line Revisited," *Journal of Strategic Studies* 11 (June 1988): 149–76.

39. Inbar, "Israel's Strategic Thinking after 1973," 38–39, 44.

40. Ibid., 44–45. After 1967, Israel believed it enjoyed "secure borders," which minimized the need for a territorial defense. Moreover, Moshe Dayan, the minister of defense during this period, belittled the importance of this military structure. In contrast, in the post-1973 period, the need to fight on the defensive was clearer, and senior officers, such as Maj. Gen. Rafael Eitan, the chief of the Northern Com-

mand, were supporters of the territorial defense concept. Eitan became chief of staff in 1978.

41. Interview with Rabin; Interview with Dr. Zeev Bonen, 31 March 1997. See also Saadia Amiel, "Deterrence by Conventional Forces," *Survival* 20 (March/April 1978): 58–62. Amiel served in the 1970s as director of Long-Range Planning at the Ministry of Defense.

42. Yitzhak Rabin, Lecture at the National Security College, 14 March 1988, Library of the National Security College, transcript 5732, pp. 9–10.

43. Yitzhak Rabin, Lecture at the National Security College, 28 July 1986, Library of the National Security College, transcript 6539, p. 6.

44. Dov Goldstein, "Interview with Rabin," *Maariv*," 25 September 1974.

45. See appendix A: Rabin, "After the Gulf War."

46. Yitzhak Rabin, Lecture at the National Security College, 11 March 1986, Library of the National Security College, transcript 6536, p. 17.

47. Yitzhak Rabin, Lecture at the National Security College, 5 August 1988, Library of the National Security College, transcript 5749, p. 3. A subcommittee of the Knesset Committee for Defense and Foreign Affairs spent much effort in the mid-1980s to reevaluate Israel's strategic thinking and the IDF's military doctrine. Its members included Benyamin Begin, Dan Meridor, and Yossi Sarid.

48. Yitzhak Rabin, Lecture at the National Security College, 11 July 1993, Library of the National Security College, transcript 454, p. 6. For an argument that the American victory was primarily the consequence of a flawed strategy rather than the result of technological disparity, see Lawrence Freedman and Efraim Karsh, "How Kuwait Was Won: Strategy in the Gulf War," *International Security* 16 (fall 1991): 36–37. For a sober analysis of the technological and organizational dimensions of the Gulf War, see Gene I. Rochlin and Chris Demchak, "The Gulf War: Technological and Organizational Implications," *Survival* 33 (May/June 1991): 260–73. For an analysis of one tank battle during the Gulf War, see Stephen Biddle, "Victory Misunderstood: What the Gulf War Tells Us about Conflict in the Future," *International Security* 21 (fall 1996): 139–79.

49. For similar conservative Israeli views of the RMA, see Brig. Gen. Dr. Yitzhak Ben-Israel, "Back to the Future," *Maarachot,* no. 329 (March–April 1993): 2–5 (the author served as head of R&D in the IDF); see also Zeev Bonen, "Sophisticated Conventional War," in *Advanced Technology and Future Warfare,* Mideast Security and Policy Studies No. 28 (Ramat Gan: BESA Center for Strategic Studies, Bar-Ilan University, 1996): 19–30 (the author served as president of the Israeli Weapon Development Authority [RAFAEL]). For a summary of the American views on RMA see, Eliot A. Cohen, "A Revolution in Warfare," *Foreign Affairs* 75 (March/April 1996): 37–54.

50. See the next chapter for the debate over the need for a nuclear deterrent.

51. Yitzhak Rabin, Lecture at the National Security College, 30 June 1983, Library of the National Security College, transcript 7038, p. 3.

52. Yitzhak Rabin, Lecture at the National Security College, 11 March 1986, Library of the National Security College, transcript 6536, pp. 4–5.

53. See appendix A: Rabin, "After the Gulf War."

54. "Rabin and Sadat Interview," NBC, 5 April 1975. See also Dov Goldstein, "Interview of the Week with Rabin," *Maariv,* 18 April 1975. This position was also a veiled threat, particularly toward the United States, that Israel could initiate a more destabilizing regional scenario if weapons became unavailable and if Israel was pushed into an untenable geographical position.

55. *Maariv,* 2 September 1974.

56. Interviews with Haber, 11 August 1997, with Maj. Gen. (Res.) Shlomo Gazit, 26 February 1998, and with Haim Assa, 21 December 1997. See also Yoel Ben-Porat, "Intelligence Estimates: Why Do They Fail?," in *Intelligence and National Security,* ed. Zvi Ofer and Avi Kober (Tel Aviv: Maarachot, 1988), 226.

57. Yitzhak Rabin, Lecture at the National Security College, 28 July 1986, Library of the National Security College, transcript 6539, p. 10.

58. Yitzhak Rabin, Lecture at the National Security College, 30 June 1983, Library of the National Security College, transcript 7038, p. 2.

59. Rabin, "The Quality That Guarantees Power," 40.

60. Yitzhak Rabin, Lecture at the National Security College, 28 July 1986, Library of the National Security College, transcript 6539, p. 15.

61. Ibid.

62. For red lines in Israeli strategic thinking, see Micha Bar, *Red Lines in Israel's Deterrence Strategy* (Hebrew) (Tel Aviv: Maarachot, 1990).

63. Yitzhak Rabin, Lecture at the National Security College, 30 June 1983, Library of the National Security College, transcript 7038, p. 9.

64. Ibid., 10.

65. Yitzhak Rabin, Lecture at the National Security College, 28 July 1986, Library of the National Security College, transcript 6539, p. 5.

66. "Interview with Yitzhak Rabin," *Maariv,* 2 June 1972, p. 15. For a study critical of the need to establish reputations in deterrence relationships, see Jonathan C. Mercer, *Reputation and International Politics* (Ithaca, N.Y.: Cornell University Press, 1996).

67. Interview with Yuval Neeman, 23 June 1996. See also Yitzhak Rabin, "The Indirect Approach in the War of Independence," *Maarachot,* no. 151 (April 1963). For this method of offensive warfare, see Basil H. Liddell-Hart, *Strategy: The Strategy of Indirect Approach* (London: Faber and Faber, 1946). Liddell-Hart's book was translated into Hebrew and published by the IDF Publishing House in 1956. In all probability, Israeli military leadership in the first few years of the state's existence had little, if any, acquaintance with the works of Liddell-Hart. See Tuvia Ben-Moshe, "Liddell-Hart and the Israel Defense Forces: A Reappraisal," *Journal of Contemporary History* 16 (1981): 369–91.

68. For the new rationale underlying these two operations, see Yitzhak Rabin, "Yigal Alon: Commander and Strategist in the War of Independence," *Maarachot* 272 (1980): 1, 54.

69. Maj. Gen. Aharon Yariv, chief of intelligence, maintained that the Egyptian involvement in Yemen precluded an Egyptian-Israeli war. See interview with Maj. Gen. (Res.) Yeshayahu Gavish, chief of the Southern Command, quoted in Uri Milstein and Dov Doron, *Shaked Patrol* (Hebrew) (Tel Aviv: Miskal, 1994), 141.

70. Yitzhak Rabin, with Dov Goldstein, *Pinkas Sherut* (Hebrew) (Tel Aviv: Maariv, 1979), 154–55, hereafter cited as Rabin, *Memoirs.*

71. Quoted in Brecher, *Decisions in Israel's Foreign Policy,* 327.

72. The collapse was preceded by several reproaches from Israeli leaders, including David Ben-Gurion. See Rabin, *Memoirs,* 149–50, 166, 170–72, 178.

73. Rabin, "Why We Won the War," 5. For an analysis of the 1967 War, see Chaim Herzog, *The Arab-Israeli Wars: War and Peace in the Middle East* (London: Arms and Armour Press, 1982), 145–91.

74. Rabin, "Why We Won the War," 4.

75. Interview with Maj. Gen. (Res.) Uzi Narkis, 19 January 1997. For the events leading to Dayan's appointment as defense minister on 2 June 1967, see Brecher, *Decisions in Israel's Foreign Policy,* 398–418.

76. For this incident and Rabin's role in it, see Rabin, *Memoirs,* 121–25. See also Israel Tal, *National Security: The Few against the Many* (Hebrew) (Tel Aviv: Dvir, 1996), 136–38.

77. "Interview with Chief of Staff Yitzhak Rabin," *Bamahane,* 2 May 1965, p. 19. See also Moshe A. Gilboa, *Six Years, Six Days: Origins and History of the Six-Day War* (Hebrew) (Tel Aviv: Am Oved, 1968), 46.

78. He was disappointed by the poor performance of Israeli tank gunners and entrusted Maj. Gen. Israel Tal, at that time commander of the Tank Corps, to rectify the situation immediately. The improvement in the efficiency of gunnery, which was achieved in a short time due to the systematic and assiduous work of Tal, served Israeli tanks well later, in the 1967 war.

79. For the political and strategic context of the escalation toward the 1967 war, see Avner Yaniv, "Syria and Israel: The Politics of Escalation," in *Syria under Asad,* ed. Moshe Maoz and Avner Yaniv (New York: St. Martin's Press, 1986), 162–68.

80. Rabin, *Memoirs,* 124.

81. Yitzhak Rabin, "The Challenge: To Be the Leader," *IDF Journal* 19 (winter 1990): 3 (adapted from a speech delivered to graduates of the IDF Staff College, August 1989).

82. Yitzhak Rabin, Lecture at the National Security College, 28 July 1986, Library of the National Security College, transcript 6539, p. 2. For the detonation theory in Palestinian thinking, see Yehoshafat Harkabi, *Fedayeen Action and Arab Strategy,* Adelphi Papers No. 53 (London: International Institute for Strategic Studies, 1969), 25.

83. Ibid.

84. Interview with Maj. Gen. (Res.) Rehavam Zeevi, 2 September 1997.

85. Yitzhak Rabin, Lecture at the National Security College, 18 July 1985, Library of the National Security College, transcript 6940, p. 5.

86. Yitzhak Rabin, Lecture at the National Security College, 14 March 1988, Library of the National Security College, transcript 5732, p. 3.

87. See Benjamin Netanyahu, ed., *Terrorism: How the West Can Win* (London: Weidenfeld and Nicolson, 1986).

88. "Minister of Defense Speaks Out on Terrorism, Security, and Violence," *IDF Journal* 15 (summer 1988): 5–6.

89. *IDF Journal* 3 (fall 1986), 34.

90. "Minister of Defense Speaks Out on Terrorism, Security, and Violence," 6.

91. Leah Rabin, *Rabin: Our Life, His Legacy* (New York: G. P. Putnam, 1997), 193.

92. For the Israeli retaliation policy, see Dan Horowitz, "The Control of Limited Military Operations: The Israeli Experience," in *International Violence: Terrorism, Surprise, and Control,* ed. Yair Evron (Jerusalem: Leonard Davis Institute for International Relations, Hebrew University, 1979), 258–76; Shimshoni, *Israel and Conventional Deterrence,* 34–122; William O'Brien, *Law and Morality in Israel's War with the PLO* (New York: Routledge, 1991), 33–76; Benny Morris, *Israel's Border Wars, 1948–1956: Arab Infiltration, Israeli Retaliation, and the Countdown to the Suez War* (Oxford: Clarendon Press, 1993). For the distinction between deterrence by punishment and deterrence by denial, see Glenn H. Snyder, *Deterrence and Defense* (Princeton: Princeton University Press, 1960), 13–14. See also Richard K. Betts, "The Concept of Deterrence in the Postwar Era," *Security Studies* 1 (august 1991): 30–34.

93. Yitzhak Rabin, Lecture at the National Security College, 28 July 1986, Library of the National Security College, transcript 6539, p. 12.

94. *IDF Journal* 3 (fall 1986), 35.

95. Ibid., 34.

96. For Israel's retaliatory policy in this period, see Shlomo Aronson and Dan Horowitz, "The Strategy of Controlled Retaliation: The Israeli Example," *Medina Umimshal* (Hebrew) 1 (summer 1971): 77–100; Shimshoni, *Israel and Conventional Deterrence,* 34–122; Morris, *Israel's Border Wars, 1948–1956,* 173–354.

97. Yitzhak Rabin, "From the Battles over the Water to the Six-Day War," in *The IDF: An Encyclopeadia for Army and Security* (Ramat Gan: Revivim, 1981) (Hebrew), 186. For his specific criticism of the 1956 Kalqilia raid, see Rabin, *Memoirs,* 96.

98. Rabin, "From the Battles over the Water to the Six-Day War," 186.

99. Yitzhak Rabin, Lecture at the National Security College, 30 June 1983, Library of the National Security College, transcript 7038, p. 9. The Samoa operation ended with only one Israeli soldier dead, but with much greater Jordanian damage and casualties than anticipated because of unexpected Jordanian military involve-

ment. Political reverberations within Jordan were similarly unintended by Israeli leaders. For this raid, see Zeev Schiff and Eitan Haber, *Israel, Army, and Defense: A Dictionary* (Hebrew) (Tel Aviv: Zmora, Bitan, Modan, 1976), 384–85. Weizman, the chief of operations in the General Staff, supported the change in the IDF retaliation policy. See Ezer Weizman, *On Eagles' Wings* (New York: Macmillan, 1979), 197.

100. Aryeh Brown, *Moshe Dayan and the Six-Day War* (Tel Aviv: Yediot Aharonot, 1997) (Hebrew), 224–25. The raid against several Palestinian training bases and headquarters in the vicinity of Karameh, which sparked Jordanian military involvement and resulted in many casualties, elicited much criticism within the IDF. See Schiff and Haber, *Israel, Army, and Defense*, 277–78.

101. Interviews with Zeevi, Gazit, and Maj. Gen. (Res.) Yitzhak Hofi, 21 May 1998.

102. Rabin, *Memoirs*, 520.

103. *New York Times*, 3 December 1975, A1.

104. Quoted in O'Brien, *Law and Morality in Israel's War with the PLO*, 158.

105. Rabin, *Memoirs*, 455, 520.

106. Yitzhak Rabin, "Towards a New National Security Concept," in *The War on Terror and the National Security Policy of Israel, 1979–1988* (Hebrew), ed. Zeev Klein (Ramat Gan: Revivim, 1988), 172.

107. Rabin, *Memoirs*, 220–21. Because of the breakdown of the negotiations, the IDF intervened to free the hostages.

108. Ibid., 455.

109. For Rabin's account of the Entebbe raid, see ibid., 523–33. He familiarized himself with the detailed plan. Interview with Lt. Gen. (Res.) Dan Shomron, 1 July 1997. Shomron, at that time chief infantry and paratroopers officer, was the planner and the commander of the rescue operation. Defense Minister Shimon Peres also wholeheartedly supported the military operation. For a detailed account of the military and political preparations for the raid, see Motta (Mordechai) Gur, *Chief of the General Staff (1974–1978)* (Hebrew) (Tel Aviv: Maarachot, 1998), 175–292.

110. This deal evoked much criticism in Israel. See Zeev Schiff, "A Frustrating Agreement," *Haaretz*, 21 May 1985, A9.

111. *New York Times*, 1 October 1985, A1. For a description of the operational aspects of the air raid, see Moshe Ganz, "The Attack on the PLO Headquarters in Tunis," in Klein, *The War on Terror*, 167–69.

112. For a report of Rabin's briefing to the Knesset Committee on Security and Foreign Affairs, see *Maariv*, 3 October 1985. The Israeli government also considered attacking PLO bases in Jordan but preferred not to hurt Jordanian-Israeli relations. For the problematic relations between Jordan and the PLO, see Emile Sahliyeh, "Jordan and the Palestinians," in *The Middle East: Ten Years after Camp David*, ed. William B. Quandt (Washington, D.C.: Brookings Institution, 1988), 298–301.

113. Interview with Shomron.

114. See Inbar, *War and Peace in Israeli Politics*, 137.

115. Only about 10 percent of the Israeli public (the far left) opposed countert-errorist activities. See Gad Barzilai and Efraim Inbar, "The Use of Force: Israeli Public Opinion on Military Options," *Armed Forces and Society* 23 (fall 1996): 49–80.

116. For an analysis of the Intifada and its implications, see Zeev Schiff and Ehud Yaari, *Intifada* (Hebrew) (Tel Aviv: Shocken, 1990); Robert O. Freedman, ed., *The Intifada: Its Impact on Israel, the Arab World, and the Superpowers* (Miami: Florida International University Press, 1991).

117. Yitzhak Rabin, Lecture at the National Security College, 14 March 1988, Library of the National Security College, transcript 5732, p. 3.

118. Yitzhak Rabin, Lecture at the National Security College, 3 August 1989, Library of the National Security College, transcript 5393, p. 9.

119. For an early treatment, see C. Calwell, *Small Wars: Their Principles and Practice* (London: Her Majesty's Stationary Office, 1906). For low-intensity con-flict, see Sam C. Sarkesian and William L. Scully, eds., *American Policy and Low-Intensity Conflict* (New Brunswick, N.J.: Transaction Books, 1981). For an elucida-tion of the small war concept, see Stuart A. Cohen and Efraim Inbar, "A Taxonomy of Israel's Use of Force," *Comparative Strategy* 10 (April 1991): 128–29.

120. Yitzhak Shamir, *Summing-Up* (Hebrew) (Tel Aviv: Edanim 1994), 220. See also Chaim Herzog, *Living History* (Hebrew) (Tel Aviv: Miskal, 1997), 467–68.

121. Interview with Shomron.

122. Dan Sagir, "Jordan Will Return," *Haaretz* (Israel's 40th Year Magazine), May 1988, p. 26. Prime Minister Shamir made the same point (Interview with Yitzhak Shamir, 16 June 1997). For Israeli decison-making in national security and foreign affairs, see Yehuda Ben-Meir, *National Security Decision-making: The Israeli Case* (Boulder, Colo.: Westview Press, for the Jaffee Center for Strategic Stud-ies, Tel Aviv University, 1986), 65–125. This section relies partly on Efraim Inbar, "Israel's Small War: The Military Response to the Intifada," *Armed Forces and So-ciety* 18 (fall 1991): 29–39.

123. Interviews with Avraham Kostelitz, 13 May 1997, and with Shomron.

124. NBC's *Meet the Press,* 27 December 1987 (official transcript), 2.

125. Ibid., 4.

126. David B. Ottaway, "Rabin Defends Israel's Riot-Quelling Tactics," *Wash-ington Post,* 17 December 1987, A47.

127. Generally, Rabin prefered a greater use of firearms against the Palestinians but was restrained by the military and civilian legal authorities. He often com-plained about how the lawyers were limiting the IDF's freedom of action. See Yitzhak Rabin, Lecture at the National Security College, 14 March 1988, Library of the National Security College, transcript 5732, pp. 4–5; Yitzhak Rabin, Lecture at the National Security College, 3 August 1989, Library of the National Security Col-lege, transcript 5393, p. 10. For the military judicial system during the Intifada, see Amnon Straschnov, *Justice under Fire* (Hebrew) (Tel Aviv: Yediot Aharonot, 1994).

128. "Interview with Rabin," *Spectrum* 6 (March 1988): 9.

129. Glenn Frankel, "Rabin Defends Use of Tough Tactics," *Washington Post*, 19 January 1988, A12.

130. Interview with Shamir.

131. Joel Brinkley, "Israel Reaffirms a Stern Response as Violence Grows," *New York Times*, 28 September 1988, A1.

132. "Interview with the Defense Minister, Yitzhak Rabin," *Bamahane*, 30 March 1988, p. 17.

133. Rabin, "The Quality That Guarantees Power," 41.

134. Joel Greenberg, "From Bad to Worse," *Jerusalem Post*, 17 February 1989, p. 4.

135. Interview with Shamir.

136. Ibid. Interview with Shomron.

137. Yitzhak Rabin, interview on Israeli television, 13 January 1988, transcript, *Journal of Palestine Studies* 17 (spring 1988): 151.

138. Frankel, "Rabin Defends Use of Tough Tactics," A12.

139. *New York Times*, 21 January 1989, A9.

140. *Washington Post*, 19 January 1989, A37.

141. *New York Times*, 16 May 1989, A8.

142. The attempts to create islands of exclusive Palestinian authority, where the IDF was effectively prevented from entering and from having a modicum of control, were unsuccessful. Schiff and Yaari, *Intifada*, 296.

143. *Haaretz*, 5 January 1990, A6.

144. Steven Metz, "Foundations for a Low-Intensity Conflict Strategy," *Comparative Strategy* 8 (July 1989), 271.

145. Baruch Kimmerling, *The Interrupted System* (New Brunswick, N.J.: Transaction Books, 1985).

146. For an analysis of the crisis in Lebanese politics, see Walid Khalidi, *Conflict and Violence in Lebanon* (Cambridge: Center for International Affairs, Harvard University Press, 1979), and Itamar Rabinovitch, *The War for Lebanon, 1970–85*, rev. ed. (Ithaca, N.Y.: Cornell University Press, 1985).

147. Rabin, *Memoirs*, 503.

148. Ibid.

149. The United States had communicated to the Israeli government its objection to any Israeli invasion in the event of a Syrian invasion. See *Haaretz*, 20 October 1975, A1.

150. *Maariv*, 11 January 1976.

151. Rabin, *Memoirs*, 494.

152. For the developments leading to the Syrian intervention in Lebanon, see Adeed I. Dawisha, *Syria and the Lebanese Crisis* (New York: St. Martin's Press, 1980). Assad used the American channel, as well as King Hussein of Jordan, to convey messages to Israel.

153. Rabin, *Memoirs*, 503.

154. Interview with Moshe Zak, 19 June 1997.

155. Shmuel Segev, "From the 'Good Fence' to the Litani Operation," *Maariv,* 21 April 1978.

156. Avner Yaniv and Robert Lieber, "Personal Whim or Strategic Imperative: The Israeli Invasion of Lebanon," *International Security* 8 (fall 1983): 117–42; Avner Yaniv, *Dilemmas of Security: Politics, Strategy, and the Israeli Experience in Lebanon* (New York: Oxford University Press, 1987); Yair Evron, *War and Intervention in Lebanon: The Israeli-Syrian Deterrence Dialogue* (London: Croom Helm, 1987).

157. The U.S.-supported Israeli goals included expelling the PLO from Lebanon, establishing a new Christian-dominated political order, and ending the Syrian military presence. The United States even attempted to persuade Israel to refrain from withdrawing from the Beirut area in the fall of 1983. For an American perspective of the Lebanon War, see Raymond Tanter, *Who's at the Helm? Lessons of Lebanon* (Boulder, Colo.: Westview Press, 1990).

158. Rabin, *Rabin: Our Life, His Legacy,* 187.

159. Ibid., 187–88.

160. "Interview with Rabin," *Migvan* 72 (August 1982): 8. His occasional offers of advice to Defense Minister Ariel Sharon were misconstrued as support for the war.

161. Interview with Lt. Gen. (Res.) Moshe Levy, 5 July 1997. See also Yaniv, *Dilemmas of Security,* 254–62. For the May 1983 agreement, see Efraim Inbar, "Great Power Mediation: The USA and the May 1983 Israeli-Lebanese Agreement," *Journal of Peace Research* 28 (February 1991): 71–84.

162. See impressions of his interview with Anthony Lewis, "Looking for an Exit," *New York Times,* 5 November 1984, A19.

163. See "An Interview with Yitzhak Rabin," *Time,* 11 February 1985, p. 44.

164. *New York Times,* 15 January 1985, A1.

165. Yitzhak Rabin, Lecture at the National Security College, 18 July 1985, Library of the National Security College, transcript 6940, p. 11.

166. O'Brien, *Law and Morality in Israel's War with the PLO,* 56–57.

167. *Washington Post,* 22 April 1987, A24.

168. Israel's Grapes of Wrath Operation of April 1996, this time ordered half-heartedly by Prime Minister Shimon Peres, had the same strategic rationale and similar meager results.

169. *Haaretz,* 13 December 1994. Dirani was a Hizballah leader hijacked in May 1994, and the air strike at Ain Dardara in June 1994 killed scores of Hizballah members. In July 1994, the building housing the offices of several Argentinian Jewish communal organizations in Buenos Aires was blown up, and in London, two car bombs exploded, one near the Israeli embassy and the second near the office of the Joint Israel Appeal. Both acts were attributed to the Hizballah, or Iranian-sponsored terrorism.

170. *Yediot Aharonot* (Shabat Supplement), 25 July 1997, pp. 6–7.

CHAPTER 5

1. The best exposition of this school of thinking is Shai Feldman, *Israeli Nuclear Deterrence: A Strategy for the 1980s* (New York: Columbia University Press, 1982). For Israel's nuclear program and policy, see Leonard Spector, *The Undeclared Bomb* (Cambridge: Ballinger 1988); Louis R. Beres, ed., *Security or Armageddon: Israel's Nuclear Strategy* (Lexington, Mass.: Lexington Books, 1985). The most comprehensive discussion is Yair Evron, *Israel's Nuclear Dilemma* (Ithaca, N.Y.: Cornell University Press, 1994).

2. For the conventional school of thought in Israel, see Uri Bar-Joseph, "The Hidden Debate: The Formation of Nuclear Doctrines in the Middle East," *Journal of Strategic Studies* 5 (June 1982): 218–223.

3. Moshe A. Gilboa, *Six Years, Six Days: Origins and History of the Six-Day War* (Hebrew) (Tel Aviv: Am Oved, 1968), 30. See also Avner Cohen, "Stumbling into Opacity: The United States, Israel, and the Atom, 1960–63," *Security Studies* 4 (winter 1994–95): 195–241; Yair Evron, "Israel and the Atom: The Uses and Misuses of Ambiguity, 1957–67," *Orbis* 17 (winter 1974): 1326–43.

4. For Israel's position on the NPT, see Ran Marom, *Israel's Position on Non-Proliferation*, Policy Studies No. 16 (Jerusalem: Leonard Davis Institute for International Relations, Hebrew University, 1986), 26–47. These concerns were, of course, shared by other states and analysts. See Albert Wohlstetter et al., *Swords from Ploughshares* (Chicago: University of Chicago Press, 1977).

5. Dan Margalit, *I Have Seen Them All* (Hebrew) (Tel Aviv: Zmora-Bitan, 1997), 60.

6. Interview with Yuval Neeman, 18 September 1997.

7. *Maariv*, 15 March 1976.

8. Yitzhak Rabin, Lecture at the National Security College, 1 April 1981, Library of the National Security College, transcript 6412, pp. 7–8.

9. Ibid. For the evolution of nuclear strategy, see Lawrence Freedman, *The Evolution of Nuclear Strategy* (London: Macmillan, 1981); Barry Buzan, *Introduction to Strategic Studies: Military Technology and International Relations* (London: Macmillan Press, for the International Institute for Strategic Studies, 1987), 143–62.

10. *Maariv*, 30 December 1990, p. 2.

11. Yitzhak Rabin, Lecture at the National Security College, 1 April 1981, Library of the National Security College, transcript 6412, p. 8.

12. Ibid., 5.

13. Yitzhak Rabin, Lecture at the National Security College, 11 July 1993, Library of the National Security College, transcript 454, p. 16.

14. Yitzhak Rabin, Lecture at the National Security College, 1 April 1981, Library of the National Security College, transcript 6412, p. 8.

15. Yitzhak Rabin, Lecture at the National Security College, 30 June 1983, Library of the National Security College, transcript 7038, p. 4.

16. Yitzhak Rabin, Lecture at the National Security College, 18 July 1985, Library of the National Security College, transcript 6940, p. 14.

17. Yitzhak Rabin, Lecture at the National Security College, 1 April 1981, Library of the National Security College, transcript 6412, p. 8. For an elaboration of the uncertainties of such a balance in the superpower context, see Albert Wohlstetter, "The Delicate Balance of Terror," *Foreign Affairs* 37 (January 1959): 211–34. For its fragility in the Arab-Israeli context, see Efraim Inbar, *Israel's Nuclear Policy after 1973* (Los Angeles: Pan Heuristics, 1977), 35–49.

18. Thomas C. Schelling defines *brinkmanship* as manipulation of the shared risk of war. For a discussion of risk manipulation, see his *Arms and Influence* (New Haven: Yale University Press, 1966), 99–125.

19. Thomas C. Schelling, *The Strategy of Conflict,* 4th ed. (Cambridge: Harvard University Press, 1970), 37.

20. Yitzhak Rabin, Lecture at the National Security College, 30 June 1983, Library of the National Security College, transcript 7038, p. 6.

21. *Maariv,* 4 April 1980.

22. Yitzhak Rabin, Lecture at the National Security College, 1 April 1981, Library of the National Security College, transcript 6412, p. 9.

23. Ibid., 10.

24. *Maariv,* 4 April 1980; see also Yitzhak Rabin, "Making Use of the Time-Out," *Politika* (Hebrew) 44 (March 1992): 29. Allon said several times: "Israel will not be the first to introduce nuclear weapons into the Middle East, but it will not be the second."

25. Yitzhak Rabin, Lecture at the National Security College, 1 April 1981, Library of the National Security College, transcript 6412, p. 9. See also Yitzhak Rabin, Lecture at the National Security College, 30 June 1983, Library of the National Security College, transcript 7038, pp. 4–5.

26. *Bamahane,* 28 October 1954, p. 5.

27. Yitzhak Rabin, with Dov Goldstein, *Pinkas Sherut* (Hebrew) (Tel Aviv: Maariv, 1979), 127, 129–30, hereafter cited as Rabin, *Memoirs.*

28. Interview with Maj. Gen. (Res.) Israel Tal, 5 August 1996.

29. Rabin, *Memoirs,* 243.

30. Ibid., 226.

31. For the early nuclear contacts between the two countries, see Avner Cohen, "Israel's Nuclear History: The Untold Kennedy-Eshkol Dimona Correspondence," *Journal of Israeli History* 16 (summer 1995): 159–94.

32. Rabin, *Memoirs,* 251.

33. Communication from Avner Cohen. See his *Israel and the Bomb* (New York: Columbia University Press, 1998).

34. Interview with Joseph Sisco, 13 August 1996.

35. For Dayan's statements and the nuclear debate after the 1973 war, see Efraim Inbar, "Israel and Nuclear Weapons since October 1973," in Beres, *Security or Armageddon,* 61–78. This section partly relies on this article.

36. Louis Williams, ed., *Military Aspects of the Israel-Arab Conflict* (Tel Aviv: University Publishing Projects, 1975), 210.

37. *Haaretz,* 2 July 1974, p. 2.

38. "ABC Interview," 15 April 1975, ABC transcript, IV-4.

39. *Davar,* 15 March 1976, p. 2.

40. *Maariv,* 8 April 1976.

41. For Israeli decision-making, see Yehuda Ben-Meir, *National Security Decision-making: The Israeli Case* (Boulder, Colo.: Westview Press, for the Jaffee Center for Strategic Studies, Tel Aviv University, 1986).

42. Interview with Neeman, 18 September 1997. As chief scientist and chairman of the Committee for Development, Neeman secured Rabin's approval on several key decisions on "sensitive matters."

43. *Maariv,* 20 June 1974.

44. *Maariv,* 4 December 1974.

45. Interview with Yitzhak Rabin, 25 April 1979.

46. Ibid.

47. Israel wanted to procure the accurate Pershing 2 to counter the Russian Scud missiles in the service of Arab armies and was also interested in the Pershing 2 advanced homing technology. (Interview with Neeman, 18 September 1997.)

48. Williams, *Military Aspects,* 210. Both Shimon Peres, the defense minister, and Yigal Allon, the foreign minister, declared that such missiles would not carry nuclear warheads. (*Jerusalem Post,* 18 September 1975.) Israel often included ultra-sophisticated equipment on the shopping lists it submitted to the United States, knowing a negative answer was forthcoming. The reason was to reserve a place in line for the future supply of such items. See Efraim Inbar, "The American Arms Transfer to Israel," *Middle East Review* 15 (winter 1982/83): 44.

49. For the text, see "Allon's Address to the UN," *Jerusalem Post,* 1 October 1975.

50. Evron, "Israel and the Atom," 1335–36.

51. Interviews with Rabin, 25 April 1979, and Yigal Allon, 4 June 1979.

52. After Egypt's turn to the West in the aftermath of the October 1973 war, Egyptian relations with Iran improved considerably. In May 1974, Iran decided to finance an oil pipeline from Suez to Alexandria, which could serve as a substitute for the Israeli Eilat-Ashkelon pipeline. Egyptian-Iranian cooperation was strengthened during the Shah's visit to Cairo in January 1975. Iranian-Egyptian relations caused concern in Israel. It was feared that a pro-Arab Iran might stop the oil flow to Israel and increase Israel's isolation. Furthermore, Israel was in the midst of negotiations with Egypt, which involved the possibility of withdrawal from the Abu Rudeis oil fields. Relinquishing the oil fields meant an increase in Israeli oil imports. The continued flow of Iranian oil was therefore extremely important to Israel, and Allon was sent to Tehran in February 1975 to receive assurances about the continuation of Iranian oil sales to Israel. (See Shmuel Segev, "The Oil Bridge between Iran and Israel," *Maariv,* 15 May 1981.)

53. Interview with Allon, 14 November 1979.

54. Yitzhak Rabin, "The National Security Problems of Israel in the 1980s," *Maarachot*, nos. 270–71 (October 1979).

55. For the Israeli decision-making process leading to the raid, see Shlomo Nakdimon, *Tammuz in Flames* (Hebrew) (Jerusalem: Edanim Publishers, 1986).

56. *Haaretz*, 6, 9 June 1981.

57. Gad Barzilai, "Democracy in War: Attitudes, Reactions, and Political Participation of the Israeli Public in the Processes of Decision-Making" (Hebrew) (Ph.D. diss., Hebrew University, Jerusalem, 1987), 64.

58. For his detailed position on the air strike, see "Interview with Yitzhak Rabin," *Davar*, 12 June 1981, p. 14.

59. Efraim Inbar, *War and Peace in Israeli Politics: Labor Party Positions on National Security* (Boulder, Colo.: Lynne Rienner, 1991), 134–35.

60. "Interview with Yitzhak Rabin," *Davar*, 12 June 1981, p. 14. See also Leah Rabin, *Rabin: Our Life, His Legacy* (New York: G. P. Putnam, 1997), 184.

61. "Interview with Yitzhak Rabin," *Davar*, 12 June 1981, p. 14. For an analysis of the political and military implications of the Israeli raid, see Shai Feldman, "The Bombing of Osirak—Revisited," *International Security* 7 (fall 1982): 114–42.

62. Yitzhak Rabin, "War and Peace," *Spectrum* 5 (September 1987): 8.

63. Rabin, "Making Use of the Time-Out," 28. For a review of the Iraqi nuclear program, see Yiftah Shapir, "Proliferation of Nonconventional Weapons in the Middle East," in *The Middle East Military Balance: 1993–1994*, ed. Shlomo Gazit (Jerusalem: Jerusalem Post, for the Jaffee Center for Strategic Studies, 1994), 216–18.

64. Rabin, "Making Use of the Time-Out."

65. Ibid.

66. Ibid., 28–29.

67. For the Iranian nuclear program in the early 1990s, see Greg Gerardi and Maryam Aharinijad, "An Assessment of Iran's Nuclear Facilities," *Nonproliferation Review* 3 (summer–spring): 209–15; Shahram Chubin, "Does Iran Want Nuclear Weapons?" *Survival* 37 (spring 1995): 86–104; Al J. Venter, "Iran's Nuclear Ambition: Innocuous Illusion or Ominous Truth?," *International Defense Review*, September 1997, pp. 29–31.

68. Quoted in Shai Feldman, *Nuclear Weapons and Arms Control in the Middle East*, CSIA Studies in International Security (Cambridge: MIT Press, 1997), 47.

69. Interview with Lt. Gen. (Res.) Dan Shomron, 1 July 1997.

70. Yitzhak Rabin, Lecture at the National Security College, 14 March 1988, Library of the National Security College, transcript 5732, p. 2.

71. Yitzhak Rabin, Lecture at the National Security College, 28 July 1986, Library of the National Security College, transcript 6539, p. 8.

72. For a discussion of this term, see Herman Kahn, *On Escalation: Metaphors and Scenarios* (Baltimore: Penguin Books, 1968), 290. For the Syrian motivation in acquiring ballistic missiles, see M. Zuhair Diab, "Syrian Security Requirements in a Peace Settlement with Israel," *Israel Affairs* 1 (summer 1995): 82–83.

73. For the distinction between countercity (countervalue) and counterforce targeting strategies, see Schelling, *Arms and Influence,* 190–98.

74. Yitzhak Rabin, Lecture at the National Security College, 28 July 1986, Library of the National Security College, transcript 6539, p. 8.

75. *Haaretz,* 22 May 1986, A2.

76. Missile attacks against Israeli cities could also hinder mobilization of the reserve units, the bulk of the IDF.

77. Yitzhak Rabin, Lecture at the National Security College, 5 August 1988, Library of the National Security College, transcript 5749, pp. 2–3. Rabin tried to compare the experiences of the British and Germans during the strategic bombings to that of the Iranians in the spring of 1988. He admitted that he could not draw any clear conclusion (ibid., 2). For the the social dimension of strategy, see Michael Howard, "The Forgotten Dimension of Strategy," *Foreign Afairs* 57 (summer 1979): 975–86.

78. Yitzhak Rabin, Lecture at the National Security College, 5 August 1988, Library of the National Security College, transcript 5749, p. 4.

79. See Steven Rosen, "War Power and the Willingness to Suffer," in *Peace, War, and Numbers,* ed. Bruce M. Russett (Beverly Hills: Sage Publications, 1972), 167–83.

80. Yitzhak Rabin, Lecture at the National Security College, 28 July 1986, Library of the National Security College, transcript 6539, p. 8.

81. Interview with Maj. Gen. (Res.) Avraham Rotem, 14 February 1997.

82. Yitzhak Rabin, "The Quality That Guarantees Power," in *Israeli Security in the Next Decade* (Hebrew) (Efal: Yad Tabenkin, 1988), 39–40. The Israeli intelligence community was surprised by the ability of the Iraqi engineers to extend the range of their Scud missiles from 350 kilometers to 650 kilometers. See Yitzhak Rabin, Lecture at the National Security College, 14 March 1988, Library of the National Security College, transcript 5732, p. 2.

83. Rabin, "The Quality That Guarantees Power," 34.

84. For details, see Danny Shoham, *Chemical Weapons in Egypt and Syria: Evolution, Capabilities, Control* (Hebrew), BESA Studies in Mideast Security No. 21 (Ramat Gan: BESA Center for Strategic Studies, Bar-Ilan University, 1995), 9–11.

85. Yitzhak Rabin, Lecture at the National Security College, 14 March 1988, Library of the National Security College, transcript 5732, p. 12. See also the report of his Knesset presentation, *Haaretz,* 3 December 1986, A3.

86. Shoham, *Chemical Weapons in Egypt and Syria.*

87. FBIS-NEA, 21 July 1988, pp. 28–29. For the chemical weapons program in Arab countries, see Shoham, *Chemical Weapons in Egypt and Syria;* see also Danny Shoham, "The Chemical-Biological Threat on Israel," *Nativ* 10 (January–April 1997): 171–79.

88. *Maariv,* 4 March 1990. For reports of preparations against chemical attacks on civilian centers, see *Haaretz,* 16 June, 25 November 1988; *Maariv,* 26 July 1988.

89. For a criticism of this defensive policy, see Aharon Levran, *Israeli Strategy after Desert Storm: Lessons of the Second Gulf War,* BESA Studies in International Security (London: Frank Cass, 1997), 142–43.

90. *Haaretz,* 22 June 1988. For a treatment of Israeli reactions to the threat of chemical weapons, see Gerald Steinberg, "Israeli Responses to the Threat of Chemical Warfare," *Armed Forces and Society* 20 (fall 1993): 85–101.

91. FBIS-NEA, 21 July 1988, pp. 28–29.

92. For Rabin's response, see *Maariv,* 3 April 1990.

93. Yitzhak Rabin, "Deterrence in an Israeli Security Context," in *Deterrence in the Middle East: Where Theory and Practice Converge,* ed. Aharon Klieman and Ariel Levite, JCSS Study No. 22 (Boulder, Colo.: Westview Press, 1993), 13.

94. Dan Margalit, "Rabin: For Israel This Is a Deluxe War," *Haaretz,* 19 February 1991, A3. See also Reuven Pedatzur, "Beginning to Emerge from the Basement," *Haaretz,* 3 April 1991, B1.

95. *Maariv,* 30 December 1990.

96. Ibid. See also Rabin, *Rabin: Our Life, His Legacy,* 203.

97. Yitzhak Rabin, "A Smart Governmental Policy," *Maariv,* 1 February 1991, p. 3.

98. *Haaretz,* 28 August 1992.

99. Ibid.

100. Some analysts in Israel argued that Israel was successful in deterring chemical attacks from Iraq during the 1991 Gulf War. See Shai Feldman, "Israeli Deterrence during the Gulf War," in *War in the Gulf: Implications for Israel,* ed. Joseph Alpher (Boulder, Colo.: Westview Press, for the Jaffee Center for Strategic Studies, 1992), 184–208; Levran, *Israeli Strategy after Desert Storm,* 84.

101. Efraim Inbar, "Contours of Israel's New Strategic Thinking," *Political Science Quarterly* 111 (spring 1996): 57–63.

102. *Davar,* 17 January 1992, p. 18. Interview with Haim Assa, 21 December 1997.

103. *Haaretz,* 1 November 1994, A4; *Maariv,* 16 December 1994, A3. See chapter 2.

104. Efraim Inbar, "Israel and Arms Control," *Arms Control* 13 (September 1992): 214–21; Inbar, "Contours of Israel's New Strategic Thinking," 60–61. For an advocacy for the regional approach, see Gerald M. Steinberg, "Middle East Arms Control and Regional Security," *Survival* 36 (spring 1994): 126–41.

105. Rabin, "Making Use of the Time-Out," 29.

106. *Voice of Israel,* 10 January 1989.

107. *Jerusalem Post,* 5 September 1997, p. 24.

108. After President Bill Clinton's decision to seek a CTBT in July 1993, the Geneva Conference on Disarmament decided in August 1993 to give its Ad Hoc Committee on a Nuclear Test Ban a mandate to begin negotiations on a CTBT in January 1994.

109. Interview with Dr. Yitzhak Lederman, 1 April 1997. See also Gerald M. Steinberg, "Israel and the Changing Global Non-Proliferation Regime: The NPT Extension, CTBT, and Fissile Cut-Off," in *Middle Eastern Security: Prospects for an Arms Control Regime,* ed. Efraim Inbar and Shmuel Sandler (London: Frank Cass, 1995), 74–77; Feldman, *Nuclear Weapons and Arms Control in the Middle East,* 256–57.

110. *Haaretz,* 29 July 1994, A4; "United States Will Not Press Israel to Join the NPT," *Haaretz,* 17 November 1994. For the Middle Eastern aspects of the extension conference, see Shai Feldman, *Extending the Nuclear Nonproliferation Treaty: The Middle East Debate,* Research Memorandum 28 (Washington, D.C.: Washington Institute, 1995), and Gerald M. Steinberg, "Middle East Peace and the NPT Extension Decision," *Nonproliferation Review* 4 (fall 1996): 17–29.

111. *Haaretz,* 29 July 1994, A4; "United States Will Not Press Israel to Join the NPT," *Haaretz,* 17 November 1994.

112. Feldman, *Nuclear Weapons and Arms Control in the Middle East,* 248.

113. The Egyptian policy jeopardized the American preference for an indefinite extension of the NPT and introduced a new bone of contention in the Arab-Israeli relations, harming the American-backed peace process.

114. Aluf Ben, "Israel Will Agree to a NWFZ Two Years after Signing of a Comprehensive Peace Agreement," *Haaretz,* 21 February 1995, A1. Interview with Eitan Haber, 11 August 1979.

115. Aluf Ben, "A Dispute over Clinton's Initiative," *Haaretz,* 28 December 1993, A1; Aluf Ben, "Minimizing the Peace Risks," *Haaretz,* 11 February 1994, B3; Ran Adelist, "What Do We Do with It?," *Hadashot* (Weekend Supplement), 22 October 1993, pp. 1–3. Shimon Peres, the foreign minister, was willing to accept the initiative.

116. David Makovsky, "PM: Egyptian Model of Full Withdrawal Difficult to Change," *Jerusalem Post,* 24 September 1995, p. 1. See also Steinberg, "Israel and the Changing Global Non-Proliferation Regime, 77–79.

117. Efraim Inbar and Shmuel Sandler, "The Changing Israeli Strategic Equation: Toward a Security Regime," *Review of International Studies* 21 (January 1995): 41–59.

CHAPTER 6

1. For an early formulation of this thesis, see Efraim Inbar, "Contours of Israel's New Strategic Thinking," *Political Science Quarterly* 111 (spring 1996): 45–62.

2. "Address by Yitzhak Rabin," in *Towards a New Era in US-Israel Relations,* ed. Yehuda Mirsky and Ellen Rice (Washington, D.C.: Washington Institute, 1992), 1.

3. For an analysis of Middle East international politics after 1991, see L. Carl Brown, "The Middle East after the Cold War and the Gulf War: Systemic Change

or More of the Same?" in *Collective Security beyond the Cold War*, ed. George Downs (Ann Arbor: University of Michigan Press, 1994), 197–216; Efraim Karsh, "Cold War, Post-Cold War: Does It Make A Difference for the Middle East?" in *The National Security of Small States in a Changing World*, ed. Efraim Inbar and Gabriel Sheffer (London: Frank Cass, 1997), 77–106; Muhamed Faour, *The Arab World after Desert Storm* (Washington, D.C.: United States Institute for Peace, 1993).

4. Rabin's inaugural address as prime minister to the Knesset, *Knesset Minutes*, 13 July 1992, p. 44.

5. Interviews with Maj. Gen. (Res.) Uzi Narkis, 19 January 1997, and Maj. Gen. (Res.) Rehavam Zeevi, 2 September 1997. This author also noted the new style. See Inbar, "Contours of Israel's New Strategic Thinking," 48. Even though he did not write his own speeches, it was out of character for Rabin to make statements and use terminology that he was not comfortable with. Only on a very few occasions did Rabin object to the language or the content of the speeches prepared for him by Eitan Haber. (Interview with Eitan Haber, 26 June 1997.) Moreover, he also used this new language in less structured situations, such as press interviews.

6. *Knesset Minutes*, 13 July 1992.

7. "Address by Yitzhak Rabin," 2.

8. Yitzhak Rabin, "Deterrence in an Israeli Security Context," in *Deterrence in the Middle East: Where Theory and Practice Converge*, ed. Aharon Klieman and Ariel Levite, JCSS Study No. 22 (Boulder, Colo.: Westview Press, 1993), 13. For a counterargument claiming erosion in Israel's deterrent power, see Efraim Inbar and Shmuel Sandler, "Israel's Deterrence Strategy Revisited," *Security Studies* 3 (winter 1993/94): 330–58. For the notion of extended deterrence, see Janice Gross Stein, "Extended Deterrence in the Middle East: American Strategy Reconsidered," *World Politics* 39 (April 1978): 326–52.

9. "Remarks by Yitzhak Rabin to the United Jewish Appeal Luncheon," Washington Hilton, Washington D.C., Federal News Service, 17 March 1992. See also his inaugural address to the Knesset, *Knesset Minutes*, 13 July 1992, p. 44.

10. Ibid., 2.

11. Speech delivered by PM Yitzhak Rabin to graduates of the National Security College, 12 August 1993 (official text), 3 (emphasis in the original).

12. Ibid.

13. Interview with Haim Assa, 21 December 1997.

14. Yitzhak Rabin, "My National Agenda," *Maariv*, 24 January 1992, p. 12.

15. "Interview with Maj. Gen. (Res.) Uri Sagui," *Kol Hair*, 8 December 1995, p. 33.

16. Interview on Israeli television evening news, 15 February 1994.

17. See his "Peace and Security, or War" (speech presenting his government to the Knesset, 13 July 1992) in *Pursuing Peace: The Peace Speeches of Prime Minister Yitzhak Rabin* (Hebrew) (Tel Aviv: Zmora-Bitan, 1995), 68.

18. Interviews with Assa, and Imri Tov, 15 January 1998.

19. For the views of Shimon Peres, see his *The New Middle East* (New York: Henry Colt and Co., 1993).

20. *Jerusalem Post*, 21 November 1993, p. 1.

21. Appendix B: "Policy Statement by Prime Minister Yitzhak Rabin to the Knesset," 3 October 1994 (official transcript).

22. See "Interview with PM Rabin," *Bamahane*, 23 September 1992, p. 9.

23. Ibid. See also appendix A: Yitzhak Rabin, "After the Gulf War: Israeli Defense and Its Security Policy."

24. "Interview with PM Rabin," *Bamahane*, 23 September 1992. See also "Interview with Rabin," *Maariv* (Shabbat Supplement), 24 June 1994, pp. 2–3.

25. See his "Confronting the Knives of Hamas and the Axes of the Islamic Jihad" (speech to the Knesset, 21 December 1992) in *Pursuing Peace*, 81. See also appendix B: "Policy Statement by Prime Minister Yitzhak Rabin to the Knesset," 3 October 1994 (official transcript). For a sober assessment of the threat of Islamic fundamentalism, see Graham E. Fuller and Ian O. Lesser, *A Sense of Siege: The Geopolitics of Islam and the West* (Boulder, Colo.: Westview Press—A RAND Study, 1995); Efraim Inbar, "Islamic Radicalism and the Peace Process," *Terrorism and Political Violence* 8 (summer 1996): 199–215.

26. *Jerusalem Post*, 26 October 1993, p. 12.

27. "Interview with Prime Minister Yitzhak Rabin," *NBC Today*, 26 July 1994, Israel Information Service Gopher.

28. *Washington Post*, 29 October 1987, A33.

29. Interview with Yitzhak Shamir, 16 June 1997. For the Israeli "periphery doctrine"—emphasis on good relations with non-Arab countries at the fringes of the Middle East, Turkey, Iran, and Ethiopia—see Aharon S. Klieman, *Israel and the World after Forty Years* (Washington, D.C.: Pergamon-Brassey's, 1990), 91–92, 169, 236.

30. *Bamahane*, 8 August 1990, p. 7.

31. Rabin decided against such a step in order not to endanger the situation of the Jews left in Iran and not to jeopardize the efforts to rescue the Israeli pilot Ron Arad, downed in Lebanon and believed to be in Iranian hands. See *Haaretz*, 7 August 1996, A1.

32. For the time factor as a distinguishing element between hawks and doves in Israeli politics, see Efraim Inbar, *War and Peace in Israeli Politics: Labor Party Positions on National Security* (Boulder, Colo.: Lynne Rienner 1991), 14–15.

33. For his use of this term, see appendix B: "Policy Statement by Prime Minister Yitzhak Rabin to the Knesset," 3 October 1994 (official transcript).

34. Interviews with Haber, 26 June 1997, and Assa.

35. *Jerusalem Post*, 16 August 1992, p. 2.

36. *Haaretz*, 29 June 1994, A1.

37. Yitzhak Rabin, "Making Use of the Time-Out," *Politika* (Hebrew) 44 (March 1992): 29.

38. Ibid. The rationale behind this assessment, to which many Laborites and those to their left adhere, is not entirely clear. The counterargument—that radical countries in the region, which deny Israel's right to exist and oppose the peace process, will try to undo the peace process and to harm Israel with whatever means are at their disposal—sounds to me more plausible.

39. Interview with Assa.

40. "Interview with Prime Minister Yitzhak Rabin," *NBC Today,* 26 July 1994.

41. David Makovsky, *Making Peace with the PLO: The Rabin Government's Road to the Oslo Accord* (Boulder, Colo.: Westview Press, 1996), 68–69.

42. Interview with Assa.

43. For a discussion of establishing reputations, see Thomas C. Schelling, *Arms and Influence* (New Haven: Yale University Press, 1966), 55–59.

44. *Davar,* 2 September 1993.

45. Interview with Dr. Yehuda Ben-Meir, 26 June 1997. The impact of terrorist acts on the Israeli public is understudied. For exceptions, see Gad Barzilai and Efraim Inbar, "The Use of Force: Israeli Public Opinion on Military Options," *Armed Forces and Society* 23 (fall 1996): 51–54, 72. (Several terrorist acts in March 1993 and October 1994 led to greater public support for the Israeli use of force.) For a study of the interactions between media and terror, see Gabriel Weimann and Conrad Winn, *The Theater of Terror: Mass Media and International Terrorism* (New York: Longman, 1994).

46. Marvin Kalb, "The Promise and Problems of the Israeli Press" (interview with Yitzhak Rabin), *Press/Politics* 1 (winter 1996): 113.

47. "Interview with PM Yitzhak Rabin on Israel Radio," 11 April 1994, Israel Information Service Gopher.

48. Ibid.

49. "Rabin Remarks on Tel Aviv Bombing," 19 October 1994, Israel Information Service Gopher.

50. *Yediot Aharonot,* 30 January 1995, p. 9. I thank Boaz Ganor for supplying this quotation.

51. David Makovsky and Alon Pinkas, "Rabin: Killing Civilians Won't Kill the Negotiations," *Jerusalem Post,* 13 April 1994, p. 7. In the same interview, Rabin also coined the phrase "There are no holy dates," by which he refused to commit himself to end the negotiations with the Palestinians over the Cairo agreement by the agreed-upon deadline. This duality was a constant feature of Rabin's approach to the negotiations with the Palestinians.

52. *Yediot Aharonot,* 30 January 1995, p. 9.

53. See Haim Assa, *Essentiality* (Hebrew) (Tel Aviv: Hakibbutz Hameuchad, 1995), 114–15. Haim Assa served as Rabin's strategic adviser from 1992.

54. Efraim Inbar, "Israel's New Predicament in a New Strategic Environment," in *The National Security of Small States in a Changing World,* ed. Efraim Inbar and Gabriel Sheffer, Besa Studies in International Security (London: Frank Cass, 1997), 155–74.

55. For a comprehensive review of Israeli-Syrian talks in the post-1992 period, see Itamar Rabinovich, *The Brink of Peace: Israel and Syria, 1992–1996* (Hebrew) (Tel Aviv: Miskal, 1998). Rabinovich was the head of the negotiating team with Syria during Rabin's premiership and Israel's ambassador to the United States. For the Israeli-Syrian negotiations in this period, see also Moshe Maoz, *Syria and Israel: From War to Peace-Making* (Oxford: Clarendon Press, 1995), chap. 11; Efraim Inbar, "Israeli Negotiations with Syria," *Israel Affairs* 1 (summer 1995): 89–100; and Aluf Ben, "The Golan Heights File," *Haaretz,* 14 January 1997, B1. For Assad's perspective on the Arab-Israeli conflict, see Patrick Seale, *Asad: The Struggle for the Middle East* (London: I. B. Taurus, 1988). See also Moshe Maoz, *Asad, the Sphinx of Damascus: A Political Biography* (London: Weidenfeld and Nicolson, 1988). For Assad's adjustment to the post-1991 Middle East order, see Raymond A. Hinnebusch, "Asad's Syria and the New World Order: The Struggle for Regime Survival," *Middle East Policy* 2, no. 1 (1993): 1–14.

56. *Al Hamishmar,* 2 June 1992, p. 1. For a collection of his statements on the importance of the Golan Heights, see *Haaretz,* 13 September 1994, A4. For a military analysis of the Golan plateau, see Aryeh Shalev, *Israel and Syria: Peace and Security on the Golan* JCSS Study No. 24 (Tel Aviv: Jaffee Center for Strategic Studies, 1994).

57. Rabin preferred not to table a proposal for leasing the Golan Heights because it would indicate an Israeli acceptance of Syrian sovereignty over the territory. Yitzhak Rabin, Lecture to the National Security College, 8 July 1993, Library of the National Security College, transcript 454, p. 10.

58. For this speech, see *Nativ* 2 (March 1993): 22.

59. Rabin, *Memoirs,* 476.

60. Between 1968 and 1992, the span of responses rejecting the notion of withdrawing from the Golan Heights in exchange for a peace treaty ranged from 96 percent to 71 percent. See Asher Arian, *Security Threatened: Surveying Israeli Opinion on Peace and War* (Cambridge: Cambridge University Press, for the Jaffee Center for Strategic Studies, Tel Aviv University, 1995), 101–3. Since 1992, there has been an erosion in this uncompromising position, but the proportion of Israelis willing to relinquish all of the Golan did not exceed 7 percent in the 1992–94 period. Ibid., 103.

61. *Maariv,* 29 October 1991; *Yediot Aharonot,* 10 September 1992; Rabinovich, *The Brink of Peace,* 100.

62. Yossi Olmert, *Toward a Syrian-Israel Peace Agreement: Perspective of a Former Negotiator,* Research Memorandum No. 25 (Washington, D.C.: Washington Institute, 1994).

63. For the statement of Rabinovich, see *Haaretz,* 25 August 1992, p. 1. For Labor's positions on the Golan, see Inbar, *War and Peace in Israeli Politics,* 86–87, 93–94.

64. *Yediot Aharonot,* 10 September 1992, p. 2. This statement elicited strong opposition from the settlers on the Golan Heights, who launched an intensive political campaign to block such a move.

65. He spoke to a delegation of Israeli Druses on 9 September 1992.

66. *Haaretz,* 10 September 1992, A1. Peres was not involved in the negotiations with Syria, as a result of Rabin's decision to leave this matter in his own hands. Rabin preferred to deal in the same manner with the Palestinians, but Peres circumvented Rabin's initial preference by establishing a back channel at Oslo, which is discussed below.

67. *Yediot Aharonot,* 2 December 1992.

68. "Interview with Yitzhak Rabin," *Yediot Aharonot,* 4 May 1993; *Jerusalem Post,* 6 October 1993, p. 7.

69. See "Interview with Yitzhak Rabin," *Yediot Aharonot,* 4 May 1993, p. 15; David Makovsky, "PM: Egyptian Model of Full Withdrawal Difficult to Change," *Jerusalem Post,* 24 September 1995, p.1.

70. *Maariv,* 25 April 1993, p. 2.

71. Zeev Schiff, "The Pocket File," *Haaretz,* 29 August 1997, B2. Rabin's insistence that he made no commitment to withdraw from the Golan Heights in exchange for peace with Syria was technically correct because the suggestion was presented as a hypothetical deal to the Americans only.

72. Rabinovich, *The Brink of Peace,* 28, 115. Ehud Barak, former chief of staff (1992–95) and currently Labor's leader, also confirmed the content of the hypothetical discussion. (*Jerusalem Post,* 29 August 1997, p. 1.)

73. Interviews with Haber, 11 August 1997, and with Rabbi Yoel Bin-Nun, 26 November 1997.

74. Interview with Assa.

75. Assad was probably surprised by Rabin's concessions early in the negotiations and decided to insist on a withdrawal to the June 1967 line, which included territory captured by Syria from Israel in 1948. For the importance of cultural factors in international negotations, see Raymond Cohen: *Negotiating across Cultures* (Washington, D.C.: United States Institute for Peace Press, 1991), and *Culture and Conflict in Egyptian-Israeli Relations: A Dialogue of the Deaf* (Bloomington: Indiana University Press, 1990).

76. For Rabin's admission that Christopher's failure in August 1993 to bring a satisfactory reply from Assad served as the impetus for the deal with the PLO, see "The Prime Minister Speaks to David Makovsky," *Jerusalem Post,* 6 October 1993, p. 7. See also Rabinovich, *The Brink of Peace,* 115.

77. *Haaretz,* 7 October 1994, A1, A10.

78. *New York Times,* 18 May 1994, p. 1.

79. Schiff, "The Pocket File." This line was west of the international border and included areas of mandatory Palestine that had been conquered by Syria in 1948. Moreover, this line allowed Syrian presence very close to Israel's water resources (the Jordan and Yarmuk Rivers, as well as the Sea of Galilee). See Zeev Schiff, "The 4 June 1967 Trap," *Haaretz,* 21 June 1995, B1.

80. *Haaretz,* 15 July 1994, A1. This statement was not coordinated with Rabin, who kept Peres in the dark on the negotiations with Syria.

81. *Haaretz,* 28 July 1994, A1.

82. *Haaretz,* 31 October 1994, A1.

83. The security measures that Israel focused on were the size of the demilitarized zone, a reduction and redeployment of the Syrian armor, early warning stations, a verification regime, and the deployment of an international monitoring force on the Golan Heights. See Steve Rodan and Alon Pinkas, "Special Rosh Hashanah Interview with Yitzhak Rabin," *Jerusalem Post,* 5 September 1994, p. 5.

84. The establishment of Egyptian-Israeli diplomatic relations and the opening of borders between the two countries for free movement of goods and people preceded the complete Israeli withdrawal from the Sinai Peninsula. The withdrawal in stages took three years, and the evacuated area was demilitarized. For Rabin's sticking to the Egyptian precedent, see *Haaretz,* 9 September 1994, A2.

85. For an account of this meeting, see Aluf Ben, "A Photograph Not for Publication," *Haaretz,* 23 January 1995, B2.

86. Indeed, the pro-Golan lobby organized a popular movement, which later became the Third Way Party. Its leadership and constituency came primarily from the hawkish wing within the Labor Party. Two Labor MKs—Avigdor Kehalani and Immanuel Zissman—were among the Third Way's leaders. Both of them also voted in the Knesset, in October 1995, against the the Oslo II Agreement. The Third Way ran independently in the 1996 elections, gaining four seats. It was an important contributing factor in the electoral loss of the Peres-led Labor Party in 1996.

87. Interview with Haber, 26 June 1997. See also Teddy Preuss, "All Will Accept the Verdict of the Majority," *Davar,* 14 September 1994, p. 5.

88. *Yediot Aharonot,* 22 April 1994, p. 3.

89. Appendix B: "Policy Statement by Prime Minister Yitzhak Rabin to the Knesset," 3 October 1994 (official transcript).

90. Ibid.

91. *Haaretz,* 13 September 1994, A4. The proposed legislation would have required a 60 percent majority in the Knesset or a 65 percent majority in a national referendum before Israel could leave the Golan Heights.

92. *Haaretz,* 7 February 1995, A4.

93. Interview with Haber, 26 June 1997. Public opinion polls run by the BESA Center for Strategic Studies, Bar-Ilan University, and the Tami Steinmetz Center for Peace Studies, Tel Aviv University, also showed a gradual, small erosion in the opposition to full withdrawal, though the majority of Israelis remained opposed to full withdrawal. For the poll data submitted to Rabin on the issue of the Golan, see *Haaretz,* 22 September 1994, B3.

94. Interview with Haber, 26 June 1997.

95. Israeli television (Channel 1), 15 February 1994 (communicated by the Government Press Office). One example mentioned by Rabin was Syria's refusal to allow Arab MK Abd al-Wahab Darawshe to visit Damascus with a group of Arab Israelis.

96. *Haaretz,* 23 August 1994, A5, and 23 November 1994, A1.

97. *Haaretz,* 23 January 1995, B2.

98. *Jerusalem Post,* 1 February 1996, p. 1.

99. See Ben Caspit, "Beilin, the Bad Boy," *Maariv* (Shabat Supplement), 8 December 1995, p. 6. See also Yossi Beilin, *Touching Peace* (Hebrew) (Tel Aviv: Miskal, 1997), 149, 233. Such a view has been vindicated in light of the even greater efforts made by Peres, Rabin's successor, to reach a deal with Assad. For a view critical of Israel, see Helena Cobban, *Syria and the Peace: A Good Chance Missed* (Carlisle, Pa.: Strategic Studies Institute, U.S. Army War College, 1997); "An Interview with Ambassador Walid al-Moualem," *Journal of Palestine Studies* 26 (winter 1997): 81–94.

100. David Makovsky, "Asad with Bitter Coffee (an Interview with Warren Christopher)," *Haaretz,* 24 October 1997, B5.

101. Rabin had objected before to the inclusion of any residents of Jerusalem in the Palestinian delegation in order to clarify the exclusion of the issue of Jerusalem from the agenda. Peres convinced the Americans to suggest to Rabin, during his visit to Washington in March 1993, to bring Husseini into the talks in order to break the logjam in the negotiations. Peres also ignored Rabin's instructions to delay a meeting of the Oslo track. Moreover, without Rabin's permission, he offered Jericho to the Palestinians in addition to Gaza. See Makovsky, *Making Peace with the PLO,* 26, 37.

102. Interview with Assa.

103. For the Oslo talks, see Beilin, *Touching Peace,* 61–164; Makovsky, *Making Peace with the PLO.*

104. Makovsky, *Making Peace with the PLO,* 42, 51; Beilin, *Touching Peace,* 131–32. Orly Azoulay-Katz, *Sisyphus' Catch* (Hebrew) (Tel Aviv: Miskal, 1996), 211–12.

105. Azoulay-Katz, *Sisyphus' Catch,* 197.

106. For the text of the DOP, see Walter Laqueur and Barry Rubin, eds., *The Israel-Arab Reader* (New York: Penguin Books, 1995), 599–611.

107. For the Cairo agreement, see Laqueur and Rubin, *The Israel-Arab Reader,* 629–42.

108. The second agreement was partly implemented after Rabin's assassination. For an analysis of these agreements, see Max Singer and Michael Eichenwald, *Making Oslo Work,* Mideast Security and Policy Studies No. 30 (Ramat Gan: BESA Center for Strategic Studies, Bar-Ilan University, 1997), 45–66. The asymmetry in the payoffs of the Taba agreement is striking, leaving Israel little to bargain in the permanent status negotiations. This assessement led to a coalition between doves (i.e., Yossi Beilin, Ezer Weizman) and hawks (Netanyahu); the coalition demanded skipping the withdrawals and moving immediately to negotiations over permanent status issues.

109. See "Interview with Prime Minister Yitzhak Rabin," *NBC Today,* 26 July 1994.

110. Dan Petreanu, "Labor's PLO Dilemma," *Jerusalem Post,* 20 January 1989.

111. Martin Indyk, "Current Assessment of the Middle East Peace Process," speech delivered at Haifa University, 16 November 1995 (official text), 3. See also Makovsky, *Making Peace with the PLO,* 41.

112. This precise point was made by the author in his 1991 analysis of the positions of Rabin and Peres on the PLO. See Inbar, *War and Peace in Israeli Politics,* 80.

113. These commitments are included in the letter of 9 September 1993 sent by Yasir Arafat to Rabin. For the letter, see Laqueur and Rubin, *The Israel-Arab Reader,* 611.

114. He specified these goals in his lecture to the National Security College, 11 July 1993, Library of the National Security College, transcript 454, p. 10. See also "The Prime Minister Speaks to David Makovsky."

115. In a speech to the coalition members, *Haaretz,* 31 August 1993, A3. See also "The Prime Minister Speaks to David Makovsky."

116. "The Prime Minister Speaks to David Makovsky." Rabin emphasized that a deal with Syria could entail many more security risks.

117. In a speech to the coalition members, *Haaretz,* 31 August 1993, A3.

118. Ibid.

119. "The Prime Minister Speaks to David Makovsky." For the security risks embodied in such a state, see Mark A. Heller, "Towards a Palestinian State," *Survival* 39 (summer 1997): 5–22; Efraim Inbar and Shmuel Sandler, "The Risks of Palestinian Statehood," *Survival* 39 (summer 1997): 23–41.

120. *Haaretz,* 14 April 1995, A4.

121. For the importance of cities in the process of state-building, see Charles Tilly, *Coercion, Capital, and the European States, AD 990–1990* (Oxford: Basil Blackwell, 1990), 1–66.

122. See his "Without Separation There Is No Security" (speech in the Knesset on 8 April 1993), in *Pursuing Peace,* 84–85.

123. "Rabin Remarks on Tel Aviv Bombing," 19 October 1994, Israel Information Service Gopher.

124. Interview with Assa. Rabin was a formalist and did not like advisers who lacked, by their mere staff status, responsibility for the decisions taken. (Interview with Tov.)

125. Ibid. The issue at stake was the control over the entry points to the PA from Egypt and Jordan. Assa suggested that Israel monitor the incoming persons through transparent mirrors, with a right to stop suspects. This allowed the Palestinians to have the appearance of unilateral control.

126. *Haaretz Magazine,* 7 March 1997, p. 18.

127. Interview with Prof. Shimon Shitreet, 8 May 1997.

128. Ibid.

129. Interviews with Ben-Meir and with Haber, 11 August 1997.

130. *Jerusalem Post,* 21 November 1993, p. 1.

131. Interview with Maj. Gen. (Res.) Danny Rotschild, 13 March 1996. Generally, Rabin did not excel in bargaining skills, particularly not in a Middle Eastern bazaar atmosphere.

132. Leah Rabin, *Rabin: Our Life, His Legacy* (New York: G. P. Putnam, 1997), 259.

133. For the IDF position, see Shimon Schieffer and Nahum Barnea, "The IDF Looks for a Crisis with Arafat," *Yediot Aharonot* (Shabbat Supplement), 4 February 1994, pp. 1–2.

134. "The Prime Minister Speaks to David Makovsky."

135. See Semadar Peri, "Interview with Maj. Gen. Dany Rotschild," *Yediot Aharonot* (Shabat Supplement), 22 April 1994, pp. 12–13.

136. *Haaretz,* 18 May 1994, A1. In contrast, Peres minimized the importance of what Arafat said as long as the process continued.

137. See "Arafat's Remarkable Consistency," *Jerusalem Post,* 18 November 1994, p. 6; Evelyn Gordon, "Zisman: Arafat Violating Accords through Speeches," *Jerusalem Post,* 3 August 1995, p. 2; *Haaretz,* 11 August 1995, A5. Moreover, in an April 1995 speech, Arafat compared the Oslo agreements to Mohammed's agreement with the Kuraish tribe—an agreement that the prophet broke two years later.

138. Arafat's dilemma was clear. On the one hand, he preferred not to start a civil war against Islamic militias in order not to be perceived as subservient to Israel. On the other hand, the continuous existence and activities of the Hamas and Islamic Jihad undermined his own rule and the development of a political entity with monopoly over coercive means and interfered with extracting additional concessions from Israel.

139. David Makovsky and Alon Pinkas, "Interview with Yitzhak Rabin," *Jerusalem Post,* 13 April 1994, p. 7.

140. *Haaretz,* 1 September 1994, A7. Yossi Beilin said at the same party caucus meeting that the Oslo agreements would fail if Arafat did not reduce the scope of terror. (Ibid.)

141. Ibid. The civilian functions mentioned were health, welfare, tourism, and direct taxation. See also the interview with the prime minister by Steve Rodan and Alon Pinkas, "The PA Not Doing Enough against Hamas and Islamic Jihad," *Jerusalem Post,* 5 September 1994, p. 5.

142. Appendix B: "Policy Statement by Prime Minister Yitzhak Rabin to the Knesset," 3 October 1994 (official transcript).

143. *Haaretz,* 5 December 1994, A1.

144. Ibid.

145. *Haaretz,* 17 April 1995, A4.

146. *Jerusalem Post,* 24 September 1995, p. 7.

147. According to data collected for the Project on Public Opinion and National Security of the BESA Center for Strategic Studies, Israelis generally endorsed the peace process during the summer of 1995 but lent much less support to the specific policies pursued by the Rabin government. The understandings reached with the

PA drew only 30 percent support and about 40 percent opposition, whereas the rest of the public remained undecided. Thus, portraying Israeli public opinion as split into two large groups—a peace and a nationalist camp—is false. The correct formula depicting the distribution of opinions on national security in Israel is 30–40–30 percent, which means that there is a large body of security-oriented centrists. See Arian, *Security Threatened*, 256–61. This is precisely why Rabin-led Labor won the 1992 elections, whereas Peres, perceived to be more dovish than Rabin, was unable to lead Labor to an electoral victory. This formula also explains the popularity of national unity governments in Israel.

148. *Jerusalem Post*, 24 September 1995, p. 7.

149. Appendix B: "Policy Statement by Prime Minister Yitzhak Rabin to the Knesset," 3 October 1994 (official transcript).

150. *Haaretz*, 20 February 1995.

151. *Davar*, 27 September 1992; *Jerusalem Post*, 21 November 1993, p. 1; appendix B: "Policy Statement by Prime Minister Yitzhak Rabin to the Knesset," 3 October 1994 (official transcript).

152. Interviews with Maj. Gen. (Res.) Menachem Maron, 1 June 1997, and with Bin-Nun.

153. For the Knesset debate and the vote, see *Haaretz*, 24 September 1993, A1.

154. The support of the 61st MK, Alex Goldfarb of the Yeud Party (a splinter group of the right-wing Tzomet Party), was secured only after much pressure was applied. Not only was the parliamentary opposition much larger than for Oslo, but Rabin's government secured a parliamentary majority only with the support of the Arab parties, which were not part of the coalition. In Israeli political parlance, this agreement did not command a "Jewish majority," which was problematic. For the Knesset debate and the vote, see *Haaretz*, 8 October 1995, A1.

155. Efraim Inbar, "Netanyahu Takes Over," *Israel Affairs* 4 (fall 1997): 36.

156. For Jordan's road to peace, see Moshe Zak, *King Hussein Makes Peace* (Hebrew) (Ramat Gan: Bar Ilan University Press and BESA Center for Strategic Studies, 1996). For other works on Israeli-Jordanian relations, see Dan Shueftan, *A Jordanian Option* (Hebrew) (Tel Aviv: Yad Tabenkin, 1986); Aharon S. Klieman, "The Israel-Jordan Tacit Security Regime," in *Regional Security Regimes: Israel and Its Neighbors*, ed. Efraim Inbar (Albany: State University of New York Press, 1995), 127–50.

157. Zak, *King Hussein Makes Peace*, 290.

158. Azoulay-Katz, *Sisyphus' Catch*, 214.

159. "Interview with Prime Minister Yitzhak Rabin," *NBC Today*, 26 July 1994.

160. Zak, *King Hussein Makes Peace*, 293–94.

161. Ibid., 294–95.

162. Ibid., 297–98.

163. For the many agreements signed between the two countries after the peace treaty, see Zak, *King Hussein Makes Peace*, 300–301.

164. For the tension in the relations between Egypt and Israel, see Fawaz A. Gerges, "Egyptian-Israeli Relations Turn Sour," *Foreign Affairs* 73 (May–June 1995): 69–78.

165. For an inquiry into the idea that the individual may be seen as—or actually is—a set of relatively autonomous "selves," see Jon Elster, ed., *The Multiple Self* (Cambridge: Cambridge University Press, 1986).

166. Interviews with Yuval Rabin, 31 September 1997, and Yitzhak Hofi, 21 May 1988. The three of them were among the founders of the Third Way movement.

167. Beilin, *Touching Peace,* 111.

168. *Haaretz,* 3 May 1994, A1; Razi Guterman and Zisi Stavi, "Special Interview with the Prime Minister," in *Journalists' Yearbook 1994–95* (Hebrew) (Tel Aviv: Journalists' Association, 1996), 17.

169. Ibid.

170. *Yitzhak Rabin's Speech on the National Security Policy of Israel and Its International Status* (Hebrew) (Jerusalem: Information Center, Ministry of Education, 1994), 7. On 2 May 1994, he still rejected such a formulation in an interview with the CNN. See "Interview with PM Yitzhak Rabin," CNN International World Report, 2 May 1994, Israel Information Service Gopher.

171. Interview with Haber, 11 August 1997.

172. *Haaretz,* 29 June 1994, B3.

173. Appendix B: "Policy Statement by Prime Minister Yitzhak Rabin to the Knesset," 3 October 1994 (official transcript).

174. Interview with Tov.

175. Kalb, "The Promise and Problems of the Israeli Press," 110.

176. Ibid., 111.

177. *New York Times,* 21 July 1994, A16.

178. For the text of the 11 October 1993 letter to Johan Jorgen Holst, see Makovsky, *Making Peace with the PLO,* appendix XIX.

179. See Nadav Shragay, "They Have Given Up on Jerusalem," *Haaretz,* 18 January 1996, B1.

180. Steven Greenhouse, "Rabin Tells U.S. Lawmakers Aid Cuts Would Hurt Peace Effort," *New York Times,* 9 May 1995, A7.

181. The introvert Rabin made an unusual display of happiness when Jerusalem was liberated in 1967. See the testimony of Maj. Gen. (Res.) Uzi Narkis and Maj. Gen. (Res.) Uri Ben Ari, who were, in 1967, chief of the Central Command and chief of the armored Harel Brigade, respectively. *Bamahane,* 10 November 1995, p. 26.

182. *Knesset Minutes,* 29 May 1995.

183. Preuss, "All Will Accept the Verdict of the Majority," 5.

184. Yitzhak Rabin, Lecture at the National Security College, 18 July 1985, Library of the National Security College, transcript 6940, pp. 6–8.

185. Ibid., 7.

186. *Haaretz,* 20 July 1993, B1.

187. Interview with Haber, 26 June 1997. For a view that the Israeli public response to the missile attacks was rationale and low-key, see Zehava Salomon, *Coping with War-Induced Stress: The Gulf War and the Israeli Response* (New York: Plenum Press, 1995).

188. Guterman and Stavi, "Special Interview with the Prime Minister," 16–17.

189. Interview with Bin-Nun.

190. Uri Dan, "The Security Man (an Interview with Ariel Sharon)," *Maariv* (Shabat Supplement), 1 December 1995, p. 21.

191. Interviews with Maj. Gen. (Res.) Israel Tal, 5 August 1996, and with Tov.

192. Confidential correspondence. For a somewhat disquieting picture of the contemporary IDF, see Stuart A. Cohen, "Towards a New Portrait of the (New) Israeli Soldier," *Israel Affairs* 3 (spring/summer 1997): 77–117.

193. Interview with Bin-Nun.

194. Interview with Tov.

195. Yitzhak Rabin, "The Challenge: To Be the Leader," *IDF Journal*, no. 19 (winter 1990) (adapted from a speech delivered to graduates of the IDF Staff College, August 1989), 3.

196. Begin had a weakness for Jewish generals and appreciated Rabin's smooth transition of power to him in the aftermath of the 1977 elections. Rabin reciprocated in respect for this leader of the Ben-Gurion generation. See his *Memoirs*, 566, 577–78. The two also never faced each other as leaders of competing parties, thus leaving no electoral scars.

197. Appendix B: "Policy Statement by Prime Minister Yitzhak Rabin to the Knesset," 3 October 1994 (official transcript).

198. "Rabin Remarks on Tel Aviv Bombing," 19 October 1994, Israel Information Service Gopher.

199. *Jerusalem Post*, 24 September 1995, p. 7.

200. Interview with Haber, 11 August 1997.

201. For an analysis of this aspect of Rabin's personality, see Yehudit Auerbach, "Yitzhak Rabin: Portrait of a Leader," in *Israel at the Polls, 1992*, ed. Daniel Elazar and Shmuel Sandler (Lanham, Md.: Rowman and Littlefield Publishers, 1995), 288–94.

202. Dan, "The Security Man."

203. *Maariv* (Shabat Supplement), 1 December 1995, p. 21.

204. *Maariv* (Weekend Supplement), 10 November 1995, p. 32.

205. Rabin, *Pursuing Peace*, 253.

206. *Jerusalem Post*, 24 September 1995, p. 7.

BIBLIOGRAPHY

DOCUMENTS

Information Center, Ministry of Education, Jerusalem
Israel Defense Force (IDF) Archives, Tel Aviv
Israel Information Service Gopher, Jerusalem
Israel Labor Party Archives, Tel Aviv
Knesset Minutes, Jerusalem
Library of the National Security College, IDF Camp 871
U.S. Federal Broadcasting Information Service (FBIS), Washington, D.C.
U.S. Federal News Service, Washington, D.C.
USIA Official Texts, Tel Aviv
U.S. State Department Bulletin, Washington, D.C.

INTERVIEWS

Yigal Allon, Minister for Foreign Affairs (1974–77), 4 June, 14 November 1979.

Haim Assa, Strategic Adviser to the Prime Minister (1992–94), 21 December 1997.

Prof. Shlomo Avineri, Director General of the Foreign Ministry (1976–77), 17 April 1997.

Yossi Ben-Aharon, Director General of the Prime Minister Ministry (1987–92), 6 June 1997.

Dr. Yehuda Ben-Meir, MK and Deputy Foreign Affairs Minister (1981–83), 26 June 1997.

Rabbi Yoel Bin-Nun, one of the settlers' leaders, 26 November 1997.

Dr. Zeev Bonen, President of Authority for Weapon Development (RAFAEL), 31 March 1997.

David Clayman, Director of American Jewish Congress in Israel (1979–), 7 July 1997.

Leonard Davis, Director of AIPAC Office in Israel (1982–97), 13 June 1997.

Israel Galili, Minister without Portfolio (1974–77), 28 August 1979.

Maj. Gen. (Res.) Shlomo Gazit, Head of Intelligence IDF Branch (1974–78), 26 February 1998.

Eitan Haber, Adviser to Rabin and Head of the Prime Minister Bureau (1992–95), 26 June, 11 August 1997.

Maj. Gen. (Res.) Yitzhak Hofi, Commander of the Northern Front (1972–74), Head of Mossad (1974–82), 21 May 1998.

Maj. Gen. (Res.) David Ivri, Director General, Minister of Defense (1986–96), 8 July 1997.

Avraham Kostelitz, Deputy Director, General Security Services (1993–95), 13 May 1997.

Dr. Yitzhak Lederman, Spokesman of the Israel Atomic Energy Agency (1992–98), 1 April 1997.

Lt. Gen. (Res.) Moshe Levy, Chief of Staff (1983–87), 5 July 1997.

Maj. Gen. (Res.) Menachem Maron, Director General of the Ministry of Defense (1983–86), 1 June 1997.

Maj. Gen. (Res.) Uzi Narkis, Commander of Central Front (1966–68), 19 January 1997.

Prof. Yuval Neeman, Chief Scientist in the Ministry of Defense (1974–75) and Chairman of the Israeli Space Agency (1983–90), 23 June 1996, 18 September 1997.

Yitzhak Rabin, Prime Minister (1974–77, 1992–95), 25 April, 18 November 1979.

Yuval Rabin, the son of Yitzhak Rabin, 31 September 1997.

Peter W. Rodman, Senior Aide to Henry Kissinger (1970–76), 13 August 1996.

Maj. Gen. (Res.) Avraham Rotem, Chief of Training Branch (1975–78), 14 February 1997.

Maj. Gen. (Res.) Danny Rotschild, Coordinator of IDF Activities in the Territories (1991–95), 13 March 1996.

Yitzhak Shamir, Prime Minister (1983–84, 1986–92), 16 June 1997.

Prof. Shimon Shitreet, Minister of Economic Planning and Religious Affairs (1992–96), 8 May 1997.

Lt. Gen. (Res.) Dan Shomron, IDF Chief of Staff (1987–91), 1 July 1997.

Joseph Sisco, Assistant Secretary of State for Near Eastern & South Asian Affairs (1969–74) and Undersecretary for Political Affairs (1974–76), 13 August 1996.

Maj. Gen. (Res.) Israel Tal, Adviser to the Minister of Defense (1974–), 5 August 1996.

Imri Tov, Economic Adviser, Ministry of Defense (1988–), 15 January 1998.

Moshe Zak, veteran journalist, 19 June 1997.

Dov Zakheim, Deputy Undersecretary of Defense for Planning and Resources, Department of Defense (1985–87), 7 March 1997.

Maj. Gen. (Res.) Rehavam Zeevi, MK and Chief of the Central Command (1968–74) and Intelligence and Counterterror Adviser to PM Rabin (1975–77), 2 September 1997.

BOOKS

Admoni, Yehiel. *A Decade of Discretion: Settlement Policy in the Territories, 1967–77* (Hebrew). Tel Aviv: Hakibbutz Hameuchad, 1992.

Allon, Yigal. *A Curtain of Sand* (Hebrew). Tel Aviv: Hakibbutz Hameuchad, 1968.

Arian, Asher. *Security Threatened: Surveying Israeli Opinion on Peace and War.* Cambridge: Cambridge University Press, for the Jaffee Center for Strategic Studies, Tel Aviv University, 1995.

Aronson, Shlomo. *Conflict and Bargaining in the Middle East.* Baltimore: Johns Hopkins University Press, 1978.

Asia, Ilan. *The Core of the Conflict: The Struggle for the Negev, 1947–1956* (Hebrew). Jerusalem: Yad Ben Tzvi Press and Ben Gurion University Press, 1994.

Assa, Haim. *Essentiality* (Hebrew). Tel Aviv: Hakibbutz Hameuchad, 1995.

Azoulay-Katz, Orly. *Sisyphus' Catch* (Hebrew). Tel Aviv: Miskal, 1996.

Baker, James A., III. *The Politics of Diplomacy.* New York: Putnam, 1995.

Baldwin, David A., ed. *Neorealism and Neoliberalism.* New York: Columbia University Press, 1993.

Bar, Micha. *Red Lines in Israel's Deterrence Strategy* (Hebrew). Tel Aviv: Maarachot, 1990.

Barnett, Michael N. *Confronting the Costs of War: Military Power, State, and Society in Egypt and Israel.* Princeton: Princeton University Press, 1992.

Bar-On, Mordechai. *The Gates of Gaza: The Foreign and National Security Policy of Israel, 1955–57* (Hebrew). Tel Aviv: Am Oved, 1992.

Bar-Zohar, Michael. *A Bridge over the Mediterranean: The France-Israel Relationship, 1947–1963* (Hebrew). Tel Aviv: Am Hasefer, 1964.

Beilin, Yossi. *Touching Peace* (Hebrew). Tel Aviv: Miskal, 1997.

Ben-Gurion, David. *Uniqueness and Mission* (Hebrew). Tel Aviv: Am Oved, 1975.

Ben-Horin, Yoav, and Barry Posen. *Israel's Strategic Doctrine.* Paper R-2845-NA. Santa Monica: Rand Corporation, 1981.

Ben-Meir, Yehuda. *Civil-Military Relations in Israel.* New York: Columbia University Press, 1995.

———. *National Security Decision-making: The Israeli Case.* Boulder, Colo.: Westview Press, for the Jaffee Center for Strategic Studies, Tel Aviv University, 1986.

Bentsur, Eytan. *The Road to Peace Crosses Madrid* (Hebrew). Tel Aviv: Miskal, 1997.

Ben-Zvi, Avraham. *The United States and Israel: The Limits of the Special Relationship.* New York: Columbia University Press, 1993.

Beres, Louis R., ed. *Security or Armageddon: Israel's Nuclear Strategy.* Lexington, Mass.: Lexington Books, 1985.

Bialer, Uri. *Between East and West: Israel's Foreign Policy Orientation, 1948–1956.* Cambridge: Cambridge University Press, 1990.

Brecher, Michael. *Decisions in Israel's Foreign Policy.* London: Oxford University Press, 1974.

———. *The Foreign Policy System of Israel.* London: Oxford University Press, 1972.

Brown, Aryeh. *Moshe Dayan and the Six-Day War* (Hebrew). Tel Aviv: Yediot Aharonot, 1997.

Brzezinski, Zbigniew K. *Power and Principle.* London: Weidenfeld and Nicolson, 1983.

Buzan, Barry. *Introduction to Strategic Studies: Military Technology and International Relations.* London: Macmillan Press, for the International Institute for Strategic Studies, 1987.

Calwell C. *Small Wars: Their Principles and Practice.* London: Her Majesty's Stationery Office, 1906.

Carter, Jimmy. *Keeping Faith.* New York: Bantam Books, 1982.

Clausewitz, Karl von. *On War.* Ed. and trans. Michael Howard and Peter Paret. Princeton: Princeton University Press, 1976.

Cobban, Helena. *The Palestinian Liberation Organization: People, Power, and Politics.* Cambridge: Cambridge University Press, 1984.

———. *Syria and the Peace: A Good Chance Missed.* Carlisle, Pa.: Strategic Studies Institute, U.S. Army War College, 1997.

Cohen, Avner. *Israel and the Bomb.* New York: Columbia University Press, 1988.

Cohen, Raymond. *Culture and Conflict in Egyptian-Israeli Relations: A Dialogue of the Deaf.* Bloomington: Indiana University Press, 1990.

———. *Negotiating across Cultures.* Washington, D.C.: United States Institute for Peace Press, 1991.

Cohen, Yerucham. *The Allon Plan* (Hebrew). Tel Aviv: Hakibbutz Hameuchad, 1973.

Cordova, Yishai. *The Policy of the United States in the Yom Kippur War* (Hebrew). Tel Aviv: Maarachot, 1987.

Crosbie, Sylvia K. *A Tacit Alliance: France and Israel from the Suez to the Six-Day War.* Princeton: Princeton University Press, 1974.

Dagan, Avigdor. *Moscow and Jerusalem.* New York: Abelard-Schuman, 1970.

Dawisha, Adeed. *Syria and the Lebanese Crisis.* New York: St. Martin's Press, 1980.

Eban, Abba. *An Autobiography.* London: Futura Publications, 1977.

Elon, Amos. *The Israelis: Founders and Sons.* London: Weidenfeld and Nicholson, 1971.

Elster, Jon, ed. *The Multiple Self.* Cambridge University Press, Cambridge, 1986.

Erell, Shlomo. *Facing the Sea: The Story of a Fighting Sailor and Commander* (Hebrew). Tel Aviv: Ministry of Defense, 1998.

Erez, Yaakov, and Ilan Kfir, eds. *The IDF: An Encyclopedia of Army and Security* (Hebrew). Ramat Gan: Revivim, 1981.

Evron, Yair. *Israel's Nuclear Dilemma.* Ithaca, N.Y.: Cornell University Press, 1994.

———. *War and Intervention in Lebanon: The Israeli-Syrian Deterrence Dialogue* London: Croom Helm, 1987.

Faour, Muhamed. *The Arab World after Desert Storm*. Washington, D.C.: United States Institute for Peace, 1993.

Feldman, Shai. *Extending the Nuclear Nonproliferation Treaty: The Middle East Debate*. Research Memorandum 28. Washington, D.C.: Washington Institute, 1995.

———. *The Future of U.S.-Israel Strategic Cooperation*. Washington, D.C.: Washington Institute for Near East Policy, 1996.

———. *Israeli Nuclear Deterrence: A Strategy for the 1980s*. New York: Columbia University Press, 1982.

———. *Nuclear Weapons and Arms Control in the Middle East*. CSIA Studies in International Security. Cambridge: MIT Press, 1997.

Freedman, Lawrence. *The Evolution of Nuclear Strategy*. London: Macmillan, 1981.

Freedman, Robert O. *Soviet Policy toward the Middle East since 1970*. New York: Praeger, 1975.

———, ed. *The Intifada: Its Impact on Israel, the Arab World, and the Superpowers*. Miami: Florida International University Press, 1991.

Fuller, Graham E., and Ian O. Lesser. *A Sense of Siege: The Geopolitics of Islam and the West*. Boulder, Colo.: Westview Press—A RAND Study, 1995.

Gazit, Mordechai. *Israel's Weapons Procurement from the United States* (Hebrew). Policy Papers No. 8. Jerusalem: Leonard Davis Institute for International Relations, Hebrew University, 1983.

———. *President Kennedy's Policy toward the Arab States and Israel*. Tel Aviv: Shiloach Center, Tel Aviv University, 1983.

Gazit, Shlomo. *The Stick and the Carrot: The Israeli Administration in Judea and Samaria* (Hebrew). Tel Aviv: Zmora-Bitan, 1985.

Gilboa, Moshe A. *Six Years, Six Days: Origins and History of the Six-Day War* (Hebrew). Tel Aviv: Am Oved, 1968.

Golan, Galia. *Soviet Policies in the Middle East: From World War II to Gorbachev*. Cambridge: Cambridge University Press, 1990.

Gold, Dore. *Israel as an American Non-NATO Ally: Parameters of Defense-Industrial Cooperation*. JCSS Study No. 19. Boulder, Colo.: Westview Press, 1992.

Greenberg, Yitzhak. *Defense Budgets and Military Power: The Case of Israel, 1957–1967* (Hebrew). Tel Aviv: Ministry of Defense Publishing House, 1997.

Gur, Motta (Mordechai). *Chief of the General Staff (1974–1978)* (Hebrew). Tel Aviv: Maarachot, 1998.

————. *From the North and from the West* (Hebrew). Tel Aviv: Maarachot, 1998.

Haber, Eitan. *Today War Will Break Out: The Reminiscences of Brig. Gen. Israel Lior, Aide-de-Camp to Prime Ministers Levi Eshkol and Golda Meir* (Hebrew). Tel Aviv: Edanim, 1987.

Harkabi, Yehoshafat. *Fedayeen Action and Arab Strategy.* Adelphi Papers No. 53. London: International Institute for Strategic Studies, 1969.

————. *Israel's Fateful Decisions.* London: I. B. Tauris, 1988.

————. *Palestinians and Israel.* Jerusalem: Keter, 1974.

Herzog, Chaim. *The Arab-Israeli Wars: War and Peace in the Middle East.* London: Arms and Armour Press, 1982.

————. *Living History* (Hebrew). Tel Aviv: Miskal, 1997.

————. *The War of Atonement, October 1973.* Boston: Little, Brown and Co., 1975.

Horovitz, David, ed. *Yitzhak Rabin: Soldier of Peace.* London: Peter Halban, 1996.

Horowitz, Dan. *Israel's Concept of Defensible Borders.* Jerusalem Papers on Peace Problems No. 16. Jerusalem: Leonard Davis Institute for International Relations, Hebrew University, 1975.

————. *Israel's Concept of National Security: Continuity and Change in Israeli Strategic Thinking* (Hebrew). Jerusalem: Levi Eshkol Institute, 1973.

Inbar, Efraim. *Israel's Nuclear Policy after 1973.* Los Angeles: Pan Heuristics, 1977.

————. *Outcast Countries in the World Community.* Denver: University of Denver Press, 1985.

————. *War and Peace in Israeli Politics: Labor Party Positions on National Security.* Boulder, Colo.: Lynne Rienner, 1991.

Jervis, Robert. *Perception and Misperception in International Politics.* Princeton: Princeton University Press, 1976.

Kahn, Herman. *On Escalation: Metaphors and Scenarios.* Baltimore: Penguin Books, 1968.

Kampelman, Max. *Entering New Worlds.* New York: Harper Collins, 1991.

Kenen, I. L. *Israel's Defense Line: Her Friends and Foes in Washington.* Buffalo, N.Y.: Prometheus Books, 1981.

Khalidi, Walid. *Conflict and Violence in Lebanon.* Cambridge: Center for International Affairs, Harvard University Press, 1979.

Kimmerling, Baruch. *The Interrupted System.* New Brunswick, N.J.: Transaction Books, 1985.

Kissinger, Henry. *The White House Years.* Boston: Little, Brown and Co., 1979.

———. *Years of Upheaval.* Boston: Little, Brown and Co., 1982.

Klieman, Aharon S. *The Global Reach: Arms Sales as Diplomacy.* Washington, D.C.: Pergamon-Brassey's, 1985.

———. *Israel and the World after Forty Years.* Washington, D.C.: Pergamon-Brassey's, 1990.

Kober, Avi. *Military Decision in the Arab-Israeli Wars, 1948–1982* (Hebrew). Tel Aviv: Maarachot, 1995.

Laqueur, Walter. *The Struggle for the Middle East: The Soviet Union and the Middle East.* Harmondsworth: Penguin Books, 1972.

Laqueur, Walter, and Barry Rubin, eds. *The Israel-Arab Reader.* New York: Penguin Books, 1995.

Levite, Ariel. *Offense and Defense in Israeli Military Doctrine.* JCSS Study No. 12. Boulder, Colo.: Westview Press, 1989.

Levran, Aharon. *Israeli Strategy after Desert Storm: Lessons of the Second Gulf War.* BESA Studies in International Security. London: Frank Cass, 1997.

Liddell-Hart, Basil H. *Deterrent or Defense.* London: Stevens and Sons, 1960.

———. *Strategy: The Strategy of Indirect Approach.* London: Faber and Faber, 1946.

Lorch, Netanel. *The Edge of the Sword: Israel's War of Independence,* 2d rev. ed. Jerusalem: Massada Press, 1968.

Luttwak, Edward, and Dan Horowitz. *The Israeli Army.* London: Allen Lane, 1975.

Makovsky, David. *Making Peace with the PLO: The Rabin Government's Road to the Oslo Accord.* Boulder, Colo.: Westview Press, 1996.

Mandelbaum, Michael. *Fate of Nations: The Search for National Security in the Nineteenth and Twentieth Centuries.* Cambridge: Cambridge University Press, 1988.

Maoz, Moshe. *Asad, the Sphinx of Damascus: A Political Biography.* London: Weidenfeld and Nicolson, 1988.

———. *Syria and Israel: From War to Peace-Making.* Oxford: Clarendon Press, 1995.

Margalit, Dan. *I Have Seen Them All* (Hebrew). Tel Aviv: Zmora-Bitan, 1997.

———. *A Message from the White House* (Hebrew). Tel Aviv: Otpaz, 1971.

Marom, Ran. *Israel's Position on Non-Proliferation.* Policy Studies No. 16. Jerusalem: Leonard Davis Institute for International Relations, Hebrew University, 1986.

Mercer, Jonathan C. *Reputation and International Politics.* Ithaca, N.Y.: Cornell University Press, 1996.

Milstein, Uri. *Rabin File: How the Myth Swelled* (Hebrew). Ramat Efal: Yaron Golan, 1995.

Milstein, Uri, and Dov Doron. *Shaked Patrol* (Hebrew). Tel Aviv: Miskal, 1994.

Morgenthau, Hans. *Politics among Nations: The Struggle for Power and Peace.* New York: Alfred A. Knopf, 1948.

Morris, Benny. *Israel's Border Wars, 1948–1956: Arab Infiltration, Israeli Retaliation, and the Countdown to the Suez War.* Oxford: Clarendon Press, 1993.

Nakdimon, Shlomo. *A Hopeless Hope: The Rise and Fall of the Israeli Kurdish Alliance, 1963–1975* (Hebrew). Tel Aviv: Yediot Aharonot, 1996.

———. *Tammuz in Flames* (Hebrew). Jerusalem: Edanim Publishers, 1986.

Narkis, Uzi. *Soldier of Jerusalem* (Hebrew). Tel Aviv: Ministry of Defense Publishing House, 1991.

Navias, Martin. *Going Ballistic: The Build-up of Missiles in the Middle East.* London: Brassey's, 1993.

Neeman, Yuval. *The Clairvoyant Policy* (Hebrew). Ramat Gan: Revivim, 1984.

Netanyahu, Benjamin, ed. *Terrorism: How the West Can Win.* London: Weidenfeld and Nicolson, 1986.

O'Brien, William. *Law and Morality in Israel's War with the PLO.* New York: Routledge, 1991.

Olmert, Yossi. *Toward a Syrian-Israel Peace Agreement: Perspective of a Former Negotiatior.* Research Memorandum No. 25. Washington, D.C.: Washington Institute, 1994.

Organsky, A. F. K. *The $36 Billion Bargain: Strategy and Politics in U.S. Assistance to Israel.* New York: Columbia University Press, 1990.

Ostfeld, Zehava. *An Army Is Born* (Hebrew). Tel Aviv: Ministry of Defense Publishing House, 1994.

Pail, Meir. *The Emergence of Zahal (IDF)* (Hebrew). Tel Aviv: Zmora, Bitan, Modan, 1979.

Pedatzur, Reuven. *The Arrow System and the Active Defense against Ballistic Missiles.* Memorandum No. 42. Tel Aviv: Jaffee Center for Strategic Studies, Tel Aviv University, 1993.

Peres, Shimon. *David's Sling* (Hebrew). Jerusalem: Weidenfeld and Nicholson, 1970.

————. *The New Middle East.* New York: Henry Colt and Co., 1993.

————. *The Next Phase* (Hebrew). Tel Aviv: Am Hasefer, 1965.

Peres, Shimon, and Haggay Eshed. *Tomorrow Is Now* (Hebrew). Jerusalem: Keter, 1978.

Peri, Yoram. *Between Battles and Ballots: Israeli Military in Politics.* Cambridge: Cambridge University Press, 1983.

Perlmutter, Amos. *Military and Politics in Israel.* London: Frank Cass, 1969.

Porat, Yehoshua. *The Emergence of the Palestinian Arab National Movement, 1918–1929.* London: Frank Cass, 1977.

————. *The Emergence of the Palestinian National Movement, 1929–1939.* London: Frank Cass, 1977.

Porter, Bruce D. *War and the Rise of the State: The Military Foundations of Modern Politics.* New York: Free Press, 1994.

Puschel, Karen. *U.S.-Israel Strategic Cooperation in the Post-Cold War Era: An American Perspective.* JCSS Study No. 20. Boulder, Colo.: Westview Press, 1992.

Quandt, William B. *Decade of Decisions: The American Policy toward the Arab-Israeli Conflict, 1967–1976.* Los Angeles: University of California Press, 1977.

Rabin, Leah. *Rabin: Our Life, His Legacy.* New York: G. P. Putnam, 1997.

Rabin, Yitzhak. *The House of My Father* (Hebrew). Tel Aviv: Hakibbutz Hameuchad, n.d.

————. *Pursuing Peace: The Peace Speeches of Prime Minister Yitzhak Rabin* (Hebrew). Tel Aviv: Zmora-Bitan, 1995.

————. *The War in Lebanon* (Hebrew). Tel Aviv: Am Oved, 1983.

————. *Yitzhak Rabin Talks with Leaders and Heads of State* (Hebrew). Givataim: Revivim, 1984.

Rabin, Yitzhak, with Dov Goldstein. *Pinkas Sherut* (Hebrew). Tel Aviv: Maariv, 1979.

Rabinovitch, Itamar. *The Brink of Peace: Israel and Syria, 1992–1996* (Hebrew). Tel Aviv: Miskal, 1998.

————. *The War for Lebanon, 1970–85.* Rev. ed. Ithaca, N.Y.: Cornell University Press, 1985.

Reich, Bernard. *Quest for Peace.* New Brunswick, N.J.: Transaction Books, 1977.

Reiser, Stewart. *The Israeli Arms Industry: Foreign Policy, Arms Transfers, and Military Doctrine of a Small State.* New York: Holmes and Meier, 1989.

Rubin, Barry. *Cauldron of Turmoil: America in the Middle East.* New York: Harcourt, Brace, Jovanovich, 1992.

————. *Revolution until Victory? The Politics and History of the PLO.* Cambridge: Harvard University Press, 1994.

Rubinstein, Alvin Z. *Red Star on the Nile.* Princeton: Princeton University Press, 1976.

Rubinstein, Elyakim. *Paths of Peace* (Hebrew). Tel Aviv: Ministry of Defense Publishing House, 1992.

Safran, Nadav. *Israel: The Embattled Ally.* Cambridge: Belknap Press of Harvard University, 1978.

Salomon, Zehava. *Coping with War-Induced Stress: The Gulf War and the Israeli Response.* New York: Plenum Press, 1995.

Sandler, Shmuel. *The State of Israel, the Land of Israel: The Statist and Ethnonational Dimensions of Foreign Policy.* Westport, Conn.: Greenwood Press, 1993.

Sandler, Shmuel, and Hillel Frisch. *Israel, the Palestinians, and the West Bank: A Study in Intercommunal Conflict.* Lexington, Mass.: Lexington Books, 1984.

Sarkesian, Sam C., and William L. Scully, eds. *American Policy and Low-Intensity Conflict.* New Brunswick, N.J.: Transaction Books, 1981.

Schelling, Thomas. *Arms and Influence.* New Haven: Yale University Press, 1966.

————. *The Strategy of Conflict.* 4th ed. Cambridge: Harvard University Press, 1970.

Schiff, Zeev. *Whether an Israeli-U.S. Defense Treaty.* Jerusalem: American Jewish Committee, 1996.

Schiff, Zeev, and Eitan Haber. *Israel, Army, and Defense: A Dictionary* (Hebrew). Tel Aviv: Zmora, Bitan, Modan, 1976.

Schiff, Zeev, and Ehud Yaari. *Intifada* (Hebrew). Tel Aviv: Shocken, 1990.

Schultz, George P. *Turmoil and Triumph.* New York: Scribner's, 1993.

Seale, Patrick. *Asad: The Struggle for the Middle East.* London: I. B. Taurus, 1988.

Shalev, Aryeh. *Israel and Syria: Peace and Security on the Golan.* JCSS Study No. 24. Tel Aviv: Jaffee Center for Strategic Studies, 1994.

Shamir, Yitzhak. *Summing-Up* (Hebrew). Tel Aviv: Edanim, 1994.

Shapira, Anita. *The Army Controversy, 1948: Ben Gurion's Struggle for Control* (Hebrew). Tel Aviv: Hakibbutz Hameuchad, 1985.

Sheffer, Gabriel. *Resolution vs. Management of the Middle East Conflict.* Jerusalem Papers on Peace Problems No. 32. Jerusalem: Leonard Davis Institute for International Relations, Hebrew University, 1980.

Shimshoni, Jonathan. *Israel and Conventional Deterrence: Border Warfare from 1953 to 1970.* Ithaca, N.Y.: Cornell University Press, 1988.

Shoham, Danny. *Chemical Weapons in Egypt and Syria: Evolution, Capabilities, Control* (Hebrew). BESA Studies in Mideast Security No. 21. Ramat Gan: Begin-Sadat (BESA) Center for Strategic Studies, Bar-Ilan University, 1995.

Shueftan, Dan. *A Jordanian Option* (Hebrew). Tel Aviv: Yad Tabenkin, 1986.

Singer, Max, and Michael Eichenwald. *Making Oslo Work*. Mideast Security and Policy Studies No. 30. Ramat Gan: Begin-Sadat (BESA) Center for Strategic Studies, Bar-Ilan University, 1997.

Slater, Robert. *Rabin of Israel*. London: Robson Books, 1977 (paperback ed., 1996).

Snyder, Glenn H. *Deterrence and Defense*. Princeton: Princeton University Press, 1960.

Spector, Leonard. *The Undeclared Bomb*. Cambridge: Ballinger, 1988.

Spiegel, Steven L. *The Other Arab-Israeli Conflict: Making America's Middle East Policy, from Truman to Reagan*. Chicago: University of Chicago Press, 1985.

Straschnov, Amnon. *Justice under Fire* (Hebrew). Tel Aviv: Yediot Aharonot, 1994.

Tal, Israel. *National Security: The Few against the Many* (Hebrew). Tel Aviv: Dvir, 1996.

Tamir, Avraham. *A Soldier in Search of Peace* (Hebrew). Tel Aviv: Edanim, 1988.

Tanter, Raymond. *Who's at the Helm? Lessons of Lebanon*. Boulder, Colo.: Westview Press, 1990.

Tilly, Charles. *Coercion, Capital, and the European States, AD 990–1990*. Oxford: Basil Blackwell, 1990.

Touval, Saadia. *The Peace Brokers: Mediators in the Arab-Israeli Conflict, 1948–1979*. Princeton: Princeton University Press, 1982.

Tzur, Yaakov. *The Diplomatic Campaign in France, 1953–56* (Hebrew). Tel Aviv: Am Oved, 1968.

Vance, Cyrus. *Hard Choices*. New York: Simon and Schuster, 1983.

Vital, David. *The Inequality of States*. Oxford: Clarendon Press, 1967.

Weimann, Gabriel, and Conrad Winn. *The Theater of Terror: Mass Media and International Terrorism*. New York: Longman, 1994.

Weizman, Ezer. *On Eagles' Wings*. New York: Macmillan, 1979.

Williams, Louis, ed. *Military Aspects of the Israeli-Arab Conflict*. Tel Aviv: University Publishing Projects, 1975.

Wohlstetter, Albert, et al. *Swords from Ploughshares*. Chicago: University of Chicago Press, 1977.

Yaniv, Avner. *Deterrence without the Bomb: The Politics of Israeli Strategy.* Lexington, Mass.: Lexington Books, 1987.

————. *Dilemmas of Security: Politics, Strategy, and the Israeli Experience in Lebanon.* New York: Oxford University Press, 1987.

Zak, Moshe. *Israel and the Soviet Union: A Forty-Year Dialogue* (Hebrew). Tel Aviv: Maariv, 1988.

————. *King Hussein Makes Peace* (Hebrew). Ramat Gan: Bar-Ilan University Press and Begin-Sadat (BESA) Center for Strategic Studies, 1996.

Zakheim, Dov. *Flight of the Lavi: Inside a U.S.-Israeli Crisis.* Washington, D.C.: Brassey's, 1996.

ARTICLES

Allon, Yigal. "Israel: The Case for Defensible Borders." *Foreign Affairs* 55 (October 1976): 38–53.

Amiel, Saadia. "Deterrence by Conventional Forces." *Survival* 20 (March/April 1978): 58–62.

Anthony, Ian. "Politics and Economics of Defense Industries in a Changing World." In *The Politics and Economics of Defense Industries,* ed. Efraim Inbar and Benzion Zilberfarb, 1–28. BESA Studies in International Security. London: Frank Cass, 1998.

Arian, Asher. "The Passing of Dominance." *Jerusalem Quarterly* 5 (fall 1977): 20–32.

Aronson, Shlomo, and Dan Horowitz. "The Strategy of Controlled Retaliation: The Israeli Example." *Medina Umimshal* (Hebrew) 1 (summer 1971): 77–100.

Auerbach, Yehudit. "Yitzhak Rabin: Portrait of a Leader." In *Israel at the Polls, 1992,* ed. Daniel Elazar and Shmuel Sandler, 283–317. Lanham, Md.: Rowman and Littlefield Publishers, 1995.

Auerbach, Yehudit, and Hemda Ben-Yehuda Agid. "Attitudes to an Existence Conflict: Rabin and Sharon on the Palestinian Issue, 1967–87." In *Conflict and Social Psychology,* ed. Knud Larsen, 144–67. London: Sage Publications for PRIO, 1993.

Bar-Joseph, Uri. "The Hidden Debate: The Formation of Nuclear Doctrines in the Middle East." *Journal of Strategic Studies* 5 (June 1982): 205–27.

————. "Rotem: The Forgotten Crisis on the Road to the 1967 War." *Journal of Contemporary History* 31 (July 1996): 547–66.

Bar-Siman-Tov, Yaakov. "The Bar-Lev Line Revisited." *Journal of Strategic Studies* 11 (June 1988): 149–76.

Barzilai, Gad. "Democracy in War: Attitudes, Reactions, and Political Participation of the Israeli Public in the Processes of Decision-Making" (Hebrew). Ph.D. diss., Hebrew University, Jerusalem, 1987.

Barzilai, Gad, and Efraim Inbar. "The Use of Force: Israeli Public Opinion on Military Options." *Armed Forces and Society* 23 (fall 1996): 49–80.

Ben-Moshe, Tuvia. "Liddell-Hart and the Israel Defense Forces: A Reappraisal." *Journal of Contemporary History* 16 (1981): 369–91.

Ben-Porat, Yoel. "Intelligence Estimates: Why Do They Fail?" In *Intelligence and National Security* (Hebrew), ed. Zvi Ofer and Avi Kober, 223–51. Tel Aviv: Maarachot, 1988.

Ben-Yehuda, Hemda. "Attitude Change and Policy Transformation: Yitzhak Rabin and the Palestinian Question, 1967–95." *Israel Affairs* 3 (spring/summer 1997): 202–24.

Betts, Richard K. "The Concept of Deterrence in the Postwar Era." *Security Studies* 1 (autumn 1991): 25–36.

Biddle, Stephen. "Victory Misunderstood: What the Gulf War Tells Us about Conflict in the Future." *International Security* 21 (fall 1996): 139–79.

Bonen, Zeev. "Sophisticated Conventional War." In *Advanced Technology and Future Warfare,* 19–30. Mideast Security and Policy Studies No. 28. Ramat Gan: Begin-Sadat (BESA) Center for Strategic Studies, Bar-Ilan University, 1996.

Brooks, Charles D. "S.D.I.: A New Dimension for Israel." *Journal of Social, Political, and Economic Studies* 11, no. 4 (1986): 341–48.

Brown, L. Carl. "The Middle East after the Cold War and the Gulf War: Systemic Change or More of the Same?" In *Collective Security beyond the Cold War,* ed. George Downs, 197–216. Ann Arbor: University of Michigan Press, 1994.

Chubin, Shahram. "Does Iran Want Nuclear Weapons?" *Survival* 37 (spring 1995): 86–104.

Cohen, Avner. "Israel's Nuclear History: The Untold Kennedy-Eshkol Dimona Correspondence." *Journal of Israeli History* 16 (summer 1995): 159–94.

———. "Stumbling into Opacity: The United States, Israel, and the Atom, 1960–63." *Security Studies* 4 (winter 1994–95): 195–241.

Cohen, Eliot A. "A Revolution in Warfare." *Foreign Affairs* 75 (March/April 1996): 37–54.

Cohen, Eliot A., Michael J. Eisenstadt, and Andrew J. Bacevich. "Israel's Revolution in Security Affairs." *Survival* 40 (spring 1998).

Cohen, Stuart A. "The Israel Defense Force (IDF): From a 'People's Army' to a 'Professional Military'—Causes and Implications." *Armed Forces and Society* 21 (winter 1995): 237–54.

———. "Israel's Changing Military Commitments, 1981–1991." *Journal of Strategic Studies* 15 (September 1992): 330–50.

———. "Towards a New Portrait of the (New) Israeli Soldier." *Israel Affairs* 3 (spring/summer 1997): 77–117.

Cohen, Stuart A., and Efraim Inbar. "A Taxonomy of Israel's Use of Force." *Comparative Strategy* 10 (April 1991): 121–38.

Cordesman, Anthony H. "How Much Is Too Much?" *Armed Forces Journal*, October 1977, pp. 36–37.

Diab, M. Zuhair. "Syrian Security Requirements in a Peace Settlement with Israel." *Israel Affairs* 1 (summer 1995): 71–88.

Evron, Yair. "Israel and the Atom: The Uses and Misuses of Ambiguity, 1957–67." *Orbis* 17 (winter 1974): 1326–43.

———. "Some Political and Strategic Implications of an American-Israeli Defense Treaty." In *The Middle East and the United States*, ed. Haim Shaked and Itamar Rabinovitch, 371–94. New Brunswick, N.J.: Transaction Books, 1980.

Feldman, Shai. "The Bombing of Osirak—Revisited." *International Security* 7 (fall 1982): 114–42.

———. "Israeli Deterrence during the Gulf War." In *War in the Gulf: Implications for Israel*, ed. Joseph Alpher, 184–208. Boulder, Colo.: Westview Press, for the Jaffee Center for Strategic Studies, 1992.

Freedman, Lawrence, and Efraim Karsh. "How Kuwait Was Won: Strategy in the Gulf War." *International Security* 16 (fall 1991): 36–37.

Ganz, Moshe. "The Attack on the PLO Headquarters in Tunis." In *The War on Terror and the National Security Policy of Israel, 1979–1988* (Hebrew), ed. Zeev Klein, 167–69. Ramat Gan: Revivim, 1988.

Garfinkle, Adam. "U.S. Decision-Making in the Jordan Crisis: Correcting the Record." *Political Science Quarterly* 100 (spring 1985): 117–38.

Gerardi, Greg, and Maryam Aharinijad. "An Assessment of Iran's Nuclear Facilities." *Nonproliferation Review* 3 (summer–spring): 209–15.

Gerges, Fawaz A. "Egyptian-Israeli Relations Turn Sour." *Foreign Affairs* 73 (May-June 1995): 69–78.

Guterman, Razi, and Zisi Stavi. "Special Interview with the Prime Minister." In *Journalists' Yearbook 1994–95* (Hebrew), 9–21. Tel Aviv: Journalists' Association, 1996.

Handel, Michael. "Israel's Political-Military Doctrine." Harvard University Occasional Papers, Harvard University, Cambridge, July 1973.

Heller, Mark A. "Coping with Missile Proliferation in the Middle East." *Orbis* 35 (winter 1991): 15–28.

———. "Towards a Palestinian State." *Survival* 39 (summer 1997): 5–22.

Hinnebusch, Raymond A. "Asad's Syria and the New World Order: The Struggle for Regime Survival." *Middle East Policy* 2, no. 1 (1993): 1–14.

Horowitz, Dan. "The Constant and the Changing in Israeli Strategic Thinking." In *War by Choice* (Hebrew), ed. Joseph Alpher, 58–77. Tel Aviv: Hakibbutz Hameuchad, 1985.

———. "The Control of Limited Military Operations: The Israeli Experience." In *International Violence: Terrorism, Surprise, and Control,* ed. Yair Evron, 258–76. Jerusalem: Leonard Davis Institute for International Relations, Hebrew University, 1979.

Howard, Michael. "The Forgotten Dimension of Strategy." *Foreign Afairs* 57 (summer 1979): 975–86.

Inbar, Efraim. "The American Arms Transfer to Israel." *Middle East Review* 15 (winter 1982/83): 40–51.

———. "Attitudes toward War in the Israeli Political Elite." *Middle East Journal* 44 (summer 1990): 431–45.

———. "Contours of Israel's New Strategic Thinking." *Political Science Quarterly* 111 (spring 1996): 41–64.

———. "Great Power Mediation: The USA and the May 1983 Israeli-Lebanese Agreement." *Journal of Peace Research* 28 (February 1991): 71–84.

———. "Islamic Radicalism and the Peace Process." *Terrorism and Political Violence* 8 (summer 1996): 199–215.

———. "Israel." In *Middle East Contemporary Survey,* vol. 16, ed. Ami Ayalon, 499–534. Boulder, Colo.: Westview Press, 1995.

———. "Israel and Arms Control." *Arms Control* 13 (September 1992): 214–21.

———. "The Israeli Navy." *Naval War College Review* 43 (winter 1990): 100–112.

———. "Israeli Negotiations with Syria." *Israel Affairs* 1 (summer 1995): 89–100.

———. "Israel's New Predicament in a New Strategic Environment." In *The National Security of Small States in a Changing World,* ed. Efraim Inbar and Gabriel Sheffer, 155–74. BESA Studies in International Security. London: Frank Cass, 1997.

———. "Israel's Small War: The Military Response to the Intifada." *Armed Forces and Society* 18 (fall 1991): 29–50.

———. "Israel's Strategic Thinking after 1973." *Journal of Strategic Studies* 6 (March 1983): 36–59.

———. "Jews, Jewishness, and Israel's Foreign Policy." *Jewish Political Studies Review* 2 (fall 1990): 165–83.

———. "Netanyahu Takes Over." *Israel Affairs* 4 (fall 1997): 33–52.

———. "The 'No Choice War' Debate in Israel." *Journal of Strategic Studies* 12 (March 1989): 22–37.

———. "Problems of Pariah States: The National Security Policy of the Rabin Government, 1974–77." Ph.D. diss., University of Chicago, 1981.

Inbar, Efraim, and Giora Goldberg. "Is Israel's Political Elite Becoming More Hawkish?" *International Journal* 45 (summer 1990): 631–60.

Inbar, Efraim, and Shmuel Sandler. "The Changing Israeli Strategic Equation: Toward a Security Regime." *Review of International Studies* 21 (January 1995): 41–59.

———. "Israel's Deterrence Strategy Revisited." *Security Studies* 3 (winter 1993/94): 330–58.

———. "The Risks of Palestinian Statehood." *Survival* 39 (summer 1997): 23–41.

Johnston, A. "Thinking about Strategic Culture." *International Security* 19 (spring 1995): 32–64.

Kalb, Marvin. "The Promise and Problems of the Israeli Press." *Press/Politics* 1 (winter 1996): 110–15.

Karp, Aaron. "Ballistic Missiles in the Middle East: Realities, Omens, and Arms Control Options." In *Middle Eastern Security: Prospects for an Arms Control Regime,* ed. Efraim Inbar and Shmuel Sandler, 111–29. BESA Studies in International Security. London: Frank Cass, 1995.

Karsh, Efraim. "Cold War, Post-Cold War: Does It Make a Difference for the Middle East?" In *The National Security of Small States in a Changing World,* ed. Efraim Inbar and Gabriel Sheffer, 77–106. BESA Studies in International Security. London: Frank Cass, 1997.

Kissinger, Henry. "Limited War: Conventional or Nuclear." *Daedalus* 90 (fall 1960).

Klieman, Aharon S. "Adapting to a Shrinking Market: The Israeli Case." In *The Politics and Economics of Defense Industries,* ed. Efraim Inbar and Benzion Zilberfarb. BESA Studies in International Security. London: Frank Cass, 1998.

———. "Israeli Diplomacy in the Thirtieth Year of Statehood: Some Constants and Discontinuities." In *Israel: A Developing Society,* ed. Asher Arian, 43–49. Assen: Van Gorgum, 1990.

————. "The Israel-Jordan Tacit Security Regime." In *Regional Security Regimes: Israel and Its Neighbors*, ed. Efraim Inbar, 127–50. Albany: State University of New York Press, 1995.

Lanir, Zvi. "Political Aims and Military Objectives." In *Israeli Security Planning in the 1980s: Its Politics and Economics*, ed. Zvi Lanir, 14–49. New York: Praeger, for the Jaffee Center for Strategic Studies, 1984.

Levran, Aharon. "Threats Facing Israel from Surface-to-Surface Missiles." *IDF Journal* 19 (winter 1990): 37–44.

Lewis, Bernard. "Settling the Arab-Israeli Conflict." *Commentary* 63 (June 1977): 50–56.

Mearsheimer, John. "The False Promise of International Institutions." *International Security* 19 (winter 1994/95): 5–49.

Metz, Steven. "Foundations for a Low-Intensity Conflict Strategy." *Comparative Strategy* 8 (July 1989): 265–74.

Navon, Yitzhak. "The Changes in the Israeli Position on the Arab-Israeli Conflict." In *Between War and Settlements* (Hebrew), ed. Alouph Hareven and Yehiam Padan, 127–38. Tel Aviv: Zmora-Bitan, 1977.

Rabin, Yitzhak. "Address by Yitzhak Rabin." In *Towards a New Era in US-Israel Relations*, ed. Yehuda Mirsky and Ellen Rice, 1–4. Washington, D.C.: Washington Institute, 1992.

————. "Deterrence in an Israeli Security Context." In *Deterrence in the Middle East: Where Theory and Practice Converge*, ed. Aharon Klieman and Ariel Levite, 6–15. JCSS Study No. 22. Boulder, Colo.: Westview Press, 1993.

————. "From the Battles over the Water to the Six-Day War." In *The IDF: An Encyclopedia for Army and Security* (Hebrew), vol. 1, 183–208. Ramat Gan: Revivim, 1981.

————. "Making Use of the Time-Out." *Politika* (Hebrew) 44 (March 1992): 28–29.

————. "The Quality That Guarantees Power." In *Israeli Security in the Next Decade* (Hebrew), 31–41. Efal: Yad Tabenkin, 1988.

————. "Towards a New National Security Concept." In *The War on Terror and the National Security Policy of Israel, 1979–1988* (Hebrew), ed. Zeev Klein, 171–77. Ramat Gan: Revivim, 1988.

Rhynold, Jonathan. "Labor, Likud, the 'Special Relationship,' and the Peace Process, 1986–96," *Israel Affairs* 3 (spring/summer 1997): 239–46.

Rochlin, Gene I., and Chris Demchak. "The Gulf War: Technological and Organizational Implications." *Survival* 33 (May/June 1991): 260–73.

Rosen, Stephen P. "Military Effectiveness: Why Society Matters." *International Security* 19 (spring 1995): 5–31.

Rosen, Steven. "War Power and the Willingness to Suffer." In *Peace, War, and Numbers,* ed. Bruce M. Russett, 167–83. Beverly Hills: Sage Publications, 1972.

Sabin, Philip A. G., and Efraim Karsh. "Escalation in the Iran-Iraq War." *Survival* 31 (May/June 1989): 241–54.

Sadeh, Sharon. "The Rehabilitation Process of the Defense Industries." In *The Defense Industries in Israel* (Hebrew), 15–29. Ramat Gan: Begin-Sadat (BESA) Center for Strategic Studies, Bar-Ilan University, 1995.

Sahliyeh, Emile. "Jordan and the Palestinians." In *The Middle East: Ten Years after Camp David,* ed. William B. Quandt, 279–318. Washington D.C.: Brookings Institution, 1988.

Sandler, Shmuel. "The Protracted Arab-Israeli Conflict." *Jerusalem Journal of International Relations* 10 (December 1988): 54–78.

Shamir, Shimon. "Arab Military Lessons from the October War." In *Military Aspects of the Israeli-Arab Conflict,* ed. Louis Williams, 172–78. Tel Aviv: University Publishing Projects, 1975.

Shapir, Yiftah. "Proliferation of Nonconventional Weapons in the Middle East." In *The Middle East Military Balance: 1993–1994,* ed. Shlomo Gazit, 216–38. Jerusalem: Jerusalem Post, for the Jaffee Center for Strategic Studies, 1994.

Sheehan, Edward. "Step By Step in the Middle East." *Foreign Policy* 22 (spring 1976): 3–70.

Spiegel, Steven L. "U.S. Relations with Israel: The Military Benefits." *Orbis* 30 (fall 1986): 475–97.

Steinberg, Gerald. "Israel and the Changing Global Non-Proliferation Regime: The NPT Extension, CTBT, and Fissile Cut-Off." In *Middle Eastern Security: Prospects for an Arms Control Regime,* ed. Efraim Inbar and Shmuel Sandler, 70–83. BESA Studies in International Security. London: Frank Cass, 1995.

———. "Israeli Responses to the Threat of Chemical Warfare." *Armed Forces and Society* 20 (fall 1993): 85–101.

———. "Middle East Arms Control and Regional Security." *Survival* 36 (spring 1994): 126–41.

———. "Middle East Peace and the NPT Extension Decision." *Nonproliferation Review* 4 (fall 1996): 17–29.

Tal, Israel. "Israel's Doctrine of National Security: Background and Dynamics." *Jerusalem Quarterly* 4 (summer 1977): 44–57.

Wohlstetter, Albert. "The Delicate Balance of Terror." *Foreign Affairs* 37 (January 1959): 211–34.

Yaniv, Avner. "Syria and Israel: The Politics of Escalation." In *Syria under Assad,* ed. Moshe Maoz and Avner Yaniv, 157–78. New York: St. Martin's Press, 1986.

Yaniv, Avner, and Robert Lieber. "Personal Whim or Strategic Imperative: The Israeli Invasion of Lebanon." *International Security* 8 (fall 1983): 117–42.

ENGLISH PRESS

ABC News
IAF Organ
IDF Journal
International Defense Review
Jane's Intelligence Review
Jerusalem Post
National Review

NBC News
Newsweek
New York Times
Spectrum
Time
Washington Post

HEBREW PRESS AND PERIODICALS

Al Hamishmar
Bama
Bamahane
Dapei Elazar
Davar
Haaretz
Hadashot
Kol Hair
Maarachot
Maariv

Medina Umimshal Veyachasim Beinleumiim
Mibifnim
Migvan
Moledet
Nativ
Politika
Safra Vesayfa
Yediot Aharonot

INDEX

Agranat Commission, 78
airborne operations, long range, 75, 213n100
air force. *See* Israeli Air Force (IAF)
air raids: Gulf War, 177; Iraqi nuclear
   reactor (1981), 122–23; Israeli response in
   1948 and 1991, 161–62; Lebanon, 100;
   Tunis, 101–02
Allon, Yigal, 108; armored vehicles, 65;
   conventional perspective, 91; nuclear
   weapons, 114–15, 120; Rabin replacing, 3
Allon Plan, 18, 25, 152; description, 30;
   map, 32
ambassadorship to U.S., 37–42; nuclear
   program, 118; significance, 57; weapons
   acquisition, 69–71
American-Israel Public Affairs Committee
   (AIPAC), 54–56
American Jewish Congress, 55
ammunition, nonlethal, 106
annexation, West Bank and Gaza Strip,
   30–31
antimissile defense, 47
antipersonnel mines, export, 131
Arab boycott of Israel, 189
Arab-Israeli conflict: Arab losses,
   significance, 72; brinkmanship, 117;
   defense treaty with U.S., possibility, 54;
   defensible borders for Israel, 29;

deterrence, 175; deterrence by Israel,
   89–91; external actors, 174; historical
   evaluation, 18–23; incremental progress
   approach, 143; Intifada as facet, 104;
   Israeli-initiated war, considered, 173–75;
   Israeli military strength, importance, 85;
   Israeli security policy, 173; larger Arab
   forces predicted, 72; military power,
   Rabin's view, 168; missiles, 125; nature of,
   13–18; naval considerations, 69; nuclear
   weapons, 114–15; Palestinian dimension,
   104–05; Palestinian issue, 101, 157;
   Palestinian question, 23–24; "Palestinization," 22; political labels, 194n24; power-
   politics perspective, 113; psychological
   factors, per Rabin, 160; Rabin's dovish
   diagnosis, 159; Rabin's new strategy, 139;
   rapprochement in time of strength, 136;
   security policy and, 7; Soviet involvement,
   12; state-centric approach, 24–25, 33, 105,
   143; step-by-step diplomatic process,
   17–18; Syria and larger context, 145;
   terrorism's role, 97; threats, after Gulf
   War, 173; time vector, 16; U.S. elections,
   44; use of force, 86, 217n13; U.S.-Israeli
   relations, influencing, 45; U.S.S.R. role,
   per Rabin, 51, 52; victory, meaning of,
   175–76; worst-case scenario, 65

Arab-Israeli War of 1973: Soviet
influence, 12
Arab Knesset, 4
Arab League, 14
Arab military: in 1960s, 39; compared to
Israeli, 61; preemption, 174; Soviet
influence, 64
Arab Peace-Keeping Force, 109
Arab states: hostility to Israel, 14–15;
policies to Israel, 13–14; threat declining
in 1980s, 21–22
Arafat, Yasir, 136; Oslo agreements, 154,
243n137; Rabin's views, 26, 153–55;
terrorism and factionalism, 154–55;
terrorism issue, 183
Arens, Moshe, 76
Arieh project, 81
armored vehicles, 64–65; cuts, 74–75
arms control, 121, 129–31
Arms Control and Regional Security
(ACRS) multilateral forum, 130
Arrow antitactical ballistic missile (ATBM)
program, 76, 83, 127
Assa, Haim, 152
Assad, Hafez al-, 109, 112, 136–37;
American channel, 226n152; Syrian track,
143, 144–45, 146, 147, 148–49, 239nn75,
76, 79
attrition policy, Intifada, 104, 105, 106–07
attrition rates, 72–73
attrition war, 125

Baker, James, 48
balance-of-power viewpoint, 11–12
Barak, Ehud: conventional perspective, 91
Bar-Lev Line, 90
Begin, Menachem, 87, 246n196; criticized
for Sinai withdrawal, 46; "home rule" for
Palestine, 27; Rabin's views, 163–64
Beilin, Yossi, 149–50, 159
Ben-Gurion, David, 11; home-front
defenses, 177–78; IDF, 58–59; nuclear
weapons, 115; relations with Eshkol, 36;
Suez Campaign, 178; use of force limited,
86–87; U.S. relations, 34
Border Police, 104
brinkmanship, 117
British Jewish Brigade, 61
"Brookings Plan," 17
Bush, George, 50, 137

Camp David Accords (1978), 27, 30
Carlucci, Frank, 48
Carter, Jimmy, 17, 53, 109
casus belli: Jordan waters diversion, 95–96;
nuclearization, 122; "red lines" concept,
92–93; Syrian invasion of Lebanon,
108, 109
chemical weapons, 22, 126–28
Chemical Weapons Convention (CWC),
129
Christians, in Lebanon, 108
Christopher, Warren, 146, 149, 239n76
civil disobedience, 102–03, 105
Civil Guard, 99
Clausewitz, Karl von, 85, 86, 173, 219n37
Clinton, Bill, 50; Jordanian treaty, 158;
peace process, 145; weapons sales, 189
Clinton-Assad Geneva summit, 147
coercive diplomacy, 99, 127
Cold War: Egypt, perceptions of, 40; Nixon
approach, 38; Reagan administration, 47;
Star Wars, 47; threat of superpower
clashes in Mideast, 39
Cold War, end of, 137; collapse and Mideast
peace, 134; Israeli defense industry, 82
communist members, Knesset, 4
Comprehensive Test Ban Treaty (CTBT),
129–30, 233n108
computers: logistics system, 67
Conference of Presidents of the Major
American Jewish Organizations, 56–57
conventional warfare: deterrence and, 91;
versus nuclear weapons, 114–15, 116, 119,
120, 127–28, 131
counterterrorism, 98–102, 143, 225n115
Cuban Missile Crisis, 116
cumulative deterrence, 89
"current security," 173

Dayan, Moshe, 36; absolved, 78; IDF, 58;
June 1967 War, 95; military manpower,
122; military strategy, 67; nuclear issue,
119–20; paratrooper training, 63; Rabin's
evaluation of U.S. criticized, 40;
superpower clashes, 39; Yom Kippur
War, 180
decision-making: in defense matters, 2;
process, 3; Rabin's style, 152, 242n124
Declaration of Principles, Israeli-
Palestinian, 136, 150, 151, 157, 182

Declaration of Principles (DOP), Israeli-
Jordanian, 158
defense budgets: cuts, 73–75; during 1980s,
21; relations with Egypt, 21; use of force,
87–88
defense industries, Israeli, 78–83
defense minister, 3; analogies of role, 168
defense strategy: activist school, 11; self-
reliance notion, 34, 35; territorial issues,
29–30
defense treaty, U.S.-Israeli, possibility, 53–54
defensive strategy, 176; after 1973, 90;
Rabin's views, 89, 175, 218n28; "superiority of the defense," 90
"demographic problem," 30
deterrence, 89–91, 92, 93; Arab ballistic
missiles, 125; arms control with, 129;
chemical warfare, 126–28; cumulative, 89;
Gulf War, 233n100; Intifada, 103–04;
nuclear, 117; nuclear option, 141; nuclear
weapons, 116, 131–32; peace process, 141;
power-politics perspective, 113; by
punishment, strategy, 98; Rabin's views,
175; second-tier countries, 141; Sinai
Campaign, 19; U.S. extended, 135
"dialogue," military force in, 14
Diaspora Jewish life: Rabin's views, 55, 56
Dimona reactor, 118, 119
diplomatic ventures: ambassadorship to
U.S., 37–42; bicentennial visit, 46;
European, 43
direct negotiations, 20
Dobrinin, Anatoly, 42
"dormant war," 14
Dulles doctrine of massive retaliation, 116

Eban, Abba, 34; Rabin's evaluation of U.S.
criticized, 40
economic factors, 79, 159–60, 182, 215n134
Egypt, 45, 95; border changes, 30; casus
belli, 93; chemical warheads, 126; interim
agreements, 203–04n51; Iranian oil,
230n52; leadership with regard to Israel,
20; missile boats, 69; Nasser era threat, 13;
nuclear issue, 130, 234n113; peace and
military force, 16–17; peace treaty, 73,
144, 147; precedent in negotiations, 147,
240n84; Rabin on relations with, 45–46;
rapprochement with Israel, 15; Sadat
initiative, 20–21; Soviet relations, 12,

195n34; surprise campaigns, 72; U.S.
reactor sale, 120–21; U.S. relations, 130
Eilat, 30
Eitan, Rafael: conventional perspective, 91
Elazar, David, Chief of Staff, 78
Emunim, Gush, 17
energy crisis of 1970s, Israeli isolation, 42–43
Entebbe rescue operation, 100–101, 224n109
equipment: procurement vis-à-vis
maintenance, 68
escalation, 141
escalation dominance, 125, 127
Eshkol, Levi, 36; Jordanian arms, 37; Jordan
waters diversion, 96; June 1967 crisis, 95;
military guidance, 68; nuclear weapons,
115; U.S. relations, 34
Europe: chemical weapons, 129; Rabin
questioning role, 50; Rabin rejects role
of, 43

Fatah group, 23, 154
fighter planes, 48; casualties compared, 177;
counterterrorism, 100; deterrence, 141;
economic constraints, 68; F-15s and
F-16s, 73; F-15s, 83; F-151s vis-à-vis
F-16s, 77, 214n123; IAF, 66; Israeli attack
on Iraqi reactor (1981), 123; Lavi jet
fighters, 49, 80, 81–82; local production,
80; Phantom deal, significance, 69–70; retired, 74; Saudi Arabia, 55, 56; Soviet, 70
financial assistance to Israel, 189; aid levels
in 1960s and 1970s, 42; defense treaty
and, 54; late 1970s, 44; Soviet
immigration, 50; weapons sales tied, 80
fissionable materials, production, 130–31
Ford, Gerald, 52–53, 55
foreign policy, Israeli, 34
fortification programs, 90, 219–20n40
forum, territories, 103
France, 34; arms, 10, 36, 39, 117, 201n7;
inertia in relations, 36; nuclear weapons,
117; officers' cultural ambience, 35; Suez
Campaign, 178
fundamentalism, Islamic, 138, 142, 151;
Rabin on, 181–82

Galili, Israel, 91, 108, 200n141
Gavish, Yeshayahu, 64
Gaza Strip, 134
Gazit, Shlomo, 27

General Assembly of American Jewish Organizations, 56
Geneva Conference, 51, 52
Germany, 54
Golan Heights, 31, 51, 107, 134, 158–59; opposition, 148, 240nn91, 93; political parties, 240n86; withdrawal, 143–49, 163, 184–87, 238nn57, 60, 64, 239n71
"good fence" policy, 110
Grapes of Wrath Operation, 227n168
Greater Israel ideology, 170–71
Green Line, 31, 53, 137, 200n141
Gulf War (1991), 50; address by Rabin on security policy, 172–78; chemical warfare, 128; combat style, 176, 177; Israeli response, 162; as model, 91; nuclear aspects, 123; outcome as surprise, 172; political changes resulting, 133
Gur, Mordechai, 80; casus belli, 93; conventional perspective, 91; as military attaché, 195n34; preemptive strikes, 92; security zone, 112; Syrian referendum proposal, 147
Gush Emunim movement, 200n141

Haber, Eitan, 162
Halevy, Efraim, 157
Hamas, 145, 154
Hareali High School (Haifa), 63
Harriman, Averell, 96
Hashemites, in Jordan, 25, 137
Hebrew, 60
helicopters, 76–77
Hizballah, 111, 112, 141, 142; bombings, 227n169; Rabin on, 181; strikes against, 227n169
Holocaust, 127
home front, 177–78
hostages, 100
Hussein, King, 25, 28, 149; Jordanian track, negotiations, 156–58. See also Jordan
Hussein, Saddam, 15; chemical warfare, 128; chemical weapons, 127; invading Iran, 17. See also Iraq

IDF. See Israel Defense Force (IDF)
IFF (identify foe-friend) system, 80
immigration, 97, 135, 137
"indirect approach," to military operations, 94

Indo-Pakistani war, 10
infantry, Rabin's view, 67
intelligence community, 49, 92; Palestinian Authority, 143; skepticism about, 71–72
intelligence satellite program (Ofeq), 75–76, 213–14nn109, 110
International Atomic Energy Agency (IAEA), 115, 130
Intifada, 16, 22, 28, 83, 102–07; attritional approach, 104, 105, 106–07, 226n142; Israeli public's attitudes, 162; King Hussein's influence, 157; Rabin approach, 9; released prisoners, 101; stone throwing punished, 106; tougher responses, 104, 106, 225n127; U.S. Jewry, 55
Iran: arms control, 121; Egypt cooperation, 230n52; Israeli support, 53; nuclear program, 124; nuclear threat, 140; as potential ally, 139, 236n31; Scud missiles, 51; terrorism, 143, 181–82; threat of, 138–39, 140
"Irangate" affair, 49
Iran-Iraq agreement (1975), 9, 17, 193–94n11
Iran-Iraq War (1980–88), 16, 53, 73; chemical warfare, 126; missile use, 125; U.S. policy, 53, 206n113
Iraq: chemical warfare, 22, 126, 127, 128; Kurdish minority, 9; missile attacks, 128; missile technology, 76; nuclear threat, 129, 130, 138, 140; peace overtures, 15–16; relations with, 50; significance of its defeat, 135; U.S. confrontation, 178; war with Iran, 53
Islamic fundamentalism. See fundamentalism, Islamic; Islamic radicalism
Islamic radicalism, 22, 138, 142, 151; economic factors, 159–60; Rabin on, 181–82
isolation of Israel, 20, 52; as collective memory, 8–9; during energy crisis, 42–43; IDF's offensive profile, 92; mitigated, 134–35, 136, 155, 188–89; Rabin on, 8–9
Israel Aircraft Industry (IAI), 76, 80, 82
Israel Defense Force (IDF), 21, 58; under agreement with PLO, 151; army enlargement, reasons for, 71–73; budgetary constrictions, 68, 73–75, 83, 212n90; chemical warfare, 126; College of Command and Staff, 62–63; combat

style, 176; costs of war, 176–77; counter-terrorism, 99–100; expansion era, 83; Golan Heights withdrawal, 163; Intifada, unprepared for, 83; Israeli-made weapons, 81; later preparedness, 162–63; Lebanon clean-up effort, 111; Manpower Branch, 67; military decline, 60; military doctrine, 62; nuclear issue, 118; Oslo agreements, 153–54, 163; professional language, 60; protecting settlements, 31; public disappointment, 161; purpose, per Rabin, 60; Rabin as teacher, 168; Rabin commands officer training, 60–61; Rabin emphasis on large-scale maneuvers, 67; Rabin on role, 172–78; Rabin's attention to detail, 113; Rabin's career, 58–69; Rabin's contribution, 168; Rabin's influence, 59; Rabin's later influence, 170; role in peace promotion, 176; structure, 65; technological advances, 75–76; troop strength expanded, 73

Israeli Air Force (IAF), 66; 7 April 1967 air duel, 93; budget cuts, 74; defensive strategy, 91; Lebanon air raids, 100; missiles, 124; Phantom acquisition, 70; Popeye air-to-ground standoff weapon, 81

Israeli defense industry, 48, 82; arms sales, reporting, 131; Lavi jet-fighters, 49

Israeli-Jordanian peace accord, 184

Israeli society, Rabin's evaluation: war weariness, 16

Israel Military Industries (IMI), 82

Ivri, David, 80

Jackson Amendment, 55

Japan, 50–51

Jericho Plan, 25–26

Jerusalem: Rabin's position on, 160–61; as symbol, 29

Johnson, Lyndon B., 37, 40, 69

joint military exercises, U.S.-Israeli, 48

Joint Political and Military Group (JPMG), 47

Jordan, 95; counterterrorist policy, 99, 223–24n99; "home rule" for Palestinians, 27; invasion by Syria, 41; Palestinian issue, 25; PLO presence, 101–02, 224n112; tanks purchase, 37; territorial issues, 25. See also Hussein, King

Jordanian option, 25, 27

"Jordanian orientation," of Rabin, 25–28

Jordanian track, negotiations, 156–58; Rabin on, 184

Jordan River, battle, 95–96

June 1967 crisis, 94

June 1967 war. See Six-Day War

Karameh foray, 99

Katyusha attacks, 111, 112

Kehalani, Avigdor, 78

Kennedy, John F., 36

Khomeini, Ayatollah Ruhollah, 22, 138

Kissinger, Henry, 38; accord of 1975, 44–45; American-Soviet agreement, 51; Egypt-Israel compromise, 52; Israel-Europe relations, 43; Israeli nuclear program, 118; Jackson Amendment, 55; Middle East policy control, 42; opposition to preemptive strikes, 92; weapons demands, 45

Knesset, Rabin's 1994 policy statement to, 179–90

Komer, Robert, 96

Kurds, 9, 194n11

Kuwait, invasion of, 116

Labor Party, 11, 25, 28, 55; centrist role, 4; exiting power, 73; Golan Heights, 144; independent Palestinian state, 29; Rabin as leader, 133

Laskov, Haim, 60, 61, 209n14

Lavi jet fighters, 49, 80, 81–82

Lebanon, 54, 107–12; Christians, 108; civil war, 10, 87–88, 110; counterterrorist policy, 99, 100; Rabin's role, 227n157; Syrian invasion, 107–08, 226n149

left wing, 4; peace slogan, 17

left-wing orientation, Rabin's: power politics vis-à-vis, 11

Levy, Moshe, 75, 91

Liddell-Hart, Basil, 94, 221n67

Lifton, Robert, 56–57

Likud Party, 86; Palestinian statehood, 170; on terrorism, 142

lobby groups, 54–55

logistics system, upgrading, 67

long-range ballistic missiles, 124–27

Madrid Peace Conference (1991), 130, 133; Arab weakness, 136; joint Jordanian-Palestinian delegation, 157; Rabin on, 182

"Major Non-NATO Ally," status, 47

Make or Buy (MOB) guidelines, 80
Mann, Theodor, 55
Matmon-B plan, 71
McGovern, George, 39
medical cooperation, military, 47
Meir, Golda: arms from U.S., 70–71; Egypt policy, 40; Rabin's caution, 41–42; U.S. relations, 34; U.S. ties, 36
Memorandum of Agreement (1988), 48
Memorandum of Understanding (MOU): 1975 MOU, 121; 1987 MOU, 47–48
Middle East: importance of military force, 15; instability, 11; nuclear proliferation, 117–118; peace treaties, 17
military, Israeli: reserve units created, 61
military career of Rabin, 58–69; chief of staff, 59; General Staff, 62; greatest achievement, 69; large scale operations, 94–95; Northern Command, 63; Operations Branch, 64; Operations Division, 61; power to promote senior officers, 78; as primary identity, 169; significance of his contribution, 168; significance of his role, 167; territorial issues, 185; training command, 62–63
military doctrine, preemption, 92, 221n54
military force, 10; Arab states, 13; costs of war, 176–77; as "dialogue," 14; Middle East, 11–12; national interests, 13; peace process, 17; political dimensions, 85–88; preservation of treaties, 17; Rabin's views, 85; superiority as necessary, 15; units of achievement, 19. See also use of force
military power: army size, issue of, 71–73; vis-à-vis economic factors, 159–60; strength issue, 59–60, 65
military professionalism, 63
military schools, 63
missile acquisition by navy, 69; cuts, 74; missile corvettes (Saar-5 class), 77; Sparrow air-to-air, 70
missiles, 124–28; ballistic missiles, 124–25; changing conditions, 83; chemical warheads, 126; long-range ballistic, 124–27; Pershing, 121; Rabin's views, 177; threats to Israel, 76. See also missile acquisition by navy; Patriot surface-to-air missiles; Scud-B missiles; Scud III missiles; surface-to-air missiles; surface-to-surface missiles
Moledet Party, 59

Moslems. See fundamentalism, Islamic; Islamic radicalism
"Mr. Security," 3, 171
Mubarak, Hosni, 136
Muslims. See fundamentalism, Islamic; Islamic radicalism

Nasser, Gamal Abdel, 13, 40, 87
national interest, 10
nationalism, 23; Palestinian, 25
national security: military superiority vis-à-vis, 86; terrorism and, per Rabin, 97–98
NATO, terrorism, 10
navy, 68–69, 98
Negev, 49, 116
neorealism, 9–10
Netanyahu, Benjamin, 156
Nicaragua, 49
Nixon, Richard, 38, 42; arms policy, 70–71; Israeli nuclear program, 118, 119; Middle East policy, 40–41; Phantoms, 70; view of Rabin, 203n30
Nixon Doctrine, 108
Nixon-Kissinger approach, 38, 70–71; Rabin's views, 164; U.S. Jews view, 55
"no fly zone," 128
nonviolent protest, 102–03
normalization, Golan Heights, 187
North Korea: missiles to Iran, 129
Nuclear Non-Proliferation Treaty (NPT), 115, 118–19, 122, 123, 130
nuclear proliferation, 51, 117–118; Israeli, 54; Rabin's fears in 1990s, 140
nuclear weapons, 114–32; versus conventional warfare, 114–15, 116, 119, 120, 127–28, 131; Rabin's view, 115–18, 131, 168–69
Nuclear Weapons Free Zone (NWFZ), 121, 130

Obeid, Sheik, 111
October 1967 War: Rabin's contribution, 170
October 1973 War: dependence on U.S., 35; deterrence, 89; missile boats, 69; nuclear issue following, 119–22; as Rabin's greatest achievement, 69; U.S.-Israeli relations after, 42–46
offensive military forces, 176
officer training, 60–61, 62, 63; morale and dynamism, 68; paratrooper aspect, 209n31
oil: crisis, 20; supplies to Israel, 44
Operation Accountability, 112, 141

Operation Danny, 61, 209n21
Operation Yoav, 61
orthodox tradition, 8
Oslo agreements, 146, 147, 152; Arafat on, 154, 243n137; clandestine Israeli-PLO dialogues, 149–50, 151; domestic criticism, 4; Israel Defense Force (IDF), 163; Jerusalem, 161; Rabin deliberations, 152–53; Rabin's contribution, 170; Rabin's views, 156, 159; security, 153–54

Palestine: antiterrorist campaigns, 96–102; "autonomy" plan, 27; formation of a Palestinian state, 151–52, 170; "home rule" plan, 27; negotiations with, 28; non-PLO leadership, 28; Palestinian track, 146, 149–56; PLO vis-à-vis Palestinians, 28; terrorism, 109
Palestine Liberation Organization (PLO), 183; American Jewry, 56; assassination of leaders, 102; Carter policy, 53; destruction as Israeli goal, 22; deterrence by punishment, 98; Fatah violence, 154; Intifada, 105–06, 226n142; Lebanon, 99; negotiations with, opposed, 26; objectives seen, 26; Palestinian Diaspora, 29; Palestinian statehood, 29; Palestinians vis-à-vis, 28; Palestinian track, negotiations, 149; pro-Soviet orientation, 25; Rabin's later tolerance, 160; Rabin's later views, 150–52; Rabin's rejection, 26–29; Rabin's rejection of, 33; Rabin's view of threat, 141–43; Rabin's views, 159; recognition, 27; as Saddam Hussein ally, 136; status, 23, 24; as tool of Arab states, 23–24; Tunis headquarters air raid, 101–02; village of Karameh attacked, 99, 224n100; West Bank and Gaza entrenchment, 170
Palestinian Authority (PA): creation, 29; granted civilian authority, 150; Jerusalem issue, 161; Rabin-Arafat agreement, 136; territorial issue, 243n138; terrorism issue, 154–55, 183; West Bank, 152
Palestinian question: Arab-Israeli conflict, 23–24; Rabin's recognition, 23–29
Palestinians, 9; incremental approach, 156; Israeli costs of occupation, 159; in Lebanon, 107, 111; Madrid Peace Conference, 136; Palestinian orientation in Israeli foreign policy, 157; Rabin on accord with, 182–83; Shiite groups, 111

Palestinian track, 146, 149–56, 150–51, 241n101
Palmach Harel Brigade, 8, 29, 58; IDF, 61
paratroopers: morale, 67–68; Rabin's view, 67; training, 63, 209n31
Patriot surface-to-air missiles (SAMs), 51, 127
peace: imposition, viewed by Rabin, 174; Israeli interpretation of nature of, 20; Israeli sense of the term, 145; Rabin on regional conditions, 15; as Rabin priority, 5
peacemaker role, Rabin's: address to Knesset (1994), 179–90; communication skills, 169; public opinion, 169; speeches published, 5. See also Golan Heights; peace process
"Peace Now" slogan, 17
peace process: of 1990s, 22–23; grandfather role, 164–65; Iraq, 16; Israeli initiative, 18; Jordanian track, 156–58; public attitudes, 155, 162, 166, 243–44n147; Rabin and window of opportunity, 139; Rabin's doubts about future, 165, 166; Rabin's involvement, 135–38; step-by-step approach, 17–18; Syrian track, 143–49
Peled, Maj. Gen. (Res.) Mati, 26–27
Peres, Shimon, 28, 108, 109, 111; Jordanian arms, 37; local weapons production, 79, 215n137; Matmon-B plan, 71; Mideast NWFZ, 130; nuclear weapons, 114, 116, 140; Oslo talks, 149–50; Palestinian elections, 106; peace vocabulary, 135; Soviet presence, 52; spying incident, 49; Syrian track, 145, 146–47, 239n66; U.S. as ally, 35, 201n7
"periphery doctrine," 236n29
Perry, William, 124
petrodollars, 72
Phantom fighter planes, 69–70
political career of Rabin: assassination, 1, 171; assessed, 3–5; changing views, 159, 161; coalition politics, 140; decision-making style, 170; domestic impact of terrorism, 142; intergenerational tensions, 164–65; political skills, 4–5; pragmatism versus strategic thinking, 169; Rabin's significance, 167; role in Israeli history, 164
political realism, 7, 193n2. See also neorealism; realpolitik
political system: military engagements/battles and, 84

"politicide," 13, 85, 195nn38, 39
Pollard, Jonathan, 48–49
Popeye air-to-ground standoff weapon, 81
Popular Front for the Liberation of
    Palestine, 101
Precise Guided Munitions (PGM), 75, 90
preemption, 92, 221n54; Lebanon, 111;
    Rabin on, 174
preparedness, for war, 78
privatization, defense industry, 82
protest, nonviolent, 102–03
public opinion, 171; approval of Rabin, 170;
    Rabin support, 4–5

Rabin, Yitzhak: as ambassador to U.S.,
    37–42; candor analyzed, 5; childhood,
    7–8, 193n4; civilian life, 69; as defense
    minister, 46–50, 73–75; eulogies, 57;
    funeral, 57; funeral attendees, 1; as
    grandfather, 164–65; Jewishness, 8,
    193n6; mythology, 171; negotiation skills,
    44–45; paratrooper training, 63;
    pessimism, 165, 169; pro-U.S.
    orientation, 35; spying incident, 49. See
    also military career of Rabin; political
    career of Rabin
Rabinovich, Itamar, 144, 145, 146
RAFAEL Weapon Development Authority,
    80, 82
Rafah salient, 30
Reagan, Ronald, administration, 47, 49, 53
realpolitik, 31; changes, 135, 235n5;
    deterrence, 19; Nixon-Kissinger influence,
    38; origins of, 167–68; of Rabin, 9–12
"red line," Syrian invasion, 109
referendum, peace with Syria, 188
refugees, Lebanese, 112
religious perspective, return of Jews, 17
reserve units: budget cuts, 74; upgrading, 66
retaliation, 98, 101; chemical weapons, 127
Revolution in Military Affairs (RMA), 91
Rhodos talks, 14–15
right wing: impact of terrorism, 97
Rogers Plan of December 1969, 42, 52
Rubinstein, Elyakim, 157

Sadat, Anwar, 20–21, 45
scandal, foreign currency, 4, 191–92n7
Schultz, George, 48
Scud-B missiles, 125–26, 232n82

Scud III missiles, 51
"second-tier" countries, 138, 140
secrecy, need for, 11
security: after Gulf War, 172–78; as Rabin
    priority, 5; security zone, 110, 112;
    U.S.-Israeli relations, 46–52
Sella, Col. Aviem, 49, 205n87
separation, as goal, 152
settlement policy: Allon Plan, 30, 200n141;
    Green Line, 200n141; Maale Adumim, 52;
    military protection, 66, 210n42; security
    versus political, 31; Shamir era, 137; U.S.
    challenges, 52–53. See also Golan Heights
settlements, negotiated: Israeli military
    superiority, 85
Shamir, Yitzhak, 9; Gulf War, 50; Intifada,
    103; Iraqi missile attacks (1991), 128;
    Rabin supporter, 46–47; response to
    Palestinians, 105; spying incident, 49
Sharm al-Sheikh, 30
Sharon, Ariel, 162
Shiite Hizballah. See Hizballah
Shitreet, Shimon, 153
Shomron, Dan, 75, 77; chemical warfare,
    126; conventional perspective, 91;
    Intifada, 103
Sinai, 51; U.S. troops, 188
Sinai Campaign (1956), 19, 63, 85
Sinai II Agreement (1975), 12, 21, 143;
    memorandum of understanding (1975),
    contents of, 44, 45; strategic reasons for, 45
Six-Day War (1967), 19
"small war," 103
social dimensions, of war, 125, 232n77
South Lebanese Army (SLA), 111
Soviet Union: Egypt, 12; nonideological
    foreign policy, 10; Rabin's Jewish
    approach, 9; Rabin's views, 51–52;
    relations with Israel, 52; "Soviet
    umbrella," 134; supporting Arab
    militaries, 12; Syria aid, 21–22
spying incident, 48–49
"Star Wars" (U.S. Strategic Defense
    Initiative, SDI), 47, 127
status quo power, Israel as, 87
step-by-step approach, 52
strategic coordination policy, 57
strategic culture: Rabin's impact, 3
Strategic Defense Initiative (SDI), or "Star
    Wars," 47, 127

strategic policy: Star Wars, 47
strategic position: in 1980s, 21–22
strategic views: American factor, 37
submarines, 69, 77, 211n70
Suez Campaign, 34–35, 178; European eclipse, 35; reserve units, 66
superpowers: limits of force, 86; nuclear weapons, 117; weapon sales, 202n16
surface-to-air missiles (SAMs), 123; Rabin's views, 177; Syria, 124
surface-to-surface missiles, 22, 92, 121, 124
Syria, 14, 90; air duels, 96; American Jewry, 56; 7 April 1967 air duel, 93; battle over the Jordan waters, 95–96; chemical warfare, 126; counterterrorist policy, 98–99; deterrence as a possibility, 175; Golan Heights and nonbelligerency agreement, 31; invading Jordan, 41; Israeli-Syria treaty, 51; Israeli use of force restrained, 141; Lebanese civil war, 107–08; missile boats, 69; nuclear weapons, 116; PLO support, deterring, 87; possibility of war in 1990s, 139; post-Gulf-War, 136–37; Sinai II Agreement, 45; tank attack, 66–67; Tunis air raid, 102
Syrian track: peace negotiations, 143–49; Rabin on, 185–88; security measures, 240n83

Taba agreement (1995), 155, 156, 241n108, 244n154
tactical solutions, 105
TAKAM kibbutz movement convention, 148
tanks, 71; cuts, 74; force expanded, 73; local production, 80; M-48, from U.S., 118; Tank Corps, 66–67, 68, 96, 222n78
territorial issues, 29–31; accord of 1975, 44, 45; Arava, 158; Egyptian interests, 21; Golan Heights withdrawal, 143–49, 238nn57, 60, 64, 239n71; Jordan, 158; Kissinger's shuttle, 52; Palestinian track, 150; Rabin on Israel as status quo power, 14; Rabin's concessions, 134; settlement policy, 30–31; Six-Day War, 19, 25; strategically desirable areas, 30; Taba agreement, 155; terrorism, 142, 237n51
territories forum, 103
terrorism, 86, 96–102; deterrence by punishment strategy, 98; domestic impact, 141–43, 237n45; Islamic

fundamentalist, 138; negotiations, 100–101; Palestinian, 23, 183; Palestinian Authority and Arafat, 154–55; PLO renouncing, 151; Rabin on Iranian, 181–82; Rabin's view, 173; reprisals, 98; suicide bombings, 142
Third Way Party, 240n86
time vector, Arab-Israeli conflict, 16
Tiran Straits, Egypt closing, 94
Toon, Malcolm, 53
training, importance, 65
Tunisia, 101–02

United Nations (UN): Israel arms control proposal, 121; resolution equating Zionism with racism, 9, 16, 41, 100, 144
United Nations (UN) Resolution 242, 9, 16, 41, 100, 144
United States: foreign policy in election years, 44; importance of relations for Israel, 12; Israeli strategic equation, 12; Israel's dependence on, 20, 21; moral factors, 35–36; nuclear policy, 116
use of force: analyzed, 168; attitudes toward, 217n13; costs of war, 176–77; Intifada, 104; large scale operations, 94–95; Lebanon, 110–112; for limited goals, 93; modus operandi, 93–112; against nuclear infrastructure, 122–23; peace process, 141; power-politics perspective, 113; self-reliance in manpower, 53–54
U.S.-Israeli relations: American airlifts, 73; Arab boycott lifted, 189; Arab-Israeli conflict, 45; Clinton administration, 145; early warning systems, 76; five areas of support, 43; Israeli defense industry, 81; Lebanese civil war, 107–09; limits on, 52–54; Mideast peace process, 137; military partners, 41, 42; negative incidents, 48–50; nuclear issue, 118; nuclear proliferation in Mideast, 129; nuclear reactor for Egypt, 120–21; nuclear weapons, 121–22; October 1973 war, 42–46; peace process support, 163; post-1973, 43–46; Rabin as early advocate, 168; Rabin visit (1963), 36–37; strategic relationship growing, 46–52; U.S. Jews, 39, 41, 54–57
U.S. military: Rabin's views, 64; training methods, 63

U.S. weapons: ATBM program, 76; Eisenhower administration, 202n16; Phantoms, 69–70; tanks, 66

U.S.S.R., former: arms to Arabs, 36, 38; arms to Egypt and Syria, 39; collapse and Mideast peace, 134; diplomatic relations, 135; Eastern bloc, 135; immigration to Israel, 50; military doctrine among Arabs, 64; missile boats, 69; nuclear ramifications, 123. *See also* military force

victory, meaning of, 175–76

Voice of America (VOA), 49–50

war, goals of, 88; social dimensions, 125, 232n77

War, Six-Day, 19

War of Attrition (1969–70), 40, 42

War of Independence (1948), 18; "indirect approach" military operations, 94; Israeli military preparedness, 59; models of contingency planning, 61; time factor, 91–92; as war of generations, 22

Washington Declaration (1994), 158

weapons, 55; arms sales, 131; early-warning radar stations, 36; fighter aircraft, 37, 39, 40, 41; France selling, 34; IAF, 66; Israeli attack on Iraqi reactor (1981), 123; of mass destruction, 22, 114–32; procurement sources, 36–37; Rabin lobbying U.S. for, 38, 39–42; Star Wars era, 47; surface-to-air missiles (SAMs), 36; tank purchases, 66; U.S. arms availability, 36–37. *See also* armored

vehicles; arms control; chemical weapons; fighter planes; helicopters; missiles; nuclear weapons; tanks; weapons procurement

Weapons of Mass Destruction Free Zone, 130

weapons procurement: ambassadorship era, 71; Apache attack helicopters, 76–77; Arab states, 174; budget cuts, 74–75; expansion in 1970s, 73; firepower capacity, 72; first tenure as prime minister, Rabin's, 71; France, 35, 201n7; from Israeli manufacturers, 78–83; Make or Buy (MOB) guidelines, 80; Pershing missiles, 121, 230nn47, 48; pro-U.S. bias, 83; Rabin's preference, 81, 83; recent, 189; "smart" weapons, 74, 75; strategic threats to Israel, 76–77; tanks, 210n49; upgrading systems, 79

Weizman, Ezer, 210n46, 224n99

West Bank, 134; Jordanian option, 25

Western Wall, 29

World War II, 86, 173–74

Yadin, Yigal, 58

Yom Kippur War (1973): Rabin on, 180; as watershed, 19–20

Zeevi, Rehavam, 59, 208n10, 209n14

Zionism: Arab compromise, 152; Arab-Israeli conflict, 13; elite, 19; immigration, 97; perspective, 55; Rabin's background, 8; racism resolution in UN, 9, 16, 41, 100, 144